The American Humorist

First of all, there is the tricky question of what is going to be 'normal,' in a world of constantly shifting values. It is hard enough to determine what is 'normal' now.

— *James Thurber*

Not to laugh at the twentieth century is to shoot yourself.

— *Erich Maria Remarque*

The American Humorist
Conscience of the Twentieth Century

Norris W. Yates

☆ ☆ ☆

Iowa State University Press *Ames,* Iowa, U.S.A.

To my mother,

Phoebe M. Yates

and to

the memory of my father,

Willard W. Yates

Acknowledgments

I believe this book is the first attempt at a full-length study of twentieth-century American writers of humor. However, I have made use of several briefer studies included in books on larger subjects. Among these books are Constance Rourke, *American Humor*, Jennette Tandy, *Crackerbox Philosophers in American*

Humor and Satire, Walter Blair, *Native American Humor* (revised 1960 edition) and the same author's *Horse Sense in American Humor.* My debt to Blair's two books in particular extends well beyond the specific citations. *The Satirist,* by Leonard Feinberg, has furnished many ideas used in this work, and Professor Feinberg has helpfully criticized the chapter on H. L. Mencken. He is not responsible for any errors or misjudgments in my book or for how I may have warped his ideas in applying them.

Many other individuals have assisted the author in making this book. My former student, Norma Groves Soden, first called my attention to Ralph L. Curry's investigations of Stephen Leacock's influence on Robert Benchley. To James C. Austin of Southern Illinois University I am indebted for the loan of a copy of Thurber's lecture on humor before parts of that lecture appeared in Thurber's *Lanterns and Lances* (1960); to James E. Humphrey of Iowa State University for help in acquiring a partial file of the *American Mercury;* to the Alumni Achievement Fund of Iowa State University for a grant-in-aid that defrayed some of the expenses of this study; to Katharine S. White for bibliographical assistance concerning the work of E. B. White; to the *New Yorker* for information on the collaboration of Thurber and White; to Vivian Harris, librarian of Atlanta (Georgia) Newspapers, Inc., for information on Don Marquis' early career in the South; and to James E. McInnis, formerly of Iowa State University, for aid in procuring certain southern newspapers. Thanks are also heartily given to Mildred E. McHone, Eleanor June McKee, and Elizabeth Windsor of the Iowa State University library, whose help in procuring interlibrary loans has been constant over a period of years.

Once the writer's notes became a readable manuscript, Richard Gustafson, Helen Herrnstadt, and Richard L. Herrnstadt lost many hours and much adrenalin in the reading and helpful criticism of this work. Keith Huntress caught several embarrassing errors before their immortalization in print. Judy Matterson assisted in copyreading the final typescript, using, in this tedious chore, time she could ill spare. Further practical assistance came from Paula Hayne, and intangible but invaluable support has come from Phillips G. Davies, Rosemary Davies, and other friends and colleagues at Iowa State University. My pleasure in recalling their aid is curbed only by the impossibility of acknowledging them all by name.

ALCI ALIQUID ACCEPTUM REFERE

Material from the writings of Frank McKinney Hubbard is used by permission of Josephine Hubbard (Mrs. Kin Hubbard), as is the drawing of "Abe Martin" in Chapter VI.

Unless otherwise stated, all quotations from *The Best of Clarence Day,* Knopf (New York, 1948), *H. L. Mencken on Politics,* Malcolm Moos (ed.), Vintage (New York, 1960), *The Vintage Mencken,* Alistair Cooke (comp.), Third Printing, Vintage (New York, 1956), *H. L. Mencken Prejudices: A Selection,* James T. Farrell (ed.), Second Printing, Vintage (New York, 1958), and all other writings of H. L. Mencken are used by permission of Alfred A. Knopf, Inc.

Material from *The Lives and Times of Archy and Mehitabel* by Don Marquis is reprinted by permission of the publisher, Doubleday and Company, Inc.

Unless otherwise stated, material by Dorothy Parker is from *The Portable Dorothy Parker,* copyright 1944 by Dorothy Parker, and used by permission of The Viking Press, Inc.

Material from the writings of James Thurber is copyrighted by James Thurber and quoted here by permission of Mrs. Helen Thurber. This includes the drawings on page 274.

Material from *How to Be a Hermit* by Will Cuppy is used by permission of the publisher, Liveright Publishing Corporation.

Unless otherwise stated, material from the writings of E. B. White is used by permission of E. B. White and of Harper and Brothers.

An excerpt in Chapter 19, from p. 108 of *The Best of*

S. J. Perelman, appeared in "Slow—Dangerous Foibles Ahead," by S. J. Perelman, copyright 1939 by S. J. Perelman, and is reprinted from *The Best of S. J. Perelman* by permission of Random House, Inc. An excerpt in Chapter 19, from the "Introduction" by Sidney Namlerep, to *The Best of S. J. Perelman* is copyright 1947 by S. J. Perelman and reprinted by permission of Random House, Inc.

All other writings of S. J. Perelman are used by permission of the author, S. J. Perelman.

Unless otherwise stated, material quoted from the writings of Ring Lardner is used by permission of Charles Scribner's Sons.

The introductory quotation by Erich Maria Remarque is from *Three Comrades,* Little, Brown (Boston, 1937), p. 198, and is used by permission of the author.

Unless otherwise stated, all quotations from the *New Yorker* are used by permission of that publication.

Quotations from *The Benchley Roundup, Chips Off the Old Benchley, 20,000 Leagues Under the Sea,* and *Benchley Beside Himself* are used by permission of Harper & Row, Inc.

ACKNOWLEDGMENT FOR THE SECOND PRINTING

I am indebted to Mrs. James Thurber for assistance in correcting several misstatements in the first printing about James Thurber, Dorothy Parker, and Robert Benchley, and for sharpening my critical judgment about these writers. Final responsibility for the content of this book of course rests on me alone.

NORRIS W. YATES

Ames, Iowa, 1964

Contents

Introduction

This book is not an attempt to tell what humor is or why some pieces are more humorous than others. As E. B. White says, "Humor can be dissected, as a frog can, but the thing dies in the process and the innards are discouraging to any but the pure scientific mind." Nor is this volume a collection of humor; it is a discussion of the work of certain humorists of the printed word, a slice of literary history. In it, an attempt is made to set forth what humorists in the first half of this century believed concerning such important phenomena as man, society, and the cosmos. Humor and satire must have norms and standards by which to treat men, events, and institutions. What were the norms and standards by which American humor and satire, from 1900 to 1950, was written?

In framing a series of answers to this question, I have had to deal with another, closely related: when these norms and standards were not merely abstract propositions, how were they implied in characters, situations, episodes? The closest thing to a "key" that can be found to the printed humor of this period is the humorists' use of character types. Three character types that occur and recur may be considered the chief carriers of values for the humorous writers treated here, and will be discussed in close connection with the elucidation of these values. One type is the rustic sage who lets fall his wisdom in maxims and/or yarns as if he were talking to the crowd around the crackerbarrel in a rural store. He was more prominent in nineteenth- than he has been in twentieth-century humor. He might be a loafer but was sometimes a small-businessman or professional man. The second type is that respectable citizen, a pillar of his community, who differs from the mindless mob of his fellow Babbitts in being public spirited rather than self-absorbed. Whether a liberal or conservative, he takes public affairs seriously and tries to think his way, rationally, through all problems he encounters. He usually owns and runs his own enterprise; in this and in other ways he is a nineteenth-century product that has survived into the twentieth century. In humor he sometimes is merged with the crackerbox philosopher.

The third type existed sporadically in the nineteenth century but was refashioned and has gained new importance in the twentieth; this is the worried Little Man of whom Mr. Milquetoast and Dagwood Bumstead are examples in cartoon humor. In social status he is lower than the entrepreneur, being a clerk or

junior executive (usually very junior) rather than the proprietor
of his own business. He is the version in story or essay form of
Jimmy Hatlo's Tremblechin, bullied by Mr. Bigdome at the office
and badgered by Little Iodine or her mother at home.

When oversimplified by abstraction from their contexts, these
three types may easily be distinguished from each other. When
made flesh by the words of their creators, they appear in all sorts
of guises. Not only do the first two types sometimes become
mutually indistinguishable, but one or both occasionally blend
with the third. None of this amalgamation is surprising, because
the three have certain similarities. First, they are all of the middle
class—and what that means in humor will be shown later. Second,
they are American variants of a type and norm in classical satire,
the *vir bonus*—the good, plain man—who, as Professor Maynard
Mack has pointed out in the *Yale Review* (1951), also functions
as one of Alexander Pope's *personae*, or masks, in his satires.
Third, this plain man cuts a poor figure at home, harassed as
he is by his unmanageable wife and children. Fourth, all three
of these American types often shape up in varying degrees as in-
digenous versions of the wise fool. This world-wide figure is not
so much a type as a function; almost any sort of humorous character may function as the wise fool in one of two ways, either as the
naïf, or simple fellow with direct, clear insight like the child who
saw that the emperor had nothing on at all, or as the "eccentric"
jester who slashes his alleged betters with satire that would sting
if it didn't come from an apparently stupid or disreputable
character.

Fifth, the three types embody similar values: a golden
mean, everyday common sense, personal integrity, monogamous
marriage, a stable family life, a measure of personal and political
freedom. All three types also embody certain value-combinations
that are unstable, such as a respect for literacy joined with a
distrust of culture, a love of freedom but a distrust of what men
do with it, a suspicion of science and gadgetry but an involvement with them, a distrust of suburban comfort and status yet
a relishing of the same. When the authors themselves are not

fully aware of these instabilities, the result is sometimes confusion. When they are fully aware, the result is comic irony. In
either case, these three types represent the ethical elite, those who
think and who try to be "good" men, in contrast to the hypo-
critical and unthinking masses.

That such loaded value-terms as "freedom," "the common
man," and "culture" may be defined in very different ways by
different writers does not alter the allegiance of these writers to
the terms or to their definitions of them. Likewise, the different
language in which different humorists dress their type-figures
should not prevent the reader from recognizing familiar outlines.
Although this book is not primarily concerned with language
and other aspects of style, notice has been taken that most of the
crackerbox loafers and entrepreneurs spoke or wrote in dialect or
in an informal prose not far above the level of dialect; the solid-
citizen types (and their authors, when wearing the citizen's mask)
affected the same informal, fairly colloquial kind of speech; and
the creators of the Little Man presented him and had him speak
in more urbane and more cultivated but no less lively accents. In
1900 it was difficult to write correctly and also excitingly; vigor
and propriety in style were far apart. Malcolm Cowley has said
in *Evolutionary Thought in America* (ed. by Stow Persons) that,

> In America during the late nineteenth century culture was set
> against daily living, theory against practice, highbrow against
> lowbrow; and the same division could be found even in the
> language itself—for one side spoke a sort of bloodless literary
> English, while the other had a speech that was not American
> but Amurrken, ugly and businesslike, sometimes picturesque
> but not yet a literary idiom.

Ring Lardner, H. L. Mencken, and the crackerbox humorists
helped to make "Amurrken" a literary idiom. Somewhat later,
the writers who made the most use of the Little Man took the
pale English of gentility and infused it too with vigor, without
sacrificing any of its "correctness." In the main, the colloquial
idiom has remained associated with the crossroads sage and the

solid citizen, and "college" English has become the medium of the Milquetoast type-figure. The language of their creators will therefore be treated, in passing, as the specific authors are surveyed for their values and for their use of characters.

Two introductory chapters are intended as a brief and highly compressed summary of certain social and political trends in the first half of our century insofar as these trends bear directly on the central values and main types in American humor. To these chapters is appended a discussion of John Kendrick Bangs, the most popular as well as the most representative of the genteel humorists at the turn of the century. The next four chapters are devoted to five crackerbox humorists of the twentieth century (in one chapter two of these writers are considered). A chapter on those changes in American taste (a section which might be entitled "An Exercise in Convenient Oversimplification") that bear most obviously on humor between 1910 and 1920 is followed by a discussion of three writers who developed in different ways but whose outlook remained recognizably that of the small town. A general account of the rise of the *New Yorker* brand of humor follows, and after that come seven chapters on humorists in the *New Yorker* tradition, with emphasis on how they often embodied their values in the Little Man.

Selection of the writers to be discussed has been a problem. Doubtless many a reader will find a void or a brief reference where a chapter on his favorite humorist should be. Where, for example, are Harry Leon Wilson and Ellis Parker Butler, whose depictions of bumpkins and Little Men were so popular once upon a time? Where is Langston Hughes with his crackerbox oracle of Harlem, Jess B. Semple ("Simple")? Where is Franklin P. Adams, landmark of columnists? Where is Donald Ogden Stewart, prince of parodists? Where is Damon Runyon, Broadway local-colorist? Where are Corey Ford and his aging Little Man, Thorne Smith and his Cosmo Topper? Where are Christopher Morley, Heywood Broun, C. E. S. Wood, Anita Loos, George Jean Nathan, Don Herold, Emily Kimbrough, Cornelia Otis Skinner, Margaret Halsey? Weren't there other stars in the

New Yorker galaxy—Alexander Woollcott, Frank Sullivan, John McNulty, Wolcott Gibbs, to name a few? Where are the versifers —Carolyn Wells, Gelett Burgess, Samuel Hoffenstein, Ogden Nash, Phyllis McGinley? How about the writers who have gone in for broad farce, like H. Allen Smith, Marion Hargrove, and Max Shulman? How about those satirists who rank also as "serious" novelists, such as Sinclair Lewis and John P. Marquand?

Two partial replies can be made: separate discussion of more writers would have turned this book into an encyclopedia rather than a literary history, and, the writers chosen at least could not be left out of any study of twentieth-century American humor.

Some further comments on the purpose of this book may help to remove false expectations on the part of the reader. First, in emphasizing the ideas, values, and character types stressed by the humorists, I have not confined myself to treatment of their humorous work but have discussed whichever pieces—humorous or serious—throw the most light on the chosen topics. In consequence, many items written without humorous intent have here received detailed analysis. Second, I have tried to refrain from overtly judging humor as humor (one man's humor is apt to be another man's boredom anyway), except where such judgments have seemed to contribute to the analysis of types and value-standards. The book, of course, is shot through with implicit judgments because such judgments are inherent in the selection of the material. *Caveat lector.*

Third, all historical study involves some distortion, if only by virtue of the need for selectivity just mentioned. Part of my plan has been to find and follow the main currents of thought in modern American humor of the printed word. Consequently, I have laid stress on similarities and continuities rather than differences among the writers discussed. Some differences are outlined, but to capture the uniqueness of each writer—and every humorist worth his salt is essentially unique—one must read, not discussions of that writer, but his works.

PART ONE

*Genteel Humor
and Some History*

VOLUME XXVII.   ·LIFE·   NUMBER 681.

A SCHEMER.

He: I'm Afraid I Couldn't Make You Happy, Darling, On Only $2,000 A Year.
She: Oh, It's Plenty! With Economy I Can Dress On $1,500 And Just Think, Dear,
We Can Have All The Rest For Household Expenses!

The "Gibson girl" and the "Gibson man," created in Life *by Charles
Dana Gibson, were popular middle-class types in American humor. In
this drawing, certain assumptions about the social and financial status
of these two types are made explicit.*

This cartoon appeared in *Life*, XXVII (January 16, 1896), 35.

1

Humor in the Nineties

The decade of the eighteen-nineties was not a brilliant period in American literary humor. Most of the famous fun-makers of the later nineteenth century were dead or past their prime as writers. David Ross Locke (Petroleum Vesuvius Nasby) had died in 1888; Henry Wheeler Shaw (Josh Billings) died in 1885 but had published little of note since 1881; Robert H. Newell's humorous output had been small since his *Orpheus C. Kerr Papers* (1862–1868). The southern humorist Charles H. Smith (Bill Arp) scribbled industriously if weakly until 1903, but Eugene Field, whose column "Sharps and Flats," in the Chicago *Daily News*, was widely quoted, died in 1895, and Edgar W. (Bill) Nye followed him the next year.

In this decade Mark Twain wrote three major satires, *Pudd'nhead Wilson* (1894), *The Man That Corrupted Hadleyburg* (1900), and *The Mysterious Stranger* (1898–1906; published in 1916). But none of these ranks with *Huckleberry Finn*. Only Edgar Watson Howe and Ambrose Bierce could be said to be at their peak as writers of humor and satire. Howe had once written a serious novel, *The Story of a Country Town* (1883), in which he became the forerunner of Hamlin Garland, Brand Whitlock,[1] Sherwood Anderson, Sinclair Lewis, and other writers of fiction who castigated the small town. But in the eighteen-nineties Howe was writing the sour proverbs for his Atchison (Kansas) *Globe* that made him widely known as the "Sage of Potato Hill" and now remind one of the sayings Mark Twain put into "Pudd'nhead Wilson's Calendar." In 1897 Bierce began to set down the cynical and witty definitions that were later collected as *The Devil's Dictionary*.[2]

THE CRACKERBOX ORACLE

All these writers made much use of the dominant type-character in nineteenth-century American humor, the cracker-box philosopher.[3] The eighteenth-century ancestor of this folk-oracle is Benjamin Franklin's Poor Richard, and the ancestor of the Poor Richard type is, as Franklin made clear, innumerable sententious philosophers and witty peasants of all ages. In America during the nineteenth century the crackerbox type appeared in a variety of guises. He might be a Yankee wiseacre like Seba Smith's Major Jack Downing or James Russell Lowell's Parson Hosea Biglow; a backwoodsman of the southern frontier like Davy Crockett, or an adventurer on some other frontier like

Bret Harte's stage driver, Yuba Bill. He might edit or write for a small-town newspaper as did Bill Nye, Robert J. Burdette (the "Burlington *Hawkeye* man"), or Alec Sweet (Col. Bill Snort).[4] In any case, all variations of the crackerbox type have certain features in common:

(1) They are predominantly of rural or small-town origin (though in the later part of their authors' careers, these characters appeared in periodicals in large cities).

(2) They are "just folks"—representatives of a mass of Americans who are between the extremes in wealth, education, interests, and mastery of the English language. As such, they are shy on book l'arnin' but long on common sense and mother wit. They articulate the unarticulated wisdom of the plain people. "I knew that already; it sure is so," readers may well have thought as they chuckled over Josh Billings' remark that "Evrybuddy that writes expeckts tew be wize or witty—so duz evrybody expect tew be saved when they die; but thare iz good reason tew beleave that the goats here after will be in the majority, just az the sheep are here."

(3) Their techniques include the anecdote or short (often "tall") tale, the homely metaphor, and the proverb or wise saw. Many of the crackerbarrel humorists wrote in a generalized rural dialect, and some made frequent use of grotesque misspellings. Thus Josh Billings uses the proverbial style, the domestic metaphor, rural dialect, and tricky orthography in commenting on the difference between English and American tastes in humor:

> So with their [Americans'] relish of humor; they must hav it on the half-shell with cayenne.

> An Englishman wants hiz fun smothered deep in mint sauce, and he iz willin tew wait till next day before he tastes it.[6]

(4) They are prone to overstatement rather than understatement. Thus Sut Lovingood refers to General Winfield Scott as "commander in chief of all the earth" and describes him as "an awful mixture of gold, feathers, iron, noise, gas, and leather."

(5) They often play the role of "wise fool," or shrewd ignoramus. Ringing a change on the tradition that out of the mouths
of babes, outcasts, and imbeciles often comes the audacious
truth, the humorous writers frequently made the country-store
philosopher expound unwelcome truths behind a protective
mask of character deficiency or of linguistic, logical, or factual
error. Sometimes the "inferiority" of this jester lies merely in his
illiteracy, as in the cases of Artemus Ward or Josh Billings;
sometimes it is manifested when he appears too stupid or un-
sophisticated to see the broader implications of his own statements. Thus Huck Finn notices that the hogs have the run of a
certain country church, and he says, "Most folks don't go to
church only when they've got to; but a hog is different." Sometimes the "fool" is conceited or downright vicious, and then he
is often made to expound views that the author really wishes
to oppose. In promoting these views, this character actually
turns the reader against them; Walter Blair points out that
Locke's Copperhead preacher, Petroleum Vesuvius Nasby, was
intended to boost the Union cause by the rascality and egotism
he showed in defending Secessionist sentiments.[7]

The uncouthness of the crackerbox philosopher had a special
value for his authors in that it enabled them to poke fun without giving offense. Walter Lippman has remarked that, "The
best servants of the people, like the best valets, must whisper unpleasant truths in the master's ear. It is the court fool, not the
foolish courtier, whom the king can least afford to lose."[8] The
crossroads oracles carried on the tradition of the court fools and
jesters in satirizing their readers in an era when the common
man was the uncrowned king, at least in the official mythology.
Too, they could, at the same time, flatter the people by giving
them a sense of superiority over the unlettered or conceited rube
even as this hayseed told them their faults. Moreover, any
criticism would tend to be directed at the fictitious oracle
rather than at the real but shadowy writer behind him. Thus the
writer could criticize his readers up to a point but still amuse
and hold them.

The wise fool was an especially effective disguise when he was made a member of some minority group distrusted or looked down upon by the majority. Hans Breitmann, created by Charles Godfrey Leland, and Yawcob Strauss, by C. F. Adams, were German and expressed themselves in pseudo-"Dutchy" dialect; Private Miles O'Reilly was Irish; Uncle Remus was a Negro; Benjamin Shillaber's Mrs. Partington and Marietta Holley's Samantha Allen were women; Huck Finn and Tom Sawyer were boys. The newspaper and magazine readership of America was still predominantly masculine, native-born, adult, and of Anglo-Saxon descent, and such creations appealed to them.

THE SOLID CITIZEN

A less prominent brand of late nineteenth-century humor than the crackerbox variety featured a different basic character type. Although somewhat wider in its variations than the rustic, this figure could be most sharply distinguished from him by the following attributes:

(1) He tended to live in the city or in the suburbs, especially when he appeared in periodicals of national circulation.

(2) Economically he was a little bit better off than "just folks." He was an idealized figure of the common man, representing not what most native-born Americans thought they were but what they hoped to become—a business or professional man who owned his own home (or could if he wanted to), and earned a substantial income which gave him some, but not too much, leisure. The idealization was not so extreme that the common reader could not easily identify himself with this figure. The solid citizen of humor in the eighteen-nineties was not rich, and he expected to better himself yet a good deal. The caption of the drawing by Charles Dana Gibson shown on page 18 concerns a young man who is worried about making his future wife happy on "only $2,000 a year." The girl expects to put fifteen hundred dollars of that money on her back. At that time, two thousand dollars represented an income that was comfortable but left little margin for luxuries. The man in this drawing is

a young variation of the middle-class individual who is or should be out to better his lot. As was often the case—in humor, at any rate—he shows more sense about financial matters than the girl.

(3) He was a model of good manners, avoiding the uncouthness of the rustic and the snobbery of the *nouveau riche*, with both of whom he was often placed in contrast. In deportment, and in clothing too, Gibson defined this character clearly in the "Gibson man" and the "Gibson girl," both of which he evolved for *Life* between 1887 and 1890. The young men and women in popular advertisements as well as in some humor came to be modeled largely upon the Gibson man and upon what Frank Luther Mott calls this "woman of refinement and gentle breeding." The Gibson male was a clean-cut fellow in sober broadcloth or in sporting flannels; he was usually a family man or about to become one through decorous courtship of the Gibson girl. Both were sturdily built; readers got in them vigor without coarseness and curves without sex. Although the laugh was frequently on them, "She [the Gibson girl] and the Gibson man became popular middle-class ideals,"[9] and the Gibson man may be said to have grown into Father Barber, of "One Man's Family."

(4) The norms of the solid citizen included language usage on a certain level. Regardless of the periodicals in which he appeared or of whether he was self-educated or college-trained, he and his wife (or sweetheart) and kin express themselves in correct prose of the "quality" magazines. Their fastidiousness in language kept these characters—and their authors, when the latter wrote in their own persons—from becoming as lively examples of humor as the somewhat less respectable crossroads oracles. Samuel Cox, an ex-Congressman and a connoisseur of political humor, had noted in 1876 that well-bred humor was becoming "a barren simper." "Our humor needs to be democratized. Our genteel laughter needs crossing with that of hearty toil.[10] A generation later, the laughter was still decorous. John Ames Mitchell, the Harvard graduate who founded and edited *Life,* said that the Gibson girl would never use poor grammar when

out of the picture.[11] The same was surely true of her masculine counterpart. Moreover, no distinction need be made between the level of diction of the solid, literate citizen and that of his creators. By contrast, a wide gap is frequently found in crackerbox humor between the literate verse or prose of the narrator (who is usually, though not always, identified with the author) and the illiterate speech of the rustic sage.

(5) Along with correctness in speech, the solid citizen showed a moderate acquaintance with culture. He could quote Shakespeare and the novelists whose works helped to fill his library—Scott, Dickens, Trollope, Thackeray, Bulwer, and possibly George Eliot. His acquaintance with music and the fine arts was limited, but he respected the arts as such, although he mistrusted painters, musicians, poets, and novelists as unstable, and he was suspicious of people too enthusiastic about these unprofitable occupations. Sketchy though his cultural background was, it placed him in sharp contrast with the crackerbarrel philosopher, who garbled Shakespeare and who distrusted culture categorically.

(6) Since he was an idealization in status and deportment, this solid citizen could less easily be made to play the fool—even the wise fool—than could the crackerbox oracle. He could be badgered and frustrated by his wife and family, as was Father Day a few years later, but the household definitely functioned as a means to serve him, not he them, and, like as not, his wife and children revealed themselves as irresponsible of mind and fickle in taste unless guided by the steady Victorian hand of the dominant male. Such a mental lightweight is the girl in the Gibson drawing who wants to spend three-fourths of her prospective husband's income on dress. Henry James' Daisy Miller was a mental and moral featherhead.

Whether the laugh was on him or not, the solid citizen in humor demonstrated certain judgments on the part of his authors regarding the good life. Those judgments which differed most clearly from the crackerbox humorists assumed the necessity of living in the city or suburbs, of "breeding" (in the sense of good manners), and of literacy. All three judgments are found in *The Suburban Sage* (1896), a string of sketches by Henry Cuyler Bunner that first appeared in *Puck*. The comic difficulties of the householder in these pieces mainly concern building the house, moving in, borrowing yard tools, commuting, golf, pets, real-estate promoters, and the unfamiliar loneliness of the new home at night (which also bothered Thurber's Mr. Monroe). By comparison with some of the workmen and promoters whom he depicts, the manners of this suburban citizen are impeccable. The language of his speech and reverie too is correct in grammar and diction, though informal in tone.

The "Autocrat" of Oliver Wendell Holmes had been a solid citizen in the values he embodied, despite his outspoken snobbishness in speaking of the uneducated, self-made man. In theory, the Autocrat rejected the self-made man, not so much because he was self-made and uneducated, but because he was likely to lack the social graces. The same concern for deportment is reflected in an anecdote in *Puck* which tells how a well-bred family was embarrassed by the boisterousness of a "Cousin in the Navy." Another joke in the same magazine runs:

> PRUYN.—Then you do not approve of the Universalist doctrine?
>
> MRS. DE PISCOPAL.—Oh, I have nothing to say of their orthodoxy; but I'm sure they're not sufficiently exclusive![12]

In the first item, most of the humor evolves from the crudeness of the sailor; in the second, from the snobbishness of the matron. In both, the implied point of view is that of one who assumes a norm between the two extremes. Contributors of magazine humor in the eighteen-nineties were, on the whole, less snobbish than Holmes had been in the *Autocrat,* but they were no less in earnest about the golden mean in manners and in attitudes toward social classes different from one's own.

The reader may compare the crackerbox type of character and the solid citizen by using Bathless Groggins in the present-day comic strip "Abbie An' Slats," and Judge Parker or Rex Morgan, M. D. (in the strips of those titles), as examples of the rustic sage and the urban citizen, respectively. Groggins differs from the "pure" crackerbarrel type only in having adventures that link him also with the rogue-hero of frontier humor. Despite the air of modernity in "Judge Parker" and "Rex Morgan, M. D.," the leading characters in these strips are also survivals of the nineteenth century. One is a jurist and one a physician, and each thereby retains some of the independence associated with the solid entrepreneur of two generations ago. Each is also an idealized model of stability and manners, and his high level of education is revealed in his speech as well as in the nature of his profession.

A NEW TYPE

In the first quarter of the twentieth century the two types were gradually to blend and form a new type, the "Little Man." This new character, who is still the major type-figure in American humor, resembles the solid citizen more than he does the crackerbox oracle, although he incorporates certain qualities of both and soon acquired some important traits basic to neither. (The crackerbarrel philosopher, like the solid citizen, has also survived as a distinct type alongside, as it were, the Little Man.) Despite the differences between the rustic philosopher and the urban citizen, the merging of the two should now surprise no one. In the eighteen-nineties the two types had much in common. Both embodied the belief that Henry F. May in *The End of American Innocence* says was most important among Americans until about the time of World War I—that moral values were fixed and absolute in nature. Both appeared on occasion as wise fools, the rural sage because of his ignorance and illiteracy, and the solid citizen—less often—because of deviations from reason and taste, deviations that included pomposity, arrogance, excessive good nature, and the inability to comprehend or manage his family. Both figures were of the middle class, and through them their authors usually took cautious, middle positions on subjects of popular interest. Thus both types were used to satirize the snobbery of the "Four Hundred" but also to make game of minority immigrant groups, and both types deplored political corruption but were skeptical of the more zealous reformers. More important, both venerated the Christian ethic, civil law and order, the family, home, Mother, and the sanctity of all women so long as women stuck to their two prescribed roles of ingénue and homemaker. In short, with a very few iconoclastic exceptions, both embodied the genteel tradition and the cult of decorum on which it rested.

In the later synthesis of the two types, the dominance of the solid citizen is shown in the way certain traits observable in this citizen during the eighteen-nineties became the major traits of the Little Man by the middle nineteen-twenties. In the nineties these traits were most easily observed in humor about the suburbanite. Traits shown by Bunner's suburban homeowner reappear, treated with more stress and more astringency when the middle-class citizen is recast by Ring Lardner, Don Marquis, Robert Benchley, and James Thurber. These traits include an overconcern with status, a concomitant distrust of manual laborers, inability to cope with household finances, and a nagging sense that one's wife is too much for one. Bunner's narrator reflects, "I know, of course, that I, myself, am managed at home, but I do not know just how it is done, and I am not likely to be let to know." Mild perplexity in Bunner's man becomes anxiety-neurosis in Thurber's, but the line of development between them is continuous.

THE PERIODICALS OF LITERATE HUMOR

Because the substantial citizen is the more obvious of the Little Man's two ancestors, it might be well to look further at some of the periodicals by which the humor that featured this citizen originally reached its public.

Much crackerbox humor first appeared in daily newspapers, but in the eighteen-nineties, apart from an occasional light essay masquerading as a book review, most of the more urbane and decorous humor—synonymous with that stressing the solid citizen—was confined to the magazines. The "quality" monthlies, chief of which were the *Atlantic,* the *North American Review,* the *Century, Scribner's, Harper's Monthly, Harper's Weekly,* and after 1895, the *Bookman,* printed a quota of humorous short fiction and essays each year. Most hospitable to humorists were the "Editor's Drawer" (conducted for a while by John Kendrick Bangs) of *Harper's Monthly,* and *Harper's Bazaar.* Contributors of humor to one or both outlets included Charles Battell Loomis, H. G. Paine, James Barnes, Hayden Caruth, Charles Dudley Warner, Joseph C. Lincoln (an early favorite of Thurber's), and Thomas L. Masson.

The humor in the "Editor's Drawer" probably reached a larger body of readers than that in the comic weeklies, and the humor in the quality monthlies as a group probably reached a public as large as that of the largest urban daily newspapers of the time; certainly it found a readership greater than that of the comic weeklies. Frederick Lewis Allen has estimated the circulation of *Harper's Monthly* in 1890 as between 100,000 and 200,000, whereas the peak circulation attained by *Life* in the eighteen-nineties may barely have touched 10,000. The circulation of *Harper's Bazaar* was undoubtedly much smaller than that of the firm's more famous monthly, but in 1892 only ten daily newspapers had circulations of more than 100,000, the New York *World* topping the list with 374,741 and the Chicago *Daily News* running second with 243,619. The era when Hearst and Scripps would each have dailies that counted their circulation in the millions yet lay ahead, and the biggest circulations in journalism were achieved by the magazines, of which the *Ladies' Home Journal* ranked all others in 1892 with 700,000 subscribers.[13]

The magazines that were primarily humorous fed a much smaller public—the circulation then attained by *Life* (1883–1936) may, as noted, barely have touched 10,000. However, this periodical, and *Puck* (1877–1918), *Judge* (1881–1939), and *Vanity Fair* (1868–1936) were weeklies and put out fifty-two issues a year as compared to the twelve for the monthlies, and the amount of polished humor that reached any public at all through these weeklies was therefore much larger than that appearing in the quality monthlies. The stream of "refined" humor in general was augmented by that in several less long-lived periodicals of the decade, notably *Truth*, *Clips*, the *Lark*, the *Wave*, and the *Wasp*. Gelett Burgess edited the *Lark* and published his "Purple Cow" therein.

The humor in the comic weeklies was indistinguishable in kind from that in the monthlies. Thomas L. Masson, one of the frequent contributors to the "Editor's Drawer" of *Harper's Monthly*, was only one of many such writers who also appeared regularly in *Life;* later he edited that magazine. *Life* (not to be confused with the present-day Luce magazine of that name)[14] was intended to be a satiric weekly of "higher artistic and literary merit" than *Puck* or *Judge,* but all three operated on about the same level of taste. Like *Harper's Monthly* and *Harper's Bazaar,* the weeklies did use some crackerbox material—as, for instance, Chucky the slum philosopher in Alfred Henry Lewis' *Verdict* (1898–1900)—but they paid much attention to finish of style and to subject matter of interest to people of some cultivation. *Life* has been dubbed "a product of the university wits" by Mott, the most thorough of American magazines; in finely cut English, *Life* crusaded against a wide assortment of what its editors considered breaches of decorum and of right reason, including fads in women's fashions, the snobbery as well as the vulgarity of the *nouveau riche*, Christian Science, the bicycle craze, and cruelty to animals. From time to time, of course, subjects of this kind were also treated in dialect by various newspaper writers. But authors in *Life* also had much to say about such "highbrow" matters as whether the specimens of art and architecture donated to the Metropolitan Museum of Art by General di Cesnola were spurious or genuine, and whether the realism of William Dean Howells, Henry James, and Stephen Crane was a welcome addition to formal literature. With some exceptions, most of the humorous participants in the struggle over realism, a struggle carried on throughout the literary world near the end of the cen-

tury, showed their gentility of taste by attacking this new phenomenon; they felt that "realistic" fiction was dull, amoral, lacking in heroes, excessively detailed and analytical, and irreverent
toward the past and toward things American.[15]

Most political humor in the nineties came from crackerbox
oracles. At first, *Life, Puck,* and *Judge* printed a good deal of
political satire, though not necessarily from the crackerbarrel.
The iniquities of Tammany Hall, the "folly" of Free Silver, and
the questionable tactics of well-known candidates of all the
major parties were among the main targets of these three magazines in the eighties and nineties. The moderately Republican
Judge originated the emblem of the "full dinner pail" which was
used as a symbol of the association of prosperity with McKinley
in the campaign of 1896. However, in that same year, Harry
Leon Wilson, the new editor of *Puck,* began to cut down on the
frequency of political topics in that periodical, and by the turn
of the century all three magazines were devoting less and less
space to politics. This trend continued until all were primarily
nonpolitical. Perhaps these magazines were following the lead
of *Vanity Fair,* which seems to have ignored politics consistently
throughout the decade. Among the monthlies, the same was true
of *Harper's Bazaar* (which, after all, reflected a male image of the
ideal Victorian woman). Thus, in the eighteen-nineties, the
magazines of humor were moving away from one of the traditional preoccupations of crackerbox humor.

The comic weeklies and the quality monthlies nourished a
number of cultivated satirists and wits who now lie in obscurity
alongside most of their cruder brethren of the newspapers.
John Kendrick Bangs, the first literary editor of *Life* (1884–
1888), worked on three Harper publications, edited *Puck* for a
short while (1904–1905), and for several years was chief reviewer
for the *Bookman.* Significantly, he also briefly edited (1903) the
Metropolitan, a magazine that preceded the *New Yorker* in trying to capitalize on the "smartness" and urban local color of the
metropolis. Clarence Day, Jr. wrote for this magazine a few
years later, after it had become a mildly socialistic, muckraking

organ. Henry Cuyler Bunner edited *Puck* from 1878 until his death in 1896 and contributed his "short sixes" stories and his sketches of suburbia to that magazine. Wilson, his successor, collaborated with Booth Tarkington in writing comic plays, and later wrote *Bunker Bean, Ruggles of Red Gap,* and *Merton of the Movies.* Oliver Herford has been called the wittiest contributor to *Puck* in its first two decades; he sparkled also in *Life.* Carolyn Wells' light verse could be found in several of the monthlies and weeklies. Except for specialists in literary history and for an occasional admirer among the next generation of humorous writers (Herford, for example, has been praised by Don Marquis and E. B. White), these writers lie as neglected as do Thomas L. Masson, R. K. Munkittrick, Charles Battell Loomis, H. W. Phillips, and Williston Fish.[16]

Was it topicality that killed their humor? Their contemporary, Mr. Dooley, was topical, and George Ade was scarcely less so in his *Fables in Slang.* Perhaps these cultured humorists of the nineties were just too polite. The genteel magazines had to wait until much later for rejuvenation by more pungent talent that had in part developed in the breezier medium of the personal newspaper column.

COLUMNS AND COLUMNISTS

If the reference by Samuel Cox to American humor as "genteel laughter" had been amended to read "genteel chuckles," it would have better fitted the atmosphere of the quality monthlies. Frank Moore Colby, writing after the turn of the century, chided these magazines and possibly the humorous weeklies for the stuffiness of their language: "Distinguishable English sometimes may be found in an American newspaper; it is never found in an American literary magazine. In some corner of a newspaper you may find a man writing with freedom and a sort of natural tact, choosing the words he really needs without regard to what is vulgar or what is polite."[17] In that last sentence, was Colby referring to the humorous newspaper column? He should have been, for between 1900 and 1920 the humorous column of the urban daily, conducted in each case as the personal organ of one writer, grew to become the most important single medium of American humor.

One reason for this importance was the freedom enjoyed by the personal columnist within the space allotted to him. Over a period of, say, a week, a typical column might include informal comments ranging from one-sentence quips to essays of several hundred words on any topics that had caught the columnist's fancy. These topics might be drawn from current headlines, from the author's reading, from his personal life and observation, or from all three sources combined, and they ranged in variety from golf to Greek myth. The columnist's range often equaled that of Addison and Steele—with whom, too, his work had stylistic affinities.

Another reason was that the humorous column had grown out of the crackerbarrel gossip of the small-town newspaper but, in "graduating" to the big-city daily, had left behind some of the crudities of the rural press. In combining the informality of the rustic oracles with the literacy of the better magazines, the metropolitan column doubtless filled a need felt by many people who had been reared in the country but had migrated to the city. Thomas D. Clark says that millions of such people continued to read small-town papers,[18] but many must have rejected such fare and yet longed for reading that would be chatty without being "countrified." In addition, many city-bred readers welcomed the humorous column as a relief from the impersonality or sensationalism of the news and the seriousness of the editorials.

A third reason, then, was that both those humorists who clung to the crackerbox approach and those who were developing in a more urbane tradition found major outlets in this kind of column—at the price of smartening their styles, in the case of the rustics, and loosening it in the case of the more cultivated sort. It may be significant that the first columnists to become well known in the twentieth century as humorists got their start with columns on papers in the Midwest or South, closer in spirit to large bodies of rural readers than were the New York City papers. Chicago was particularly rich in columnists. Eugene Field set an example, until his death in 1895, with "Sharps and Flats," his column for the *Daily News* in which he sometimes used dialect and sometimes wrote in "correct" prose but always reflected a certain suspicion of big-city life and ways, especially book learning. George Ade wrote "Stories of the Streets and of the Town" for the *Record* in informal but literate prose, except when he chose to introduce characters who spoke in dialects either rural or urban. Finley Peter Dunne introduced Mr. Dooley in a column for the *Evening Post.* Later, Ring Lardner, who, like Ade, had been reared in a small town and had migrated to the city, took over the sports column of the *Tribune,* "In the Wake of the News," and began to brighten it with an idiom that was not a regional dialect and was certainly not "correct," but rather was the speech of the semi-literate man everywhere in America. Elsewhere, H. L. Mencken began his "Knocks and Jollies" feature of the Baltimore *Morning Herald* (1901), and Don Marquis conducted personal columns in Atlanta, first for *Uncle Remus's the Home Magazine* and then in the daily *Journal.*

Some of these men, like Kin Hubbard in Indianapolis, continued throughout their careers to rely mainly on crackerbox characters for presentation of their material and views. Others, like Lardner and Marquis, developed well beyond the crackerbarrel tradition. Young columnists in the polite, cultured vein also found their opportunities in the newspaper column. In fact, the turn of the century may also have marked the turn of a corner in personal journalism and in humor. James Gray says:

> Bert Leston Taylor, who died in 1921, had set a new fashion in his editorial-page feature of the *Chicago Tribune* called "A Line-o'-Type or Two" [1900–1921]. Urbane, civilized, a little aloof, Taylor delighted his readers by pointing out the absurdities of American social life. A reference in a small town paper to a "quiet wedding" brought from him the comment: "Unmarred by the usual screams of the bride-

groom." His disciple Franklin P. Adams began his career in Chicago on the *Journal* [1903] and carried it to its finest point when "The Conning Tower" appeared in the New York *World* during the 1920's, offering a most attractive glimpse into the human studies of a studio habitué. Adams was a gourmet of gossip; his reliable taste created a new standard for the columnist-critic. Another Chicago columnist Keith Preston contributed to the *Daily News* witty translations from Horace.[19]

Urbanity and learning were becoming more and more acceptable as the number of city-dwellers rose, and the number of people with some education rose even more phenomenally.[20] By 1914, Don Marquis's "The Sun Dial" was only one of several columns in New York that followed Adams' example in commenting on weighty subjects in an urbane—but never "heavy"—style. Erudition without dullness was also a specialty of Mencken when he began "The Free-Lance" in the Baltimore *Evening Sun* in 1911 and used the mask of a rational but hot-tempered citizen as a shield from behind which to jab at both the average, unthinking fellow in the street and at the academic highbrow.

Thus the informal newspaper column had much to do with revitalizing American humor just before and after 1900. And during the first third of the new century it was partly in the newspaper column—which often reached a nationwide audience through syndication—that the crackerbox philosopher continued to spin yarns and to coin or re-coin proverbs, the solid citizen went on exemplifying "solid" values, and a third type, the Little Man, that absorbed traits from the other two types, became more and more prominent.

THE SQUIRE.

He's gone, the little village store
  Seems drear without him there;
The stove is cold, they've swept the floor
  And put aside his chair.

For Spring has come, the leafy grove
  Shows Winter drear is done;
The chronic loafer needs no stove,
  He's basking in the sun.

But then, in Summer's torrid days,
  The store keeps cool and dim;
He'll come back to his wonted ways
  And place long held by him.

There once again he'll arbitrate
  A nation's destinies,
And nonchalantly confiscate
  The crackers and the cheese.

R. I.

2

The Decline of the Common Man

Here, on the same page in *Puck*, are examples of two main character types in American humor: on the left, the crackerbox
philosopher; on the right, an early version of the Little Man and
his helpmeet, harassed by their environment. This type of couple
did not become prominent until the second decade of the twen-

A PROBLEM IN FINANCE.

MRS. FEWROCKS.—What are you so worried about, dear?

MR. FEWROCKS.—I am trying to figure out how we can live well enough to keep our creditors from getting suspicious, without living so high that we'll attract the attention of the income-tax inspectors.

tieth century. The "Squire's" title and his leisurely mode of life, and the clues about the income of the couple suggest middle-class standing for both types.

The gradual shift of focus in humor during the first third of the twentieth century from the crackerbox philosopher and the solid citizen to the less secure Little Man may be followed in the works and careers of the humorous writers discussed in the chapters that follow. How that shift of focus affected the values associated with the older type-figures, the hardiness of certain of these values, and the intensification in the Little Man of attitudes not usually considered desirable—insecurity, anxiety, fear, neurosis—may also be thus observed. However, to throw this change in emphasis into sharper relief, an attempt is made in this chapter to sketch the common man as depicted by certain writers outside the field of humor, to compare his image with its humorous counterpart, and to show how that image has changed in both humorous and nonhumorous writing. Whether this imaginary man fits the real man of flesh and blood, one cannot easily say. Not that the imaginary common man is irrelevant to the real one; the images of the ordinary man that are acceptable to a society made up largely of ordinary men are bound to have some relevance to these men as they actually are. However, the extent and nature of that relevance are matters too complex to be treated here. One can suggest only that the picture of this man in American humor bears some resemblance to the portrait drawn by writers in other fields.

SHRINKAGE AND DISINTEGRATION

Basically, the changes in this archetype have involved a shrinkage of the type in relation to its environment and a humbling in this mythical character's conception of himself. Economically this common man of the myth has become less independent; socially he has lost ground, and psychologically he feels less secure. In the late nineteenth century he was either a blend of Poor Richard and Honest Abe or such a plain but well-to-do businessman as Henry James' Christopher Newman; in either case he tended to be self-made, self-employed, and self-reliant; he lived in, or at least came from, a rural area, and, for better or worse, he was an active citizen and voter. By the middle of the twentieth century he had become a salaried, white-collar hack who still owned his own home but not his business, who lived in the city or commuted from a suburb, and whose relationship to the community and the State was mainly the passive one of consumer, both of goods and of propaganda. Moreover, he experienced much confusion of values and at times even doubted his own identity. As a citizen he had shrunk; as a personality he was threatened with disintegration.

This decline is only one of many changes in American geography, economy, science, politics, art, and social institutions, especially the family. At the risk of oversimplification, a very few of these changes may be summarized here. In 1890 the Bureau of the Census announced that the frontier no longer existed. Long before, a movement of "back-trailers from the middle border" (Hamlin Garland's phrase) had developed. This vast, invisible migration of rural and small-town people to the cities generated a counter-migration of the more successful back to the suburbs or the country. As Don Marquis put it,

> i have observed
> a queer cycle in human affairs
> a boy comes to the city
> from the country
> when he is twenty years old
> and works his nerves into tattered
> dishrags
> for forty years
> just to get money enough
> so that he can go and live
> in the country again and nurse
> his nervous breakdown[1]

This counter-movement was part of the decline in numbers of what both C. Wright Mills and Richard Hofstadter have called the "old" middle class—self-employed businessmen and farmers —and the rise of the "new" middle class—white-collar people on salary. Figures on this decline differ, but the proportion of the old middle class to the less self-reliant new seems to have gone down steadily from 1870 to about 1940.[2] The expanding suburbs were filling largely with the new middle class.

Related to these changes in physical environment and in social class was the political transmutation of the United States from an assemblage of state and local governments into a centralized maze illustrating what Louis D. Brandeis called "the curse of bigness." Possibly the change reflected most sharply in humor has been the rise of modern industry, especially as manifested in the automobile and in the mass media of communications—radio, movies, television, and advertising. The partnership of Big Technology with Big Business appears with particular blatancy in these fields, in which it is relatively easy to see how goods are mass-produced for an "affluent society" that is tempted by the mass media to consume them. A Harvard economist, John K. Galbraith, coined the phrase just quoted, but the ex-cowboy Will Rogers had much the same thing in mind when he quipped, "We are the first nation in the history of the world to go to the poorhouse in an automobile."

Concerning the more intimate spheres of the family and of individual personality, the changes most relevant to the new Fall of Man have been the impact of Darwinian biology, the "emancipation" of women, the rise of social science—especially the "progressive" education of children—and the boom in psychology, particularly of the Freudian persuasion with its emphasis on ripping open those parts of the personality that once were private. All of these phenomena are reflected in American humor by the shrinkage of the "common American," once the imperious Father of Clarence Day, Jr., now the henpecked Walter Mitty of James Thurber.

Let us look further at the early and late images of this archetype in the twentieth century. During the ground swell of political and social reform that pushed Theodore Roosevelt and

William Howard Taft into trust-busting and Woodrow Wilson
into the Presidency in 1912 on a ticket that included curbing
the great corporations, both reformers and conservatives felt that
they were working for the self-reliant citizen and entrepreneur
who had climbed a little way up the ladder of success and was
striving to go farther. Wilson hoped to bring about an era of
"new freedom" in which fair play would be assured for "the man
who is on the make," and deplored the possibility that his
children must be "employees or nothing." [3] Nicholas Murray
Butler, a staunch Republican, was no less insistent that "The
American is self-reliant by nature and by tradition," though he
somewhat illogically stressed that "The people have invested their
savings very largely in the stocks and bonds of railways and industrial corporations." [4] In any case, Butler seemed to take for
granted that the typical American was a small-businessman. A
writer in *McClure's* magazine referred to "the huge array of hard-
working, sober, intelligent men who, actuated by the most laud-
able sort of ambition, desire to climb from the precarious position
of employees to the more secure position of owners or part-own-
ers of industry."[5] William Allen White, a Republican with Progressive leanings, made a sharp distinction between "farming and
storekeeping and . . . many of the outdoor trades which require
alert minds" and the "other millions, bound to machines" who,
he implied, suffered from "arrested mental development."[6]

In addition to seeing the American as a member of the "old"
middle class, most spokesmen before the First World War associated him also with a rural background. White's statement reveals
a rural bias as well as a predisposition toward the small enterpriser as custodian of American values. Self-reliance, business
enterprise, and rural origins are also linked in Butler's saying
that "The American type is seen at its purest and best in any one
of the hundred or more small cities and towns in the Middle
West." [7] The statement of Butler, who was president of a university in New York City, was amplified by the Rev. Orison Swett
Marden, who asserted that "The sturdy, vigorous, hardy qualities,
the stamina, the brawn, the grit which characterize men who do

great things in this world, are, as a rule, country bred," [8] and by Meredith Nicholson, a novelist from Indiana, who called his native Midwest the "Valley of Democracy."

That the typical American was in the upper-middle income bracket economically and in the middle class socially was also assumed by popular commentators—including both those who did and those who did not deny the existence of class lines in America. White thought that if one eliminated "the submerged tenth" from consideration one would have left "the average man who lives on $75 a month" [9] (The average wage earner's income for 1910, the year in which White published his statement, has since been computed at $558 for the twelve-month period).[10] When a "Gibson man" in *Life* worried about being unable to make a girl happy on "only $2,000 a year,"[11] the salaried white-collar worker in manufacturing was probably making an average at that time (1896) of only slightly over one thousand dollars per annum. [12] The irony of Gibson's caption must have been relished by a fair percentage of the readers of the magazine.

Booth Tarkington too was confused in his notions of who were the "average" people. In *The Gentleman From Indiana* (1899), the heroine terms the people of Plattville "Just one big jolly family," and decries those who "speak of country people as the 'lower classes.' How happy this big family is in not knowing it is the lower classes!" Yet an important sequence of the plot depends on the conflict between the respectable town of Plattville and the northern poor-whites of Six-Cross-Roads, a settlement which, in the author's own words, "bears the same relation to the country that the slums do to a city." Meredith Nicholson was equally naïve in his reference to "the normal, the real 'folksy' bread-and-butter people who are, after all, the mainstay of our democracy." By these people Nicholson apparently meant those who lived in homes "that cannot imaginably be maintained on less than five thousand dollars a year." [13] Randolph Bourne reminded him that these "folks" were "the prosperous minority of an urban minority," and asked, "Could class division be revealed in plainer terms?" [14]

George Ade was more general in defining the middle classes of Chicago as all persons "who work either with hand or brain, who are neither poverty-stricken nor offensively rich. " [15] However, like most other commentators, Ade evidently thought of the common man as a *producer,* whether with hand or mind. Before the plush nineteen-twenties, relatively few writers stressed the average man's role as *consumer* of commodities, of services, and of ideas mass-produced and mass-marketed. One exception was William Graham Sumner, who, in 1883, had characterized the "Forgotten Man" as the hard-working citizen whose function is, above all, to pay, through his labor and his taxes, for the follies of reformers and idlers.[16] The Forgotten Man is the consumer-as-victim because he pays for something and gets nothing. Another exception was Walter Weyl, a spokesman of the reform movement that the successors of Sumner denounced. Weyl emphasized that the role of consumer ought to unite the motley democratic mass against the corporate trusts. He pointed out in 1912 that such catch-phrases as "the 'plain people,' " the " 'straphanger,' " "the 'man on the street,' " "the 'taxpayer,' " and "the 'ultimate consumer' " were coined as part of the political battle against the trusts' capacity to injure the consumer.[17]

Consumption is surely a more passive role than production, but Weyl's ideal common-man-as-consumer was still energetic and aggressive. Weyl was urging the average man to fight for his right to a just price as the means to the good life. Two other liberals, Charles Beard and James Harvey Robinson, wrote their textbook *The Development of Modern Europe* (1907–1908) "to enable the reader to catch up with his own times; to read intelligently the foreign news in the morning paper" [18]—that is, to assist the consumer of mass media in his battle for knowledge and integrity.

A few years later Robert Benchley was impugning the middle-class man's knowledge as mostly misinformation and his integrity as shaky, and Ring Lardner was suggesting that his knowledge was nil and his integrity even less.

THE MYSTERIOUS UNIVERSE AND THE COMMON MAN

The average man, at least as he was presented by some of his self-appointed spokesmen before World War I, was the core of a stable, democratic community that in turn was sustained by a rational, orderly cosmos presided over by a benevolent Deity (if one believed in the New Testament) or a nexus of beneficial natural laws (if one preferred Mr. Darwin or Mr. Ingersoll). Calvin Coolidge recalled that his philosophy professor at Amherst in the early nineties had believed and taught that a divine order prevailed in the universe, an order in which man had been set at the head of all living beings. "On that precept rests a faith in democracy that cannot be shaken," [19] said the man who broke the Boston police strike. Part of the fighting faith of Justice Louis D. Brandeis was his belief that the "eternal principles of liberty, fraternity, justice, honor" underlay economic and legal affairs and provided guiding lights for all to steer by.[20] A belief in progress was both explicit and implicit in such views, as Henry F. May has pointed out. Ella Wheeler Wilcox, a minor poetess, proclaimed in 1901 that

> We shall break each bond and fetter
>   That has bound us heretofore,
> And the earth is surely better
>   Than it ever was before.[21]

William Allen White and Walter Lippmann did not feel that progress came so easily and automatically as this verse implied, but they did believe that the good fight would be won because of what White called "the enlightened selfishness of the people— their public altruism." [22]

Nevertheless, Darwinism, with its stress on competition and strife in nature; social Darwinism, with its use of this doctrine of the "survival of the fittest" in nature as a justification of dog-eat-dog competition among nominally Christian businessmen; and Freudian psychology, with its stress on the irrational within man himself, were corroding the earlier image of a rational being at the apex of an orderly cosmos. Spread among intellectuals largely by Herbert Spencer, the philosopher, and Émile Zola, the novelist, and by popularizers of philosophy like Thomas Henry Huxley and Max Nordau, this new picture especially gripped the imagination of literary men. Stephen Crane stressed the indifference of the universe to man:

> A man said to the universe:
> "Sir, I exist!"
> "However," replied the universe,
> "The fact has not created in me
> A sense of obligation."

And without benefit of Freud he emphasized the irrational impulses from the mindless depths of the self that motivated his coward-hero in *The Red Badge of Courage*. Mark Twain reduced man's status in the universe even further, suggesting in *The Mysterious Stranger* that man was but "a homeless thought, wandering forlorn among the empty eternities." Frank Norris, Jack London, and Theodore Dreiser depicted man as merely an articulate animal, at the mercy of nature by virtue of both his uncontrollable passions and his unpredictable environment. John Dos Passos concentrated on the big, brutal city and its effect on this confused animal, and John P. Marquand stated that the main character in all his fiction was the badgered American male—"and that includes me—fighting for a little happiness and always crushed by the problems of his environment." [23] Marquand's statement could be applied with little change to the average American as delineated by Lardner, Marquis, Benchley, Thurber, E. B. White, and Perelman.

This view that man is but an animal and as such is part of a cosmic Nature composed merely of matter and/or force, and indifferent to human problems, is loosely termed "naturalism" by writers of literary history. Naturalism means that, "In Zola's words, 'men are but phenomena and the conditions of phenomena.'" [24] Like Christianity, it is rarely found in the pure state but exists in an unstable mixture with other world views, some of which are logically irreconcilable with this one. For example, Dreiser, London, and Dos Passos believed that man's actions were controlled by his heredity and environment; but part of the time these writers were also socialists and believed that human animals, working in cooperation, could exercise rational control over their environment and thus build a better world. Despite this contradiction, the naturalistic image of man was a compelling one among writers.

Naturalism received aid from the Freudians in altering the Christian and rationalist pictures of man. "There were many versions of Freud," warns Henry F. May, and most of them in America at first presented Freud "chiefly as a liberator of the soul, or at least the creative psyche." [25] However, Max Eastman wrote in 1921 that according to Freud and his followers men were "great surging tanks full of lust and suppressed carnal hungers, which they draw up into their minds." [26] This may have been an oversimplification of Freud's total view, but it represents an important element in the impact of his work and writings on many individuals in the nineteen-twenties. Even some of the writers who criticized the Freudian approach, as did Thurber and White in *Is Sex Necessary?*, made use of Freud's views on the irrational basis of personality. Thurber's Mr. Monroe and Walter Mitty are ruled in large part by aggressions that well up from their unconscious substrata, aggressions that are expressed in dream-fantasies of wish-fulfillment.

Thus the first half of the century saw much change in the images of the average man at work, at home, as a citizen, and as part of the cosmos. In relation to his work, this man was no longer David Harum leisurely swapping horses; he was Dagwood Bumstead diving for the bus in the morning, feet up and face contorted with frantic effort. In the home he was no longer the patriarch and master but merely the last among equals and certainly not self-reliant—if it weren't for Blondie, Dagwood would never roll out of bed in the morning. Moreover, the new type appeared less often as a breadwinner than as a mere consumer of gadgets and gimmicks forced on him by brash salesmen and high-pressure advertising. Frequently he became a mere accessory to his wife's merry purchase of hats, dresses, and other mysterious equipment.

As citizen, the Little Man was a consumer and victim who often appeared in political cartoons as a frail little fellow, with a face either chinless or bewhiskered after the fashion of the nineteenth century. He cringed before such monsters as Government, Big Business, Labor, the National Debt, or War Clouds. In certain prose portraits by H. L. Mencken, Ring Lardner, Damon Runyon, Corey Ford, Dorothy Parker, James Thurber, E. B. White, Will Cuppy, and S. J. Perelman, this man has lost all touch with or interest in social and political problems. He has become "privatized"—not reactionary but *in*actionary, as Professor Mills says.[27]

In his relation to the universe, perhaps the closest thing to an archetypal image of middle-class man became the patient on the analyst's couch. The Heavenly Father was replaced by Dr. Freud. And yet, few of the humorists believed that all was lost. As the reader examines the images of the American drawn by the humorists discussed in the following chapters, he will see over and over again that these writers have tended to present not one but two images—that of a mass-man or mob-man, and that of a sensitive, thinking man and citizen. Though their versions of the two types may differ vastly, each writer stresses the contrast between them and embodies positive values in his image of the thinking American. This image and those values will receive special stress in the rest of this book.

The cartoonist Jay N. ("Ding") Darling here portrays the Little Man in dismay at the political scandals of the nineteen-twenties and prayerfully grateful for "such men as Hoover, Hughes, Wallace and Coolidge." ("Wallace" was Henry A. Wallace, liberal editor of Wallaces Farmer and father of Henry A. Wallace, Vice President of the United States during the second term of Franklin D. Roosevelt, 1937–1941.) The gasoline lamp in the upper cartoon and the kerosene lamp in the lower suggest a rural setting, but the garb of this man is not that of a farmer, and the total impression is of the composite citizen irrespective of setting. (Courtesy Des Moines Register, Feb. 24, 1924.)

3

John Kendrick Bangs,
University Wit

One of the most prolific and certainly the most popular of
the "university wits" in the eighteen-nineties was John Kendrick
Bangs. Among those humorists who made use of the solid citizen
to exemplify decorum and morality, Bangs is also one of the few
whose work is not wholly forgotten (*A House-Boat on the Styx*

and *The Idiot* may still be found in even the smaller school and
public libraries).

THE WAYS OF COLLEGE MEN

Bangs was still an undergraduate at Columbia when he helped
John Ames Mitchell, a Harvard man, get out the first issue of
Life in 1883. During the four years that Bangs was literary
editor of *Life,* the Ivy League was well represented among his
associates on the magazine, who included Brander Matthews
(Columbia), Frank Dempster Sherman (Columbia), and Henry A.
Beers (Yale). Matthews and some of the others admired Mark
Twain, and Bangs as a boy was suspended from school for "turning the solemn function of declamation into a riotous orgy of
giggling" by reading in class a piece by John Phoenix, one of the
more restrained frontier humorists of the eighteen-fifties.[1] But by
and large the writing of Bangs and his colleagues represented a
more urbane, cultivated approach to American humor than that
of Mark Twain and the newspaper humorists, for whom the
country print shop had, like as not, been the prep school, and life
with a small "l" their Yale and their Harvard. The diploma
would have made a better symbol for Bangs' humor than the
composing stick.

Bangs was born in Yonkers, "located at that time about fifteen
miles from New York City, but now its too proximate next-door
neighbor."[2] The humorist's father was a well-to-do lawyer, and
the family tree was intertwined with the history of New England,
one ancestor having been a Pilgrim Father and another a president of Wesleyan University. Though mild fun-poking at high
society was part of Bangs' stock in trade, he was not above a bit
of racial and rural snobbery: "I also attribute my sturdy Americanism to my Westchester County birth, for, as I understand the
situation, to be born in New York City is an almost certain in-
dication of an alien strain whose prenatal affiliations are mainly
either Slavic or Neo-Tipperarian."[3] Like most of the humorists
discussed in this book, Bangs felt that his values were those of an
earlier, purer America, and in his genial fashion he defended
them against what he believed to be the encroachments of the

upper crust on the one hand and the unwashed alien on the other.

Bangs' family moved to Manhattan when John was four, and he grew up as a city-dweller. Following his graduation from Columbia in 1883, he studied law for a year, but was soon back with *Life*. In the next twenty-four years he worked at various editorial jobs for *Life, Harper's Monthly, Harper's Weekly, Harper's Bazaar, Literature* (another Harper publication), the *Metropolitan, Puck* (of which he was editor for a year, 1904– 1905), and the *Bookman*. Having reached comparative affluence through his editing and writing, Bangs moved his family back out to Yonkers and became a commuter. In 1907, at the age of forty-five, he moved still farther from the city and became a pillar of Ogunquit, a village in Maine. With this background and career, it is altogether fitting and proper that Bangs could say, "It is not necessary to be vulgar to be amusing," and his son could assert that "Bangs was rather of the *genteel* tradition but none the less American for that."[4]

Bangs' sixty-odd volumes of essays, tales, fantasies, parodies, plays, verse, and juvenilia consistently reflect his belief in the status quo of an earlier generation. The most entertaining chapter in *A House-Boat on the Styx* is, in part, an attack on Darwinian biology through *reductio ad absurdum*—the shade of Samuel Johnson declares that if Adam and Eve, as early human products of evolution, had tails, their first sin undoubtedly consisted in swinging by these appendages from the forbidden tree. The presence of the serpent in the biblical account is explained by the fact that " 'The serpent was the tail.' " Likewise, the ghost of Baron Munchausen insists that if monkeys do talk, they must do so in various languages:

> There are French monkeys who speak monkey French, African monkeys who talk the most barbarous kind of Zulu, monkey patois, and Congo monkey slang, and so on. Let Johnson send his little Boswell out to drum up information. If there is anything to be found out he'll get it, and then he can tell it to us. Of course he may get it all wrong, but it will be entertaining, and we'll never know any difference.

In the final chapter of *House-Boat,* this haven for harassed males is "captured" by the "New Women" of Hades, led by Xantippe, the termagant wife of Socrates. Here, and in *The Pursuit of the House-Boat* and *The Enchanted Typewriter,*[5] Bangs uses Xantippe to show his distrust of the crusade for female suffrage and other rights for women. He felt that the "New Woman," once she got her "rights," would be more of a martinet than husbands had ever been.

Throughout seven slender volumes[6] the Idiot also voices his distrust of new ways. The Idiot is a broker's clerk who indulges in "coffee and repartee" with his fellow-boarders at the breakfast table. He wears the white collar, but he is not a white-collared Little Man. Unlike the losers depicted by Benchley and Thurber, he is on the way up in his profession, and he eventually becomes a partner in the business of his father-in-law. That is, he is first seen as making his way and later as an entrepreneur. Moreover, his nickname is apt only as irony; his wit and logic get the best of every argument. Thus he is also a cultured variety of the wise fool.

Being the only man among the boarders who thinks for himself and says what he thinks—and the latter practice is the largest part of his "idiocy"—he speaks with the voice of reason and taste on the music of Wagner, bad poets, pedantic grammarians, the property tax, the proposed income tax, yellow journalism, high doctor bills, the arrogance of scientists, the New Woman, and many other topics. His "independent" thought usually locates him in the middle ground between extremes; thus he says that, "In the chase for the gilded shekel the education of experience is better than the coddling of Alma Mater," but he adds, "In the satisfaction—the personal satisfaction—one derives from a liberal education, I admit that the sons of Alma Mater are the better off." The reasonableness of his views is often disguised by whimsy through which he keeps his friends off balance. This whimsy frequently includes playing with the English language; on one occasion he baffles the group with the word "sciolist," and on another he descends to slang:

"Pouf!" said the Bibliomaniac. You are a reactionary, Sir."
"Ubetcha," said the Idiot. "First principles first, say I."

Bangs confessed that "With *The Autocrat* in one hand and a pair of scissors in the other, 1 created the Idiot."[7] Holmes' suave tyrant was a variety of the solid citizen, and the Idiot is a young man who is becoming one. So too is George Ade's "Artie." Both he and the Idiot already have sane, "solid" opinions, although Artie is more uncouth in language and somewhat more so in person than is the broker's clerk. Most of the characters on the *House-Boat* too are variations of the same traditional archetype.

Artie deserves mention here because his slanginess, which really amounts to an urban dialect, links him also with the crackerbox philosophers, and he thereby illustrates how the crackerbarrel sage and the substantial citizen were related despite their different levels of diction. Both exemplified moderation and horse sense in practical matters, and reason and responsibility whenever principles were involved. Both also were authoritative commentators on the passing parade of events and customs. Sometimes the two types even echo each other verbally. "I see by the paper this morning," begins the Idiot on one occasion, and Mr. Dooley's frequent "I see be th' pa-apers" leaps into mind. True, Dooley differs from the Autocrat and the Idiot in being genuinely ignorant of many details concerning the public affairs on which he pontificates, but he is usually aware of his ignorance, and his native good sense is equal to theirs. It is not surprising that certain young contemporary humorists were tending to merge the two types.

THE SUBURBANITE IN POLITICS

Bangs wrote much of his work from the standpoint of the fairly well-to-do suburban householder—even the Idiot has become one in *The Idiot at Home*. Bangs is thus in line with several earlier humorists of suburbia, including Frederick Swartwout Cozzens, whose *Sparrowgrass Papers* (1855) dealt with the problems of developing a farmstead near Bangs' own home town of Yonkers. Bangs also shows similarities to Hayden Caruth, who

contributed letters from "a country place" to *Harper's Monthly,*
and Henry Cuyler Bunner's *The Suburban Sage* (1896). With
Bangs, these writers anticipated the humor about suburbia by
Irvin S. Cobb, Robert Benchley, James Thurber, and E. B.
White, among others. Usually as a backdrop to the white-collar
citizen and his family, the suburb is a continual theme in humor
from the nineteenth century to such recent works as Eric Hod-
gins' *Mr. Blandings Builds His Dream House* (1946), Max Shulman's *Rally Round the Flag, Boys!* (1957), and Margaret Halsey's
This Demi-Paradise (1960).

In *The Booming of Acre Hill* (1900), Bangs voices the perennial complaint of the dignified older resident whose district is
being exploited by a new and blatant mode of promotion. As a
result of this promotion, the vicinity around his home has declined from an upper-middle-class to a lower-middle-class area:

> To-day Acre Hill is gridironed with macadamized streets
> that are lined with houses of an architecture of various de-
> grees of badness. Where birds once sang, and squirrels gam-
> bolled, and stray foxes lurked, the morning hours are made
> musical by the voices of milkmen, and the squirrels have
> given place to children and nurse-maids. Where sturdy oaks
> stood like sentinels guarding the forest folk from intrusion
> from the outside world now stand tall wooden poles with
> glaring white electric lights streaming from their tops. And
> the soughing of the winds in the trees has given place to the
> clang of the bounding trolley. All this is the work of the
> Acre Hill Land Improvement Company.

In this plaint, there is surely something akin to the grumbling of
Henry, Charles, and Brooks Adams about the get-rich-quick
tactics of the Vanderbilts and their ilk, something akin also to
those novels of John P. Marquand in which the Apleys and their
generation are contrasted with the new generation of less scrupu-
lous but more energetic businessmen. Bangs was only one of many
spokesmen for a class that was Nordic, native-born, prosperous,
and "proper," but was being shoved aside by the ambitious and
the hungry (including the alien), none of whom as yet had either
the means or the taste for Bangs' way of life.

Much of Bangs' political satire is the same sort of well-bred protest. *Three Weeks in Politics* (1894) is based largely on Bangs' own experience as a "Goo-goo" (Good Government man)—the name given amateur reformers by the old pros who generally ran the wards. Bangs had run for mayor of Yonkers and been defeated. Written shortly thereafter, this book takes the reader through the experiences of a citizen who is lured into a similar campaign by promises that he will be allowed to clean up the mess at city hall. The more obvious abuses of campaigning are reviewed, such as mudslinging from the platform, buying the support of the saloon crowd through "standing treat," and countenancing "repeaters" at the polls. Eventually Bangs' *persona* learns that he has been tricked into fronting for one gang of cynical grafters who merely hope to oust the other gang from power. The experience leaves him soured on politics in general. Bangs is especially acrid concerning the shameless appeal to the illiterate by both sides.

His urge to reform had severe limits, and in one of his more interesting fantasies, "A Glance Ahead, Being a Christmas Tale of A.D. 3568,"[8] he parodies the blueprint for state socialism outlined in Edward Bellamy's *Looking Backward* (1888), with possible jibes at William Dean Howells' *A Travelor From Altruria* (1894), and at the science fiction of H. G. Wells. However, Bangs' sketch is less striking as an attack on socialism than in its predictions of the role of applied science in the super-state of the future. The earth, we learn, is now heated and cooled from a central station and the temperature is kept at about seventy degrees. Ships run regularly to Mars, but are overcrowded in holiday time. Children have long been abolished and the world's population is regulated scientifically. "When Dr. Perkinbloom discovered how to separate man's mental from his physical side, by means of this little door in the cranium, all the perishable portions of man were done way with," and human bodies are now manufactured by a process the secret of which the inventor is permitted by the Government to retain, "although the factories are maintained under the supervision of the Tailor-General."

Thirty-one years before Aldous Huxley published *Brave New World*, Bangs anticipated the world super-state and the "Bokanovsky process" of decanting babies. In a later piece, *Alice in Blunderland* (1907), Bangs poked fun at ownership of property by municipalities. His distrust of reform also cropped out in his parody of *The Jungle*, by Upton Sinclair, whom Bangs renamed "Dopeton Hotair." In this work he referred to *Everybody's Magazine*, one of the muckraking periodicals, as "Busybody's Magazine," and to George Bernard Shaw as a "Megotist" and as "the acknowledged leader of the Neo-Bunkum School of Right Thinking."

Bangs was no friend to the wealthy "Rockerbilts" and the "Bondifellers"; indeed, he accused them of irresponsible speculation and of indifference to "squalid misery." But his utterly middle-class outlook is shown in his discussions of the "servant problem," one of the favorite humorous themes of the Victorian era. For example, *Paste Jewels* (1897) consists of seven tales about the difficulties with "help" experienced by a suburban family, and the chief implication of these stories is that one should be stern but fair with hired domestics (like Father Day perhaps). In the next to the last tale, a sort of climax is reached when papa's Christmas gift to the family is to fire the cook, maid, and hiredman. That Bangs ignored what servants in real life might think of such a "gift" shows how effectively his outlook was screened by the privet hedges of the middle-class householder.

Francis Bangs labeled his biography of his father *John Kendrick Bangs, Humorist of the Nineties,* and although the elder Bangs poured out a stream of humor almost until his death in 1922, the title fits. In genial and genteel prose and verse he defended the status quo of the McKinley era against the snobbery and irresponsibility of great wealth, the zeal of reform groups in his own social bracket, and the machine politics of the masses as well as their pushiness and general illiteracy. Long before his death, the rougher humor of Ade, Dunne, Mencken, and Lardner had made Bangs seem quaint and insipid, although the targets of their satire and his remained much the same. Yet Bangs interests us, not only for his rearguard action but as a foreshadower of new trends in humor. During the first ten or fifteen years of the new century, the humorous tradition which Bangs represented, consisting of decorum in conduct, correctness in language, and unashamed learning, all incorporated in a narrative *persona* of dignity, moderate means, and eminent respectability, became dormant. It would revive—with less mellowness and more tension, but also with more vigor.[9]

PART TWO

Crackerbarrel Survivals

4

George Ade,
Student of "Success"

The unity of humor about middle-class man is rippled on the surface by contrasts between midwestern and eastern humor, between humor of cultivated and colloquial groups, and between that of self-educated writers and those trained in universities. In general, the best known specialists in "low" language were self-educated midwesterners. During the first fifteen years or so of the new century, the urbane wit and humor of such cultivated easterners as John Kendrick Bangs, Clarence S. Cullen, Miles Bantock, Frank Moore Colby, and Harry Thurston Peck—all of whom adopted the upper-middle-class male of considerable culture as their most sympathetic type—was overshadowed by the satire in dialect or slang of George Ade, Finley Peter Dunne, and Kin Hubbard, writers whose language identifies them with the crackerbox tradition but whose basic character type in every case had many traits of the solid citizen as well as of the crackerbarrel philosopher (this citizen, however, was denied by his authors the culture to be had from books). During the following ten years or thereabouts, the humor of cultivation was still overshadowed by the gravelly prose and uncouth character types of Will Rogers and Ring Lardner, two more humorists from the hinterland, while the erudite but ungenteel satire of H. L. Mencken and Don Marquis captured a fair share of attention. Of these seven writers, only one (Ade) had a university degree, and only one (Mencken) came from the eastern seaboard. Six were from the Midwest, and one (Rogers) came from the western fringe of that area.

All this is a way of suggesting that the rural crackerbox tradition and the humor of urbanity and urban living were, in some writers, undergoing a process of blending. By the end of the nineteen-twenties, a new crop of humorists, some from the Midwest and some from the East but all with university diplomas and all writing mainly for magazines in eastern cities, would have reestablished a style with crackerbox informality but with university standards of diction, grammar, and allusiveness as an important medium for printed humor. This humor would also present an urban or suburban citizen with considerable education—though with less social standing and less inner security than the older "pillar of the community" type—as its most sympathetic character.

But when George Ade first arrived in Chicago, these germinating trends were evident to few.

TO THE BIG CITY

In 1893, Frederick Jackson Turner delivered his paper on "The Significance of the Frontier in American History," in which he stressed, among other things, that the frontier was now at an end. However important to homesteaders and historians, this idea meant little to a small-towner in Chicago whose frontier was real enough, even though it included scenes like this one:

—in the foreground a morgue for empty bottles, barrels, and old packing-cases; in the middle distance a row of chimneys, and in the distant prospect the stately uplift of the Polk Street Station tower outlined against the western sky.[1]

Such, in the words of John T. McCutcheon, was the view from the ten-by-twelve hall bedroom occupied by that cartoonist and by George Ade during their first months in Chicago. Ade and McCutcheon were living their parts in the great American country-to-city, bottom-to-top drama of achieving success and paying its price. They conquered their frontier and watched others trying to do the same—and McCutcheon drew them and Ade wrote about them.

Ade was born "in 1866 in a little Indiana town framed with cornfields." [2] Kentland, which squatted near the Illinois line about seventy miles south-southeast of Chicago, was the type of small town that appears in many of Ade's fables in slang, with "the Corn-Fields sneaking up on all sides of it, trying to break over the Corporation Line." Ade's father was a blacksmith, a storekeeper, and a Methodist. George's mother joined the Campbellites, but Fred C. Kelly asserts that "the household was happy and harmonious." Perhaps it was. In the story "To Make a Hoosier Holiday," Ade depicts a town whose chief product is the ill will springing from a continual squabble between folk of the Methodist and Campbellite churches, but this discord need not necessarily have affected the Ade household.

In high school, Ade showed a flair for composition and wrote at least one effusion that has been printed,[3] the gist of which

was: "Friends, remember this; in the tough, earnest battle of
life the big potatoes will go to the top and the small ones will go
to the bottom. . . . And so it is everywhere, life is but a basket
of potatoes. When the hard jolts come, the big will rise and the
small will fall. The true, the honest and the brave will go to the
top. The small-minded and ignorant must go to the bottom."
Much of Ade's humorous writing as an adult was one long "Oh,
yeah?" to such classroom moralities, but as will be seen, he never
wholly abandoned them.

For a while Ade went neither to the top nor the bottom; he
went to Purdue. In 1887 he emerged with a B.S., but, as so often
happens, his subsequent jobs bore little relation to the nature of
his degree. He worked as a reporter on two newspapers in
Lafayette, Indiana, and briefly held a job with a patent-medicine
firm. Three years out of college, he finally grew restless and went
to Chicago.

In the early eighteen-nineties, Chicago had just passed the
million mark in population and was also becoming a literary
center. Theodore Dreiser, just twenty-one, went to work for the
Globe as a reporter in 1892. Henry Blake Fuller wrote *The Cliff-
Dwellers* in 1893; in the same year Robert Herrick, soon to be a
novelist of the same moderately realistic sort, joined the faculty
of the University of Chicago. In journalism and in humor the
city already could boast concentration of talent. When Ade
began writing his own column in 1893—the same year in which
Turner read his paper—for the *Record* (later the *Record–Herald*),
Eugene Field's column, "Sharps and Flats," was a feature of the
Daily News, Bert Leston Taylor was doing "A Line o' Type or
Two" for the *Tribune,* and Finley Peter Dunne had started to
write sketches in Irish dialect for the *Evening Post.* Moreover,
the newspaper humorists were a fairly close-knit crew. Ade told
Franklin J. Meine that "I knew Field and Dunne rather inti-
mately. We were all members of the old Chicago Press Club, but
in the Nineties a number of us purely professional newspapermen pulled out and started an independent Newspaper Club of
our own." [5] Field and Dunne were both included in this im-

portant new group, the "Whitechapel Club," in which the crackerjacks of the city's press traded wit and ideas. Ade might have become a successful humorist in any city, but Chicago certainly offered him a special brand of stimulation.

"STORIES OF THE STREETS AND OF THE TOWN"

The second act of Ade's personal drama of success began in November, 1893, when he was given a two-column feature department all his own in the *Record*, entitled "Stories of the Streets and of the Town." For this department he wrote sketches that gained him local popularity and included pieces that remain among his more interesting work. He conducted this daily feature for seven years, and supplied it with an immense amount of material, including straight news, parodies, verse, dialogues, and fiction. Some of the fictional sketches were eventually collected in book form, often with revisions, as *Artie* (1896), *Pink Marsh* (1897), *Doc' Horne* (1899), *In Babel* (1900), and *Bang! Bang!* (1928).[6]

Many years later, Ade wrote of the nineties:

> At that time Chicago was the stew-pan of creation. It was a roaring, brawling multitude of suddenly assembled specimens from all parts of the world. The saloons kept open 168 hours every week. The downtown district was polka-dotted with gambling houses and poolrooms. The levee district swarmed with riff-raff. In the red-light region vice was noisy and unashamed. To offset this brazen cussedness, Chicago had the civic pride and unselfish public spirit which made possible the Columbian Exposition. It was the home of entertainment and the newcomer could get a liberal education while he waited.[7]

To get some of that liberal education between 1893 and 1900, one could do worse than read Ade's column. True, Ade purged his pieces of anything that might offend many readers of the paper. Politics he left to the editorial writers, and pleas for or against social reform were usually conspicuous by their absence. Off-color words and jokes were outlawed from his otherwise convincing re-creation of street language, and so were the more lurid and suggestive details of life among the riffraff. Ade's realism, like that of Fuller and Herrick, was genteel.

Nonetheless, it deserves more than a smirk. Graphically Ade described office buildings, canals, street crowds, saloons, dance halls, hotels, markets, family circles, and police courts. Occasionally he could be forthright in his depiction of the drab aspects of city life:

> In front of the police-station the street was a dismal slime. A fine rain beat into the black puddles and helped to soften the islands of mud. Dripping trolley-cars went by, hissing in disgust, the dirty water lifted by the wheels. Now and then, through the fog and drizzle, some one came wading, stamped his feet on the mucky stone sidewalk and entered the station.
>
> Within the sheltered arch there was a smell of wet clothes. The men who stood there had their coat-collars turned up and their hats pulled down. They stood and looked out at the rain with deadened eyes. The hallway beyond was gloomy, and the men against the wall talked in growls.
>
> At first the court-room seemed like a cavern, with dim shapes moving stealthily, their soggy feet making little noise on the floor. When the eye became more accustomed to the gloom, there were two sections of benches facing the high place where the magistrate was to sit.
>
> The water dripped on the sills outside. The walls beyond were rain-soaked and blurred by fog. Along the benches the men and women sat motionless—immersed in melancholy.

In another police court scene, Ade mentions "chalky women with their hats pulled forward, who showed a weary and smiling contempt for this familiar process of taxation." Obviously Ade was not untouched by the drift toward Émile Zola's type of frankness, a drift which included Crane, Norris, and Dreiser (though *not* Bangs and his school of humor).

At first Ade stuck to straight reporting, but gradually he included more and more fiction, usually based on character types whom he conducted through loosely interrelated adventures.[8] No longer bound by literalism, Ade would de-individualize a character whom he had actually observed and make him a representative type by blending in him various traits from other specimens he had seen and heard. Even thus had Mark Twain, with greater skill, made Tom Sawyer a blend of three different boys in Hannibal, Missouri.

In constructing these types, Ade was mingling traits of the crackerbox philosopher with those of the substantial citizen, as were also Finley Peter Dunne, George V. Hobart, and E. W. Townsend. First, there is Artie, who is city born and bred and whose favorite term of abuse is "farmer." However, his courtship of Mamie Carroll reminds one of "The Courtin' " by James Russell Lowell and of *Major Jones's Courtship* by William T. Thompson—two pieces which featured the crackerbox motif of the awkward suitor. Artie is also at one with his crossroads counterparts when he speaks in aphorisms—"Take a guy that bellers at kids and bluffs women and put him against a man of his own weight and he's a cur . . ."—and in homely metaphors— "When you come to know the town [Chicago] it's as common as plowed ground." On the other hand, Artie is like Bangs' Idiot and Townsend's Chimmie Fadden in being a young scrambler for success and status. His job is low-paying but steady, and he means to keep it until he can do better. He subscribes wholly to the official credo of success—"I ain't one o' them beefers that's got it in for people just because they've got the coin and make a front with it. I'm out for the stuff myself." Yet his integrity, sense of moderation, and chivalry toward women are such that one reviewer hailed Ade's book about him as "immeasurably more wholesome than all the stories like 'George's Mother' [by Stephen Crane] that could be written by an army of the writers who call themselves realists." [9]

Two types more in the crackerbarrel mode are Doc' Horne and Pink Marsh. Doc's forum is the lobby of the Alfalfa Hotel, where he can spin tall tales about his past that make his hearers forget the present shabby setting. One of his yarns is a well-worn

backwoods piece about how a horse got mired in a country road
and sank out of sight, "and they had to dig about five feet before
they came to the saddle." [10] Pink Marsh is a bootblack and is
also one of the first examples in humor of a northern, city Negro
portrayed as a central character. [11] Often Pink is a white man's
stereotype of the grinning, shiftless "stage darky," but he can also
philosophize as a wise fool, especially in the few instances where
Ade skirts the race issue. Pink says once, "I don' mean to 'sinuate
'at a cullud man ought to do anything 'at a white pusson does,
but what ahgament I make, Misteh Cliffo'd, is 'at he's got right
to do it undeh ouah law." Concerning the breakup of a Negro
entertainment by some Irish thugs, Pink says wryly, "We got mo'
rights 'an anybody, but it sutny ain't safe to use 'em."

Ade did not neglect genuinely rural types, but he tended to
treat them briefly if sometimes vividly. One country girl, Effie
Whittlesy, gets work as a domestic in the city and finds out with
pleasure that she is from the same rural area as her employer.
The wife acts snobbish about this; the husband doesn't, a difference in attitude toward class distinctions which appears in some
of the fables in slang about successful husbands—usually rural
types—and socially ambitious wives.

Of significance equal to his treatment of crackerbox characters
in an urban environment are Ade's occasional portrayals of
middle-class city people when they stop work and try to play. In
such cases one sees Weyl's common-man-as-consumer, but not as
Weyl and other Wilsonians and Progressives hoped and felt that
this man would act. Ade's critical view of the average American
at leisure much more closely resembles that of Ring Lardner.
The moderately well-fixed Barclay family are stuffy and snobbish,
and the conversation of Ollie and Freddie, gilded youths-about-
town, anticipates in its vacuity some of the dialogues Lardner
was to re-create twenty years or so later:

> "Who's that?"
> "Vesta Tilly."
> "That's right. I think she's great."
> "She's dog-goned fine."

"I liked Yvette Guilbert too."

"Yes, I think she's elegant."

"Did you think she was good-looking?"

"No, I didn't think she was, but Billy Pendleton says he thinks she's good-looking."

"The dickens he does! No, I don't think she is."

"Neither do I. She's good, though."

"Yes, I always thought she was elegant."

Ade preceded both Lardner and Dorothy Parker in depicting the "working girl," whom he treated realistically, yet sympathetically. On the one hand, there is the shopgirl who tattles on another no less obnoxious and gets her fired. On the other, there is Min Sargent, who walks resolutely into an office and talks her way into a clerical job. She is "red-cheeked, bright-eyed, curly-haired, shirt-waisted, straw-hatted. Her nose had just the slightest tilt upward." Here is a self-reliant type in petticoats—a fit mate for Artie if he didn't already have Mamie. Ade makes clear that Min lives with her parents; presumably her morals are therefore impeccable—unlike those of Sister Carrie, a more famous female entrepreneur.

Incidentally, the working girl in fiction from the eighteen-nineties until at least after the First World War must generally be considered an entrepreneur, whether she is an actress, office-worker, shopgirl, or contributor to the "social evil." She is not usually self-employed, but whether she is ambitious for a career or is merely marking time until the right man comes along, she is breaking new ground as a climbing member of an under-privileged group,[12] and as such, is emphasized as having the degree of initiative then commonly associated with free enter-prisers.

In themselves, Ade's "Stories of the Streets and of the Town" form a neglected body of work uneven in quality but often note-worthy for its realistic treatment of city life. As a part of the de-veloping "new humor," the stories included crackerbox types in the city, young men and women who would undoubtedly become solid citizens, and average city people of some affluence and leisure. They also featured some of the characters and thematic material that reappeared in the more famous fables in slang.

FABLES IN SLANG

Ade later claimed that he was bored and just fooling around one day in 1897 when he filled his "Streets and Town" column with his first fable in the vernacular.[13] Friends liked it, but not until ten months later did he try this line again. Then Herbert Stone, his book publisher, urged him to do some more. The first collection of *Fables in Slang* was published in 1899 and sold an impressive if not amazing seventy thousand copies in its first year. It was followed by nine more volumes of fables in the next twenty years,[14] before Ade stopped writing these tales and retired on the fortune they had brought him.

The medium was as old as Aesop and had been honored by Marie de France and La Fontaine. In Ade's own lifetime, Ambrose Bierce had contributed satirical fables to *Fun,* a London periodical, as early as 1872, and Guy Wetmore Carryl *(Fables for the Frivolous,* 1898) and Josephine Dodge Daskam *(Fables for the Fair,* 1901) were also working this vein. Philip Nordhus mentions another fabulist, George T. Lanigan, as a possible influence on Ade.[15] By 1882, Eugene Field was writing the "Tribune Primer" pieces for the Denver (Colorado) *Tribune*— pieces which, though not exactly fables, set a precedent in parodying the McGuffey readers, and in 1893, Harry Leon Wilson wrote a parody of McGuffey for *Puck.*

The McGuffey readers, with their free capitalization and sugary moralizing, were certainly Ade's main inspiration. But another group of tales may also have stimulated him, either consciously or unconsciously. Ade had contributed to *Puck*[16] and was undoubtedly scanning the other humorous magazines, including *Life,* as possible takers of the stuff that he didn't feed into his column. In 1896 a series of "Fables for the Times" appeared in *Life,* written by Henry Wallace Phillips. They consisted of Aesopian plots reworked as satires on contemporary topics, much in the manner of Bierce. Phillips had will rather than talent, but one of his efforts may be reprinted, if only as a sample of his standard prose in contrast to the uncouth diction of Ade's fables:

THE OLD MAN, HIS SON AND THE ASS[17]

An old man and his little boy were once driving an ass to the market place. "What's the mater with one of you riding?" said a passer-by. So the man put his boy on the ass and they went on. The next person they met said it was a shame to see a boy ride while an old man walked. The man lifted the boy off and got on himself. This also excited adverse comment, and the man took the boy up behind him. The next critic was a member of the S.P.C.A., and he upbraided them both roundly, saying that they would better carry the ass than he them. Thereupon they tied the ass's legs to a long pole and carried him between them. While crossing the bridge, into town, the man stumbled and the ass fell into the water and was drowned. They promptly sued the city for damages, and compromised on $263, more than eight times the value of the ass.

Immoral: Hard luck cannot touch smooth people.

Phillips' moral has a cynical twist, as Ade's often had.

And here is the opening of Ade's "Fable of How He Never Touched George":

A comic Lover named George was sitting on the Front Porch with a good Side Hold on your old friend Mabel. They were looking into each other's Eyes at Close Range and using a rancid Line of Nursery Talk.

It was the kind of Conversation calculated to Jar a Person.

George murmured that Mabel was George's own Baby-Daby and she Allowed that he was a Tooney-Wooney Ittle Bad Boy to hold his Itsy-Bitsy Bun of a Mabel so tight she could hardly breave. It was a sort of Dialogue that Susan B. Anthony would love to sit up Nights to Read.

Ade found that "it was a great lark to write in slang—just like gorging on forbidden fruit," and his recipe for a fable was "one portion of homely truth, one pinch of satire, a teacupful of capital letters, well spiced with up-to-date slang and garnished with woodcut drawings."[18] In consequence, the language of gentility took a beating that was probably good for it in the long run, even as wholesome flagellation would have benefited certain little boys in the McGuffey readers.

Ade's formula for his fables changed little, and by 1900 his ideas too had become set in their essentially nineteenth-century mold. Consequently, these tales, although written during more than two decades, may be treated as a single group.

William Dean Howells has said that all of Ade's fables concerned two themes, "the Girl Proposition and the Money Proposition."[19] He might better have said that their two main topics were the Success Proposition and the War Between Men and Women, with the two themes often closely interrelated.

Success: its requirements, nature, and rewards—this complex topic had appeared fragmentarily in "Stories of the Streets and of the Town." A number of the fables ask whether the requirements of success really do include the morality taught in the schoolroom. Work hard, live right, and money and fame will be yours—hadn't that, in essence, been the great American sermon on the mount of eminence, from Franklin to Andrew Carnegie and Horatio Alger, Jr.? "What! is nobody idle? Then little boys must not be idle," [20] said McGuffey. Ade's reply to such admonitions included several fables about pairs of contrasting characters in which the "bad" or idle one succeeded and the "good" one didn't. In nearly every case, the successful member of the pair went to the top mainly because he was able to manipulate other people, largely through "putting up a front" of affability and aggressiveness; if he "worked," it was to maintain that front. Ade's first fable, about "Sister Mae, Who Did as Well as Could Be Expected," was of this order. Mae "lacked Industry and Application," but she used her looks and charm to marry wealth and break into society. Eventually she took her industrious sister out of a sweatshop "and gave her a Position as Assistant Cook at five Dollars [a week]." The moral was, "Industry and Perseverance bring a sure Reward."

In another fable of contrasting careers, "The Bookworm and The Butterfly Who Went into the Law," the dashing man-about-town prospers as a lawyer and hires his studious brother to do the real work for him while the dasher reaps the credit. In another story between the same covers (in *Forty Modern Fables*), pure "front" enables a doctor who is a good mixer and a flashy dresser to acquire a lucrative practice while his quiet, hard-working colleague gets a reputation for irresponsibility because he has accumulated no property and doesn't press his patients for their overdue bills. The gullible, unmoral public are implicitly satirized here, as elsewhere in Ade's work.

In other fables Ade further suggested that a ruthless expediency which included pandering to the lowest tastes of one's public or one's customers was often a requirement of success in any field. A certain preacher enthralls his congregation only when he inflates his sermon with rhetoric and fake learning. A writer soars to popularity through a sentimental poem entitled "When Willie Came to Say Good Night," while his more solid efforts in prose remain comparatively unknown (this fable was based on Eugene Field's success with "Little Boy Blue"). A "Canny Commercial Salesman" talks about predestination to a devout grocer, and the grocer's sales resistance crumbles.

Yet Ade declared that the fable of Sister Mae, and by implication, his other fables, "was not intended to corrupt the morals of Methodist families and teach babes in arms to grow up to be poker players." Wasn't it? In many of these tales the "unofficial" philosophy works. A self-made political boss tells the pupils at a school of which he is a "tough trustee" that he has succeeded by "doing the other fellow." "Self-made Hezekiah" makes his million and gives a pious talk with no sense of the inconsistency between his chicanery in business and his piety outside the office. Ade ironically stresses that Hez did make money. In "The Fable of the Two Mandolin Players and the Willing Performer,"

a nervy suitor wins the girl and a good job in her father's firm
on the basis of aggressiveness rather than manners.

However, Ade's fables are often less cynical than the action
suggests at first reading. Ade did not so much reject the Mc-
Guffey quadrivium of honesty, perseverance, industry, and frugality as merely claim that these qualities, by themselves, did not
guarantee success. The fact that "pull" gets a top job for the
playboy son of a major stockholder while the "Patient Toiler"
who had hoped for the post remains in a lower spot does not
mean that hard work in itself is valueless; "Essie's Tall Friend"
is fired for neglecting his job to moon around a girl. In a sense,
Sister Mae does not lack industriousness; to this quality she adds
the ability to make the most of her natural advantages. Industry
and perseverance bring rewards only if resourcefulness and aggressiveness are added. "Honesty" is dissected by Ade into at least
two meanings, public and private. Ade suggests that honesty
in the public pursuit of success is an idle word, yet none of his
self-made men and women are dishonest in their private lives.
He accepted the divorce between business and morals which was
part of the ideology of "rugged individualism," although he
did not examine the biological and economic bases of this ideology as Theodore Dreiser did in his three novels about Frank
Cowperwood. Nor did Ade care to inquire whether there might
not be, after all, a connection between the need for ethics in
one's private life and a need for some rules in business and in
public office. Ade was content to stress the naïveté in the school-
books' applications of private morality to the quest for success.
His ridicule of this naïveté and his lack of interest in broader
ethical problems constitute the extent of his cynicism—and possibly of his own naïveté.

THE SELF-MADE MAN'S WOMENFOLK

A major topic in fiction just before and after the turn of the
century was the social aspirations of the successful man's family.
The wife and offspring of the *nouveau riche* often wanted to

climb far above the level of the husband and father who had made the money. He, however, tended to remain a solid citizen with plain, "countrified" tastes. Henry James observed that "This failure of the sexes to keep pace socially" was "perhaps more suggestive of drama . . . than anything else in the country." [21] Booth Tarkington and Edith Wharton—far apart in other ways—were also examining the family life of the *nouveau riche* during the years when George Ade was doing likewise in his narrower medium.

Ade showed two different feelings about the self-made man. He often portrayed this man as strictly a money-maker, dull outside his speciality; yet he frequently sympathized with this breadwinner when depicting his family troubles. He once wrote, "When Providence is directing the Handouts, she very often slips some Squarehead the canny Gift of corraling the Cush, but holds out all of the desirable Attributes supposed to distinguish Man from what you see in the Cages at the Zoo." He also sketches a self-made executive who died of a broken heart because he couldn't play golf well, and a "Business Slave" who built an expensive country-place which he never got around to using. Ring Lardner could have been no more critical of these conspicuous consumers, though Ade tended to be genial where Lardner was often bitter. Yet, when dealing with family groups, Ade was likely to depict the successful entrepreneur as an affectionate husband and father with basically sound views concerning the home, who is bewildered nonetheless by the strange antics of his social-climbing wife and offspring. The father's role as "the Producer" is emphasized; he is "Old Ready Money," the man who signs the checks—he alone of all the family has done something solid in his life. The father of Tillie is "The antique Hay-Maker who had been sending the Money," and he is baffled when Tillie, home from finishing school "with a tan-colored Automobile," high-hats her dad on account of his informal dress and says, ". . . if you expect to meet any of my Friends who are coming to see me during the Holidays, you will have to ring a few Changes

on your Grammar, Pronunciation and Accent." Another good
provider, with a "steel-trap Jaw and a cold glittering Eye," is
putty in the hands of his wife and daughters, who study piano
and French and drag him into high society. Both of the girls
eventually marry titled Europeans who, Pop knows, are dead-
beats, "cheap at any Price."

Ade especially distrusted the newly rich womenfolk who
"went in" for culture and for "uplifting" the lower classes.
Personally, Ade had enjoyed the study of literature at Purdue,
even writing an essay for the college monthly on "The Literature
and Learning of the Anglo-Saxons." As a newspaperman his
wide reading included Macaulay and Maupassant, the latter of
whom he admired for his "short, simple, direct sentences, no
words wasted, and how quickly he can make a scene or a person
seem real." [22] But in his humor, Ade expressed the self-made
man's attitude toward letters and the arts, an attitude summed
up by the tycoon in Booth Tarkington's *The Turmoil* who shouts
at his son, "Poems and essays! My Lord, Bibbs, that's *women's*
work." Thus the women in Ade's fables go in for the heavier and
more precious authors while their husbands remain defensively
middlebrow or lowbrow. One matron likes Henry James, Walter
Pater, Maeterlinck, and Browning; her husband reads "Horse
Papers and the Comic Supplement" (where, after 1915, he could
have seen Jiggs and Maggie in George McManus' *Bringing Up
Father*—cruder counterparts of Ade's characters). In "The Fable
of What Happened the Night the Men Came to the Women's
Club," the wives try "to cut a seven-foot Swath through English
Literature from Beowulf to Bangs, inclusive" and to acquire a
smattering of ignorance about Wyclif, Milton, and Mrs. Browning. Actually the club functions mainly as an instrument of
social intrigue. The men are soon bored by the paper of the
evening on "Woman's Destiny—Why Not?" and listen instead to
the latest story brought to town by a traveling salesman. Before
long they are singing "those low-down Songs about Baby and

Chickens and Razors." Ade implies that such male tastes are the healthy ones—for men, anyway—and that formal literature should be classed with social reform as a mere plaything of affluent females with nothing to do.

Ade's distrust of formal culture annoyed H. L. Mencken, who praised him as a writer but said, "he is unable to avoid rattling his Philistine trappings a bit proudly; he must prove that he, too, is a right-thinking American, a solid citizen and a patriot, unshaken in his lofty rectitude by such poisons as aristocracy, adultery, *hors d'oeuvres* and the sonata form." Perhaps Ade had to prove his Philistinism mostly to himself. According to Fred Kelly, Ade as a boy longed to play the cello. "One of his elder sisters started to give him lessons on the melodeon, but his father put his foot down on such nonsense. There was a general distrust of any male who could make music." In *More Fables,* Ade satirizes his own early yearning. "Lutie" has a long-haired boy friend who plays the cello; she also thinks she has a voice good enough for the concert stage. Her mother thinks so too, but dad disagrees. After expensive lessons, Lutie makes her concert debut and the critics flay her alive. Dad, the only sensible character in the tale, seizes his chance, stops the lessons, and boots out the cellist boy friend.

In thus punishing the boy in the story, is not Ade castigating a part of his private self in order to preserve his public role as a tough-minded man of the "people" (the hardheaded, thinking few, not the mindless mass)? If Ade had ever given vent to the "long-hair" urge he showed as a boy, he would have become "abnormal," according to the standards he defended in his humor, and would no longer have been able sincerely to satirize highbrow culture. Doubtless a Freudian analyst would also be able to detect, in Ade's linking of culture with effeminacy, a sublimation of an Oedipal pattern. This sort of speculation would be stimulated by the fact that Ade was a lifelong bachelor and seems to have had no serious affairs of the heart, despite the frequency with which marriage and courtship appear as themes in his writings. However, the patient is many years deceased and is therefore difficult to psychoanalyze.

Whatever its hidden motivations, Ade's distrust of culture was certainly associated with a dislike of social reform and reformers. Ade squinted critically at the urge to "uplift" the less affluent, an urge that was growing in the Populist period and was strong in the succeeding Progressive era. His contempt for common people en masse blocked any possible sympathy for reform in his attitude. "Give the People what they Think they want," is the ironic moral of one of his earlier fables. Twenty-one years later his skepticism about the common herd had not lessened: "The Plain People are worth dying for until you bunch them and give them the cold Once-Over, and then they impress the impartial Observer as being slightly Bovine, with a large Percentage of Vegetable Tissue." In the era of Wilson's "New Freedom," these sentiments belong to the strain of conservative dissent which included John Kendrick Bangs and H. L. Mencken. In their different styles, all three humorists defended the ideal—that is, the uncommon common man who had made something of himself. An irony of history is that the reformers against whom they defended him carried in their own minds an idealized image of the same man as still "on the make," and merely thought of themselves as clearing from his path the unfair obstructions placed in it on the one hand by the "malefactors of great wealth," and on the other by those who were ignorant, unassimilated, and uninspired by the American goal of economic success.

A "COMPOSITE" MAN

From Ade's fables one might put together a composite character who would represent all the values Ade stood for. Such a type would resemble none of Ade's characters exactly but would have all the traits exhibited by those individuals whom he treated sympathetically. This composite type would be a male from a small town who rose by his own efforts to eminence and wealth in the business world. He would never forget "the Homely Doctrines that were called to his Attention by means of a Hickory Gad some forty years earlier in the Game," but somewhat inconsistently, he would be willing to play the business game the way it is played in "an Era of Horseless Carriages, Limited Trains, Colonial Extension, Corners in Grain, the Booming of New Authors, Combinations of Capital, the Mushroom Growth of an Aristocracy of Wealth, and the Reign of Tailor-Made Clothes." In other words, he would have adapted himself to the pursuit of success at a time when the blacksmith shop and the country store were being replaced by the assembly line and the mail-order house. He himself would not have been trapped in the assembly line or the office cages because, although ordinarily a quiet fellow, he could put up a brash front in pursuit of the main chance.

His tastes and his language would remain essentially those of a character in the crackerbox tradition. Unlike his author, he would never have been near a college campus—except maybe as a trustee, after he had made his pile. Unlike the *personae* of Bangs and Mencken, he would not have read much except for newspapers, and his taste in music would remain at the level of "When the Corn is Waving, Annie Dear." He would be married to a wife who might once have shared his tastes and feelings but is now a social snob who dabbles in culture and in reform politics. His children would devote most of their limited energy to conspicuous consumption of the old man's wealth, like the couple who "worked in every one of the Louies until the Gilt Furniture gave out." This composite father would be baffled by the motives of his wife and offspring, but like Jiggs or Father Day, and unlike Thurber's males, he would sometimes use horse sense or his power of the purse to rescue his family from the difficulties in which they involved themselves.

Ade knew the role of paterfamilias only at second hand, but the theme of success he knew from the "inside." Ade may be seen as the founder of a one-man firm which made a product that sold well and raised the head of the firm to affluence. This enterpriser was uncommon in his ability but remained common in most of his tastes and values. Looking at Ade the man as an entrepreneur and solid citizen helps one to understand why Ade the humorist often laughed *with* rather than *at* the self-made man and *at* rather than *with* the critics of that figure.

5

Mr. Dooley of Archey Road

George Ade's archetype of the self-made man was born in the city room of a Chicago newspaper in the eighteen-nineties. So was Mr. Dooley, voice of the people, and scourge of the people too.

The migration of millions of people from country to city carried American humor along with it, but rural humor did not change its overalls for a boiled shirt when it moved into the city. Despite his urban background and his distrust of the country, where he once spent a night with "dogs an' mosquitos an' crickets an' a screech-owl," Mr. Dooley is rightly designated a crackerbox philosopher.[1] Elmer Ellis, the biographer of Mr. Dooley's creator, Finley Peter Dunne, has said that Dooley's saloon "was in a village-like area of one-story business buildings, shanties, cabbage patches, and goat pastures." Neighborliness—the neighborliness of the small town—was the word for Archey Road and its oracle.

(American humorists and their readers put such a high value on neighborliness that after the Dooley vogue had passed, Harold Ross founded a magazine for urban readers that preserved the same air of back-fence gossip, as if New York were, as E. B. White claimed, a series of neighborhoods. Eustace Tilley with his top hat and monocle may have become a symbol of the *New Yorker* type of humor, but the symbol was misleading. Despite the difference in idiom, there is more than a little similarity between the chattiness of Mr. Dooley and the informal prose White and Thurber put into the "Talk of the Town.")

Besides the tradition of rural horse sense, another strain helped to produce Dunne's Irish barkeeper. Dooley is the successor of "a long line of humorous characters who had talked in the dialect of recently Americanized foreigners."[2] Hans Breitmann and Yawcob Strauss had been German-American dialect philosophers created by Charles Godfrey Leland (1824–1903) and Charles Follen Adams (1842–1918) respectively. The Irish-American was represented in humor by Private Miles O'Reilly during the Civil War, by Edward Harrigan in the latter part of the century, and by many other comics in the newspapers and on the stage. Shortly after Mr. Dooley had become popular, Augustine Daly began to publish verses about Irish and Italian immigrants, and Wallace Irwin introduced Hashimura Togo, a shrewd commentator in yet another dialect, in *Letters of a Japanese Schoolboy* (1907–1909). Most of these clowns played the wise fool from time to time, as did the native American sages.

Finley Peter Dunne was the son of a self-made Catholic Irish immigrant who had begun as a carpenter and risen to some affluence as an owner of Chicago real estate. The author himself was born in Chicago in 1867, received a schooling that stopped short of college, and knocked about the newspaper world of his home city as reporter, editorial writer, and city editor on six different papers. He became editor of the *Evening Journal* in 1896 and moved to New York to edit the *Morning Telegraph* of that city in 1900. He was working on the Chicago *Post* in 1892 when he tried a few dialect editorials based on the personality of an Irish saloonkeeper, James McGarry, who in the editorials became "Colonel McNeery." Dunne put the actual sayings of McGarry into the mouth of Colonel McNeery—probably with some revision—until McGarry objected. Dunne then moved the saloon of his sketches from Dearborn Avenue out to Archer Avenue, which became "Archey Road," and during the next year he created Mr. Dooley, a composite of a number of Chicago Irishmen whom he knew. He continued to use Dooley off and on after he had moved to the *Journal*, but attracted no special attention with him outside the Chicago orbit until his first book, *Mr. Dooley in Peace and War*, was collected and published in 1898.[3]

The crackerbox tradition, even including the use of immigrant dialect, does not account for all of Mr. Dooley's characteristics. As Dunne describes Martin in the preface to this first book, there emerges a neighborhood oracle who is also a businessman—small but independent—and a respected citizen:

> Among them [the Irish] lives and prospers the traveller, archaeologist, historian, social observer, saloon-keeper, economist, and philosopher, who has not been out of the ward for twenty-five years "but twict." He reads the newspapers with solemn care, heartily hates them, and accepts all they print for the sake of drowning Hennessy's rising protests against his

logic. . . . His impressions are transferred to the desensitized
plate of Mr. Hennessy's mind, where they can do no
harm. . . .

He is opulent in good advice, as becomes a man of his
station; for he has mastered most of the obstacles in a business career, and by leading a prudent and temperate life has
established himself so well that he owns his own house and
furniture, and is only slightly behind on his license. . . . His
conduct of the important office of captain of his precinct
(1873–75) was highly commended, and there was some talk
of nominating him for alderman. . . . But the activity of
public life was unsuited to a man of Mr. Dooley's tastes; and,
while he continues to view the political situation always with
interest and sometimes with alarm, he has resolutely declined
to leave the bar for the forum. . . . "Politics," he says, "ain't
bean bag. 'Tis a man's game; an' women, childher, an' pro-
hybitionists'd do well to keep out iv it." Again he remarks,
"As Shakespeare says, 'Ol' men f'r th' council, young men
f'r th' ward.' "

The irony with which the author indicates Dooley's self-impor-
tance suggests that here is a clown who is not to be taken seriously.
But despite the irony, he appears as a fusion of oracle and citizen.
Dunne's variations in creating this blend are important in giving
Dooley's ideas their mixture of sympathy and critical severity.
First, Dooley is a bachelor (like many crackerbox sages), and his
age is indefinite but great—indeed, in the number of his years,
Dooley verges on the larger-than-life, on the mythical. This
bachelorhood and his age lend him a degree of detachment in
viewing the social scene, as does also the independent nature of
his business and the fact that it is not quite respectable. On the
other hand, this slight lack of respectability and the additional
fact that he belongs to two minority groups, the Irish and the
Catholic, put Dooley closer to the underside of life in America
than any other humorous spokesman, with the possible exception
of Archy the cockroach. Hennessy is a common laborer in a steel
mill and Dooley patronizes him a good deal, but their man-to-
man relationship is not seriously impaired thereby. The lives,
loves, griefs, and joys of Archey Road, with its firemen, police-

men, and other small wage earners, are important to the saloonkeeper, and he suggests that in this area a visiting dignitary such
as the Kaiser may find as valid a cross section of the "real"
America as anywhere. Dooley may be ignorant of much of
America, but there is more truth than he knows in his pompous
suggestion. The reader can see that in the tour offered by Dooley
and his mates, the visiting VIP would meet a number of small-
businessmen like the saloonkeeper himself and would look into
establishments where he would view many workingmen like
Hennessy:

> We've arranged th' programme as far as Ar-rchey road is con-
> sarned. Monday mornin', visit to Kennedy's packin' house;
> afthernoon, Riordan's blacksmith shop; avenin', 'Th' Two
> Orphans,' at the Halsted sthreet opry house. Choosdah,
> iliven a.m., inspiction iv th' rollin' mills; afthernoon, visit to
> Feeney's coal yard; avenin', 'Bells iv Corneville,' at th' opry
> house. Winsdah mornin', tug ride on th' river fr'm Thirty-
> first sthreet to Law's coal yard; afternoon, a call on th' tan-
> neries, th' cable barn an' th' brick yards; avenin', dinner an'
> rayciption be th' retail saloonkeepers. . . . we'll show him
> what gayety ra-aly is, an' inform him iv th' foundation iv
> our supreemacy as a nation.

The fact that his license fees are not quite paid up suggests
that Dooley is not much more secure economically than Hennessy,
who shovels slag. Further, Dooley's trade depends primarily on
the manual laborers of the area—he could not afford to lose touch
with them even if he wanted to. However, his freehold status,
precarious though it may be, puts him in a position to lecture
his customers from a slight psychological point of vantage. And
lecture he does, one of his frequent targets being the ignorance
and fickleness of the public as a whole, regardless of social classes.
"Jawn, ye know no more about politics thin a mimber iv this
here Civic Featheration [for reform]," he says to Mr. McKenna
when that specimen of the people has been fighting in the streets
for his candidate. On the inertia with which the public, recently
so strongly for the Boers, now received a Boer mission seeking aid

against the British, Dooley says, "The enthusyasm iv this coun-thry, Hinnissy, always makes me think iv a bonfire on an ice-floe. It burns bright so long as ye feed it, an' it looks good, but it don't take hold, somehow, on th' ice." When the plain folk vent cer-tain prejudices born of ignorance, Dooley scourges them with irony—without losing his identification with them. Hennessy, referring to Captain Dreyfus, declares, "I think he's guilty. He's a Jew." Whereupon Dooley goes into a wise-clownish parody of the Dreyfus trial: " 'Jackuse,' says Zola fr'm th' dureway. An' they thrun him out. . . . That's all I know about Cap Dhry-fuss' case, an' that's all anny man knows. Ye didn't know as much, Hinnissy, till I told ye." Hennessy then asks in bewilderment, "What's he charged with?"

> "I'll niver tell ye," said Mr. Dooley. "It's too much to ask."
> "Well, annyhow," said Mr. Hennessy, "he's guilty, ye can bet on that."

In his ignorance and narrow-mindedness, Hennessy resembles Ade's "Plain People," Mencken's *homo boobiens,* and Lardner's average man. Dooley in part conceals his own ignorance, but he knows he is ignorant, and this alone is enough to set him off from the herd, with Ade's more sensible patriarchs, Mencken's skepti-cal *persona,* and Lardner's Gullible, after that character has be-come not quite so gullible. In all four authors, two types of "ordinary" American—mass-man and thinking citizen—are con-trasted.

The conscientious, thoughtful type of citizen was a postulate of the Wilsonian-Progressive spokesmen. Richard Hofstadter says of the Progressives:

> At the core of their conception of politics was a figure quite as old-fashioned as the figure of the little competitive entrepreneur who represented the most commonly accepted economic ideal. This old-fashioned character was the Man of Good Will, the same innocent, bespectacled, and mustached figure we see in the cartoons today labeled John Q. Public—

a white collar or small business voter-taxpayer with perhaps a modest home in the suburbs. William Graham Sumner had depicted him a generation earlier as "the forgotten man," and Woodrow Wilson idealized him as "the man on the make . . ."[4]

The leading trait of this ideal citizen was rationality; ". . . he would study the issues and think them through, rather than learn about them through pursuing his needs. Furthermore, it was assumed that somehow he would really be capable of informing himself in ample detail about the many issues he would have to pass on, and that he could master their intricacies sufficiently to pass intelligent judgment."[5] Dunne, in causing Dooley to admit his own ignorance of complex issues, is debunking the Progressive ideal of the intelligent, "well-informed" citizen at the same time as he satirizes the other type of common man in the person of Hennessy. Not only does Mr. Dooley's reason desert him at times—as when he wants to throw bricks at various old enemies—but he can't possibly keep well informed. All he reads is the "pa-apers," and the data in his mind are a weird mixture of truth and misinformation. Here, suggests Dunne, is the "ideal" citizen of the liberals as he really is.

Dunne's personal history of participation in the journalism of reform shows that he was not a cynic, and in his humor he was merely trying to show that the social education of the man in the street was far more difficult than most of the Progressives believed. In causing Dooley at least to recognize his own limitations at times, Dunne implied that the intelligence of the better sort of common man is not enough; it must be accompanied by humility as well as by information. A skeptical point of view toward all politics, Dunne suggested, is also helpful in piercing the smoke of "patented political moralities." Part of this skepticism consists in seeing the economic issues underlying the political surface. Using the old technique of twisting a familiar maxim, Dooley says, "I tell ye, th' hand that rocks th' scales in the grocery store, is th' hand that rules th' wurruld." Dooley also knows that the real issue beneath the wrangle over the tariff status of Cuba *libre* is American beet sugar vs. Cuban cane sugar—"We freed Cubia but we didn't free annything she projooces."

The reformers had also better learn that what little relationship politics has to the laboring poor is that of the wolf to the lamb. Some of Dooley's most caustic quips are merely different ways of pointing out this relationship:

> If these laws ar-re bad laws th' way to end thim is to enfoorce thim. Somebody told him that Hinnissy. It isn't thrue, d'ye mind. I don't care who said it, not if 'twas Willum Shakespere. It isn't thrue. Laws ar-re made to throuble people an' th' more throuble they make th' longer they stay on th' stachoo book.

> Di-plomacy has become a philanthropic pursoot like shopkeepin', but politics, me lords, is still th' same ol' spoort iv highway robb'ry.

> Th' modhren idee iv governmint is "Snub th' people, buy th' people, jaw th' people."

> A vote on th' tallysheet is worth two in th' box.

> Whin a man's broke an' does something wrong, th' on'y temple iv justice he ought to get into is a freight car goin' West.

> I care not who makes th' laws of a nation if I can get out an injunction.

> Th' supreme coort follows th' iliction returns.

The shrewdness of Dooley's realism at times may be gauged by his ironic defense of machine bosses: ". . . pollytics is th' poor man's college. A la-ad without enough book larnin' to r-read a meal-ticket, if ye give him tin years iv polly-tical life, has th' air iv a statesman an' th' manner iv a jook, an' cud take anny

job fr'm dalin' faro bank to r-runnin' th' threasury iv th' United
States. His business brings him up again' th' best men iv th'
com-munity, an' their customs an' ways iv speakin' an' thinkin'
an' robbin' sticks to him." In discussing the question of whether
the Boers should have granted the British minority in South
Africa voting rights or not, Dooley shows a ward heeler's sense
of expediency: " 'I'd give thim th' votes,' said Mr. Dooley. 'But,'
he added significantly, 'I'd do th' countin'.' " In this instance
Dooley intends no irony and neither does his author. The fact
that the friction between the Boers and the British ignited a
bloody war lends special point to Dooley's words. The illegal
compromises of boss rule might not always be the worst way after
all. Concerning machine politics, Dunne had some of Ade's
tolerance. Let the worst abuses of boss-ism be curbed, and Dunne
would show little of the prosperous suburbanite's holy horror
at the system itself that Bangs expressed after he had spent *Three
Weeks in Politics.*

ON REFORM

Dooley thus may not be exactly the kind of citizen who
could easily be "educated" to vote a straight Progressive or
liberal-Democratic ticket, but he does have political insight and
a social conscience. That Dunne himself had a social conscience
is attested by his crusade against crooked politicians in Chicago
—it was during such a crusade that Mr. Dooley was conceived—
and by his writing for the *American Magazine* during its muckraking days and for the *Metropolitan* after that magazine had
become a moderately socialist periodical. However, Dunne also
made his small-businessman tell the Good Government reformers that the vast majority of working people have too hard
a struggle with poverty and the day's work to bother about far-
off and complicated questions like the "Nicaragoon Canal," the
Monroe doctrine, Roosevelt's Janus-faced attitude toward the
trusts, irrigation in the West, the Indian question, and expansion of the merchant marine. Identifying himself with these

workers, Dooley says, "None iv these here questions inthrests me, an' be me I mane you an' be you I mane ivrybody. What we want to know is, ar-re we goin' to have coal enough in th' hod whin th' cold snap comes; will th' plumbin' hold out, an' will th' job last." When Seth Low, president of Columbia University, rode into the mayoralty of New York on an anti-Tammany ticket in 1902, Dooley warned that candidates are not elected because of their fancy platforms, reform or otherwise. A man is 'ilicted because th' people don't know him an' do know th' other la-ad; because Mrs. Casey's oldest boy was clubbed be a polisman, because we cudden't get wather above th' third story wan day, because th' sthreet car didn't stop f'r us, because th' Flannigans bought a pianny, because we was near run over be a mail wagon, because th' saloons are open Sundah night, because they're not open all day, an' because we're tired seein' th' same face at th' window whin we go down to pay th' wather taxes. Th' rayformer don't know this."

In this analysis of why the masses vote irrationally, their precarious lot is given heavier weight than their petty envy and dissipations. Occasionally Dunne even suggests that the working masses, despite their ignorance, are the backbone and hope of the nation. Behind the fool's mask, Dooley says of the stock-market panic of 1907, "I wanted to rush to th' tillygraft office an' wire me frind J. Pierpont Morgan: 'Don't be downcast. It's all right. I just see Hinnissy go by with his shovel.' " And he advises Hennessy to "be brave, be ca'm an' go on shovellin'. So long as there's a Hinnissy in th' wurruld, an' he has a shovel, an' there's something f'r him to shovel, we'll be all right, or pretty near all right." Though foolish in pretending that he and Morgan are on familiar terms, Dooley is sensible in warning the rich not to think the country as a whole is ruined and in neatly summing up the labor theory of value. At another time he suggests that "Ohio or Ioway or anny iv our other possissions" don't make headlines "because they'se nawthin' doin' in thim parts. Th' people ar-re goin' ahead, garnerin' th' products iv th' sile, sindin' their childher to school, worshipin' on Sundah in th' churches an' thankin' Hiven f'r th' blessin's iv free governmint an' th' protiction iv th' flag above thim." When they came back from what John Hay called the "splendid little war" with Spain, they didn't pose as heroes to gain political office. "Most iv thim put on their blue overalls whin they was mustered out an' wint up an' ast f'r their ol' jobs back—an' sometimes got thim." (By contrast there was Theodore Roosevelt, whose book about his wartime experiences ought to be called, said Dooley, "Alone in Cubia.") Hennessy and his class are, by and large, as sound as they can be in their unpromising circumstances. Mr. Dooley in some ways falls short and in some ways goes beyond that social responsibility that the Progressives expected to find in the thinking citizen, but if they will at least listen to him, their efforts at reform might be more effective.

NEITHER SHANTIES NOR LACE CURTAINS

The quest for wealth and status was not flatly rejected by Dunne, any more than by Ade, as a valid goal for the common man, but like Ade, Dunne stressed its limitations as an achieved goal. In the city of "Bathhouse John" Coughlin, "Hinky Dink" Kenna, and "Big Bill" Thompson, Dooley's comments on successful men were likely to concern shanty Irish who had risen by the traditional method of the immigrant Celt—politics. Dooley tells how Flanagan, starting at one end of a shovel, fights his way to wealth and power in the wards, and stays on top through a blatant but courageous hypocrisy that cows lesser men. Flanagan's career is a study worthy of Ade in how far amorality and audacity may carry one. In another such study, Dooley's emphasis falls on how the boss somehow lost the love and companionship of his woman, who remained a plain laborer's housewife while her husband rose beyond her. In telling this story, Dooley remarks on the relativity—and therefore the ultimate inconsequence—of class status: "Aristocracy, Hinnissy, is like rale estate, a matther iv location. I'm aristocracy to th' poor O'Briens back in th' alley, th' brewery agent's aristocracy to me, his boss is aristocracy to him, an' so it goes, up to th' czar of Rooshia." Dunne's sympathies in this case are with the woman, but he did not forget that women's heads too may be turned by success— "If a man is wise, he gets rich an' if he gets rich, he gets foolish, or his wife does."

Dooley has not done badly as an entrepreneur, but he has little hope of getting rich. Consequently he can afford a middle attitude in which he does not reject wealth and power as undesirable goals but sees clearly the penalties they exact. With compassion he satirizes the pretensions of the rich, as he does those of the poor, frequently emphasizing the basic humanity of both. He points out the single-mindedness of Higgins the "millyionaire" who gets no enjoyment out of luxury: "He mus' be up an' doin'. An' th' on'y things annywan around him is up an' doin' is th' things he used to get paid f'r doin' whin he was a young man." The well-to-do don't often land in court, but when they do they must "stand in th' clear sunlight iv American justice, . . . an' be smirched," whereas the humble may not get justice, but they at least escape widespread persecution by the press —"No wan cares to hear what Hogan calls: 'Th' short an' simple scandals iv th' poor.' " Of the socialites at Newport, Rhode Island, Dooley says that, ". . . they ain't much diff'rence between th' very rich an' th' very poor. . . . No, sir, they ain't th' breadth iv ye'er hand's diff'rence between Mrs. Mulligan and Mrs. Ganderbilk." Both must have a social circle of which they can feel a part, or their lives aren't worth living. Without sentimentalizing poverty, then, Dooley sharply questions those among both the rich and the poor who think wealth important in itself, and he does not reject the success-philosophy wholly, but counsels against its whole-hog acceptance. This may be a reasonable attitude for almost all men, but it seems especially appropriate for a citizen who has had a little success and who has to work steadily just to keep that, let alone gain more.

When he touched on the struggle between management and

labor, Dooley likewise expressed views acceptable to citizens who felt themselves in the middle brackets. There were three such groups of citizens: skilled workers who hoped to rise into management or at least into the white-collar ranks; the new middle class of salaried white-collar workers, and the old middle class— the self-employed managers of small enterprises, a class which included Dooley himself. All three groups had reasons for feeling disengaged from the strife between union labor and corporate management. Despite his compassion for the laborers in industry, Dooley often says things that may have pleased some large employers but must surely have pleased many people in these three categories. Dooley deplores strikes, sympathizes with the nonunion man who cannot strike, informs McKenna that, "A prolotoorio, Jawn, is the same thing as a hobo," and says of capital and labor, "They're so close together now that those that ar-re between thim ar-re crushed to death." "Abe Martin," the crackerbox sage of Indianapolis, implied a similar view,[6] and one thus sees how attitudes appropriate to the crackerbarrel philosopher and his rural audience might also fit the solid citizen and his urban readers. One sees further how Dooley could make shrewd comments in the role of the levelheaded citizen even though at times he betrays the ignorance and confusion that, Dunne felt, too often impeded this levelheadedness as a social force. One sees finally that this citizen may speak for other middle groups besides the small entrepreneur, though he speaks most obviously for that class.

FRIENDS AND FOILS

Besides the comments on politics, labor, and reform, Dunne has something to say about history, science, progress, Ireland, the Negro question, medicine, progressive education (Dooley was against it), music (Dooley's views on grand opera resemble those of the middlebrow narrators depicted by Bangs, Ade, and Lardner), sports, the wild West, family life, and many other topics. But not all of Dunne's views are voiced through Mr. Dooley;

minor characters also play their parts. These characters populate
Archey Road and thus give it reality; they are also foils for the
saloonkeeper's wit and humor—his "straight" men. In addition,
they represent humorous types other than the crackerbarrel
philosopher. Hennessy and McKenna embody the less admirable
traits of the plain people; Hogan is the eternal pedant, "who's
wan iv th' best-read an' mos' ignorant men I know." Hogan is
Archey Road's version of Ichabod Crane and of Dr. Obed Battins
(in James Fenimore Cooper's *The Prairie*). Father Kelly, the
parish priest, is a common-sense philosopher in his own right,
and often is quoted when Dunne wishes to stress Dooley's ignorance or narrow-mindedness rather than his shrewdness.
Father Kelly is also used to make Dooley more convincing as an
individual. William Dean Howells had said of Dunne, "He
knows that there are moments when his philosophical spectator
of events must lapse into a saloon keeper . . ."[7] When this occurs,
the priest is there to provide whatever wisdom Dooley lacks.
Since the priest is an educated man, he can do this, especially
when cultural matters are concerned, and Dunne, the author,
need not take a definite stand.

For instance, Dooley distrusts all books because they are re-
mote from life. "They're on'y three books in th' wurruld worth
readin',—Shakespeare, th' Bible, an' Mike Ahearn's histhry iv
Chicago. I have Shakespeare on thrust, Father Kelly r-reads th'
Bible f'r me, an' I didn't buy Mike Ahearn's histhry because I
seen more thin he cud put into it. Books is th' roon iv people,
specially novels." Dooley assures Father Kelly that, "There's
more life on a Saturdah night in th' Ar-rchy Road thin in all th'
books fr'm Shakespeare to th' rayport iv th' drainage thrustees."
The priest, who himself thinks Dickens is better reading than
morbid lives of martyred saints, replies (according to the bar-
tender's report of their conversation):

> "What ye say is thrue an' it's not thrue," he says. **Books is**
> f'r thim that can't injye thimsilves in anny other way," he

says. "If ye're in good health, an' ar-re atin' three squares a
day, an' not ayether sad or very much in love with ye'er lot,
but just lookin' on an' not carin' a"—he said rush—"not
carin' a rush, ye don't need books," he says. "But if ye're
a down-spirited thing an' want to get away an' can't, ye need
books. 'Tis betther to be comfortable at home thin to go to
th' circus, an' 'tis betther to go to th' circus thin to r-read
anny book. But 'tis betther to r-read a book thin to want to
go to th' circus an' not be able to," he says.

This ranking of experience ahead of books, as if books did not
offer their own kind of experience, was the "official," activist view
in Mr. Dooley's America, and for the moment, the priest rather
than the saloonkeeper becomes the spokesman for the conventional attitude, if not necessarily for the author's. Dooley tries
to use the priest's own faith against Father Kelly's argument,
saying, "Th' Apostles' Creed niver was as con-vincin' to me afther
I larned to r-read it as it was whin I cudden't read it, but believed it." Each man has a point, and Dooley, by having to be
corrected in part, gains momentary reality as an individual
rather than merely as a stereotyped wise man or even wise fool.
Meanwhile the author avoids committing himself.

At times the priest equals Dooley in the pithiness of his
aphorisms (always as quoted in the saloonkeeper's language). Of
whisky, Father Kelly says, "It has its place . . . but its place is
not in a man's head. . . . It ought to be th' reward iv action, not
th' cause iv it. . . . It's f'r th' end iv th' day, not th' beginnin'."
Concerning yellow newspapers he remarks, "They ain't any news
in bein' good." Of education—"Childher shudden't be sint to
school to larn, but to larn how to larn." Of Thanksgiving—"He
says 't was founded be th' Puritans to give thanks f'r bein' presarved fr'm th' Indyans, an' that we keep it to give thanks we
are presarved fr'm th' Puritans."

Though Dunne cautiously approved of giving women the
vote, he joined most of his fellow humorists in satirizing other
aspects of the New Woman. He struck his blows through Father

Kelly as well as through Dooley. When Molly Donahue surprises
Archey Road by riding a bicycle and wearing a divided skirt,
the priest quashes her ambition with, "Molly . . . ye look well
on that there bicycle. . . . But 'tis th' first time I ever knowed
ye was bow-legged."

Dunne types Father Kelly more distinctly by giving him some
of the traditional inconsistencies of the comic clergyman. The
good father preaches against the Corbett-Fitzsimmons prizefight,
but dances for joy upon learning that Fitzsimmons won. He takes
a dram during Lent, but restricts himself to only half a lump of
sugar in it. He is not liked by quite everybody in the parish—
the tubercular Shaughnessy for instance—and his ministrations
seem ineffectual in reducing the amount of sin along Archey
Road. Witty, tolerant, good but not too good, Father Kelly is
the most vivid of Dunne's minor characters. One should bear in
mind too that the priest, like Dooley, has a status close to and
yet above that of the workingman.

Undoubtedly the priest's combination of orthodoxy and
common sense reflects the author's liberal brand of Catholicism.
After his youth Dunne seldom went to Mass or confession, but he
remained on good terms with members of his family who were
clerics or nuns, and Professor Ellis says, "Peter Dunne remained
a Catholic Christian in sympathy and partisanship all his life.
His friends sometimes remarked that his attitude toward his
church was in one respect like that toward his family. He himself criticized both at times, but he permitted no one else to do
so in his presence."[8] Dunne's loyalty to the faith appears when
he makes the pedantic Hogan a proponent of Darwinism and has
Dooley say, concerning Hogan's views, "Most iv th' people iv
this wurruld is a come-on f'r science, but I'm not. Ye can't con-
vince me, me boy, that a man who's so near-sighted he can't read
th' sign on a cable-car knows anny more about th' formation iv
th' earth thin Father Kelly." On the other hand, the "foolish"
literalness of this "wise" statement reduces the likelihood of giving offense to the defenders of science.

A SKEPTICAL REFORMER

Dunne's attitudes often seem ambiguous and inconsistent. He was skeptical of reform and reformers, but in Chicago he crusaded against municipal and financial evils, singling out in particular the city's perpetual crime wave; bosses Frank Lawler, "Bathhouse John" Coughlin, and "Hinky Dink" Kenna; gambler Mike McDonald; traction magnate Charles T. Yerkes (later to be used by Dreiser in *The Financier* as the basis for Frank Cowperwood), and the excesses of the Pullman company in the great strike of 1894. Sometimes Dunne struck at these targets through editorials written in his own person; sometimes through Mr. Dooley in sketches never collected in book form. In fact, one reason for Mr. Dooley's leap into being was Dunne's desire to hit corruption hard and yet not alarm the timid publisher of the Chicago *Post*. He could accomplish both ends by putting his criticism into the mouth of a comic Irishman, resentment of whom would not easily be transferred to an author who kept himself out of these pieces.

In later years, Dunne, usually through Dooley, slashed at crooked life-insurance executives, exposed by Charles Evans Hughes and Louis D. Brandeis, as zealously as he ridiculed the overearnest crusader against vice, Theodore Parkhurst. He satirized "Idarem" (Ida M. Tarbell), "Norman Slapgood" (Norman Hapgood), and other muckrakers for their sensationalism—and shortly thereafter, joined Miss Tarbell, Lincoln Steffens, and others in the purchase of the *American Magazine* for muckraking purposes. He wrote in both correct English and in the dialect of Dooley for the *American* from 1906 to 1910, and in 1911 he contributed editorials in correct English regularly to the *Metropolitan,* another organ of protest, yet he was the most conservative member of the editorial staff on both magazines.[9] As a result of his palpable hits on Roosevelt's egocentric book *The Rough Riders,* Dunne acquired a personal friendship with the volatile President, a friendship not abated by Dunne's joining the muckrakers. He compared business to murder and highway robbery, but could also say of the businessman, "He is what Hogan calls th' boolwarks iv pro-gress, an' we cudden't get on without him even if his scales are a little too quick on th' dhrop."

Actually Dunne's views were not so much inconsistent as cautious—skeptical, if one prefers. Neither he nor his colleagues on the *American Magazine* wanted or expected any radical changes in society. To some extent, Dunne shared the self-made businessman's belief in the trinity of self-reliance, opportunity, and progress, but he was too close to the working poor to expect any startling benefits therefrom for "the Hennessys of the world who suffer and are silent." The future might bring "a great manny changes in men's hats an' the' means iv transportation but not much in annything else." One will "see a good manny people still walkin' to their wurruk." Even those workingmen who did "get on" might not behave so much like the "new citizen" of reform propaganda as like the common man of Ring Lardner. If Hennessy were to get rich, says Dooley, here's what would happen:

> "Ye'd come back here an' sthrut up an' down th' sthreet with ye'er thumbs in ye'er armpits; an' ye'd drink too much, an' ride in sthreet ca-ars. Thin ye'd buy foldin' beds an' pian-nies, an' start a reel estate office. Ye'd be fooled a good deal an' lose a lot iv ye'er money, an' thin ye'd tighten up. Ye'd be in a cold fear night an' day that ye'd lose ye'er fortune. Ye'd wake up in th' middle iv th' night dhreamin' that ye was back at th' gas-house with ye'er money gone. Ye'd be prisidint iv a charitable society. Ye'd have to wear ye'er shoes in th' house, an' ye'er wife'd have ye around to rayciptions an' dances. Ye'd move to Mitchigan Avnoo, an' ye'd hire a coachman that'd laugh at ye. Ye'er boys'd be joods an' ashamed iv ye, an' ye'd support ye'er daughters' husbands. . . . Ye'd be a mane, close-fisted, onscrupulous ol' curmud-geon; an', whin ye'd die, it'd take half ye'er fortune f'r ray-queems to put ye r-right. I don't want ye iver to speak to me whin ye get rich, Hinnissy."
>
> "I won't," said Mr. Hennessy.

This could have been a paraphrase in Irish dialect of one of Ade's more pessimistic fables. *Ecce homo boobiens!* In such passages about the common man, Dunne has irony and pity but no sentimentality.[10] Dooley, the solid citizen, may advise Hennessy, but little hope is offered that he will influence him. Even if he does, this influence will not necessarily be sound.

Kin Hubbard did his own drawings for his column on "Abe Martin,"
whom he represented as a pensive loafer.

From Fred C. Kelly, *The Life and Times of Kin Hubbard*, Farrar, Straus and
Young (New York, 1952), facing p. 62.

6

Kin Hubbard
of Brown County, Indiana

To prove that crackerbox humor still flourishes in the nation's newspapers, one need only point to such syndicated craftsmen as Sydney J. Harris ("Strictly Personal"), Fletcher Knebel ("Potomac Fever"), William E. Vaughan ("Senator Soaper"), "Aunt Het," "Cy Cology," and "Country Parson." Newspaper humorists with crackerbarrel traits who have dealt in the short, anecdotal essay rather than the aphorism include "Spider" Rowland of the (Little Rock) *Arkansas Gazette* and Harry Golden of the *Carolina Israelite*. One who expresses himself through both proverb and narrative is "Simple" (Jess B. Semple), a wise fool created by Langston Hughes. Simple lives in Harlem but appeared first in the Chicago *Defender*.

PLACE: RURAL AMERICA

Another contributor to this far-from-dead tradition was Frank McKinney Hubbard, whose "Abe Martin" was a fixture of the American scene from 1904 until the author's death in 1930. For the first collection in book form of Abe's proverbs and paragraphs, James Whitcomb Riley wrote a poem as enthusiastic in praise of his fellow Hoosier as it was mediocre in wit and verse. Riley's blessing did not stop Brander Matthews and E. V. Lucas, learned critics of note, from also praising Hubbard and his creation. George Ade wrote an essay about Hubbard in which he compared Abe to Josh Billings and Artemus Ward but preferred Abe because "Abe Martin is up to the minute."[1] Fred C. Kelly, Hubbard's biographer, believes that Ade's essay was the deciding factor in getting the big feature syndicates interested in Abe. Anyway, in 1910, shortly after Ade's essay had appeared, Hubbard signed a contract with a syndicate and was soon known and quoted from coast to coast.

Six years later, Hubbard signed with a new syndicate for "more money than I had ever supposed there was." His daily "box" of two or three proverbs under a drawing of Abe appeared in three hundred papers and in nearly two hundred cities and towns. In the probable size of his readership he was the only humorist of his time who may have rivaled Will Rogers. The cowboy philosopher himself said that Hubbard "is writing the best humor in America today."[2] At the time of his sudden death from a heart attack, there had been no perceptible decline in his popularity; on the day that he died the flags over the city hall and the state house at Indianapolis were put at half-mast.

Hubbard had been born in Bellefontaine, Ohio, where his father edited and published a small newspaper. He showed some talent for drawing, and in 1901 he got a modest job as cartoonist with the Indianapolis *News*. In the main, he drew small comics and caricatures, usually political in nature, for which he also supplied captions. His material was usually relegated to the back page.

Sometimes, as he told Kelly, he "would stick in a country character in a hotel lobby and have him making comments on some of the bigwigs." He caused such a character to comment on the Roosevelt-Parker campaign in 1904, and after the election he disliked the prospect of dropping him. "So, on the day after election, with no more campaign stuff to be used for a while, I used this country fellow in a small picture by himself." He did this on November 9, 1904, and in the following weeks he experimented with various rustic character types and names, including that of Abe Martin. On December 17, the latter name was adopted permanently, along with the character of the small-town loafer whose sketch thereafter appeared above the column. A few weeks later Abe announced, "I'm goin' ter move ter Brown County tomorrow," and the place of his residence was thereafter fixed.

Hubbard's column usually consisted of a drawing of Abe with a caption under it that consisted often of two unrelated sentences. For example: "Tipton Bud's niece died from a successful operation yesterday. 'Peck's Bad Boy' delighted two large houses et Logansport th' other day an' yet we say thet th' world is gittin' better." Sometimes the sentences did form a continuity, but the paragraph was rarely longer than three sentences. Thus, in 1906 when Roosevelt Republicans were riding high, Abe said, "There goes old Ez Pash. By ginger, he's a old timer. He kin remember when it wuz all right t'be a Dimmycrat."

About once a week a short essay appeared under the drawing, usually with the by-line of one of Abe's Brown County neighbors. Beginning in 1906, a yearly collection of Hubbard's drawings and sayings was published as a comic almanac, after

the manner of Josh Billings' nineteenth-century "Allminax."
These little books had varying titles, such as *Abe Martin's
Almanack; Abe Martin of Brown County, Indiana; Back Coun-
try Folks; Short Furrows,* and *Abe Martin Hoss Sense and
Nonsense.* One of these volumes appeared every year from 1906
until 1930.

What sort of character did Hubbard create and sustain for
so long as his *alter ego?* Unlike Josh Billings, who in other respects is a prototype of Abe, Hubbard's man is created partly
through drawings. Hubbard's cartoons usually show Abe in
oversized brogans or gumboots, baggy pants, and a shapeless
black coat from the sleeves of which protrude big, floppy hands.
A nondescript hat is generally perched on the side of his head,
and one hand thoughtfully grasps his jaw. In some of the earlier
drawings Abe had the chin whiskers of the stereotyped farmer,
but these soon disappeared, and the permanent type is a rather
disreputable but genial loafer. Through this wise fool who stood
somewhat outside of society, Hubbard could vent feelings and
ideas that might have offended various persons and groups had
they come in standard newspaper prose direct from the author.
Likewise Finley Peter Dunne put his satire into the mouth of an
Irish saloonkeeper.

Hubbard's version of Brown County was actually a composite of the real Brown County, which lies in south central
Indiana, and of Bellefontaine, Ohio. Certain names of buildings,
such as Melodeon Hall, and many of the names of Abe's ac-
quaintances, usually altered in part, were based on actual buildings and names in Bellefontaine. Kentucky also contributed
something to Abe's composite community; Hubbard told Kelly
that "One good source of old-fashioned names, I found, was
Kentucky jury lists." But purely regional dialect and mores were
left out or blended into the standardized picture. Leaders from
any part of rural America who had migrated to the city could
feel that here was the world of horse troughs and horse sense that
they had left behind.

Even as Dunne made Dooley quote the sense and nonsense

of his neighbors in Archey Road, Hubbard added other characters to Abe's environment. "Often I had things to say," Kin
remembered, "that Abe Martin would not be likely to say, so
from time to time I quoted various neighbors of his." Or he
caused Abe to quote them. Using both methods, Hubbard
peopled Brown County with a great many characters, a random
list of whom forms a pastoral symphony of names—Barton
Crosby, Tapley Bray, Lemmie Peters, Martin Tingle, Elmer
Titus, Bentley Gap, Wes Whipple, Miss Bonnie Grimes,
Ike Lark, Wash Pusey, Squire Marsh Swallow, the Rev. Wiley
Tanger, Stew Nugent, Schuyler Wiggins, Ludlow Mapes, Burly
Sapp, Pony Mopps, and Yile Hurst. Nearly all of Abe's neighbors are one variety or another of crackerbox philosopher acting
as wise fool: nearly all have in common an ability to coin
aphorisms, but nearly all are ignorant and incompetent in other
respects. Old Ez Pash employs compression and wit in saying,
"When you hear some smart alex blowin' off 'bout his 'ideal
home life' you kin bet your boots thet he travels er belongs t'
all th' lodges." However, he maintains, in an argument, that
George Washington's Secretary of State was Tony Pastor. Tell
Binkley makes shrewd remarks on fads in medicine—"I believe
ther's been more change in doctors than ther has in women. . . .
An jest think o' th' things that ails us today that nobuddy used
to have"—but he is a failure at the dubious professions of selling
tornado insurance and real estate. "Miss Germ Williams says
peroxide blondes ort t' be tagged jist like oleomargarine," but
she herself is an old maid who has little taste as a milliner and
even less an an organist. Another old maid, Miss Fawn Lippin-
cut, writes a column on courtship and marriage for a local
newspaper, and her advice is often sound. Other makers or
resharpeners of wise saws are Tipton Bud and Tilford Moots
(farmers who let their wives do most of the heavy outdoor work),
Uncle Niles Turner, an aged loafer and liar, and Miss Mame
Moon, a muscular suffragette. Two who might be termed
crackerbox intelligentsia are "the Hon. Ex-Editur Cale Fluhart,"
who has failed several times in his attempts to edit newspapers

on a profitable basis, and Alex Tansey, the schoolteacher, who
never quite finished his second year in high school.

Like earlier wise fools in the crackerbox tradition, the people
of Brown County acknowledge the ideals of industry, frugality,
integrity, and common sense, and the institutions of the home,
family, and respectable womanhood. For Hubbard the man,
these ideals were never tarnished; in this respect he shared only
part of the skepticism of Ade and Mencken. These two writers
had doubts of the theoretical validity of some of these ideals
unless the ideals were critically refined; they doubted also that
these values would prevail in the practical world. Hubbard
shared the latter view but not the former. Fred Kelly, who
knew Hubbard personally, says, "When Kin told his children
as he often did, 'Be good and you'll be happy,' he believed it."
Consequently the lip service paid by his characters to these ideals
is not castigated as hypocrisy but is presented through them as
wisdom by a writer who can also laugh at the weakness and
confusion shown by these characters (and by people like them)
in failing to live up to that wisdom.

NOT PROGRESS, MERELY CHANGE

John Chamberlain has said of Mr. Dooley that "Certainly
a dandy course in pre-war American history could be taught
by taking Mr. Dooley as a three-times-a-week plain English text."[4]
Though briefer per item, Kin Hubbard's coverage of the current
scene probably included more items than Dunne's. Kin had an
especially good nose for those aspects of ordinary daily life
undergoing the most drastic changes. The automobile was the
main agent of change in rural America during the first third of
the century, and Kin had a lot to say about it. Among humorists
he was not alone, of course, in dealing with this topic; jokes
about the horseless carriage appeared in daily newspapers and
in *Life* and *Puck* before 1900, and during the long reign of the
Model T Ford, quips and anecdotes about the flivver were standard filler in newspapers and magazines. Hubbard's first volume
is spotted with quips such as, "It looks like th' ortomobile wuz

goin' t' do way with hoss sense ez well ez th' hoss." Before long, the new machine had become one of his major symbols of waste and extravagance. Hubbard understood fully what the Lynds reported later—that auto ownership was "a great symbol of advancement for the Indiana worker."[5] Abe rapped this new form of status-worship with, "Tell Binkley jumped into his new $3,000 tourin' car an' hurried as fast as he could t' th' poor farm but arrived too late t' see his mother b'fore she died." In 1923, Kin used one of his wise fools, "th' Hon. Ex.-Editur Cale Fluhart," to point out relationships between the automobile and the loose living of the Jazz Age. Cale did not deny that the automobile, like alcohol, was a blessing when properly used, but it was being badly misused:

> Nine-tenths of our crimes an' calamities are made possible by th' automobile. It has unleashed all th' pent-up criminal tendencies o' th' ages. It's th' central figure in murders, hold-ups, burglaries, accidents, elopements, failures an' abscond-ments. It has well nigh jimmed th' American home. . . . No girl is missin' that wuzn' last seen steppin' in a strange automobile. . . . An' ther hain't a day rolls by that some-buddy hain't sellin' ther sewin' machine, or ther home, or somethin' t' pay on an automobile. . . . Maybe th' jails an' workhouses are empty, but that's not because th' world is gittin' better. It's because all th' criminals escape in automo-biles.[6]

The final overstatement is a typical device by which the reader is reminded that the speaker need not be taken seriously. Nevertheless, this bit of wise-foolery does not materially blunt Hubbard's main point.

He had written in 1911 that, " 'Bout th' only thing a news-paper don't have t' exaggerate is a automobile accident." Tragic proof of these words came eight years later when the family car plunged into a creek and the Hubbards' year-old baby was thrown out and drowned. Kin's views about automobiles had been long fixed by this time, and the tragedy did not alter them. He continued to suggest that the automobile was mainly an agent of speed, physical danger, crime, and conspicuous consumption, but he also continued to own and to drive a car, and he often emphasized that the more things changed, the more people remained the same. In 1928, Abe commented on the ways in which the radio, movies, and the automobile were modernizing the small town, and said, "People are no worse'n they ever wuz. They jest used t' couldn' put the stuff over with a horse an' buggy." In his views on the auto, Kin stuck to the middle of the road. If the new machine brought mere change rather than progress, it was not necessarily a change for the worse.

Hubbard's comments on the home and family were somewhat more conservative than those on the automobile and on other new devices. He felt that the American home was breaking up and that family ties were loosening, and he did not like these trends. At first he seemed sympathetic to the unmarried girl's gradual emancipation from the home; in this he shared the attitude of Hamlin Garland in *Rose of Dutcher's Coolly* (1895), Sinclair Lewis in *The Job* (1917), and Booth Tarkington in *Alice Adams* (1921). Abe remarked in 1906 that " 'Cause ther hain't no place like home is th' reason so many girls work in th' stores an' offices." Furthermore, "We never hear nuthin' 'bout a 'eight-hour day' fer mother." But as time went on, Hubbard, like many males, sympathized with woman's narrow role only until she tried to broaden it. He echoed the skepticism of Ade and Dunne toward the New Woman who showed a desire to ape masculine pursuits. "I never seen a 'athletic girl' that thought she wuz strong enough t' do in-door work," Abe said in 1907. Although he did not ignore the difficulties involved in marriage —"Two kin live unhappier than one," he said in one of his new twists of old proverbs—in 1906 he viewed with alarm the rising divorce rate: "Th' devorce court shows thet th' old ketch, 'two livin' cheaper'n one,' hain't makin' a hit fer some reason." For the next twenty-four years he worried about the divorce problem and about the role of women's clubs, the automobile, movies, the legitimate stage (of which he had a small-townsman's distrust), bridge, golf, lipstick, suggestive song hits, and other innovations in breaking up the home. The lures of the city and of social snobbery were not neglected—"Between th' exodus from th' city t' th' country club, an' th' migration from th' farm t' th' city, it looks like we wuz up agin it." Abe called the "flapper" of the nineteen-twenties, "sweet an' interestin'" but added that "we hope she gits safely thro' an' marries an' lives as happy as could be expected," and he also declared, "Th' average girl would have t' go some t' be as bad as she's painted." In all these comments, Hubbard's belief in the desirability of close family ties and of harmony in the home are as definite as his fear that the family and home are disintegrating.

THE PEOPLE—YES?

Hubbard said less about politics than did Mr. Dooley, but the sum of his political comments is nevertheless large. He was typical among humorists in being moderate in his political loyalties and in often separating these loyalties from those of Abe and the other Hubbard masks, or *personae*. He was a Democrat throughout the era of Bryan and Wilson, but was on friendly terms with the insurgent Republican Senator from Indiana, Albert J. Beveridge, and these terms did not alter when Beveridge joined the Progressives. On occasion, Kin tossed satirical darts at Beveridge, Bryan, and Wilson, as well as at the four Republican Presidents who held office during the humorist's career. Local leaders and "spear carriers" of all three of the major parties were also ridiculed, usually for their excessive partisanship and extravagant promises: "This is fine corn weather, an' ez old Milt Whitehill would say, 'corn makes whiskey, an' whiskey makes Dimmycrats an' Dimmycrats make parrymount issues.'" On the page facing this comment in Abe's almanac for 1906 is, "The Republican party is goin' t' give us a purty good termater crop after all."

The basis of Hubbard's political satire was not party loyalty but a skepticism about the optimistic myth of the rational, informed citizen, a skepticism not greatly different from that of Ade, Dunne, Rogers, Mencken, and Lardner. This citizen, Hubbard felt, really did exist, but not in the mass, and his enlightened views seldom prevailed. Abe said that a retired farmer was the most lonesome fellow around—except for "an exemplary citizen," and "Politics has reached th' level where we're goin' some if we kin even git good, efficient people t' vote, t' say nothin' o' runnin' fer office." Abe echoes Dooley in commenting on how little the average man really cares about the big, complex issues: "Secretary Mellon says that prohibition, flappers, an' business generally, are all right, but what most o' th' country wants t' know is how th' roads are goin' thro' Georgy t' Floridy?" Hubbard is even more severe than Dunne in his criticism of the common man; Dooley had at least offered the excuse of poverty and hard work for the common man's ignorance, but Hubbard sees him as just plain frivolous—more interested in a vacation trip than in public affairs.

At times, Hubbard could be as scathing as Mencken in his contempt for mass indifference and stupidity. Abe twists a saying of Lincoln into, "You can't fool all th' people all th' time, but you kin fool enough o' them all th' time t' huld your head up in society." A statement that "You kin lead a fellar to the polls, but you can't make him think," does not flatter the public in the implied comparison. By contrast, an invisible fraternity of the few good men who really do think and are fit to deal with important issues is encouraged by Abe's comment, "We mustn' git excited o'er what 'th' people' want, fer they don't know what they want. Th' thing t' do is slip 'em what they ought t' have, an' let 'em rave. If 'th' people' ever rule we're gone up."

Hubbard could not follow Ring Lardner into consistent pessimism; despite personal setbacks, Kin enjoyed life too much. One of his last sayings was, "Well, sir, I've been through the Cleveland panic, the Roosevelt dull season, an' the Hoover overproduction, an' my expeı ience is that things allus straighten 'emselves out." Nor was his recurrent skepticism a mood that grew and developed with the years; from the beginning it represented one side of his nature and one aspect of his times and owed little to the wave of popular disillusion that marked the nineteen-twenties. Though most of the quotations in the previous paragraph were stated in the twenties, one was taken from Abe's almanac for 1906 and another from that for 1912.

The moderate nature of Hubbard's skeptical pessimism was undoubtedly acceptable to many of his readers at all times in his career. His artfully two-sided use of wise-fool types must also have helped. Once Hubbard had Abe say, ironically:

> It's a source o' great pleasure fer any true American t' know what a vast amount o' knowledge is on tap under th' saddle-colored dome o' th' average terbacker-saturated, be-whiskered an' venerable country town loafer when affairs o' his country are under discussion. . . . While these old town pump wiseacres hain't got th' remotest idee whose goin' t' put up fer th' hearse when they shuffle off, they know jest what's got t' be done t' make this nation secure if we're goin' t' back up Secretary Lansin'.[7]

Abe voices the substantial citizen's mistrust of the indigent, but Abe himself is a loafer much like those at whom he scoffs, and so are many of his fellow-spokesmen in Brown County. Hubbard really wanted his utterances to be taken seriously, but he invites those who might be offended to consider the disreputable sources of the statements that offended them.

George Ade contrasted the successful entrepreneur of simple tastes with that character's unstable family and with the mob of "plain people." Finley Peter Dunne contrasted the uneducated but shrewd small entrepreneur with an audience representing a mass of wage earners habitually swayed by their ignorance and prejudices. Will Rogers favorably compared the big executive or political leader who remained ordinary in his feelings with the flighty and brainless electorate. H. L. Mencken compared the

thoughtful man of property—the Forgotten Man—with his far
more numerous counterpart, *boobus americanus,* to the disad-
vantage of the latter. Usually in a nonpolitical context, Ring
Lardner depicted a few solid citizens of the old middle class
who were self-critical enough to realize and to profit by their
mistakes; by contrast, he depicted many average men and women
who were shallow, egotistical, and often vicious. Although the
prosperous and thoughtful citizen is shadowed forth too rarely
in Kin Hubbard's sayings for that citizen to appear as a sharply-
defined type, the same contrast between the occasional man of
thought and the vast body of dolts appears in his work that
runs through the otherwise diverse humor of these other writers.
In Hubbard's case, contrast is depicted within the setting of the
American small town, whose way of life Kin felt was shaken,
but not destroyed—yet—by the pressures of the new century.

7

The Crackerbarrel Sage in the West
and South: Will Rogers and Irvin S. Cobb

As a frontispiece to the revised edition (1960) of his book, *Native American Humor,* Walter Blair has drawn a circle of nineteenth-century humorists seated around a potbellied stove, evidently swapping yarns. If Professor Blair had added one of George Ade's self-made men, and portraits of Abe Martin, Will

Rogers, Irvin S. Cobb, and possibly E. W. Howe, O. O. McIntyre, Walt Mason, and Ellis Parker Butler, he might have emphasized a point made in the text and in his *Horse Sense in American Humor,* the point, namely, that the nineteenth-century hot-stove tradition in American humor continued unbroken into the twentieth. This tradition—associated, as seen, with rugged individualism in business, caution in politics, and stability in the home— reached a new high in popularity in Will Rogers. Not without certain modifications, however.

ANOTHER SUCCESS STORY

For one thing, Rogers gave a western tinge to the tradition. Some earlier humorists had written humor while living in the West—George Horatio Derby (John Phoenix) in California; Edgar Wilson (Bill) Nye and M. C. Barrow in Wyoming, for example—but no humorist had achieved a national reputation while presenting himself as a western character. Rogers, on the other hand, began early to bill himself as "the cowboy philosopher," and although he got his start in humor on the eastern vaudeville circuits, he came honestly by his lariat and his western saddle. His father, Clem Rogers, was one of the first—and last—of the cattle barons during the brief period of the open range and the trail drive. Will once remarked, "My father was one eighth Cherokee and my mother one fourth Cherokee, which I figure makes me about one eighth cigar-store Injun." Many times Rogers stressed that his people were the first Americans and had met, not sailed on, the *Mayflower.* He came from both the economic and the ethnic heart of the Old West.

Kin Hubbard once said that, "No feller ever ort t' get too great t' register from th' little town where he lives." Rogers was born in a ranch house near Claremore, Oklahoma, and he always put down that town as his native place when he registered at hotels. His father was wealthy, but even in his teens Will preferred to make his way alone, and, after some country schooling and a two-year stay at Kemper Military Academy, he worked as a roughneck in the oil fields, punched cows in Texas and in

Argentina, and traveled with a Wild West show in Africa, China, and Australia. As a result of the latter job, he began to appear on the stage as a trick roper. Probably by 1910 he was making wisecracks on current topics to pep up his act, and it was his homely verbal comedy as much as his rope tricks that got him a role with Ziegfeld's *Follies* in 1915.

Will's first two books, *The Cowboy Philosopher on the Peace Conference* (1919) and *The Cowboy Philosopher on Prohibition* (1919), were mostly collections of what he had said on the stage. In 1922, both the New York *Herald* and the McNaught Syndicate approached him with the notion that he should write a weekly humorous feature. He began for McNaught by imitating Mr. Dooley and presenting two quaint characters talking over the news, but he found he could not create characters—except for his own *persona*—nor write narrative. He tried putting his humor into epigrams and brief paragraphs, much as he had done orally, and his rise to popularity as a writer was shortly under way. Two years later he still had not quite learned that his natural media were the quip and the editorializing paragraph. When he added a daily feature he at first imitated the anecdotal style of Irvin S. Cobb, but he soon reverted to his natural methods.[1]

Both features were soon running in dozens of newspapers; it is said he eventually reached one hundred million readers a year. In addition to the daily paper, Rogers' humor reached the public through the stage, the lecture circuit, the movies, and the radio. When he was killed in a plane crash in 1935, Senate majority leader Joseph E. Robinson announced that Rogers was "Probably the most widely known citizen in the United States." [2]

Why did Rogers capture the public on a scale that probably surpassed even Mr. Dooley and Abe Martin? Blair has suggested that his cowboy origins helped. Through them he embodied a figure that people liked to feel was more representative of American life as a whole than was any farmer type; moreover (says Blair), he reached the public through more media than any other humorist had used. Other commentators have stressed that he was always just a little, but never too far, ahead of the main drifts of public opinion. Thus he was an early supporter of Wilson but quickly became cool to the League of Nations; he advocated "normalcy" before Harding—who might himself be called a crackerbox type—had unintentionally coined the word; he tried to sting the Hooverites into more action but became a traffic cop in blue jeans warning the Roosevelt cavalcade not to go too fast and too far.

It should be added that Rogers, at least in his role as a public man, was close kin to the mythical citizen on the make praised by William Graham Sumner, idealized by the Progressives, placed in a city tavern by Dunne, given wealth and a flighty family by Ade, and brought back to the village square by Hubbard. Behind the chaps and the lariat the public recognized the same familiar figure. Furthermore, Will knew how to impersonate—perhaps one should say, to *be*—several different varieties of this man. Thus, when he discussed prohibition, he appeared as a practical citizen who minded his own business and was skeptical of both the extreme wets and drys; in this role he appealed to millions who were sick of the whole issue. When he needled the public for its complacency during the nineteen-twenties and called for moderate reforms that would reduce political immorality and help the farmer, he appeared more like the enlightened citizen the Progressives had postulated, and masses of readers who were disgusted with the corruption in high places but apathetic when it came to doing something about it responded sheepishly and joyously.

George Ade had advised that to get on, one should keep on being a country boy. Rogers strove consciously to perpetuate the image of a rube from the wide-open spaces seeking his fortune. He reproved Percy Hammond, drama critic for the New York *Herald Tribune,* with, "Percy, I am just an old country boy in a big town trying to get along. I have been eating Pretty regular, and the reason I have been is because I have stayed an old Country boy." (Hammond was from Cadiz, Ohio.) In reply to criticisms from Ed Sullivan, columnist on the New York *Daily*

News, Rogers referred to "us country columnists." Like Kin Hubbard and O. O. McIntyre, Will often used his rural background to suggest the wise fool, especially with regard to literacy and letters. "Grammar and I get along like a Russian and a Bathtub," he said, and he made a point of never having got beyond McGuffey's Fourth Reader (which was not true). However, he also stated that his public was not "buying" grammar but ideas —and left unspoken the thought that possibly he had a few worth expressing, "fool" though he might be where language was concerned.

About formal literature: "Vergil must have been quite a fellow, but he didn't know enough to put his stuff in English like Shakespeare did, so you don't hear much of him any more, only in high school and roasting-ear colleges, where he is studied more and remembered less than any single person." When it came to pictorial art, Rogers was far behind Mark Twain, who in *Innocents Abroad* had admired a few paintings. From overseas, Rogers wrote in 1926, ". . . I don't care anything about Oil Paintings. Ever since I struck a dry hole near the old home ranch in Rogers County, Oklahoma I have hated oil, in the raw, and all its subsiduaries. You can even color it up, and it don't mean anything to me. I don't want to see a lot of old Pictures. . . . So when I tell you about Rome I just want you to picture it as it is, not as it is in the guidebooks, but as an ordinary hard-boiled American like you and I would see it." Rogers here flattered the Babbitts—"hard-boiled" Americans all—in language much like theirs. In 1934, when Diego Rivera was dismissed by Nelson Rockefeller for putting Lenin and other radical figures into his murals at Rockefeller Center, Rogers sided with the millionaires and with the conservatives in art, in contrast to E. B. White (a graduate of Cornell), who spoofed both sides in a poem on the controversy. When the common man was threatened with culture, Rogers, like Dunne, was often there to defend him.

In Rogers, the professional humorist and the man were unusually close. "All I know is what I read in the papers," was almost a literal truth, according to Mrs. Rogers. Will really had been a cowhand, and whenever he visited his old haunts in Oolagah and Claremore, he was received by the local ranchers and townspeople with an affection that gives a true ring to such statements as "I am mighty happy I am going home to my people, who know me as 'Willie, Uncle Clem Rogers' boy.' " On the other hand, the public image and private man did not match perfectly. Will's visits to Oklahoma after he became famous were brief, though fairly frequent. In addition, Lowell Thomas claimed that "The only pose in Will Rogers was the pretense that he was an ignorant and illiterate fellow," and P. J. O'Brien writes that "Underneath Will Rogers' mask of 'ignorance' was a well-mannered and cultured man with a shrewd, trained mind." Both Irvin S. Cobb and Homer Croy qualify the epitaph chosen by Will, "He joked about every prominent man in his time, but he never met a man he didn't like." Cobb says that although Will certainly liked most people, he could express his dislike of a few in salty language and the epitaph probably referred to prominent politicians only. Croy asserts that Rogers had two fist fights.[3]

Yet Rogers surely meant what he said when he told Max Eastman, "I don't like to make jokes that hurt anybody."[4] Even in unguarded moments he rarely made such jokes. His kindliness, and the verifiable nucleus of truth in his claim to be "just folks" render his personality and his *persona* closer to each other than those of any other humorist examined in this book.

POLITICS AND DETACHMENT

Without an exhaustive and probably impossible study of public opinion during Rogers' career, it is not feasible to test the hypothesis that Rogers accurately voiced the immanent attitudes of the "big Honest Majority" in politics. If one goes ahead and assumes that he did so, Will's political opinions offer basic clues to what that majority were thinking and feeling. If one rejects the hypothesis, Will's public image and his views at least offer one more humorist's portrait, not only of the crackerbox oracle but of the solid citizen trying to think things through. This citizen shows traits of the man idealized by the conservative who distrusts reformers and asks only to be let alone, and traits also of his counterpart in the liberal mythology who participates in reform movements for the sake of getting the great corporations and militant unions to let him alone.[5] Rogers tried to embody both images at once without sacrificing the approval of either faction. He declared once that, "I am just progressive enough to suit the dissatisfied. And lazy enough to be a standpatter." The pretense of laziness, a trait which is part of the stereotype of the wise oaf, helped to mask his inconsistency.

One of Rogers' favorite tactics was to enact the role of a presumptuous ass who has created for himself a fictitious government job or who assumes that he is the familiar of whatever President is in office. In this tactic he resembled Jack Downing, Davy Crockett, and Sut Lovingood. Like Crockett but unlike the other two, Rogers could, in part, support his pose of hobnobbing with leading political figures by pointing to the facts. Eminent politicians were eager to be interviewed by him. Whether wholly serious or exaggerated for humorous effect, much of his "advice" suggested the *naïf* who is unaware that he may give offense and who consequently speaks frankly in telling the President or some other prominent official what the "folks back home" are thinking. In fact, this *naïf* assumes that his boss in the White House will be glad to hear him, since they both are just two good men who need to talk things over. The offhand manner of Rogers with Presidents also reminds one of Mr. Dooley's "me frind Mac" (McKinley) and "me frind Teddy." Rogers addressed the stately Wilson as "Pres." and wrote Coolidge that he was too busy to bother with seeing him, but he shrewdly warned Wilson against taxing the public to pay a veterans' bonus, and he voiced the isolationism of millions in the twenties by telling "Cal" that, "If we would stay at home and quit trying to prowl around to various [international] conferences and conventions somewhere, we would be better off." [6]

On the whole, Will (because of his essential detachment from political strife) was closer to the conservative than to the liberal

citizen, especially before the Great Slump. Aloofness toward
factions was necessary if Will was indeed to speak for all the
people, but it also stemmed from his real indifference to the outcome of party squabbles. His detachment was reflected in his
view of politics as entertaining spectacle (an approach close to
H. L. Mencken's). "Politics," he declared, "is the best show in
America." From 1920 to 1932 he did not miss a national convention of either major party—but he went as an observer only.
He received two votes in the balloting for the presidential nom-
inee of the Democrats in 1928, but he himself never voted in an
election. More than once he said, "This country runs IN SPITE
OF parties . . ." (the emphasis is his). During the Smith-
Hoover presidential contest he wrote a weekly column for *Life*
as part of the burlesque compaign in that magazine for Will
Rogers, candidate of the Anti-Bunk party. Earlier he affirmed
that "No Element, no Party, not even Congress or the Senate
can hurt this Country now; it's too big. . . . It's just the same
as it was, and always will be, because it is founded on right and
even if everybody in Public Life tried to ruin it they couldn't.
This Country is not where it is today on account of any man.
It is here on account of the real Common Sense of the big
Normal Majority." The complacency of that majority during
the Harding-Coolidge era is voiced in this statement of 1925;
some of the moral apathy with which that majority received the
disclosures of the Teapot Dome oil grab was criticized by Will
in 1928:

> Its awful hard to get people interested in corruption un-
> less they can get some of it.

> They [politicians] are great Guys personally, and they
> know in their own heart that its a lot of "Boloney," and if
> they are smart enough to make us feed em, why then we are
> the Yaps, not them.

In the hungry thirties Rogers affirmed his faith in the two-
party system, but the final sentence in that affirmation reveals

that he is still not deeply involved with the outcome of party battles. In June, 1934, he said, "So the whole thing is just a revolving wheel. One party gets in and through a full stomach and a swell head over-steps themselves and out they go. And the other gets in. And that's as it should be. For there would be no living with one of 'em if they knew the other one dident exist."

A STRONG, PATERNAL HAND

Outside the realm of party politics, Rogers' views were indeed neither conservative nor liberal, but composite. He walked in the middle of the road, holding a view commonly labeled conservative: that government is essentially a business; and holding another, commonly held to be part of the Progressive-New Deal ideology, that a powerful, centralized federal government is a good thing. Neither view changed much with the times. "It's simply a mercantile business in town—that's all the Government is," Rogers said in the *Saturday Evening Post* of March 20, 1929, several months before the stock-market crash, and in 1935 he stated, "Business rises above politics in this country." Will's conservative and liberal views had in common a kind of executive paternalism: "If we were run by the Manager form of Government we would soon be paying so little taxes we would be lonesome," he said. He thought that the only way out of the Teapot Dome scandal was "to do as the Movies did, appoint a Will Hays to Wet Nurse the Oil Industry, and see if he can keep their Nose clean." By "Manager" government, Will meant the type of management that ran Standard Oil or General Motors, firms that the Senate and Congress would "bankrupt in two years" if they tried to run them.

According to Homer Croy, Henry Ford's "Peace Ship" in 1915 gave Rogers the chance for "his first big successful joke at the expense of a public figure." Will also made his share of cracks about the tin-lizzie. However, Ford soon became for Rogers a symbol of administrative know-how and power. Will was more than half serious in pushing the Ford-for-President movement in 1923. He said, "I expect if it was left to a vote right now by all the people, Mr. Ford would be voted for by more people than any other man." Concerning a report that every man working at the Ford plants had "to have his breath smelled every morning," Will, though admitting the strictness of the rule, declared that it was "absolutely necessary" and affirmed, "Now Mr. Ford is a very smart man and in passing these rigid rules I bet you he knows where to stop."

In 1929, Rogers spoke more cautiously of Ford: "It will take a hundred years to tell whether you have helped us or hurt us, but you certainly didn't leave us like you found us." However, in the following year he said, "I have always wanted to see Ford elected President," and in 1933, his verdict on the motor executive was, "More common sense than all of 'em." Evidently the cowboy philosopher thought that "Uncle Henry" was efficient but still simple of heart and tastes, like Ade's self-made tycoons and could therefore be trusted to run the Government in the interests of the common man without too much help from the commen men in Congress who lacked Ford's efficiency.

Rogers also admired the personality and policies of Benito Mussolini, who, he thought, was like Ford in being an efficient business manager. Will reflected the views of many Americans during the nineteen-twenties; Abe Martin said in 1927, "Nearly ever'buddy I've talked to would like t' borrow Mussolini fer a day or two. . . ." (Perhaps the emphasis should fall on the final phrase.) After interviewing the Duce in 1926, Will wrote:

> Some over home say a Dictator is no good! Yet every successful line of business is run by a Dictator.
> This Fellow has been to Italy just what Henry Ford has been to all those old Ash cans and empty bottles and old pig iron; he molded them into a working machine by his own mind and Dictatorship.

Rogers praised the Duce for ending unemployment and beggary, for his shipbuilding program, for his "No Strike in Italy" policy, and for his realistic rearmament of that country. He was facetious about the fascists' quelling some of their opponents by forcibly dosing them with castor oil—"Then you don't want to forget that that Castor oil will live on after he [Mussolini] has gone, and that, applied at various times with proper disscretion, is bound to do some good from every angle." [7]

Rogers cared little for Hitler or for Huey Long, yet he was not opposed to modern authoritarianism as such. He did not favor the adoption of Soviet methods in the United States but he respected the Bolshevik aim of distributing wealth more equally. "Dictatorship is the best government in the world provided you have the right dictator," he wrote in 1933, having in mind the charges that Roosevelt had assumed dictatorial powers. The year before his death Will praised Dollfuss for his suppression of the attempted Nazi *Putsch* and said, "The Austrian chancellor has been visiting Mussolini and learning a lot. This fellow Benito is running a free school for dictators. They all come to him to learn how to put it over." (Before long Mussolini was visiting Hitler.) Will did not explicitly approve of the invasion of Ethiopia, but he criticized the British for their inconsistency in objecting to this action of a fellow imperialist.

Will's respect for executive power is surprising in a man who could hit hard, in his role as presumptuous clown, at both bigbusinessmen and politicians: "I tell you, the more I hear these big men talk, the more I realize I am the only one that is trying to uphold the rights of the common people." But Will was used to the one-man rule of the cattle empire; his point of view was that of the lone entrepreneur who distrusts both corporate wealth and organized labor, and looks to the executive branch of the Federal Government as the only force capable of keeping both off his back. Rogers' attitude toward labor is represented by his approval of the people who cooperated to keep the wheels turning during the general strike in Great Britain in 1926. His rural background undoubtedly contributed something to his distrust of labor unions, though he admired Samuel Gompers for his executive efficiency in building and running a huge organization.

Rogers' belief that the executive branch of a government is

apt to work better than its legislative branch is also surprising
in that he voiced it often during the nineteen-twenties, when
the Chief Executives of the United States were relatively inactive
and undistinguished and the Congress included such unusually
able leaders as LaFollette, Borah, Johnson, Glass, McNary,
Bankhead, and Norris. Perhaps the fact that some of these leaders were specialists in preventing rather than in initiating action
had something to do with Will's preference for the executive
branch as a force for getting things done. However, one aspect
of this preference was his qualified belief in what is now called
the welfare state. When the boom in agriculture collapsed after
World War I, he pleaded for federal relief for the farmers. In
1924 he made the then radical suggestion that the Government
move to protect children from infantile paralysis. Later he
praised Hoover's attempts to prod Congress into activity, and
still later he applauded the "Happy moratorium!" declared by
Roosevelt on bank debts (One Indiana banker's complaint to the
Lynds revealed how some of Rogers' punches had hit home. He
told the investigator that "Will Rogers didn't help any when he
said it was a good idea for people to forgive their debts so that
everybody could start clean again").[8] Rogers approved of the
National Recovery Act, and also of the Administration proposals
for the Tennessee Valley Authority and for the Bonneville
power project—"He [President Roosevelt] told that the people
could make their own electric energy cheaper than they were
getting it. And say, by Monday morning he had the companies
talking 'new rates.' " Although he was not given to summing up
his New Dealism or any other views in neat principles, he clearly
felt that the ordinary man should be protected from the powerful corporations by a benevolent state concentrated largely in a
strong Chief Executive.

Because Rogers' executive paternalism has been generally
neglected, it is here emphasized perhaps to the point of distortion. It existed alongside his somewhat contradictory view
that whoever is in political office does not really matter much:
"Nobody is making history. Everybody is just drifting along with

the tide. If any office holder feels he is carrying a burden of responsibility, some Fly will light on his back and scratch it off for him some day." However, Will was most likely to make such statements during national conventions or at election time, in order to reduce tensions and preserve good feeling. He instinctively steered toward a middle ground.

AN OLD-FASHIONED MODERN MAN

Like most crackerbarrel philosophers, Rogers sometimes showed, under the mask of the wise fool, a mixture of shrewdness and of genuine naïveté. He saw all too well the inability of Congress to act when action was needed, and he appreciated the potentialities for good of a strong executive. Yet he wanted that executive to rule a vast and complex nation by the simple code of the individual rancher, a code surviving from pioneer days. He insisted that "the whole N.R.A. plan should be written on a post card. . . . The minute a thing is long and complicated it confuses. Whoever wrote the Ten Commandments made em short." This simple view recalls Davy Crockett, who had served briefly as a magistrate and who allegedly wrote, "I gave my decisions on the principles of common justice and honesty between man and man, and relied on natural born sense, and not on law learning to guide me; for I had never read a page in a law book in all my life." [9] Crockett finally fled civilization to the West from which Rogers came.

Other inconsistencies also stand out in Rogers' attitudes. Will was a crackerbox sage who had discarded the crackerbox for mass media rendered possible by modern technology—media that helped the ex-cowpuncher to earn, at one time, around $20,000 a week. Over one of these media, the radio, he delivered possibly his most often-quoted comment, a slam at another triumph of applied science: "We are the first nation in the history of the world to go to the poor house in an automobile." Yet he took a keen interest in aviation, another modern form of transportation which, like the automobile, was tying the far-flung prairies closer to the urban life that Will distrusted. Ironically, Rogers' interest in this new form of transport led to his death near Point Barrow, Alaska, when a plane piloted by Wiley Post, with Rogers as a passenger, crashed on August 15, 1935.

Not the least of Rogers' inconsistencies was the fact that under his approval of the welfare state ran a counter-current of skepticism about the liberal icon of progress. A letter of inquiry from Will Durant in 1931—when Rogers was anticipating the New Deal in his advocacy of farm relief and stricter regulation of banks—called forth one of Rogers' few statements of basic principle. He wrote to Durant, "Nothing don't mean anything. We are just here for a spell and pass on. Any man that thinks that Civilization has advanced is an egotist. Fords and bathtubs have moved you and cleaned you, but you was just as ignorant when you got there. We know lots of things we used to didnent know but we dont know any way to prevent em happening." [10] Such a distrust of the common man's "progress" must have met with the approval of Mencken, who also had a letter to Durant in the same volume. Rogers added, "Indians and primitive races were the highest civilized, because they were more satisfied, and they depended less on each other, and took less from each other. We couldent live a day without depending on everybody. So our civilization has given us no Liberty or Independence." His skepticism became almost nihilistic:

> Suppose the other Guy quits feeding us. The whole thing is a "Racket," so get a few laughs, do the best you can, take nothing serious, for nothing is certainly depending on this generation. Each one lives in spite of the previous one and not because of it. And dont start "seeking knowledge" for the more you seek the nearer the "Booby Hatch" you get. And dont have an ideal to work for. Thats like riding towards a Mirage of a lake. When you get there it aint there.

A man who believed in God but belonged to no church, Will closed his letter to Durant with an extremely vague comment on the supernatural basis of ethics: "Believe in something for another World, but dont be too set on what it is, and then you wont start out that life with a disappointment. Live your life so that whenever you lose, you are ahead." The philosophy indicated in this letter eliminates the significance of society; it is frontier individualism carried to the point of anarchy. In its denial of progress, knowledge, and ideals, it also clashes with the assumptions of the Progressive-New Deal tradition. Here, despite his humanitarian leanings, Will suggests the conservative rather than the liberal citizen.

The fact that Rogers' popularity reached new heights during the depression suggests that the public was in the mood for a strong if unstable mixture of New Dealism, wry humor, and grass-roots skepticism. If one adds to this mixture a respect for the Man on Horseback (like a cattle king) who Gets Things Done; nostalgia for one's rural origins; an inconsistent readiness to make use of modern technology; a pungent, proverbial style; and most important, the elusive essence that makes a man Will Rogers rather than just another ranch-hand; then one has the combination for becoming the best-liked humorist of his generation.

A NOTE ON IRVIN S. COBB

Will Rogers and Irvin S. Cobb probably tossed out some of their wittiest sayings in conversations with each other that now are lost. They met in New York around or before 1915 and were still friends when they co-starred in *Steamboat Round the Bend,* the last film Rogers made before his death. They had much in common besides their gifts of repartee: each came from a highly self-conscious region just outside the Midwest; each preferred rural ways to urban; each regarded himself as a spokesman for the best type of American, namely the self-made citizen of rural middle-class background. Further, each was quite literate but enjoyed a pose of semiliteracy; each rose rapidly to popularity (though Rogers' popularity far exceeded Cobb's), and each used several media—including newspapers, magazines, the lecture circuit, radio, and movies—to reach his audience.

One difference between the two was that Rogers, as he freely admitted, could not tell a story effectively, whereas Cobb was first and last a storyteller. Even in his familiar essays Cobb was apt to fall into narrative, but unlike Rogers, he rarely uttered any quotable epigrams. As a southerner who was primarily a yarn-spinner, Cobb had fewer affinities with Josh Billings, Kin Hubbard, and other newspaper masters of the one- or two-sentence quip than with an earlier tradition, that of the pre-Civil War humorists of the southern frontier, including A. B. Longstreet, William T. Thompson, Johnson J. Hooper, T. B. Thorpe, Joseph G. Baldwin, and George Washington Harris (whose *Sut Lovingood Yarns* Cobb had read as a boy in his home town of Paducah, Kentucky).[11] These writers relied less on the aphorism and more on the quaint character and the tall tale, often as told in dialect by a narrator within a setting given in the author's more formal prose. In his nostalgic evocation of a phase of the southern past, Cobb also was related to local colorists like Richard Malcolm Johnston, Joel Chandler Harris, and Thomas Nelson Page.

Regardless of the medium, Cobb tried hard to speak for the ordinary good man, who, for him, was usually the small-town possessor of a little property and prestige. For the encyclopedia, *Twentieth Century Authors,* he wrote, "I give thanks daily that, in the main, my tastes always have been rather vulgar and my preferences for simple people and commonplace things." His daughter Elisabeth Cobb made a shrewd guess at why he was thus thankful. Apologizing for Irvin's sympathy for Mussolini during the nineteen-twenties, she made comments which apply to more than one humorist:

> In some ways I think that this blindness was a deliber-
> ate limitation of vision . . . and the reason was that the
> majority of the people of the United States were for Mus-
> solini, and what the United States liked Irvin Cobb liked. He
> was, both deliberately and instinctively, Mr. Average Cit-
> izen. . . . So when I insisted that he look at Italian Prim-
> itives, and he all but literally shut his eyes, muttering that he
> would give every old master that ever lived for one Reming-
> ton or a couple of Charley Russells. . . . I thought he was
> being exceedingly stupid. Now I think that it was I who was
> the stupid one. The man was unconsciously protecting his
> prejudices because he needed them in his business.[12]

His main business was the writing of more than sixty volumes, less than half of which were primarily humorous. Much of his output was commercial fiction which depended on contrived plots and surprise endings of the O. Henry type and had only a glaze of local color. As a humorist, Cobb is significant in making use of all three major type-figures in the humor of his time: the crackerbox sage, the solid citizen, and the Little Man. His most effective crossroads type is Judge Priest, a paternal fixer-up of other folks' troubles and a pillar of law, justice, and mercy in a town that must have been much like Paducah, Kentucky in the eighteen-nineties. Cobb affirmed that the genial Judge was a blend of at least three men he had known as a boy, but Priest also bears some resemblance to earlier southern crackerbox types like William T. Thompson's "Major Jones" and Charles Henry Smith's "Bill Arp," in their later, more philosophical versions. Will Rogers reminded Cobb of one of the models for Priest, "old Judge Bishop, the Southern circuit Judge," [13] and Rogers played Judge Priest in the film of that title.

Though a native Kentuckian and a Confederate veteran who is proud of having ridden with Forrest, Judge Priest is intended to represent what is best in the average American of any region. Cobb insisted that millions of southerners were

> just such folk as allowing for certain temperamental differences—created by climate and soil and tradition and by two other main contributing causes: the ever-present race question and the still living and vivid memories of the great war—might be found as numerously in Iowa or Indiana or any other long-settled, typically American commonwealth as in Tennessee or Georgia or Mississippi, having the same aspirations, the same blood in their veins, the same impulses and being prone under almost any conceivable condition to do the same thing in much the same way.[14]

Paducah had been pro-Confederate during the Civil War, and Cobb called it "an average southern community." The Judge and his three cronies—Dr. Lew Lake, ex-Sergeant Jimmy Bagby, and storekeeper Herman Felsburg (Jewish, but a thorough southerner and likewise a veteran of Forrest's cavalry)—embody Cobb's belief that the respectable middle-class whites of the small southern community manifested Americanism in its least adulterated form. Cobb's view preceded by several years that of John Crowe Ransom and the other southern intellectuals who presented essentially the same ideas in the symposium *I'll Take My Stand* (1930).[15]

Judge Priest is indeed a blend of southern and of more widespread traits. As a southern man he is paternalistic in politics; he "reigned as a benevolent despot over a generally satisfied community." To Negroes he is the kindly master who keeps them in their place but dispenses impartial justice to black and white alike. He approves of the "old" Ku Klux Klan of Reconstruction days, but condemns the "new" Klansmen of the nineteen-twenties as "ruffians." [16] As southerners, the Judge and his cronies are continually reminiscing about the War, but as Americans of the old, pure sort they help to straighten out young folks by exemplifying the courage, honesty, simplicity, and hospitality of ante bellum days. The Judge is also a "representative" American in being self-made and in rejecting some of the less reconstructed portions of the Old South, such as lynching and the Code Duello. On the one hand, he opposes wealthy urban politicians (of both northern and southern vintage), skinflint bankers, and southern "gentlemen" who presume on their ancestry; on the other, he helps to foil disorderly elements of the lower classes—lynch mobs, illiterate voters, backwoods bullies, and grifters of all kinds. In both kinds of role he represents the upright man of some property.

William Allen White branded Cobb's view of Confederate days "a nice blend of hiccuping nostalgia and conscious, deliberate, downright deception," [17] but he admitted that he enjoyed the Judge Priest tales. That many other northerners did too is suggested by the fact that George H. Lorimer of the *Saturday Evening Post*, Ray Long of *Cosmopolitan*, and editors of other national magazines kept calling for more Judge Priest stories, over a span of twenty-seven years, until Cobb had marketed over seventy. Perhaps the nation-wide cult of the Old

South manifested in the movie *The Birth of a Nation* (1915) and in a string of prose romances culminating in Margaret Mitchell's *Gone With the Wind* (1936) also helped to sustain the demand for more tales about Judge Priest.

It was when he turned from fiction to the familiar essay that Cobb most often presented himself as the bewildered Little Man of the city or the suburbs. Cobb came to New York in 1904 and before long was Joseph Pulitzer's highest-paid reporter and feature writer. For obscure reasons that may have been glandular, he gained weight during his late twenties and early thirties, until he could cast himself as the comic fat man in essays for the *Saturday Evening Post,* some of which were collected in *Cobb's Anatomy* (1912), *Cobb's Bill-of-Fare* (1913), and *"Speaking of Operations—"* (1915). In the last-named work, Cobb used a real and unpleasant experience as the basis for one of his most popular books. Here his character as fat man is less prominent than his role as the patient in a high-powered urban hospital—the Little Man at the mercy of modern technology. Unsettled by pain, the narrator submits meekly to being poked, punched, thumped, cross-questioned, and finally shunted off to a specialist. Though "full of quavery emotions" as he goes to see this great personage, Cobb becomes pompously resolute in hanging on to his hat and umbrella—items that symbolize what few shreds of freedom and dignity he still possesses and which he is determined not to lose without a struggle. Eventually he is conscious of being dehumanized by a massive, impersonal system, of being "already in the card-index class." He learns that to the system, this cutting up of his insides will be a "small matter," and he goes home "in a dazed state."

At the appointed time he returns, full of the forced jauntiness shown later by Benchley and Perelman.[18] But from the moment he has abandoned control over his carcass to the hospital staff, his dignity as a human being has vanished, and the patient's progress is depicted in imagery that further suggests the dehumanizing process. The orderly shaves him "on one of my most prominent plane surfaces"; then, "Having shaved me, the young

man did me up amidships in a neat cloth parcel." Before the
ether suffocates him, he feels that the medicos are golfers and he
is the ball.

Cobb's victim resembles that of Stephen Leacock, who had
done a piece about doctors in *Literary Lapses* (1910), and anticipates that of Benchley in being, not just an object of sympathetic
laughter, but a norm of common sense and a defender of human
dignity as represented by his own, however ridiculous. From his
bed, the victim as writer exercises his common sense and strives
to salvage his dignity by noting the ridiculousness of his white-
coated tormentors. He satirizes their secretiveness, their callousness, their breezy commercialism, their overspecialization, and
their tendency—at that time drawing unfavorable comment from
many sources—to operate when operation was perhaps not always
necessary. One doesn't feel well, and one's doctor "steps into the
next room and begins greasing a saw." At about the time *"Speaking of Operations—"* was written, Charlie Chaplin was playing
film roles in which, as Gilbert Seldes said, ". . . he stood always
against the authorities, always for his small independent freedom." [19] For the Little Man in Cobb's book, the "forces" of
hospital administration and of medical technology were the
authorities.

In *The Abandoned Farmers* (1916), the Little Man becomes
an exurbanite. Early in their married life the Cobbs had lived
in John Kendrick Bangs' home town of Yonkers, "one of the most
suburban of suburbs," according to Elisabeth Cobb. In 1914,
after much searching, they bought a run-down estate near Ossin-
ing in northern Westchester County—one of the older "exurbs"
discussed by A. C. Spectorsky in *The Exurbanites* (1958). The
search, the rebuilding, the furnishing, the farming, and the
gardening are recounted in detail while the narrator moans over
the financial damage and the cussedness shown by the land, live-
stock, and building materials. Though gulled by the real-estate
promoters, Cobb's *persona* strikes back in a parody of their
jargon:

> And oh, the thrill that permeates your being when you
> see the first furrow of brown earth turned up in your field,

or the first shovel-load of sod lifted from the spot where your home is to stand! And oh, the first walk through the budding woods in the springtime! And the first spray of trailing arbutus! And the first spray of trailing poison ivy! And the first mortgage! And the first time you tread on one of those large slick brown worms, designed, inside and out, a chocolate éclair!

Though a loser in his battles with nature and with commerce, Cobb would rather be what he now is, "a landed sucker," than a flat-dweller. Thus he shapes up finally as a fairly comfortable, self-satisfied fellow who is less secure than the crusading narrator of Bangs' *The Booming of Acre Hill* but more secure than the neurotics of Benchley, Thurber, and Perelman. Having ultimately got what he wanted, Cobb's Little Man is less than half badly off.

Thus Cobb re-created the crackerbox oracle in a southern environment, and as a solid citizen rather than a loafer. He also presented a version of the character who was to supersede the crackerbox philosopher and the solid citizen as the major type-figure in American humor. Nearly forgotten though his writing is now, Cobb deserves a nod for having been one of the first nationally known humorists to present the Little Man as a victim of the twentieth century.

PART THREE

"Sophisticated" Skeptics

8

Innocence and Change, 1910-1920

According to Henry F. May, the American credo in the fifteen years or so before World War I can be summed up in three articles of faith: first, "the reality, certainty, and eternity of moral values"; second, a belief in progress; and third, a respect for culture (culture is defined as "a particular part of the heritage from the European past, including polite manners, respect for traditional learning, appreciation of the arts, and above all an informed and devoted love of standard literature." No American humorist, whatever he may say, has entirely abandoned the first article. To do so he would have had to abandon humor itself, since humor requires fixed standards by which it may be identified. However, a number of American humorists in the second decade of the twentieth century did question this article, nearly all gave the second a thoroughly irreverent re-examination, and a fair percentage chucked out most of the last one. For example, Ambrose Bierce, E. W. Howe, George Ade, Will Rogers, H. L. Mencken, Ring Lardner, and Don Marquis all doubted in varying degrees the absolute certainty of moral values. John Kendrick Bangs, Kin Hubbard, and Finley Peter Dunne each had his own version of absolute morality (more often implicit than explicit), but they agreed with their more iconoclastic brethren in questioning the widespread belief in progress—more specifically, in questioning the assumptions of Progressivism about the "promise of American life," and in squinting satirically at certain liberal images, particularly the New Citizen and the New Woman (although Mencken and Marquis occasionally praised the "flapper" for her sophistication and daring). Gelett Burgess crossed to the liberals' camp in 1912 on the woman-suffrage issue; Clarence Day, Jr. wrote for a socialist magazine (the *Metropolitan*), and also for the *New Republic*, but even Burgess and Day took a dim view in general of man's immediate progress and felt any basic improvement in human nature would come during ages of time.

As for the third article in the credo, few humorists showed a belief in the traditional culture. The crackerbox writers tended to regard it with either suspicion or indifference. This statement includes the writers who exploited the dialect of immigrant or racial minorities, like Montague Glass with his stories about "Potash and Perlmutter"; Wallace Irwin with his letters from "Hashimura Togo," a Japanese schoolboy; and Octavus Roy Cohen with his tales of carefree Negroes who more or less re-

sembled Ade's Pink Marsh. (These writers appeared mostly in
the "slick" magazines of large circulation, like the *Saturday Evening Post, Collier's,* and *Cosmopolitan,* and they did tend to accept the idea of moral absolutes.) Ring Lardner belongs with the
crackerbox writers in his satirical aloofness to cultural developments, even though the "poetic renaissance" first gained headway
in his own city of Chicago.

Conversely, from the few humorists who spoke through characters of some education, one expects—and gets—more interest in
culture as an issue. A neglected phase of the revolution in letters
going on during this period was a quiet, steady revival of the
genteel tradition in humor which seemed to bring no major
changes at first, but which, as one could see by the time the
New Yorker was started in 1925, had eventually amounted to a
revolution. The centers of this revival were the *Smart Set,* after
Mencken and Nathan had taken the magazine over in 1914; the
daily columns of Christopher Morley in the New York *Evening
Mail* and of "F. P. A." (Franklin Pierce Adams) in the New York
Tribune; and, from about 1916 on, in the work of several young
contributors to *Life* and *Vanity Fair,* the most promising of
whom were Robert Benchley and Dorothy Parker, assisted by the
cartoonists George Herriman, Gluyas Williams, Rea Irvin, Gar-
diner Rea, Anne Harriet Fish, and many others. The creation of
a friendlier attitude among humorists toward culture was not
obvious as first. Although sympathetic to new poets, novelists,
and playwrights, most of the humorists did not often take up the
cudgels for such cultural "causes" as Van Wyck Brooks announced in *America's Coming-of-Age,* and they were cool toward
free verse and postimpressionist painting. Only "Owen Hat-
teras" (Mencken and Nathan) beat the drums systematically
for new writers and attacked decorum and didacticism categorically. Mencken and Nathan stood for culture, but insisted
on redefining it to exclude "Puritanism," which to them stood
for most of what passed for Victorian and American literature.
Some of the more genteel humorists, especially Benchley, were
also helping to redefine the traditional culture by refusing to

revere it as a tradition and by insisting that each "standard" author prove himself afresh to the educated but casual reader.

With respect, then, to their attitude toward the three main points of the American credo, the leading humorists of this decade frequently appear in different categories, but the general trend is one of skepticism and change. Their skepticism of most political and social creeds is apparent in their choice of masks— of *personae*. Without exception, these humorists frequently wore masks belonging to various thinking citizens of the property-owning middle class, and whether the citizen-type portrayed in each case was conservative or liberal, bachelor or family man, illiterate or erudite, crackerbox oracle or professional bookman, wise fool or conscious ironist, competent performer of all tasks or neurotic fumbler, he stood in sharp contrast to the incompetent, irrational mass and its self-important leaders. Moreover, this *alter ego* of the writer always stood for ideals of reason, integrity, independence, and citizenship, no matter how far short this comic *persona* might himself fall in living up to these ideals.

Three writers who got their start during this decade stand out as skeptics and as defenders of Rational Man. These writers— H. L. Mencken, Ring Lardner, and Don Marquis—have affinities with the crackerbox tradition and also with the younger men who used the Little Man, but they belong clearly with neither group. Chronologically, the active careers of these three ended before or during the middle nineteen-thirties, when most of the Little Man-*New Yorker* "school" of humorists were at the peak of their careers or had not quite reached that peak. Psychologically, despite having passed most of their careers in large cities working for metropolitan periodicals or national syndicates, Mencken, Lardner, and Marquis may be thought of as essentially small-town philosophers. They retained the perpetual astonishment, the almost childlike wonder, that one rightly or wrongly associates with small-townsmen viewing the great world for the first time, and two of the three—Lardner and Marquis—seem never to have gotten over their disappointment at this world's not being all they had hoped. To the end, they showed the bitterness of blasted innocence. The third, Mencken, was "innocent" in his happy unawareness that there was anything in this world or the next that could not be fitted comfortably into the intellectual framework of rigid materialism derived from his youth in the nineteenth century, and he defended this framework with the dogmatism of a village atheist, if that villager had read a lot of books and acquired an outsize vocabulary.

9

The Two Masks of H. L. Mencken

Iconoclasm may be associated with bitterness, as it often is in the satire of Howe, Bierce, Lardner, and Marquis, but it may also be associated with cheerfulness and gusto, as in the case of Henry Lewis Mencken. Frederick Lewis Allen recalled in *Only Yesterday* that reading Mencken for the first time gave one "the

sort of intense visceral delight which comes from heaving baseballs at crockery in an amusement park."[1] Allen's image suggests
an ordinarily quiet, respectable citizen discharging tensions in a
way that is boisterous but prescribed and socially acceptable, and
a glimpse of Mencken's background further suggests the solid
citizen. "I was a larva of the comfortable and complacent bour-
geoisie," Mencken wrote in *Happy Days*. Despite the irony, he
tended consciously to make this complacency a part of his credo.

A MILITANT BOURGEOIS

The other side of this self-satisfaction was a bias against the
rabble. Van Wyck Brooks feels that this bias came mainly from

> his almost exclusively German Baltimore childhood, as the
> son of a German cigar-manufacturer who had married a Ger-
> man-American wife and who usually took him on Sundays
> to German beer-gardens. . . . He acquired early the bourgeois
> traits that made him a good citizen, methodical, the most
> orderly of mortals, never late for trains, who never failed to
> appear in time for dinner, one who respected punctuality
> and solvency in others and who spent his life in one house
> in Baltimore.[2]

In addition to the middle-class and German elements in his
background, Mencken's rapid rise by his bootstraps in his chosen
profession undoubtedly played its part in fixing his attitudes.
With little help or encouragement from his family, Henry forced
his way into a reporter's job on the Baltimore *Morning Herald*
and worked up until, at twenty-four, he was the youngest managing editor of a major newspaper in the United States. For him
the Horatio Alger myth was a reality. The paper was sold the
next year (1906) to the *Evening Herald,* but after five weeks with
that periodical, Mencken took a better job on the *Evening Sun*.
With the *Sunpapers* he remained almost continuously, in some
capacity or other, until invalided by cerebral thrombosis in
1948.

As a young journalist he found time to write short stories and poetry that deserve neglect by all except the specialist. He tried to write satirical fables in slang, like those of George Ade—"miserable botches," he called them later. He first "stirred up the animals" with his column, "Knocks and Jollies," in the *Herald* and with his satirical editorials for the *Sun*. He aimed at a higher level of readership with his books on George Bernard Shaw (1905) and on *The Philosophy of Friedrich Nietzsche* (1908), as well as with the book-review column which he began to write for the *Smart Set* in the latter year. He sharpened his satire in "The Free-Lance," a daily column in the *Evening Sun,* from 1911 to 1915, but his pro-German views caused that department to be discontinued. However, when he and George Jean Nathan assumed joint editorship of the *Smart Set* in 1914 Mencken had a new and broader medium for his attack on the Philistines and the puritans. He also had a fully developed style with which to conduct that attack.

As part of their assault, Mencken and Nathan made a specialty of printing the efforts of little-known American authors, including the first works of Eugene O'Neill, F. Scott Fitzgerald, Maxwell Anderson, and Mark Van Doren to appear in a major commercial journal. The *Smart Set* was also, as Carl Dolmetsch says, "one of the most important periodicals of general circulation in this country as a purveyor of European literary influences." Among the major Europeans who first reached an American public through the *Smart Set* was James Joyce, with two stories from *Dubliners*.

Meanwhile Mencken was writing books, composed partly of reworked "Free-Lance" and *Smart Set* pieces, in which he beat the tom-toms for James Huneker, Theodore Dreiser, Joseph Conrad, Sinclair Lewis, and other authors who, he felt, were unduly neglected. A hard worker, he was also laying the beginnings of a reputation as a philologist with the first version of *The American Language* (1919). After Hearst bought the *Smart Set,* Mencken and Nathan left the magazine, and with some backing from Alfred A. Knopf, founded a new monthly, the *American*

Mercury (January, 1924). The battles for Dreiser, Conrad, and
Lewis were largely won by this time, and Mencken's interests
were shifting from the literary to the political and social arenas.
He made the *Mercury* a repository for lively but solid articles
and essays of social, historical, and political interest, although
new fiction, poetry, and literary criticism were not entirely neglected. Mencken unloosed his own satire and invective chiefly
in the editorial and book departments. From the start, Mencken
was the dominant partner, and after a year, Nathan relinquished
his joint editorship. The magazine then became Mencken's personal medium as editor and writer, and remained so until he resigned his editorship in 1933.

Although his *Treatise on Right and Wrong* was published
the next year, Mencken's humorous career may be said to have
closed when he severed his connection with the *Mercury*. The
editorial grind was beginning to bore him, and, at least by 1928,
his repeated attacks on a few targets—puritanism, prohibition,
Babbittry, the farmer—had begun to bore the readers. Moreover,
after 1929, the shuffle of feet on breadlines tended to drown the
sound of Mencken's conservative blasts.

After leaving the *Mercury*, he turned again to the revision
and expansion of *The American Language*. This revision, along
with political reporting, the compiling of a dictionary of quotations, and the writing of three volumes of autobiography, occupied most of his later years.

ARISTOCRAT AND SOLID CITIZEN

It is much easier to find out what Mencken was against than
what he was for. Several students of Mencken claim that "he
had found a philosophy in Nietzsche,"[3] but Ernest Boyd, Isaac
Goldberg, and William Manchester have offered evidence that
Mencken's basic ideas were formed and fixed before he encountered the writings of the German philosopher. Indeed Manchester says, referring to Mencken's ideas, "It is amazing how
little the man had changed since boyhood . . ." Alastair Cooke
suggests that in Mencken's "Free-Lance" column for the *Sun-*

papers, Nietzsche's direct influence was partly stylistic and partly inspirational rather than ideological. "Nietzsche suggested the outlandish metaphors," and both Shaw and Nietzsche inspired him to become, in Cooke's words, "the native American Voltaire, the enemy of all puritans, the heretic in the Sunday school, the one-man demolition crew of the genteel tradition."[4] Cooke feels that Shaw taught Mencken more than did Nietszche. But there is no doubt that Mencken was deeply involved with the German, particularly with his concept of the superman, and that Mencken's political and social views included a concept of aristocracy expressed frequently with the aid of such Nietzschean terms as "Übermensch," "Sclavenmoral," and "Der Wille zur Macht."

Mencken's ideal aristocrat or gentleman, chiefly as set forth in *The Philosophy of Friedrich Nietzsche,* differs importantly from the two models of the aristocrat that were endemic in nineteenth-century America (one should remember too that Mencken's aristocrat sometimes bore little resemblance to Nietzsche's). As summarized by E. H. Cady in *The Gentleman in America,* these two models were "the cavalier" and "the Christian gentleman." The cavalier was a sportsman, a drinker, a duelist (though he dueled only for grave breaches of honor and after all honorable means had been used to avoid the clash), and something of a rake. On the whole, this ideal was overshadowed by that of the Christian gentleman, of whom Robert E. Lee was often cited in the South as an example. The Christian gentleman was none of these things. Both types were forthright with their peers, gentle with their inferiors, and courteous to all; both were responsible servants of the State and leaders of the people. Mencken's gentleman owed nothing to the State; in fact he was above the State because in these latter days the State was dominated by the rabble. Moreover, Mencken's aristocrat was too thrifty and prudent to be a cavalier, and too much of a materialist and evolutionist to be greatly swayed by the Christian ethic.

Mencken also differed radically from earlier concepts of the gentleman in his emphasis upon self-reliance, energy, intelligence, and efficiency—attributes not excluded from the earlier ideals but not stressed either. The cavalier and the Christian gentleman might or might not be wellborn, but they certainly needed affluence, if only to make the other virtues possible. Mencken, on the other hand, emphasized that the gentleman should be able to rise to affluence through his own superior energy. Instead of taking his cues from any elaborate upper-class conventions, "The strong man—which means the intelligent, ingenious and far-seeing man—would acknowledge no authority but his own will and no morality but his own advantage." He would be self-made in a very American sense, like the more ruthless of Ade's tycoons.

However, by intelligence Mencken did not necessarily mean mere ambition to rise in business, nor did he mean "culture"—a knowledge of standard authors and of polite manners. He meant intellectual creativity. The real supermen, he suggests, are not such captains of industry as Rockefeller and Morgan, but men like Louis Pasteur, Thomas Henry Huxley, Abraham Lincoln, Otto von Bismarck, Charles Darwin, Rudolf Virchow, Ernest Haeckel, Thomas Hobbes, Niccolo Machiavelli, William Harvey, and Edward Jenner. Mencken especially praises Jenner as a man of will and action as well as of creative ideas: "That Jenner himself, when he put forward his idea and led the military caste to carry it into execution, was an ideal member of the first caste is plain." Such intellectual aristocrats possessed, for Mencken, "an unmistakable air of fitness and efficiency."[5] The implied definition of the latter term was the ability to put one's creative theories into practice.

This idea of the gentleman underwent changes in Mencken's subsequent writings but was clearly recognizable when used as a value-base in argument or in satire. Mencken invoked it centrally in opposing the socialism of Robert Rives La Monte in *Men vs. the Man* (1910), a debate in print between the two authors. Elsewhere the gist of Mencken's criticisms of Woodrow Wilson, William Jennings Bryan, and Theodore Roosevelt was that these leaders were not gentlemen: Wilson was an uplifter and a cad;

Bryan was a peasant, and Roosevelt, though he had energy and
will power, was an uplifter and a demagogue who, in trying to
improve the common people, merely stooped to their level and
thereby showed himself a "pseudo-Junker." In "The Sahara of
the Bozart," Mencken sorrowed over the South's having lost its
old aristocracy "down the red gullet of war." The poor white
trash now rule, and the result is that, "Down there a poet is
now almost as rare as an oboe-player, a dry-point etcher or a
metaphysician." The ghost of what aristocracy remains, Mencken
said, is helpless because

> It is impossible for him [the true gentleman] to stoop to
> the common level. He cannot brawl in politics with the
> grandsons of his grandfather's tenants. He is unable to share
> their fierce jealousy of the emerging black—the cornerstone
> of all their public thinking. He is anaesthetic to their the-
> ological and political enthusiasms.

The present-day aristocrat who tries to mix effectively in politics
in the South or anywhere else in America straightway loses his
integrity, intelligence, and self-reliance.

In the realm of literary criticism too, Mencken often used his
notion of the gentleman as a balance in which to weigh writers,
their critics, and their public, and to find them wanting. Over
and over Mencken claimed that "America has no intellectual
aristocracy," only the populace on one hand and a fake aristocracy, the ruling plutocracy, on the other, with the middle zone
occupied by "an indistinct herd of intellectual eunuchs, chiefly
professors." In "Puritanism as a Literary Force," Mencken identified the aristocracy as those who felt, through literature, something of the ecstasy praised by Nietzsche, "that dionysian spirit,
that joyful acquiescence in life, that philosophy of the *Ja-sager*
which offers to Puritanism, today as in times past, its chief and
perhaps only effective antagonism." The modern puritan, Menck-
en said, was not so much opposed to this philosophy as unconscious of it; he represented "a commonwealth of peasants and

small traders" who were "almost wholly unchecked by the more sophisticated and civilized ideas of an aristocracy."

When Mencken praised a particular writer, he was likely to find elements in him of Nietzsche's superman as revised by Mencken. He hailed Conrad as a pessimistic Slav who refused to accept the Christian slave-morality of the Anglo-Saxon race and was "far more resolute" than Dreiser because, "He [Conrad] is, by birth and training, an aristocrat." However, Dreiser, despite his crudities, had the creative drive and intelligence of the superior being: "There is in him, hidden deep-down, a great instinctive artist, and hence the makings of an aristocrat." Dreiser was a "natural" aristocrat corrupted by his rural midwestern upbringing. Conversely, when Mencken criticized a writer, he was likely to find that he belonged outside of the highest caste in certain respects. Thus Dreiser often had moments when he became "once more the Indiana peasant, snuffing absurdly over imbecile sentimentalities, giving a grave ear to quackeries, snorting and eye-rolling with the best of them." Similarly, Mencken was distressed by George Ade's lack of interest in European culture as typified by Ibsen and Mozart, but decided that Ade was "a peasant touched by the divine fire." He concluded that Ade, like other American satirists, might be an exception to the rule that the creative aristocrat cannot afford to stoop to the common level; perhaps the satirist of the "booboisie" does have to lower himself in order to gain the necessary insight into his material. Obviously Mencken had to do some rationalizing for his theory of the aristocrat to cover Ade and Lardner as well as Conrad and Huneker. Inconsistency, however, never troubled Mencken for long.

Mencken's concept of the gentleman, like his view of the solid, thoughtful citizen, can be fully understood only if seen as it meshes with his other basic ideas. A few hints of these ideas can be given here. The evolutionary materialism associated with his rejection of Christianity has already been noted. This world view possibly owed something to the European tradition of anticlericalism as brought over by his father and grandfather, and it was certainly indebted to Henry's early reading of Darwin, Spencer, and Huxley. Part of this view was a belief in fixed natural law as the ultimate authority. One such law was the survival of the fittest, and Mencken felt that an "aristocracy of efficiency" would fulfill this law. An aristocracy of this kind "would re-establish the law of natural selection firmly upon its disputed throne, and so the strong would grow ever stronger and more efficient, and the weak would grow ever more obedient and tractile."

In applying this view to the social scene, Mencken resembled his favorite social Darwinist, William Graham Sumner. Sumner had felt that just as unbridled competition in nature resulted in the survival of the fittest, so would the removal of all barriers to competition among men cause the ablest men (Mencken's "natural" aristocrats) to emerge in business, politics, and the arts.[6] Sometimes Mencken affirmed that such a removal of barriers would operate by allowing the laws of heredity to fulfill themselves—i.e., he inclined toward those Darwinists who defined nature as heredity and race, rather than environment: "The precise form of an individual's activity is determined, of course, by the equipment with which he came into the world. In other words, it is determined by his heredity." Joseph Conrad, Mencken felt, was a better writer than H. L. Mencken simply because he was born with more talent. At other times, Mencken spoke as an environmentalist, denouncing the stifling mediocrity of the writer's milieu in America.

Whether writing about nature or nurture, Mencken was a frank racist. Without the ridiculous intervention of the puritans, the uplifters, and others who tried to flout natural law, Negroes would have no illusions about their ability to rise, and large bodies of Americans of nearly pure Anglo-Saxon stock—a strain Mencken held to be inferior to the Teutonic—including the vast majority of New Englanders and nearly all the southern white trash, would sink to their proper level in society, politics, and the arts. So would bad writers, political demagogues, evangelists, and other spokesmen of the booboisie.

Whenever Mencken slid into his deterministic mode, he tended to pooh-pooh any belief in progress, especially as voiced by Wilsonians, Progressives, Anti-Saloon Leaguers, Bryan Democrats, social gospelers, and professors who thought Emerson and Longfellow were great writers. He declared that ". . . you will never find a first-rate race or an enlightened age, in its moments of highest reflection, that ever gave more than a passing bow to optimism." Inconsistently, he stated at other times that human history included a good deal of progress; "the priest-ridden middle ages were 'unspeakably foul,' while the nineteenth century (which Nietzsche abominated) 'witnessed greater human progress than all the centuries before it saw or even imagined.' "[7] When one also considers Mencken's zeal in support of literary freedom and against censorship—for example, his support of Dreiser when *The Genius* was suppressed, or his deliberate courting of arrest in the "Hat-Rack" case—one feels that even to himself Mencken's views on progress were not wholly clear. It is hard to accept entirely his own explanation of his combativeness —that he fought only for amusement. This explanation does reveal a further connection between his intermittent determinism and his concept of the gentleman. Belief in determinism and disbelief in progress allowed him to claim that, since gentlemen could do nothing to improve the world, their only recourse was to be amused by it. As a writer, he declared, his function was to provide that amusement. He and Nathan proclaimed the *Smart Set* "the Aristocrat of Magazines" and its intended readership to be the "civilized minority," whom they defined as "persons of taste," and Mencken informed Dreiser that "We are not trying to shock 'em but to entertain 'em."[8] In the first number of the *American Mercury*, Mencken insisted that ". . . many of the great problems of man, and particularly of man as a member of society, are intrinsically insoluble . . ." He qualified his pessimism just enough to allow that the *Mercury* might be of some nonessential use to the struggling artist by working the *lex talionis* upon "the obscurantists who occasionally beset him. . . . The business is amusing and now and then it may achieve some by-product of good." Three years later he claimed merely that the *Mercury* "is read wherever a civilized minority survives the assaults of the general herd of yawpers and come-ons. Its aim is to entertain that minority—and give it some consolation."[9] Consolation, that is, for its inability to change a predetermined world. The fact that the *Mercury* occasionally accepted essays or articles by intellectuals writing in the tradition of militant reform, such as Harry Elmer Barnes, Melville J. Herskovits, and Zechariah Chafee, Jr., merely suggested that doing good might indeed be a valid by-product but that liveliness of style—for there was little dull prose in the *Mercury*—was possibly a more important criterion of acceptance than conformity to the ideology of the editors.

THE GENTLEMAN MANQUÉ

Mencken professed to see himself primarily as an entertainer, and this conception of himself at least fitted his declarations of skepticism and determinism. He wrote to Burton Rascoe:

> Few doctrines seem to me to be worth fighting for. I can't understand the martyr. Far from going to the stake for a Great Truth, I wouldn't even miss a meal for it. My notion is that all the larger human problems are insoluble, and that life is quite meaningless—a spectacle without purpose or moral. I detest all efforts to read a moral into it. I do not write because I want to make converts. In point of fact, I seldom make one—and then it is embarrassing. I write because the business amuses me. It is the best of sports.[10]

In the same letter he asserted that from Robert I. Carter, his boss on the old Baltimore *Herald,* he had learned that the first aim of the critic was to be interesting. To interest the crowd, the critic must be bellicose. "Hence, when I have to praise a writer, I usually do it by attacking his enemies. And when I say the crowd I mean all men. My own crowd is very small and probably somewhat superior, but it likes rough-house just as much as a crowd around a bulletin-board."

To conceive of himself as an aristocrat and at the same time as a crowd-pleaser was not the most logical approach in the world. True, at least one trait of Mencken's ideal aristocrat is also found in the entertainer. The same letter includes,

> The calm, Judicial judgment makes me laugh. It is a symptom of a delusion of infallibility. I am often wrong. My prejudices are innumerable, and often idiotic. My aim is not to determine facts, but to function freely and pleasantly—as Nietzsche used to say, to dance with arms and legs.

The dionysian joy of the aristocrat is suggested here, but where is the intelligence and farsightedness which Mencken felt to be part of the equipment of Jenner, Pasteur, Huxley, *et al.*? It was hard to insist on those qualities while laughing at oneself as a buffoon and a fool, or while maintaining that one would never stand up for any great truths—especially if one insisted elsewhere on his own superiority. Besides resembling Will Rogers in his views about the meaninglessness of life, Mencken also was like Rogers in reducing his own stature as writer to that of a fool who is, anyhow, wise enough to ridicule the pretensions of all enthusiastic actionists, whatever their creeds or parties (Mencken of course expressed his views in far more erudite prose, and, in public at least, he lacked the practical humanitarianism that qualified Rogers' general skepticism). One could say that Mencken saw himself less as a gentleman than as a jester at a court of gentlemen. Moreover, in this letter and elsewhere Mencken minimizes the distinction between the aristocracy and the mob. He would rather anger than please the mob, but in allowing them to influence his style and ideas he is doing just what he accused Roosevelt and Wilson of having done—compromising himself to get a following among the booboisie. He may not have wanted converts, but he certainly wanted a "following" of attentive readers. Perhaps an entertainer could only be a gentleman *manqué*.

In Mencken's public references to himself as writer, his materialistic determinism did not alter, but his concept of the gentleman did, no less than in his private letters. "I am totally devoid of public spirit or moral purpose," he was fond of saying, with his tongue not wholly in his cheek. After claiming he hadn't "the least lust to improve American literature," he argued plausibly, "if it ever came to what I regard as perfection my job would be gone." The job, that is, of entertaining readers of taste with his denunciations of imperfection. In "On Being an American," he called the American people a "timorous, sniveling, poltroonish, ignominious mob of serfs and goose-steppers." Would not one expect him, then, to follow Henry James, Ezra Pound, and Harold Stearns into exile? "Yet I remain on the dock, wrapped in the flag, when the Young Intellectuals set sail." Why? Because, to be happy, Mencken felt that he must be

> *a*. Well-fed, unhounded by sordid cares, at ease in Zion.
> *b*. Full of a comfortable feeling of superiority to the masses of my fellow-men.
> *c*. Delicately and unceasingly amused according to my taste.

The degree of literal truth in all these statements is not here important. In reality, Mencken's attachment to a single dwelling place and routine surely had more to do with his reluctance to follow Harold Stearns and some of the other authors of *Civilization in the United States*—the "Young Intellectuals" to whom Mencken refers—abroad, than did the reasons just quoted, even though Mencken had contributed one essay to that volume.[11] More significant, however, is the implied self-portrait of a rather passive intellectual gourmet with none of the energy and will of the superman. In further calling himself "complacent (perhaps even to the point of offensiveness)," Mencken combined a neat bit of understatement with mild ridicule of himself (one may assess the understatement by glancing at the compilation by

Mencken and his wife of choice abuse aimed at the man and his ideas entitled *Menckeniana: A Schimpflexikon).*

Occasionally the notion of the aristocrat itself became the object of his ridicule. In *A Little Book in C Major* (1916), a small volume of gnomic sayings that probably owes its form to Ambrose Bierce's *The Devil's Dictionary,* he quipped,

> A man becomes a gentleman the moment the betting odds on his word of honor pass 3 to 2.
> A gentleman is one who never strikes a woman without provocation.

In "The Jazz Webster" (*A Book of Burlesques,* 1916), Mencken defined a gentleman as, "One who never strikes a woman without provocation; one on whose word of honor the betting odds are at least 1 to 2."

That Mencken could see the humorous side of his ideal does not suggest that he abandoned that ideal even temporarily. In the same book he also said, "The great difficulty about keeping the Ten Commandments is that no man can keep them and be a gentleman." His meaning is not entirely clear, but in several discussions of "honor," he emphasizes that a gentleman might be forced by his code to bear false witness in order to protect a friend or a guest from unworthy laws like the Volstead Act. Too, Mencken's gentleman, being an atheist and a materialist, would have little use for the first and second commandments. However, Mencken's occasional ridicule of the notion of aristocracy does indicate a certain detachment concerning his ideal. He may have cultivated that detachment mainly for purposes of humor; at any rate he meant the title of six of his books, *Prejudices,* to be more than a catchword.

THE FORGOTTEN MAN

Mencken often allowed the ideal of the aristocrat in his writing to fade into the background and be eclipsed by a different kind of intellectual elite, the hard-working, conservative citizen for whom he sometimes borrowed the label, "The Forgotten

Man." The phrase was the title of a lecture delivered in 1883 by Sumner in which the Yale economist propounded rugged individualism in business and a hands-off philosophy in government. Whether Mencken owed the concept as well as the label to Sumner does not matter; in any case, the ideal had more of a native American flavor than the aristocrat of Nietzsche. Sumner characterized the Forgotten Man as the citizen who has accumulated a little substance through "industry, economy, and virtue." This man is the victim of reformers and humanitarians because he pays, through taxes, for their schemes. Sumner divided the mass of people into two types: the lazy, idle, and incompetent, and "the clean, quiet, virtuous, domestic citizen, who pays his debts and his taxes and is never heard of out of his little circle." This type is the real producer of all wealth, and the only way to benefit him, other than by simply letting him alone, is to support those political measures that protect capital (and capitalists) against the depredations of philanthropists and reformers who would reduce the supply of available capital by draining it off to the shiftless nonproducers.

Mencken had made the same division long before he began to quote Sumner, and his own attitude toward economics was wholly in accord with the assumptions of laissez faire and social Darwinism hinted at in Sumner's essay and developed fully in the professor's more technical treatises. However, Mencken reworked this concept of the ideal common man for his broader purposes. In this lecture, Sumner's purposes had been primarily political and economic whereas Mencken wrote not only in these fields, but on religion, on culture, and on almost every other aspect of human affairs.[12] In religion, Mencken's man was an aggressive and wordy skeptic, whereas Sumner very briefly and incidentally describes his Forgotten Man as supporting the church of his choice. In culture, Mencken's man read widely and exercised a discriminating taste in prose; he was also a lover of classical music, especially German. In his indifference to most painting and in his distrust of poetry as a sentimentalizing of the untrue, this man strangely resembled the Babbitts whom his creator kept denouncing.

The differences between the images of Mencken and of Sumner arose mainly because Mencken's man was drawn with more detail than Sumner's; the similarities were more obvious than the differences. In politics, both remained aloof from party involvement, but expressed hostility toward government interference with the liberties of the individual. In economics, both stood for free and unlimited competition, among individuals and among corporations. Sumner says little about this man's intelligence, but both Sumner and Mencken shared a dogmatic faith in intelligence—a faith which oddly resembled that of the liberals—and in natural law. Above all, both authors saw the uncommon common citizen as victimized by *boobus Americanus* (the term is Mencken's, of course) and by the cads and crackpots who led the hordes of that species.

Mencken's closeness to Sumner has been worth dwelling on because it shows his closeness to nineteenth-century social Darwinism, even as his use of the ideal aristocrat shows his affinity with biological Darwinism. Since the two creeds were interrelated, Mencken found no difficulty in slipping off the mask of the aristocrat and putting on that of the ordinary, rational citizen. Further, both were supposed to share the same skepticism, intelligence, industry, thrift, will power, independence in tastes and habits, and the same conviviality after working hours. The solid citizen was indeed aristocracy of a sort—not the equal of Nietzsche's ideal, but the best that America could produce:

> Here [in America] the general average of intelligence, of knowledge, of competence, of integrity, of self-respect, of honor is so low that any man who knows his trade, does not fear ghosts, has read fifty good books, and practices the common decencies stands out as brilliantly as a wart on a bald head, and is thrown willy-nilly into a meager and exclusive aristocracy.

In Mencken's list of intellectual aristocrats, Lincoln was the only American. Mencken also suggested that thoughtful Americans could regard the superman as an ideal for the future only, if at all. Locating the dominant class in the future was a device (probably unconscious) by which Mencken left himself free to define that class in the present much as he pleased, and to wear whatever mask he chose.

Not only did Mencken's image of the solid citizen as aristocrat have a native American stamp, but it bore some resemblance to that citizen as envisioned by other humorists. Delete the phrase concerning this man's reading from the quotation above, and the passage could stand as a sketch of the composite "hero" in many of Ade's fables, or of Ring Lardner's Gullible. This hero or anti-hero also resembles the small-town editors who dosed the yahoos with proverbial pungencies in Mark Twain's *Pudd'nhead Wilson* and in the writings of E. W. Howe.[13] There are differences—besides having more culture, Mencken's man is less bewildered than Ade's capitalists or Lardner's temporarily gullible protagonist, and less bitter than the editorial *personae* of Twain and Howe. He is Mencken's creation, not anybody else's. Yet all these characters are close kin in their respect for the "common decencies" of courtesy, kindness, loyalty to friends, and minding one's own business.

In his rhetorical practice, Mencken seldom haggled over terminology, but emphasized one or the other of his two images or fused them, whichever strategy served his purpose. Perhaps one should say rather that he emphasized whichever side of his single, Janus-faced image served his turn—the face of the aristocrat or of the solid citizen. In his editorial for the first issue of the *Mercury*, he tried to induce as many readers as possible to subscribe to the magazine without sacrificing his goal of appealing primarily to the "civilized minority." Consequently he fused the two images and ascribed to his hoped-for readers both solidity and intellectual refinement, implying that he, the writer, was also as they were: "The reader they [the editors, Mencken and Nathan] have in their eye, whose prejudices they share and whose woes they hope to soothe, is what William Graham Sumner called the Forgotten Man—that is, the normal, educated, well-disposed, unfrenzied, enlightened citizen of the middle minority." This citizen stood in the middle in that he was beset by evangelists and reformers on one side and by an irresponsible and venal government on the other. The Forgotten Man is caught between the "Liberals" (reformers) and the "Tories" (the large daily newspapers, the organs of the business clubs, and the "reviews of high tone," by which the editors of the *Mercury* may have meant the *North American Review,* the *Dial,* and/or the *Bookman).*[14] Expanding the metaphor, they added,

> There is no middle ground of consolation for men who be-lieve neither in the Socialist fol-de-rol nor in the principal enemies of the Socialist fol-de-rol—and yet it must be obvious that such men constitute the most intelligent and valuable body of citizens that the nation can boast. The leading men of science and learning are in it. The best artists, in all the arts, are in it. Such men of business as have got any imagina-tion are in it. It will be the design of the *American Mercury* to bring, if not alleviation of their lot, then at least some solace to these outcasts of democracy.

The melding of the citizen with the aristocrat is not accom-plished smoothly; a Forgotten Man whose ideas are mere "prej-udices" and who is "normal" does not readily suggest the intel-lectual and business elite, with "imagination." All members of this mythical elite would doubtless qualify more clearly through what they oppose than what they support. They might at least find unity in their scorn of Lorelei Lee, Anita Loos' blonde whom gentlemen preferred; Lorelei felt that a friend was wasting time by going to luncheon "to meet a gentleman called Mr. Mencken from Baltimore who really only prints a green maga-zine which has not even got any pictures in it." Lorelei is a fe-

male specimen of the Great American Boob, against whom nearly
eighty thousand readers could feel they were striking a blow
when they bought the *Mercury* each month during its peak year
of 1927. This was only about half the circulation of the *Atlantic*
or *Harper's*[15]—but the magazine kept comfortably in the black
until the depression years, when most periodicals lost money.

The mask of the solid citizen, as Mencken used it, was flexible
enough to be altered in several ways, always according to how it
would increase the impact of the piece he was writing. It was a
rhetorical device first, and an ideological exhibit only secondly.
Sometimes he stressed the ordinariness of himself, or rather of
his comic self-image. In "On Being an American," he contrasted
himself with the "Young Intellectuals" partly through presenting himself as "a loyal and devoted Americano, even a chauvin-
ist, paying taxes without complaint, obeying all laws that are
physiologically obeyable, accepting all the searching duties and
responsibilities of citizenship unprotestingly" [!]. He was, he suggested, a better citizen than the worshippers of Harding, or than
Rotarians, Klansmen, and Anti-Saloon Leaguers. Sometimes he
presented himself as the working journalist or writer. In
"Gamalielese," an attack on the prose style of Warren G.
Harding, Mencken announced that he was qualified to judge the
great man's style because "I have earned most of my livelihood
for twenty years past by translating the bad English of a multi-
tude of authors into measurably better English." But he solemnly
abandons all claim to qualification for judging the great man's
ideas (thus ostensibly rejecting the mask of the intellectual superman)—and then proceeds to mix considerable criticism of Harding's ideas with ridicule of the presidential prose style. The
mask of the ordinary citizen has functioned as a device of irony
and satire.

In "The Husbandman," Mencken took the viewpoint of "a
reader of the *Congressional Record*"—a role which suggested the
editor of a magazine devoted largely to public affairs—and
thereby hinted without saying that he was an expert in political

matters. This position lent authority to his raucous attack on the American farmer as "a tedious fraud and ignoramus, a cheap rogue and hypocrite, the eternal Jack of the human pack." In "The Ulster Polonius," Mencken stated (inaccurately) that he had written the first book about Shaw's plays, and "I read them pretty steadily, even to-day, and with endless enjoyment." His purpose in this essay is to emphasize that Shaw is not an original thinker but merely has a talent for presenting commonplace ideas "so scandalously that the pious get all of the thrills out of the business that would accompany a view of the rector in liquor in the pulpit." To put his criticism across forcefully, Mencken thus adopted the point of view of a Shavian critic of pioneer achievements and long experience who still clings to the master but is skeptical of his ideological pretentiousness— His Shavian Majesty's loyal opposition. Midway in the essay, Mencken briefly changes his mask for that of a citizen who is skeptical in religion but not conspicuous in other ways. His purpose here is to demonstrate that Shaw's apparently novel view of one specific idea—the doctrine of the Atonement—is not novel at all. In the preface to *Androcles and the Lion,* Shaw had held that acceptance of this doctrine tends to weaken a man morally, whereas rejection of it strengthens him by throwing him back upon his own moral courage. Mencken says that Shaw's view

> suggests itself so naturally that I myself once employed it against a chance Christian encountered in a Pullman smoking-room. This Christian was at first shocked as he might have been by reading Shaw, but in half an hour he was confessing that he had long ago thought of the objection himself, and put it away as immoral. I well remember his fascinated interest as I showed him how my inability to accept the doctrine put a heavy burden of moral responsibility upon me, and forced me to be more watchful of my conduct than the elect of God, and so robbed me of many pleasant advantages in finance, the dialectic and amour . . .[16]

Each time Mencken altered some detail of his mask, he implicitly identified himself with one group or another among his readers. Thus in "The Husbandman," he insists that rural fundamentalists, led by "the mountebank, Bryan," are preparing to embark on a crusade "against what remains of American intelligence, already beleaguered in a few walled towns." If these peasants win, "The city man, as now, will bear nine-tenths of the tax burden; the rural total immersionist will make all the laws." Here Mencken suggested that the elite were primarily city-dwellers. However, his numerous defenses of Baltimore remind one more of the small-townsman.[17] In "On Living in Baltimore," he wrote as "the normal man of Baltimore" and stressed that the main advantage of Baltimore, with its relative stability, was to strengthen the home and even to make that man's circle of friends "a sort of extension of his family circle." In this argument he made his elite include all Baltimoreans who were lovers of home, family, and friends—three phenomena popularly supposed to have their roots in the small town—in contrast to the vast majority of New Yorkers, who have lost "the instinct to make a permanent home." Mencken thus deliberately broadened his definition of the superior minority because his main purpose was to defend Baltimore by attacking New York.

Yet another change in the details of the mask may be seen in *In Defense of Women,* which appeared in book form in 1918, after fifteen states had granted women full suffrage. Here the solid citizen (H. L. Mencken) presented himself as a genteel sybarite, so far as sex was concerned. Mencken devoted much of the book to a depiction of woman as the sex which dominates through superior intelligence and ruthlessness. The average man is depicted as a weak-minded poser whose "puerile ego" enables him to conceal from himself his mawkishness and his sexual timidity—a creature bearing some resemblance to Thurber's Mr. Monroe and Walter Mitty. Having thus shown the American male and his consort as they were, Mencken rounded off his book by showing them as he—or at any rate his *persona*—would like them to be. Mencken claimed that in his own case an ideal relationship with a woman would not include passion, because it was "too exciting and alarming for so indolent a man," and he didn't want to be mothered because he was "too egoistic." What, then, remained? He described himself as sitting on a divan, at the close of a working day:

> At the edge of the divan, close enough for me to reach her with my hand, sits a woman not too young, but still good-looking and well-dressed—above all, a woman with a soft, low-pitched, agreeable voice. As I snooze she talks—of anything, everything, all the things that women talk of: books, music, the play, men, other women. No politics. No business. No religion. No metaphysics. Nothing challenging and vexatious—but remember, she is intelligent; what she says is clearly expressed, and often picturesquely. . . . Gradually I fall asleep—but only for an instant. At once, observing it, she raises her voice ever so little, and I am awake. Then to sleep again—slowly and charmingly down that slippery hill of dreams. And then awake again, and then asleep again, and so on. . . . In the end, when the girl grows prettily miffed and throws me out, I return to my sorrows somehow purged and glorified. I am a better man in my own sight. I have grazed upon the fields of asphodel. I have been genuinely, completely and unregrettably happy.[18]

Even if a reader did not know that Mencken was the least indolent of men, or that (according to Charles Angoff) he had been heard to boast of sexual activity more vigorous than what is described here, the inconsistency of this self-portrait with the aggressive, energetic nature suggested elsewhere in the book, and the parody of the language of sentimentality and morality in the last four sentences should make all but the dullest readers suspect that they were being spoofed by means of a mask which caricatured the writer behind it.

Whether Mencken depicted himself (or his ideal reader) as a working journalist, a village-atheist type of scoffer at religion, an urban taxpayer, a home-lover, or merely a passive connoisseur of female conversation, the basic character suggested is always the diligent, hardheaded citizen. Always, too, whether he elevated

that citizen to the role of Nietzschean aristocrat or not, Mencken
followed the same basic plan in his more humorous essays—that
of contrasting the thinking minority with the "inflammatory and
fickle mob" and the charlatans who led them. In a general way,
the author always identifies himself with the thinker, but he
often disarms the reader by caricaturing this thinker, and in
doing so, practices the ancient humorous technique of laughing
at himself.

It is not always easy to spot the caricature. The creator of Mr.
Dooley obviously could not be an illiterate saloonkeeper, but
the *alter ego* of Mencken resembles the man just enough to have
taken in countless readers. Moreover, the positive image is usually
kept in the background; Mencken's way of supporting any man
or value was mainly to charge full tilt at the opposition.

To show in detail how Mencken practiced the art of self-
caricature and likewise the techniques of invective, oversimplification, exaggeration, the hoax, and the grotesque metaphor,
would require a full-length critical study. In stressing only two
of the ways by which he made humor out of his prejudices—his
use of comic masks and his contrast of an elite of rational
citizenry with the "human kohlrabi"—I hope to have pointed a
way along which others will travel farther.

10

The Isolated Man
of Ring Lardner

Mencken may have drawn more abuse because of his arrogance
and bluster, but in his satire of mass-man he was no more severe
than Ring Lardner, whom he praised for "meticulous histological
study of a few salient individuals of his time and nation."
Mencken probably meant character types; actually Lardner's

athletes, salesmen, clerks, barbers, nurses, newspapermen, and song writers were variations on a single type, the white-collar American of the lower middle class. Sometimes this type is shown in his teens; sometimes he is elderly and retired. Occasionally he is portrayed as having done unusually well financially, and more often than not, he is shown during his leisure time. Either at work or at play, he is self-centered and ignorant, and his speech and his ideas are usually limited by a fifth- or sixth-grade education—a limitation more typical in 1913, when Lardner was on the brink of his career as a humorist, than it is today.[1]

Compared to Mencken or to Don Marquis, Lardner's own interests as a humorist were narrow. Unlike Mencken, Lardner confined his range of topics largely to the limited interests of his mass-man. With few exceptions, Lardner tended either to ignore more sensitive or more intelligent types, or to fall into the sentimentality of his own middle-class lout when he tried to delineate them. Although exposition rather than evaluation is the main task of this volume, one cannot help suggesting that Lardner too often shared the values and interests of his basic character type.

Sometimes Lardner depicts this type as a hick from the small town (like Ade's rubes), and sometimes as a dweller in the city or in suburbia. Lardner knew all three areas well. He was born and reared in Niles, Michigan (then a town of about 4,000), eleven miles by horse and buggy from South Bend, Indiana. His father was a wealthy and conservative real-estate operator, but lost most of his fortune in 1901, a year of panic on Wall Street and of a dip in the business cycle generally. The family was not reduced to poverty, and the home life of the Lardners remained one of at least average security and harmony.[2] However, Ring eventually had to get out and hustle. He made a halfhearted attempt to major in engineering at Armour Institute, then drifted through a series of odd jobs and into sports writing for newspapers. By 1913 he had risen to the authorship of a humorous sporting column for the Chicago *Tribune*, "In the Wake of the

News," a column which he conducted until 1919. In it he developed a satirical style through thumbnail character sketches, monologues, and bits of dialogue, finally building this style into a full-fledged literary idiom.[3] During these six years, the "Wake" became the most popular column in Chicago; "People quoted it, and Ernest Hemingway and James T. Farrell, who were then in their teens, imitated the Lardner dialect in their high-school papers." [4]

Ring's first book was a collection of light verse, *Bib Ballads* (1915, probably inspired by the *Bab Ballads* of W. S. Gilbert), which mainly concerned his own small children. Meanwhile, Lardner's letters of a bush-league ball player were appearing in the *Saturday Evening Post,* and these came out between hard covers in 1916. This volume was followed by several more collections of stories and reportage before Ring's growing reputation brought him a contract with the new Bell Syndicate to do a weekly column. Shortly thereafter, the Lardner family moved to Greenwich, Connecticut, a suburb of New York, and later to Great Neck, Long Island, where their near neighbors included F. Scott Fitzgerald and his family. According to Donald Elder, "During the year and a half that Fitzgerald lived as Ring's neighbor in Great Neck, from 1922 to 1924, they were almost constant companions." [5] In *Tender Is the Night* Fitzgerald may have depicted Lardner in the person of Abe North, a musician frustrated by a career of fragmentary achievements.

By 1926, Ring's weekly column appeared in more than a hundred and fifty newspapers; among humorists only Will Rogers and possibly Kin Hubbard could have reached more readers. However, Lardner was tired of newspaper work, and he dropped his column for Bell the next year, though he later took other column jobs because his family needed the money. Throughout the nineteen-twenties and in the early thirties, his work continued to reach millions of readers through the *Saturday Evening Post, Collier's, Cosmopolitan,* and *Liberty.* Toward the end of his career he placed a number of sketches in the

New Yorker, and during the last fifteen months of his life he wrote a column on radio programs for that magazine, entitled "Over the Waves."

"Did any small-town boy rise faster, higher?" Maxwell Geismar has asked. But his decline was almost as rapid. Heavy expenses ate holes in Ring's large income, and despite his fame, he suffered frequent fits of depression and alcoholism. Like Don Marquis, he sank into constant ill health during several years of grinding out copy to pay the bills. He died of a heart attack in 1933, famous and forty-eight. His last extant letter is a friendly note to H. L. Mencken.

TWO TYPES OF COMMON MAN

Who was the "average man" of Lardner? Usually he was the white-collar worker away from the office—not the idle rich, but the " 'idle common man.' " [6] Howard Webb suggests that much of Lardner's satire between 1913 and 1916, when his style and interests were crystallizing into form, was directed at "the Progressive Myth of the New Citizen. . . . This emergent New Citizen— the term was William Allen White's—was viewed as upright, intelligent, and self-restrained, as one who took a broad view of matters and evidenced a disinterested concern with the needs of his community." He was often equated with the midwesterner; and as a man on the way up rather than one already up, he distrusted the plutocracy:

> This image, [in Webb's words] or rather this combined image—the Middle Westerner as the typical New Citizen— Lardner's writing criticized. It reported an aspect of the social scene which contradicted the Progressive myth. Lardner's white-collar worker was a man with a comfortable quantity of cash and leisure who was concerned almost exclusively with his own well-being and prestige. He was on the make all right, but not in the way Wilson thought. The so-called New Citizen, as Walter Weyl observed, was motivated not so much by his hatred of the plutocracy as by his role as consumer. He was becoming a social rather than an economic entrepreneur; his goal was to acquire social

prestige rather than to amass a fortune. In Lardner's portrait, he competed on the new frontiers of consumption, and making money was no more important to him than where, why and for what to spend it.

Thus Jack Keefe is on the make economically, but is equally hungry for the prestige that playing in the big leagues will give him, and in his obsession with how his money is to be spent as well as with how it is to be made, he ranks as a competitive consumer. As both consumer and status-seeker, he belongs with such Babbitts as the Hatches, Fred Gross, the Thayers (of "Liberty Hall"), Mr. Frisbie, Conrad Green, and the two garrulous vacationers in "Sun Cured."

Occasionally, however, Lardner portrays a different type of common man, one who resembles the "Old Ready Money" of George Ade—the paterfamilias who is dragged into the status chase and across the new frontier of consumption by his womenfolk. Wiser than they, he sooner or later repents of his folly and tries to restrain the women from theirs (sometimes Sinclair Lewis' Babbitt also resembles this type, especially at the end of Lewis' novel, where he supports Ted against the gabbling females). Though childless, Gullible and the narrator of *The Big Town* are each this sort of character; so are Father, in "The Golden Honeymoon," and Tom Carter—who had made his money by developing a paint, like Howells' Silas Lapham—in "Old Folks' Christmas." Lardner nearly always makes this type the spokesman of his own values in any given story. In so doing, he shows toward these heads of families about the same mixture of irony and sympathy as Ade and Lewis toward theirs.

Sometimes Lardner's much more frequent (and obnoxious) type of common man becomes the double of the author, especially in Lardner's essays and columns as distinguished from his short stories. Donald Elder calls this common-man-as-*persona* "the 'wise boob,' the average man of common sense, cynical, humorous, a conceited wiseacre, but genial and likable. He has a certain innocence which often appears to border on stupidity, and tastes that are so commonplace that they are pleasantly vulgar." He has close kinship with traditional crackerbox commentators, "from the Yankee pedlar to Mr. Dooley." He is like them in being at once an embodiment of the virtues and a burlesque of the follies of the average man; therefore he feeds the average man's ego but also stimulates that man's counterbalancing tendency to laugh at himself if the laugh on him isn't too hard.

In addition, he vicariously gratifies the average man's desire for self-expression. Many of Lardner's columns must have made readers feel, "Yes, that's just what I thought, and I could of said that if I could write good."

Maybe this character is more often fool and oaf than wise man, in contrast to Mr. Dooley, who is usually more wise than foolish:

> Marred life is a job just the same as like a telegraph operator or a embalmer and every employ is entitled to 2 wks. vacation per annum and if the husband takes a 2 wks. vacation trip every summer and vice versa, why they will get so as they won't miss their regular jobs ½ as much as if they was on it all the wile. For inst. I knew a couple where the husband use to go South for a mo. every Winter and one time he didn't come home at all and all of his relic's friends was feeling sorry for her where as she didn't know he was still missing till one night in August when a bat got in the house and she screamed and nobody told her to shut up.

The opening clause of this excerpt may be considered common sense, if one ignores the similes. The subliterate English, the proverbial style, and the use of an anecdote to illustrate a point are characteristic of the crackerbarrel philosopher. Exaggeration carries the sense into nonsense, assisted by the violent yoking of two ordinarily dissociated similes. Moreover, the grim anecdote is tossed off so callously that the narrator reveals himself to be heartless as well as foolish, like the barber in "Haircut." Instead of being a *persona* and a wise fool, he is a burlesque of the wise fool. Often Ring's portrayal of the common-man-as-wise-fool thus turns into bitter burlesque; the "wise boob" is continually becoming merely the obnoxious plain man with no wisdom in him but with a good deal of sadism. Further, if Lardner did realize his closeness to his material, his uglier portraits become deliberate burlesques of himself.[7]

The crackerbox oracle often becomes a self-mockery of the author in less striking ways; Mr. Dooley is, in part, a poking of fun at his creator's genuine interest in reform, and Abe Martin sometimes burlesques his author's regret at the decline of small-town mores. The excerpt above includes a more poignant derision of Lardner's own wish to be free from family cares and vexations. His marriage was permanent and seems to have been relatively happy, but he periodically tore himself from the household and went on long trips alone, as if this sort of freedom were a driving need in him.

With regard to the social background of his characters, Lardner should not be considered class-conscious in the sociological sense; his overt emphasis is upon a particular kind of personality rather than a social class. "Jack Keefe, Fred Gross, Conrad Green, Midge Kelly—these and many other characters all have a common fault. They carry with them as they go about their business in the world of men a false image of self, on the basis of which they behave and to which they expect others to respond." [8] When these characters collide with reality, they become either merely ridiculous or, as in the case of Midge Kelly (in "Champion") and Conrad Green, "vicious paranoiacs." Such self-deluded persons may be found in any social stratum; however, Lardner confined himself to the middle-class type that he knew best.

This false image of self tends to destroy communication between man and man in much of Lardner's work. Shut up in his private self-image, the Lardner character often reacts aggressively to any contact tending to disturb that image. Lardner's fiction deals largely with such aggressors and their victims. In the nineteen-twenties, Mencken was one of the first to notice the deepening strain of bitterness in Ring's work; his characters had been at first, Mencken said, mere yaps, but of late were more often

"loathsome scoundrels." Another aspect of this bitterness was
the gradual shift in Lardner's work from stories primarily about
aggressors such as Jack Keefe, to stories containing both aggressors and victims (for example, "Haircut" and "Champion"), and
finally to tales mainly about victims, ranging from the macabre
amusement of "Large Coffee" to the pathos and scorn of "The
Maysville Minstrel" and the undiluted pathos of "Mamma." [9]
Yet Lardner's victims are often as walled in behind their self-
images as are the aggressors. Such isolation is an attribute, not
only of Lardner's characters, but of most character types in twentieth-century American humor.

YOU KNOW ME AL

Lardner's first collection of "Busher's letters" provided his
first extended portrait of the aggressive type of average man and
may serve as a representative study. It is ironic that the first
letters about Jack Keefe were rejected in the city that saw the rise
of George Ade and Mr. Dooley. Lardner sent the letters to the
Chicago *Sunday Tribune,* but the Sunday editor turned them
down and so did other Chicago editors. The reason—people
would never accept the slang. The letters likewise came back
from the *Saturday Evening Post,* until Ring sent them to the
home address of the editor, George H. Lorimer. Lorimer was a
producer as well as a promoter of dialect humor; he had written
Letters From a Self-Made Merchant to His Son (1901–1902) and
Old Gorgon Graham (1904), colloquial pieces about an unlettered but articulate pork-packer. When Lorimer accepted
the first batch of busher's letters, he had already published many
stories by Montague Glass in stage-Jewish dialect and by Irvin
S. Cobb, who made free use of southern vernacular. Some of the
Keefe letters appeared in the *Post* of March 7, 1914, and these
were followed at irregular intervals until 1919. Eventually they
were republished in three books, of which the first, *You Know
Me Al,* remains the freshest. A composite of various players
Ring met during his years as a sports reporter, Jack Keefe is
baseball's version of the semiliterate common man who is part-

way up the ladder and has time for the pursuit of prestige. In addition, he is from a small, outlying town and is a malicious burlesque of the bumpkin in the city. From Jack Downing to Abe Martin and Will Rogers, the country boy has often been shrewder and more upright than his city cousin, but Jack Keefe is saved from gross immorality only by his stupidity and pettiness. The thick shield of his ego so distorts his view of reality that his aggressions are more often than not rendered harmless, and he, ridiculous. As Howard Webb says:

> When he wins a game, his pitching must triumph over the errors of other players and misjudgments of the umpires: "I had everything and the Cubs done well to score a run. . . . The umps give them their run. . . . Then Schulte the lucky stiff happened to get a hold of one and pulled it past first base. I guess Chase must of been asleep." When he loses, the fates and his teammates have played him false: "I had a sore arm when I was warming up. . . . Weaver and Lord and all of them kept kicking them round the infield and Collins and Bodie couldn't catch nothing. . . . Crawford got the luckiest three-base hit I ever see. He popped one way up in the air and the wind blowed it against the fence." When the manager taunts: "Don't work no harder than you have to or you might get hurt and the league would blow up," Jack concludes: "I guess he thinks pretty well of me."[10]

Keefe is also a self-made and therefore comic victim. He has some ability, but he would win many more games if his managers could penetrate his ego. "If you wind up like that with Cobb on base he will steal your watch and chain," he is told, and Cobb does steal bases on Keefe almost at will. Repeated advice to improve his fielding and to bring his weight down is likewise wasted on Jack.

But Keefe as both aggressor and victim is most vividly portrayed off the diamond, especially in his courtship, marriage, and family life. He is "the irresistible lover—whose affairs end with someone else's getting the girl; the model husband—who cannot get along with his wife." [11] Egocentric, mercenary, featherheaded, the busher's wife is a counterpart of Jack himself. She also foists on him a child that is not his—an aspect of the story heretofore neglected by critics—but his self-centeredness blinds him to what is obvious, and the result is keenly ironic. The irony is comic, however, because Jack's "love" is at least nine-tenths ego-gratification; besides, his affection never displaces his obsession with money. In the letter announcing his marriage, he say, "Yes Al I and Florrie was married the day before yesterday just like I told you we was going to be and Al I am the happyest man in the world though I have spent $30 in the last 3 days incluseive."

The alert reader may see what Jack in his egotism cannot. Florrie has married Jack mainly as a way of raising her own status, and their joint pursuit of prestige leads them on a spending orgy in the big city. Florrie's sister Marie is the wife of Allen, a left-handed pitcher with the same ball club as Jack, and in a desperate attempt to slash expenses during their foolish spree, Jack and Florrie sponge off the Allens by moving in with them. The Allens return the compliment when their own sublease expires.

Jack and Florrie had been married on October 15, after a courtship of three days. A baby is born to Florrie on June 16 of the following year, just eight months and one day after the wedding. There is no hint that the birth is premature or that Jack and Florrie had had the slightest interest in each other before the evening of October 12. Two clues, reported casually by Jack to Al, point to Allen as the father. First, Florrie wants to name the baby Allen, "after his uncle and aunt Allen but which is after you old pal." Second, the baby shows signs of being left-handed, but Jack refuses to accept any such possibility, and later writes, ". . . if it looks as if he was going to be left-handed dont let him Al but make him use his right hand for every thing." This obstinacy functions in Jack's rejection of every unpleasant fact he has ever encountered—a rejection that makes him cooperate unwittingly in his own victimization by practical jokers in the club and by an adulterer in the home.

Anyway, Jack is always more interested in his own career

than in his family. In the letter announcing the birth of the baby, his opening statement is not about the great event but about his performance on the mound—"Al I beat the Athaletics 2 to 1 to-day . . ." At the end of the letter, he says, "I got a real family. Do you get that Al, a real family?" Thus the letter as a whole reveals his isolation from reality even at the hearth and in the bed. The irony recurs whenever the curtain is lifted on the Keefes at home. It also remains comic, even when Jack worries about the baby "balling pretty hard" and "haveing the collect." Any budding sympathy in the reader is nipped by fresh evidence of Jack's callousness and self-absorption. For instance, he writes to Al and Bertha, "Babys is great stuff Al and if I was you I would not wait no longer but would hurry up and adopt 1 somewheres." Indeed, whenever the irony of the common man as cuckold is not involved, the latter installments of *You Know Me Al* are a letdown. Most of them concern the efforts of managers Callahan and McGraw to gull Jack into making an around-the-world exhibition trip with their clubs, despite his fear of crossing the ocean.

   Treat 'Em Rough (1918) and *The Real Dope* (1919) depict Jack's adventures as a draftee in the American Expeditionary Force at home and in France. The style is flat and the satire less effective than Edward Streeter's letters of an illiterate private, *Dere Mable* (1918). Both writers try to show that the common man as doughboy was not always a Sergeant York, but Ring could not get much interested in the war, either as subject matter or as a clash of ideals. He was one of the considerable number of commentators whose disillusion with American ideals began before the war. The editors of the *Smart Set,* the *Masses,* and the *Seven Arts* were—for very different reasons—among the skeptics now neglected by those who treat of "disenchantment" as strictly a postwar phenomenon.

   Evidently Ring took seriously a line he put into the head of Danny Warner in *Lose With a Smile,* a set of busher's letters that appeared in the *Post* in 1932—"Life is just a game of baseball."

Lardner showed the world of sport as a microcosm of life. Elder says,

> In Ring's fiction baseball is an ordered world with definite rules of conduct; it demands skill and integrity and it has a code of honor; it also has a hierarchy—at the top, umpires and managers, authority and intelligence, always sympathetically portrayed; at the bottom, the idolatrous fans, the shifting rabble whom Ring distrusted. . . . His preoccupation with sport reflected a longing for an ideal world where the rules, if observed, guaranteed the triumph of merit; it also reflected his acute sense of the disparity between the way people were supposed to behave and the way they did. Sport provided Ring with a useful and significant scale for measuring his characters. Moreover the criteria of sport were especially valuable because everyone knew exactly what they were.

Thus Jack Keefe, Alibi Ike, "Hurry" Kane, Buster Elliot (in "My Roomy"), and Danny Warner have their counterparts in such aggressors outside of sport as Fred Gross of *Own Your Own Home,* the Lothario of "Some Like Them Cold," Lou Gregg of "The Love Nest," Conrad Green, and Kate's succession of flannel-mouthed suitors in *The Big Town.* Conversely, the harassed family patriarch has his counterparts in managers Callahan, Gleason, and McGraw (all inspired by actual figures) in *You Know Me Al,* Carey and Cap in "Alibi Ike," Dave in "Hurry Kane," and in comparatively mature players like the catcher in "Hurry Kane" and Casey Stengel (based on the real Casey Stengel) in *Lose With a Smile.* The contrast too between the sensible man and the rabble in baseball parallels that in society, although Lardner's managers and his heads of households are far less cultured and have interests less broad than Mencken's "forgotten" citizen.

Life is also reflected through golf and bridge, two pastimes of the middle class that were targets for satire even before Miles Bantock published *Many Greens* in 1900. In "Contract," Lardner emphasized the triviality of the game and showed that people who take it seriously are likely to reveal other faults besides the pettiness they show at the bridge table.

Most of Ring's tales about sport and cards have an under-current of action concerning the problems of the central charac-ter in other matters. Usually this underlying strain concerns the love-life of the athlete or player and is interrelated to his actions on the diamond, in the ring, or at the table. Much of *You Know Me Al* is devoted to the rise and fall of Jack Keefe as Casanova and as family man; Midge Kelley's knockouts are not confined to the arena; the boxing fortunes of Burke in "A Frame-Up" de-pend on his success with women; and Elmer Kane and Buster Elliot have woman trouble that affects their success as baseball players. A basic implication of the parallels drawn between sport and life is that athletes are ordinary fellows who merely happen to have strong pitching or punching arms.

THE AVERAGE MAN AS AGGRESSOR AND VICTIM

Most of Lardner's idle common men are victims as well as aggressors, and a few are merely victims. The "active" or aggres-sive victims bring most of their difficulties on themselves through their aggressions, and then aggravate the resulting frustrations by further aggression. Nearly always they are ineffective as aggres-sors because their false self-images shut them off from reality. The "true" or passive victims either do not have the desire or the power to lash out at the environment which oppresses them. In the comic-strip field, Mutt is analogous to Lardner's "active" victims. Mutt victimizes himself through his schemes for getting even with the world—schemes that usually backfire—and he bullies Jeff a good deal. On the other hand, Jeff does not much resemble Lardner's "passive" victims except in the one quality of passivity. Unlike them, he is usually gentle, with a touch of the wise boob ("Boob" as used in the early part of the century had a connotation of "booby-hatch," and Jeff originally escaped from a lunatic asylum). The pathetic element in Lardner's stories about victims is sometimes minimized by his passive victims' resembling the aggressors in their values and tastes if not in their assertiveness.

Of the active victims, Jack Keefe has been victimized by his own egotism, and in *Own Your Own Home,* a series of four stories first published in *Redbook* in 1915,[12] Fred Gross (an apt surname) and his wife Grace bring most of their troubles upon themselves, through the same attribute. However, the first reason that Fred, a Chicago detective, gives for wishing to move out of the city proper draws the reader's sympathy:

> Charley we made up our minds to buy a place some wheres out in the subburbs & build a house not a grate big house of corse but a house where a man can move a round in with out bumping in to the walls all the wile and have enough ground so the children wont half to be cooped up all the day like in a flat but can run around & get some exercise.

His motives resemble those of the suburbanites portrayed by Bangs, Cobb, and Benchley. Other elements in the first third of the narrative belong to the same vein of suburban humor—the difficulties with the bank; the unforeseen and mounting costs of construction; troubles with the architects, the contractor, and the millwork people. All these elements tend to pull the unwary reader of *Redbook* (sometimes, no doubt, a suburban housewife) into identification with Fred and Grace, despite such early clues to Fred's character as his explanation to brother Charley of why he and Grace aren't buying Charley and his wife any Christmas presents this year—they are strapped from paying out on the new house and lot. However, before the tale is half over, the couple's main reason for moving comes to light. They are middle-class snobs. Of their new neighborhood Fred writes, ". . . as soon as we get acquainted we can for get all a bout the people we knowed in Chi & not never think a bout them." Perhaps too rapidly, the main interest in the story shifts from the house to the Grosses' difficulties with their neighbors. These difficulties arise largely out of the couple's own crude efforts to climb socially. H. C. Bunner, in the nineties, had ridiculed the quest for status in the suburbs by showing how it led buyers to victimize themselves through clever promoters. Lardner's treatment of suburban snobs is like Bunner's in its aim, but is angrier in tone and fuller in content. In addition to the promoters, the Grosses' fellow-suburbanites also help them to trip themselves up. The Hamiltons next door, whom Fred conceives to be among the city's "best people," politely ignore their new neighbors; consequently, Fred is easily made a fool of by Martin, his neighbor on the other side. In character Martin is a copy of Gross, and both are specimens of Lardner's obnoxious practical joker. Martin plays pranks on Gross himself and lets him think the joker is Hamilton; he even puts Fred up to childish and cruel tricks in retaliation. At Martin's suggestion, Fred hangs a smallpox quarantine sign outside the Hamiltons' door on a night when the Hamiltons are having a party to which he and Grace are not invited.

Another reaction of Fred and Grace to the snubs of their neighbors is the buying of a car. To Lardner, as to Kin Hubbard and to Mencken, the automobile was a symbol of conspicuous waste. Fred writes, "I guess some of these here smart alex a round Allison wouldent set up when they seen me breezeing a long in the little speeder and theyd wave there hands good morning in the hopes Id ask them to ride down town. Fine chance the cheap stiffs. . . . Im not going to take no cheap skates along that cant afford cars of there own." Conspicuous consumption is here identical with aggression. Another phase of their offensive is criticism of their neighbors for being drunk and noisy. But when Grace and Fred finally make enough contacts to be able to throw a party of their own, it turns into a booze-fest that includes fox-trotting on the sidewalk. The local watchmen arrest Fred, but he thinks Hamilton is behind the arrest.

Thus the frustrations of Fred's status-hunt merely stimulate him to further aggressions. His one crumb of comfort comes about through Hamilton, who finally understands how Gross has been deluded by Martin and has a frank man-to-man talk with him. Hamilton is the only person in this neighborhood of middle-class boors who tries to communicate with another individual or shows any other qualities of the rational, "good" man, and he is a minor figure whose example and advice are wasted on Fred. Hamilton's gesture means, to Fred, only that he has attained the social level of his uppity neighbor at last.

The rational man too is often both victim and aggressor, though less extreme in either role than Jack Keefe or Fred Gross. For example, *Gullible's Travels* mainly is about how the title character got over his gullibility. Gullible allows his wife to drag him to *Carmen* and to *"Armour's Do Re Me"* (*L' Amore Dei Tre Re*) and he finds grand opera as silly as had some of Ade's father-types.[13] Yet, he says later, "Well, I'll own up that I enjoyed wearin' the soup and fish and minglin' amongst the high polloi and pretendin' we really was somebody. . . . The next stage was where our friends wasn't good enough for us no more." The third stage in Gullible's fall from democratic grace is a longing for Palm Beach on the part of his wife, who plays Eve the temptress to his Adam and persuades him they should go there to hunt the "quality." Gullible is soon disillusioned about the futility of trying to crash "society," but his wife won't give up the quest until she gets a snub all the more brutal for being unintentional. In the corridor of the hotel, she encounters Mrs. Potter, the noted socialite from Chicago, and the *grande dame* actually speaks to her:

> "Are you on this floor?" she says.
> "Yes," says she, so low you couldn't hardly hear her.
> "Please see that they's some towels put in 559," says *the*
> Mrs. Potter from Chicago.

It is implied that Mrs. Potter's mistake is quite natural because of the incurable "commonness" manifested in Mrs. Gullible's dress, speech, and mannerisms. Back home once more, even the "Missus" looks forward to resuming the rummy games with their old friends, the Hatches. The Gullibles now see themselves as they really are—ordinary folks. Gullible has been a self-victimized aggressor whose ability to keep in touch with reality is strictly limited (he gives up the status-chase because his wife suffered a setback, not because of any spontaneous eruption of common sense on his part) but at least he is not totally impervious in defeat, unlike Keefe and Gross. This citizen (whose margin of affluence has come through some shrewd investments in "Crucible Steel") is one of the few Lardner characters whose self-image has, to some degree, been penetrated and altered by reality.

THE AVERAGE MAN AS MERE VICTIM

In their inertia and in their recessiveness, Lardner's more passive victims superficially resemble the Little Man caricatured in "The Timid Soul" and in Thurber's story, "The Secret Life of Walter Mitty." However, Mr. Milquetoast is wholly benign, and Thurber's types are more sensitive, articulate, and self-conscious than Lardner's mediocrities. Most important, Thurber's men have not entirely lost the awareness of right reason and right conduct, however often they fall short of these ideals. Most of Lardner's common men, including the more pathetic victims, never have had that awareness and never acquire it.[14]

Frequently Lardner contrasted the negative, indrawn type of common man with a brassy, outgoing aggressor. Often the latter was a practical joker—an obsolete kind of humorist with roots in the small town. In some ways Lardner may never have left Niles, but he rejected many aspects of Niles, including the practical joker. Thus, Stephen Gale, the "Maysville minstrel," is made "the victim of quite a joke." Stephen is an overworked bookkeeper and bill collector for a gas company. He is victimized by his boss—"Stephen earned the $22.50 per week which he had been getting the eight years he had worked for the gas company." But his main victimizer is Charley Roberts, a traveling salesman, with whom Stephen is contrasted. Stephen is a mousy fellow whereas Roberts is a wisecracker and kidder. Roberts discovers that

Stephen writes poetry, and lures him into submitting a serious
piece to a humorous column; then he forges a letter from an
imaginary editor encouraging Stephen to write more. Stephen
quits his job "so I can devote all my time to my poetry." His
verse is on about the level of Miss Fawn Lippincutt, one of Abe
Martin's neighbors in Brown County, Indiana:

> The Lackawanna Railroad where does it go?
> It goes from Jersey City to Buffalo.
> Some of the trains stop at Maysville but they are few
> Except the 8:22 . . .

When a couple of these masterpieces are returned by the post
office from their nonexistent destination, Stephen realizes he has
been tricked. He is lucky to get his old job back.

Stephen resembled his tormentor Roberts in believing that
success lay solely in making money. He read poetry only because
he was too poor to go to the movies. It was not love of poetry
that inspired him to write but the notion that by publishing his
poetry he could make money like Edgar Guest—a notion common
enough in the big cities but Lardner chooses to present it as a
sample of the intellectual level of the small town. Stephen falls
into temptation because he is too much like the tempter. His
main virtue, if it can be called such, is merely the passivity that
at least keeps him from forcing his standards on any audience,
even if it also condemns him and his wife to poverty and ex-
ploitation.

In "Liberty Hall," the Ben Drakes are contrasted with the
possessive Thayers; in "Mr. and Mrs. Fix-It," another of Lardner's patient husbands, and to a lesser extent his wife, are oppressed by the well-meaning but domineering Stevenses. Mrs.
Taylor and her husband in "Anniversary," Tom and his gossipy
wife in "Who Dealt," the Masons and the Johnsons in "Re-
union," the hospital patient and the talkative nurse in "Zone
of Quiet," and Paul Dickson and the joker in "Haircut" are also
paired contrasts. In each case, one person or married couple belongs to the Stephen Gale-Ben Drake type of more passive victim,

and the other person or couple to the Jack Keefe-Fred Gross-Midge Kelly-Charley Roberts type of aggressor or aggressor-victim.

The victims are seldom one hundred per cent passive. Occasionally the indrawn types lash out with a cunning or fury as futile usually as it is destructive. Ben Drake's strategem for getting away from the Thayers backfires, and presumably he hurts only himself in going on "that month's most interesting bender." Shelton in "Contract" insults his way out of one tiresome bridge circle only to land in another. Buster Elliot in "My Roomy" lacerates his fist in smashing a mirror, assaults his ex-girl-friend and her new husband with a baseball bat, and lands in an asylum. Outbursts like these resemble those of Thurber's more violent cases, including Kinstrey (the suburbanite killer in "The Whip-poor-will") and Mr. Preble, who plans to murder his spouse in the basement. In the work of both Lardner and Thurber these explosions seldom gain for the victims the recognition and stability which they crave, and in a practical sense usually leave them worse off than before. Paul Dickson in "Haircut" shoots his tormentor, and the deed is recorded as "accidental," but he kills the joker less out of resentment for Jim's pranks on him than for the cruel joke played on Julie Gregg. Ironically, one of the rare acts of altruism performed by a Lardner character is a murder committed by this boy who is mentally retarded.

WIVES, HUSBANDS, AND "FLAMING" YOUTH

Lardner criticized the plain man's wife as severely as he did the nominal head of the household. In "Say It With Oil," he gives his own version of the war between men and women. The husband-*persona* defines wives thus:

> Wives is people that thinks you ought to eat at 8 o'clock, one o'clock, and 7 o'clock. If you express yourself as having an appetite for turkey at midnight they think you are crazy.
> Wives is people that always wants to go home when you don't and vice versa.
> Wives is people that ain't never satisfied as they are always

too fat or too thin. Of all the wives I ever talked to I never run acrost one yet that was just right.

Wives is people that thinks 2 ash trays should ought to be plenty for a 12 rm. house.

Wives is people that asks you what time the 12:55 train gets to New York. "At 1:37," you tell them. "How do you know?" they ask.

Wives is people that sets on the right side of the front seat in their husband's costly motor and when he turns down a street to the left they tell him he ought to of kept straight ahead.

They are people that you ask them to go to a ball game and they act tickled to death. So along about the 7th. innings you look at them and they are fast asleep and you remind them with a delicate punch in the ribs that they are supposed to be excited. "Oh, yes," they say. "I love it." So you ask them what is the score and they say "St. Louis is ahead ain't they?" "Well," you say, "I don't know if St. Louis is ahead or ain't ahead, but the game you are watching is between Boston and New York."

The irritations described here are minor, the logic is twisted, and the language would earn a poor mark for a fifth-grader. These defects are marks of the wise fool as he says in an amusing way that wives are the aggressors and husbands the victims.[15] The narrator's attitude is an oversimplification and an exaggeration of the views developed more fully in *Gullible's Travels, The Big Town,* "Contract," and "Who Dealt?" The major faults of the wives are the same as their faults in Ade's fables—self-absorption, conspicuous waste, social climbing, and a corresponding indifference to the realistic ideal of marriage as a give-and-take proposition that is possible but seldom peaceable.

Ade and Thurber did not neglect the wife's side, nor did Lardner. Often each party to a marital disagreement is both aggressor and victim, with the man, like as not, more aggressor than victim. The complaining husband in "Say It With Oil" shows as much selfishness as he ascribes to his wife. In *Own Your Own Home,* Fred Gross shows more initiative in folly than Grace, though this is not primarily a tale of domestic strife. In "Ex Parte," the man is the initial aggressor; the wife is the victim in the sense that his tastes in conspicuous wastage prevail over hers. Neglecting to consult her, he buys her a houseful of expensive, new furniture. She turns out to prefer pseudo-antiques, and he retaliates by trying to "age" the furniture with "a pair of shears, a blow torch and an ax." Jack Keefe is probably a shade worse than Florrie, though they are two of a kind. Lou Gregg in "The Love Nest" has driven his wife into alcoholism, and the husband in "Now and Then" passes in three years from overpossessiveness to adultery. By contrast, in "Anniversary," Louis Taylor victimizes his wife through sheer indifference and neglect. Taylor is "still a model young man, sober, industrious and 'solid' "—and a self-centered bore. He is the perfect example of *homo boobiens*—a complacent prude who disapproves of liquor and thinks the local newspaper is the epitome of culture. On the evening of their wedding anniversary he sits as usual, reading aloud from the newspaper and retelling old stories she has heard many times before.[16] A friend drops in and tells a lurid but exciting tale of a wife whose drunken husband has blacked her eye. Thinking of Louis' indifference, Mrs. Taylor asks that her anniversary gift be "a punch in the eye." Of course she doesn't get it—and he doesn't get it either.

Yet one retains the impression that Lardner was, on the whole, more disappointed in American women than in American men. A few of the men—Gullible, the narrator in *The Big Town*, the chauffeur in "Mr. Frisbie"—have some shreds of self-knowledge and humility, whereas even the women victimized by their husbands are either too mercenary (like Irma in "Now and Then"), or too inert and colorless (like Mrs. Taylor), to arouse much sympathy in the reader. Elder says that, "Idealizing women as he did, he seemed more appalled by their shortcomings than by men's."[17] This idealism was directly related to Lardner's rigid moral code and to an outmoded prudishness about sex not unlike that which he burlesqued in Danny Thomas' girl (*Lose With a Smile*). This prudishness led him into what his friend F. Scott Fitzgerald called an "odd little crusade" against suggestiveness in popular songs, a crusade that caused Ernest Hemingway to refer to Ring's "Over the Waves" column about radio as "those pitiful dying radio censorship pieces." [18] The occasional treatment of illicit sex in Lardner's own writing is always focused on some aspect of the relationship other than the physical, and in his depictions of lawful wedded life sex plays almost no part.

Ring seldom expressed the sentimental admiration for the unmarried flapper that Christopher Morley and Don Marquis affirmed in *Pandora Lifts the Lid* (1924) and that Marquis voiced in *Off the Arm* (1930). "There Are Smiles" includes one of Lardner's few attractive specimens of the self-reliant modern girl— but Edith Dole's reckless driving, which is a function of her independence and modernity, brings about her death. "Mabelle" Gillespie in "Some Like Them Cold" is merely amusing as she hides her epistolary pursuit of Charles behind a transparent screen of false modesty. Ring's other flappers range from fatuous to repellent—as, admittedly, do his male teen-agers. In "Travelogue," a shy girl and a talkative girl fall into conversation with a man on a train. The talkative one tries to "snow" the fellow with stories about all the places she's been. Actually she is a self-absorbed bore and keeps repeating the same story, with only the place-names varied. The man is type-cast in the same mold and is interested only in his dental difficulties: "He opened his mouth and pointed to a large, dark vacancy where once had dwelt a molar. 'I had that one pulled in Milwaukee the day before yesterday.'" Despite his grossness, the quiet girl is charmed by his obvious preference for her company; while she has less brass she is scarcely less coarse than her girl friend.

The girls in "Zone of Quiet" and "I Can't Breathe" are female counterparts of Jack Keefe—brash aggressors completely hypnotized by their images of themselves as the most important people on earth. In the former tale the girl, a nurse, talks the ears off a patient just out from under anesthesia. In "I Can't Breathe," a teen-age vamp gets herself comically involved with three men at once. Both the daughter and the son in "Old Folks' Christmas" are types of "flaming youth" as Lardner saw it—ill-mannered, selfish, "fast," and without values except for the worship of conspicuous consumption, which with them largely takes the form of being up-to-date. They ignore their parents' hopes for a quiet Christmas with all the family together, and on Christmas Eve they are out partying until the small hours. On Christmas Day they are soon off to another party, but not before they have shown their dissatisfaction with the presents received from their parents. Caroline considers her new fur coat and jewels out-of-style, and Ted feels the same way about the roadster his father has bought for him. In the evening they bring some friends of their own "set" home for a petting party which leaves the living room looking "as if Von Kluck's army had just passed through." The old-time Christmas atmosphere of love, cheer, and family solidarity is absent.

Values other than those of expediency are absent also from the conduct of the two boys in "A Caddy's Diary":

> Well, I said it seems to me like these people have got a lot of nerve to pan Mr Crane and call him a sucker for doing what he done, it seems to me like $8000 and a swell dame is a pretty fair reward compared with what some of these other people sells their soul for, and I would like to tell them about it.
>
> Well said Joe go ahead and tell them but maybe they will tell you something right back.
>
> What will they tell me?
>
> Well said Joe they might tell you this, that when Mr Thomas asks you how many shots he has had and you say 4 when you know he has had 5, why you are selling your soul for a $1.00 tip. And when you move Mrs Doanes ball out of a rut and give it a good lie, what are you selling your soul for? Just a smile.
>
> O keep your mouth shut I said to him.
>
> I am going to said Joe and would advice you to do the same.

Perhaps one should not expect the author to have invested these mere types with the moral sensitivity of a Nick Adams or Holden Caulfield. The fact remains that they are merely aping the adults whose behavior on and off the links they have studied too well.

Incidentally, nothing illustrates the difference between the solid citizen and the middle-class oaf better than a comparison of Lardner's adult males and Clarence Day's Father as models for youth. Despite Father Day's frequent wrongheadedness, he adhered to a traditional code of duty and integrity totally lost or discarded by Lardner's corruptible golfers.

Even the more critical of Ring's literary contemporaries sometimes were "soft" on adolescents—look at Ted Babbitt, and Dick Miller (in *Ah, Wilderness!*). But Ring's teen-agers are already conspicuous consumers and social climbers—just the sort to grow up into his men and women.

Lardner's characters talk a lot, but their preoccupation with self frustrates their efforts at communication. Buster Elliot is the most extreme example of this perpetual isolation: his insecurity and hunger for recognition reinforce and are reinforced by his self-absorption. In other characters too, this hunger defeats its own ends. Jack Keefe's managers would like to help him improve his playing, but they can't penetrate his self-esteem. Hamilton would like to show Fred Gross the futility of his social climbing, but succeeds only in feeding the Gross ego. The overzealous hospitality of the Thayers and the excessive helpfulness of "Mr. and Mrs. Fix-It" earn only resentment and lies from the objects of their efforts. The most ironic examples of lack of communication are those of married couples: despite the intimacy of the married state, Mr. and Mrs. Taylor find little to say to each other; the man and wife in "Ex Parte" gratify their own tastes without mutually communicating them; after a long struggle, the narrator in *The Big Town* succeeds only partially in making his wife and her sister realize their foolishness in trying to catch a rich husband for the sister. Mrs. Gregg, in "The Love Nest," gives up the attempt to break through her husband's ego and retreats into the isolation of alcohol. The self-preoccupation of the chattering wife in "Who Dealt?" has prevented her from discovering that her husband loves another woman, and even when she has unwittingly blundered on the truth she is slow to realize it—she may never realize it. In all of Lardner's stories of wrecked or stale marriages, one partner has reduced the other to the status of a possession, or else the two are implacable rivals. In either situation, communication breaks down.

The situations in these domestic "comedies" are basic in literature, and it is platitudinous to say that isolation has been a major theme in American letters, from Franklin's *Autobiography* to the work of Saul Bellow and Bernard Malamud. Was not Franklin's celebrated retirement at forty-one and his life-long participation in scientific, fraternal, charitable, and political activities an attempt, in part, at involvement to counteract the isolation resulting from his competitive drive for success in business? Even in his time it was hard to practice "enlightened" self-interest.[19] At the height of Ring's career, a fuller statement of the common man's loneliness than Lardner could achieve within the brief compass of any one short story appeared in Elmer Rice's play, *The Adding Machine* (1923). Mr. Zero is isolated from his wife at home, from Daisy at the office, and from his counterparts in the jury box for the same reasons that most of Lardner's characters are locked within themselves—he has nothing to communicate but his own desire for recognition, and there is rarely anyone at the other end of the line but a self-absorbed creature like himself. In killing the boss, Mr. Zero too lashes out in sudden violence that defeats its own ends.

The crackerbox philosophers were detached through being wise men (or wise fools), but they communicated meanings to audiences who at least listened if they did not always understand. The solid citizen found an audience fit though few; Mencken's rational *persona* is no outsider but a participating member of the community. In contrast, Lardner's common man, and the Little Man of the *New Yorker,* are essentially mute and "privatized," to use C. Wright Mills' term. Under the stress of war, in the nineteen-forties, E. B. White's Little Man became one of the few who made a successful effort to re-establish communication and to break out of his private shell. Paradoxically,

White's man did it, like his creator, by going a little apart from the urban center and by withdrawing further into the shell.

OUT OF SOMEWHERE INTO NOTHING

The poverty and simplicity of his values may have caused Lardner to become, in Maxwell Geismar's words, "a greater iconoclast than any of the self-conscious rebels of his generation." [20] The American trinity of absolute morality, progress, and culture that had sustained the previous generation had faded in Lardner to a belief that the absolutes he had brought from Niles could prevail only in satire, as devices by which to indict the "real" world for their utter absence. Against what John Dos Passos called "heman twofisted broncobusting pokerplaying stockjuggling America," [21] Lardner put the small-town values he had grown up with—home, family, fair play, modesty, horse sense, and the Ten Commandments. Were these enough? Ring's interests did not include political and social action; he could have said with Robert Frost:

> I own I never really warmed
> To the reformer or reformed. [22]

Progressivism, socialism, and later, the New Deal, left him as unmoved as did their opposites. Nor did he have any special use for highbrow culture. In order to extract humor from the views of Gullible he had to know more than Gullible, but despite his qualified admiration for Dreiser and Hemingway, his friendship with Scott and Zelda Fitzgerald, his writing for the *New Yorker*, and his amiable relationship with Robert Benchley, Dorothy Parker, and the educated wits of the "Round Table" at the Hotel Algonquin, he was close to Gullible in many ways, especially in his attitude toward formal literature and the fine arts. As a young man Ring had ignored the *literati* of Chicago, and in his plays of "planned nonsense" he satirized *avant-garde* developments in the theater of the twenties, including the work of Gabriele D'Annunzio and Eugene O'Neill. Broadway gripped him in spite of his suspicions, and he allowed George M. Cohan to produce an expanded version of "Hurry Kane" as *Elmer the Great* in 1928. The next year, with the help of George S. Kaufman, Lardner expanded "Some Like Them Cold" into *June Moon.* Usually, however, he depicted show business as mostly "vanity, sharp practice, unscrupulous ambition, mediocrity." [23] He loved to sing and to listen to informal group singing, particularly in the barber-shop manner, but he resembled his solid citizens in caring little for most "long-hair" music, and he made grand opera a symbol of snobbery. To the bulk of painting and sculpture he seems to have been indifferent.

In religion, Ring's father was a prominent Episcopal layman, but despite an orthodox upbringing, Lardner as an adult showed little interest in the church or in the great theological and philosophical questions. It was not by the social, aesthetic, or divine gospels that Ring judged the Jay Gatsbys and George F. Babbitts of his time.

Yet the homespun values by which Lardner did judge the modern world did not wear well either. Ring never ceased to believe in the theoretical validity of these values, but he did feel more and more strongly that they were irrelevant and ineffective. Ethically Ring had no place to go. Having achieved success beyond the wildest dreams of most men, he shattered this great American icon and laughed acidly at himself, under the guise of a parody of *The Americanization of Edward Bok* which he entitled *The Story of a Wonder Man.* The few major characters in his fiction who embody positive values—Gullible, the Carters, Ella's husband in The Big Town—tend to become victims rather than aggressors, and such characters are few and far between. For compensation, these few good people have, in miniature, the same reward as the great heroes of tragedy: an increase in self-knowledge and humility. However, the vast majority of sufferers in Ring's work learn nothing from their experience. When not verging on farce, their mishaps are merely pathetic.

Part of Lardner's melancholy stemmed from a tendency toward hero-worship that would not be quenched despite perennial disappointment. When Ring castigated hero-worship as "the national disease," [24] he was criticizing himself as much as any-one. His capacity for idealism was matched by his capacity for disillusionment. Despite the satire of heroes and hero-worship in his stories of sport, he still had enough respect for the "greats" in baseball to feel a pang when members of the Chicago White Sox were discovered to have "thrown" the World Series of 1919, and two of his last pieces were tributes to Christy Mathewson, a famous pitcher, and Walter Eckersall, one of the all-time great quarterbacks. The qualities for which he most respected both players—modesty and fair play—he sought continually, but all he usually found were their opposites, in the Fred Grosses and Stephen Gales—and possibly in himself.

In his lightest pieces this disillusion smoulders. Once he wrote limericks for a book of cartoons by various hands, entitled *Regular Fellows I Have Met* (1919). These "fellows" were a cross section of the Babbittry of Chicago and other cities—self-made businessmen, doctors, lawyers, politicians, theater people, and ball-club owners and officials. The drawings and verses were intended as friendly tribute, with the humorous element sub-ordinated to this purpose. Most of Ring's limericks were friendly enough, but his "Foreward" summed up what he thought of these solid citizens:

> Well, I have tried to say something good about every reg-ular fellow in these pages, and sometimes it come hard, but if a man studies long enough you are pretty near sure to expose some good points in everybody, even if it's that they don't manicure themselves at meal times or wear a nightgown.
>
> Of course, most people has their faults and we can't all be perfect, but a few faults or a few thousand don't keep a man from being 100 per cent regular fellow. The regular fel-low, in my estimation, and kind I have wrote poetry about in this book is the bird that says: "George, let me have the check for all of this."

In the prose of a "regular fellow" the wise fool mocks himself, but behind the mask, the author grimaces at these fellows, and at us too.

Will Rogers' view that "Nothing don't mean anything" did not prevent him from enjoying his success and looking on his career with amused wonder. At times Lardner identified himself with his own version of the common man almost as completely as Rogers with his; Ring even wrote some of his personal letters "in character." But disillusionment hurt too much for him not to be bitter as well as amused and amusing. Whatever his theoretical beliefs, the implied message of his work is one of nihilism and despair. His nice guys finish last, and very few of them are even nice guys. In a wasteland of "normalcy" where there are no heroes and the common man is commonly too much of a boob—however "wise"—to be worshipped according to the democratic dogma of the liberals, there isn't much left.

Mehitabel and the Bureaucracy

Mehitabel as Tramp

The Working Reporter

BOSS, I'M ENGAGED IN A LITERARY WORK

11

The Many Masks of Don Marquis

In a biography of Don Marquis, Edward Anthony quotes Christopher Morley as saying, "The professors, very likely, will now be able to tell us *why* Don's stuff was good, and bracket it in some critical niche."[1] Judgments on whether and why a piece was good creep into the present volume only incidentally, and

Marquis' work is bracketed for expository rather than critical
convenience. In some ways his career follows the pattern of
George Ade, Will Rogers, Irvin S. Cobb, and Ring Lardner in
that Marquis too came from a small town in the Midwest and
achieved striking success in the big city.

FROM WALNUT TO NEW YORK

Marquis was born in 1878 in Walnut, Illinois (population in
1960: 1,192), and like Sinclair Lewis, was the son of a country
doctor. Another point of resemblance to his humorous contemporaries was his clinging to some of the prairie values,
notably a respect for genuine religious faith. This respect was
as strong as his skepticism concerning orthodox churches and
village morality. If Lardner retained much of the small-town
ethos, Marquis retained part of the small-town metaphysics, and
he differed from Rogers and Lardner in expressing unsatisfied
religious yearnings of his own. The contrast between these
yearnings and his naturalistic skepticism offers a clue to the
values and work of a divided and elusive personality.

This contrast appears in his attitude toward the small-town
environment. His writings on that environment are part of the
literary revolt from the village which had reached its first climax
in Mark Twain, and included Ezra Pound, Sherwood Anderson,
Sinclair Lewis, and Willa Cather among Marquis' own contemporaries. The dreariness, the prudery, the cultural sterility,
and sometimes the violence of small-town life turned many
writers, from the eighteen-seventies to the nineteen-forties, away
from their rural origins. In addition, "Marquis was by temperament a city-dweller,"[2] according to E. B. White, who knew him
fairly well. Don left Walnut at eighteen, and he never again returned to the town, even for a visit. Yet, in a sense, he carried
it with him always, as something to remember fondly and to cas-
tigate bitterly. He attacked it in his first and last books,[3] and in
much of his other fiction he drew heavily on his memories of the
town and the surrounding farm folk—memories largely uncom-
plimentary. Marquis created the "Old Soak," his most vivid por-

trait of a small-town character, and depicted him sympatheti-cally, but he used him to satirize those aspects of the small-town environment that had extended their influence into the city, especially prohibition, prudery, and religious orthodoxy.

After some wandering and some odd jobs, including brief em-ployment with a theatrical troupe, Don wrote news and edi-torials for newspapers in Atlanta, Georgia, until one of the great crackerbox humorists, Joel Chandler Harris, hired him in 1907 as assistant editor of his *Uncle Remus's Magazine.* For this, Marquis wrote, among other things, a personal column entitled "A Glance in Passing." Harris died in 1908 and his magazine did not long survive him. Marquis eventually went to New York, and in 1912 he got his big chance when offered a daily column on the *Sun.* Although Marquis was competing with Morley, "F. P. A.," and Heywood Broun, his column, "The Sun Dial," was soon one of the most widely read features in the city's news-papers.

Marquis left the *Sun* in 1922 (being succeeded there briefly by Frank Sullivan) and for two and a half years he conducted his column in the New York *Herald Tribune* as "The Lantern." Then, tired of the grind of a daily feature, he gave it up and supported himself and his family solely by writing plays and fiction. He scored a hit on Broadway with *The Old Soak* (1926), a dramatized version of the crackerbox philosopher in his column, but flopped expensively with *The Dark Hours* (pub-lished as a book in 1924; not produced until 1932), and got no-where with several other plays.[4] Financial difficulties, family tragedies, and ill health marred the last sixteen years of his life until his death in 1937 at the age of fifty-nine. The deaths of his first child, first wife, second (and last) child, and second wife did much to deepen a melancholy note discernible in his humor from the very first.

THE CAT AND THE COCKROACH

One of the ironies of Marquis' career is that he sometimes worried about being remembered mainly for creating a cock-

roach. The irony is compounded by the casualness with which
he created Archy the roach and his companion, Mehitabel the
cat. In one of his pieces for *Uncle Remus's Magazine,* Marquis
dreamed up the image of a "literary cockroach,"[5] but he apparently did not create Archy until about 1916, when a number
of poems about Archy and Mehitabel appeared intermittently in
"The Sun Dial." At first Marquis was merely using this humorous free verse as an easy way of filling his insatiable column with
short lines when he was hard up for other material. The pegs
on which the first Archy poems were hung were free verse
and reincarnation. During the poetic renaissance of 1912–1920,
vers libre, including the "Imagism" of Amy Lowell and translations from the work of Rabindranath Tagore—two poets whose
writing Marquis particularly detested—attracted much attention.
Reincarnation too was in the public eye. John Kendrick Bangs,
George Ade, and Wallace Irwin were among the humorists who
had already made game of spiritualism, transmigration, and
other ventures into the occult. Marquis' prose introduction to
the first Archy poem contains a dig at Madam Blavatsky the
theosophist, and it may well be that her particular version of
transmigration (borrowed largely from Pythagoras) supplied the
egg from which Archy was hatched in the humorist's mind. Sir
Arthur Conan Doyle, the creator of Sherlock Holmes, and
physicist Sir Oliver Lodge were interested in something occult
that they called "ectoplasm," of which Archy said,

> . . . it sounds
> as if it might be wonderful
> stuff to mend broken furniture with

In "The Coming of Archy," the columnist described how he
arrived at the office earlier than usual one morning and found
a roach jumping up and down on the keys. He couldn't work the
capital shift key and had great difficulty operating the carriage
mechanism. On reading what the bug had written, the columnist
found,

> expression is the need of my soul
> i was once a vers libre bard
> but i died and my soul went into the body of a cockroach

These early themes of free verse and reincarnation were never entirely neglected, but Archy and his feline friend soon were commenting on many other matters and playing several other roles. Through these two waifs Marquis could express provocative and even iconoclastic views without giving offense to the Dagwoods who chuckled over their newspapers on subway or streetcar. Who would mind what an alley-cat and a "poor little cockroach" had to say? Moreover, consistency did not bother Marquis much, and he freely changed the roles of his characters to fit his mood of the day. Archy most commonly vacillates among three separate though occasionally merging roles: the wise fool, the solid citizen, and the trickster-outcast. As the fool he is versifier, hobohemian, philosopher, and vessel of conceit. As middle-class citizen he waxes cautious in judgment, conventional in morals, and middlebrow in taste. As social outcast he is cynical, and the values he emphasizes are the naturalistic ones of bare survival.

Occasionally he plays a fourth role, that of a columnist very like the author himself. E. B. White lists several ways in which Archy's behavior resembled that of his creator, but Marquis usually tried to hide behind a mask of self-mockery in whatever role he chose for Archy at the moment. Marquis could thereby offer certain values to be considered seriously and yet, at the same time, make fun of them as mere prejudices or passing moods:

> please forgive
> the profundity of these
> meditations
> whenever i have nothing
> particular to say
> i find myself always
> always plunging into cosmic
> philosophy
> or something

The note of self-burlesque here is relatively moderate; on occasion Marquis could mock at himself as bitterly as Lardner. Cosmic philosophy was actually one of Don Marquis' main interests, but through the roach he often pretended to apologize for his indulgence.

ARCHY AS WISE FOOL

As bohemian poet-fool, Archy is a well of self-pity and envy. In him stirs the defense-mechanism of incompetents of all kinds:

> gods i am pent in a cockroach
> i with the soul of a dante
> am mate and companion of fleas
> i with the gift of a homer
> must smile when a mouse calls me pal

With his constant awareness of how all men's pretensions are dwarfed by the cosmos, Marquis had a tenderness for freaks and failures tempered by the same dislike of slapdash work, his own included, that was felt by Mencken, Lardner, Morley, "F. P. A.," and other able journalistic humorists. Of the "vicious circle" at the Algonquin "Round Table," Margaret Case Harriman writes, "They had no use for shoddy work of any kind,"[6] and Marquis, though not a regular diner with this circle, was a kindred spirit in that respect.

As foolish poet and philosopher, Archy is flattered when the author seeks his opinions on astronomy, archaeology, evolution, life, death, prophets, politics, literature, and many other complex topics. In delivering his views, he sometimes dodges from role to role within the same column. In one "interview" he speaks as the pompous phrase-maker ("the long arm of coincidence makes many radio connections") lies extravagantly about his literary exploits upon being told that "the stars are listening"; unabashedly plugs his sponsor, "the knockem cold roach and bug killing company"; and suddenly metamorphoses into Don Marquis himself making a crack about the egos of Theodore Dreiser and Bernard Shaw. Then as suddenly he relapses into Archy the conceited fool, and speaks of himself "as a scientist"; a moment later he makes yet another change and becomes the

responsible reader with middlebrow tastes, disliking literary
"dirt" for its own sake but taking ironic cracks at prudery also:

> oh yes the latest literary movement
> consists in going to all the fences
> and coal sheds near all the school houses
> and copying off of them all the bad words
> written there by naughty little boys
> over the week ends
> and these form the bases of the new novels
> of course these novels are kept away
> from the young so they will not be contaminated
>
> mars
> but where do the boys get the words
>
> archy
> from hired hands and the classics

Marquis often uses the "numbskull" technique of having a
character speak ineptly in favor of that which the author wishes
to satirize. By having Archy declare his intent "to see if i cannot
reform insects in general" as a "missionary extraordinary" to
"the little struggling brothers" in his phylum, Marquis hits at
overzealous missionaries spreading the American brand of "civilization" in primitive lands. Through the same technique Marquis jabs at reformers in general, pontifical radio commentators
(whom Archy impersonates as "the Cosmic Cockroach"), Senator
Bilbo, technocracy, popular-science writers, and literary fads.
Mehitabel too is a numbskull, in a different way. Through her
crude assertions that she is refined, "still a lady in spite of h dash
double l," Marquis satirizes all bumptious pretenders to social
elevation. Further, because of these claims to refinement, the
author's broader target, hypocrisy in general, is hit every time
Mehitabel sings on a fence-top, allows herself to be gracefully
seduced by a tom, scoops an eye out of that tom when the
romance is over, or abandons her kittens to be drowned.

The actors' strike of 1919, and other labor troubles, gave
Marquis a chance to portray both Archy and his boss as rogues

and fools who speak in favor of that which the author is really
against. Archy becomes a militant striker and his boss an
arrogant, double-talking employer. Archy issues an "ultimatum"
in which he threatens to

> quit you cold and go out and
> live in a
> swiss cheese i have nothing
> to arbitrate

The boss hires a roach named Henry as a scab, accuses Archy of
"sordid materialism," proclaims his own devotion to law and
order, and laments, "whither are we drifting?" In burlesquing
the language of labor disputes, Marquis adopts the "plague on
both your houses" attitude of Kin Hubbard and many another
uninvolved citizen.

ARCHY AS JOHN Q. CITIZEN

When contrasted by the author with Mehitabel, Archy sometimes appears as a sober moralist. Concerning the cat's motto,
"toujours gai," Archy muses,

> boss sometimes i think
> that our friend mehitabel
> is a trifle too gay

After Mehitabel has told him of how Percy the tomcat double-
crossed her, Archy moralizes, "i think/that mehitabel s unshel-
tered life sometimes/makes her a little sad." Primly he asserts a
little later,

> it appears to me boss
> that mehitabel is still far
> from being the quiet
> domestic character you and i
> had hoped she might become

and still later,

> . . . i think if some
> cheerful musical family
> in good circumstances were to
> offer mehitabel a home

> where she would be treated in
> all ways as one of the family
> she has reached the point where
> she might consent to give up
> living her own life

As John Q. Citizen, Archy is always sensible enough, but not as penetrating as Mencken's sound thinker. Marquis is essentially on Archy's side, but rarely without mocking overtones. Archy in this role is a little pompous and is inclined to oversimplify problems. George F. Babbitt once professed to offer brotherly love as the panacea for all social and personal difficulties; with equal shallowness, Archy suggests domesticity and security, not seeing that their price would be the sacrifice of the freedom and *joie de vivre* that is everything to Mehitabel. Like Lewis, Marquis has a friendly quarrel with middle-class man, whom he satirizes but sometimes presents as a norm, somewhere between *homo boobiens* and the man of reason but with more of the latter in him than the former.

Once in a while Archy is helped by Mehitabel in his support of conventional wisdom. Judge Ben Lindsey had advocated "companionate marriage," which he defined as "legal marriage with legalized birth control and with the right to divorce by mutual consent for childless couples."[7] In opposition to this proposal, Archy quotes Mehitabel as saying, "any kind of marriage means just one dam kitten after another." In his book Lindsey complained that his plan had been misrepresented by the label of "trial marriage." Possibly in direct reply, Marquis had Archy quote Mehitabel thus:

> trial marriage or companionate
> marriage or old fashioned american
> plan three meals a day marriage
> with no thursdays off
> they are all the same thing
> marriage is marriage
> and you cant laugh that curse off

At times this insect with horse sense composes maxims or "archygrams" in crackerbox fashion. Of abstract painting he says—his role as a Greenwich Village poet forgotten for the

moment—"i may be a / critic but still i know what i / dont like."
Archy could equal Ade, Dooley, or Abe Martin in giving an
old saw a new edge:

> the servant problem
> wouldn t hurt the u s a
> if it could settle
> its public
> servant problem

and,

> every cloud
> has its silver
> lining but it is
> sometimes a little
> difficult to get it to
> the mint

Archy as citizen had relatively little to say about the crash
of 1929, but the depression of the thirties furnished plenty of
roach-food for thought. One of the contradictions in Marquis'
personality was that this intuitive sympathizer with the down-
and-out rarely spoke for the legitimately unemployed who
manned the breadlines and sold apples in the streets, even
though he had Archy the outcast on hand as an appropriate
spokesman. Instead, when politics, the New Deal, and the
workingman are under discussion, Archy more often puts on the
mask of the man of property. One might even say he grew
nineteenth-century whiskers.

Archy's inconsistency faithfully reflected that of his creator.
During the tinsel prosperity of the years just before the crash,
Marquis wrote in *The Almost Perfect State* (1927):

> ALAS!
> THE HOURS WE WASTE
> IN WORK
> AND SIMILAR
> INCONSEQUENCE!
> FRIENDS,

                    I BEG YOU
                  DO NOT SHIRK
                  YOUR DAILY
                      TASK
                  OF INDOLENCE

(Marquis himself was a hard if intermittent worker.) Yet, after
the crash, with nearly ten million people out of work, he could
compose Archygrams behind which lurked the ghost of Poor
Richard:

> a great many people
> who spend their time mourning
> over the brevity of life
> could make it seem longer
> if they did a little more work

Marquis satirized Mencken's *A Book of Prefaces* with his
own *Prefaces* (1918), and he distrusted Mencken's pro-German-
ism, but in some ways he was as much an old-fashioned indi-
vidualist as the Baltimore bombshell. He scoffed at the "Moral
Uplift" early in his career and at the New Deal later. He had
Archy criticize the farm as well as the financial programs of the
Roosevelt Administration and jibe at "new deals and old deals /
and square deals and crooked deals / and ideals and idealists,"
concerning all of which Archy says, with a skepticism equal to
that of Bierce, Howe, or Mencken,

> it has been my observation
> and experience and that of my family
> that nothing human works out well

THE TRICKSTER

Not all of Marquis appears in Archy the wise fool or Archy
the custodian of middle-class norms. Something of Marquis
the dreamer, cynic, and questioner of norms, appears in the
trickster who scuttles through many of the poems. The trickster-
hero and outcast has many incarnations in world folklore, including Reynard the Fox of the medieval beast-epics, Anansé

the spider of West African folktales, Br'er Rabbit in the stories
of Uncle Remus, and Raven and Coyote in American Indian
folk narrative.[8] The trickster is weak physically and must live
by his wits in an environment dominated by his enemies. He
cannot afford to obey their rules and he is therefore a social
outcast. As such, Archy knows "what family skeletons" hang in
the closets of "the lordly ones," and he admits that

> my point of view
> is somewhat
> wried
> i am a pessimistic
> guy
> i see things from the
> under side

Something of the "blackness ten times black" of the disappointed
idealist—a blackness that Melville attributed to Hawthorne and
that Lardner and Thurber showed at times—deeply colors the
humor of Marquis. In certain moods he was as thorough a naturalist and social Darwinist as Mencken, but he was far less
complacent than Mencken, as is shown by his frequent use of
Archy's outcast role to suggest that all men are in the same relation to nature (meaning, for Marquis, the cosmos) as the roach
is to the hostile "society" of humans and other animals in which
he skips precariously about. Men and insects are alike in being
forced to obey universal natural law. The trickster is in part
a means by which Marquis gave guarded expression to his
skeptical naturalism, and this attitude, or rather group of attitudes, needs to be defined.

As outcast, Archy ponders four of the tenets held in common
by most of the writers loosely termed naturalistic, from Émile
Zola to Norman Mailer. First, nature is a perpetual struggle for
survival. Archy demonstrates this in his own foot-to-mouth existence; he even has to scurry into the typewriter to avoid being
eaten by Mehitabel. Second, nature is utterly indifferent to man.
With biting irony, Archy records the delusions to the contrary
of a toad named Warty Bliggens:

a little more
conversation revealed
that warty bliggens
considers himself to be
the center of the said
universe
the earth exists
to grow toadstools for him
to sit under
the sun to give him light
by day and the moon
and wheeling constellations
to make beautiful
the night for the sake of
warty bliggens

Third, man himself is merely an insignificant and inferior part of nature and shows it in his purblindness, irrationality, and pride. Of Warty Bliggens' self-importance, Archy says, "similar / absurdities / have only too often / lodged in the crinkles / of the human cerebrum." Fourth, as a segment of nature, man is not free; his fate is predetermined by chance, heredity, and environment. Far from being "the captain of my / soul the master of my fate," Archy cannot even commit suicide—being only a roach, he is too light to kill himself by falling or by hanging. His plight is an allegory of man's unfreedom.

To make the hard lot of man bearable, Marquis through Archy suggests several possible attitudes. One is a somber hedonism:

believe that everything is for
you until you discover
that you are for it
sing your faith in what you
get to eat right up to the
minute you are eaten
for you are going
to be eaten

Mehitabel's hedonism is more frenetic, but it too expresses one
of Marquis' moods:

> i know that i am bound
> for a journey down the sound
> in the midst of a refuse mound
> but wotthehell wotthehell
> oh i should worry and fret
> death and i will coquette
> there s a dance in the old dame yet
> toujours gai toujours gai

Also through Archy, however, the author reveals that some of
the spiritual atmosphere of Walnut, Illinois, still clings to him.
The roach's favorite "poem" is the same as Abraham Lincoln's
—"o why should the spirit / of mortal be proud?" The desperate
gaiety of Mehitabel and the austerity of rural evangelism as
voiced by Archy reflect valid moods of the author, and who is
to say which of his moods, if any, was the basic one?

Archy had other attitudes toward nature and toward man
as part of nature. After hearing "an elderly mother spider"
bewail the use of fly swatters "what kills off all the flies," because
"unless we eats we dies," he signs off with "yours for less justice /
and more charity." In addition to having, in certain moods,
compassion for all beings, Archy occasionally feels almost reconciled to nature's indifference:

> i find it possible to forgive
> the universe
> i meet it in a give and take spirit
> although i do wish
> that it would consult me at times

He can even sing of the harmony and beauty to be found in
nature along with the brutality. Man, he feels, has retained
the brutality but lost the harmony and beauty:

> as far as government is concerned
> men after thousands of years practice
> are not as well organized socially

> as the average ant hill or beehive
> they cannot build dwellings
> as beautiful as a spiders web
> and i never saw a city
> full of men manage to be as happy
> as a congregation of mosquitoes
> who have discovered a fat man
> on a camping trip
> as far as personal beauty
> is concerned who ever saw
> man woman or child
> who could compete with a butterfly

Because he has lost his connection with the rest of nature, man has ruined his natural environment, the American "paradise / of timberland and stream," through "greed / and money lust," and "it won't be long / till earth is barren as the moon / and sapless as a mumbled bone."

The last three comments were written after the droughts and dust storms of the thirties had begun to make people more conscious of the need for conservation of natural resources. Despite the increasing bitterness of Marquis' writings after the middle twenties, a reverence for nature and an insistence on man's need to feel a harmonious identity with it recur in his work from first to last. In 1908 Marquis had singled out in the philosophy of his late employer, Joel Chandler Harris, an element that was often present in his own thought later. Marquis wrote of Harris:

> Nothing appeared to him to be simply dead matter; his universe was all made of one stuff, and was very much alive. . . . This sense of the genuine basic kinship of all the things which exist is very familiar in all his writings, it is the quality which makes his "critters" half-human, sympathetic, understandable characters instead of merely caricatures of animals or stories about animals . . .[9]

In 1927, Marquis published *The Almost Perfect State*, a collection of pieces from his column that treated further of man's need to live in harmony with his nonhuman surroundings. In this book he declared that,

> Whenever a continent becomes so cluttered up with people that there is no longer any wild counterpoise and balance for its highest civilization, there has arisen and there arises a jungle of a poisonous and artificial sort, populated by the less fortunate human beings. . . . The real natural wilderness must come into its own again before there can be even a start at the Almost Perfect State.

Marquis therefore suggests that the United States should contain no more than from five to ten millions of people and that "the human population of the entire world should be kept well under a hundred millions." The greater part of the globe should be allowed to return to wilderness, and people would then be able to live by hunting or agriculture, as they chose. There would be little commerce or industry, and no government. "The abundant leisure of the population will be devoted to playing, making love, producing works of art, and arguing about religion." Conceivably echoing Thomas Jefferson, who had said in *Notes on Virginia* (Query XIX) that the "mobs of great cities" were like sores on the human body, Marquis declared that great cities "are as anomalous on the face of this earth . . . as warts and blackheads on an angel's nose." In Marquis' utopia, cities would disappear.

The agrarianism of *The Almost Perfect State* shows how very American was Marquis' kind of naturalism. He may have been, temperamentally, a city-dweller, but in his longing for a simple agrarian society purged of commercialism and prudery, he exemplified a major literary tradition that included, despite their differences, Thoreau, John Burroughs, Mark Twain, Robert Frost, William Faulkner, E. B. White, and perhaps Will Cuppy, who called Marquis' utopia "probably the only one fit to live in." Like many city-dwellers, Marquis may have yearned also, at times, for the small town and green fields of his boyhood, in spite of the bitter memories that often crowded into his mind. Charles Child Walcutt suggests that American naturalism was a "divided stream" of both optimism and pessimism and that the optimistic current included an ideal of perfect oneness of nature and spirit. American naturalism became pessimistic insofar as that ideal was lost or given up.[10] On the whole, the pessimistic strain predominated in *The Almost Perfect State,* as it did elsewhere in Marquis' work and in the naturalistic writers of his time generally. Man *was* hopelessly separated from nature, and Marquis had no idea how to remedy the situation. He made clear that in *The Almost Perfect State* he was just getting his kicks through utopian speculation. A few years later, Archy ended his prediction that man will make the earth barren with,

> dear boss i relay this information
> without any fear that humanity
> will take warning and reform

A FLAPPER AND AN "UPLIFTER"

In their hedonism, Archy and Mehitabel are both wise fools, but Mehitabel can play one role denied to Archy, that of the frowsier sort of flapper. As such, she is an instrument for satirizing the more lurid goings-on of unconventional womanhood, including famous actresses and movie stars, during the restless war years and the decade that followed. The ancient excuse for promiscuity—I was pure, but a villain ruined me—takes on new flavor in her mouth:

> i once was an innocent kit
> wotthehell wotthehell
> with a ribbon my neck to fit
> and bells tied onto it
> o wotthehell wotthehell
> but a maltese cat came by
> with a come hither look in his eye
> and a song that soared to the sky
> and wotthehell wotthehell
> and i followed adown the street
> the pad of his rhythmical feet
> o permit me again to repeat
> wotthehell wotthehell

The rationale that true romance needs absolute freedom also is satirized through Mehitabel. She proclaims herself never "an adventuress" but "always free footed / archy never tied down to / a job or housework"—a follower of the "life romantic." After acquiring seven kittens in Hollywood by an unknown father, she neglects them and talks about her responsibilities to her career and how her art comes before motherhood—"an artist like me shouldn't really have offspring." The transparency of her excuses and the fact that she is only a cat after all, render her personification of the flapper as inoffensive as it is exaggerated and oversimplified.

A separate book could be written on women in twentieth-century American humor, especially the New Woman of the Progressive iconology. Next to the Archy poems, Marquis' liveliest work is the monologues collected as *Hermione and Her Little Group of Serious Thinkers* (1916). Hermione resembles those daughters and wives whom Ade's males have given money and leisure to waste. Her main interest is occultism in all its current phases—psychical research, New Thought, Cosmic Consciousness, "vibrations"—but she also falls for other fads that were in the news from about 1912 to 1916. For example:

> I'm taking up Bergson this week.
> Next week I'm going to take up Etruscan vases and the Montessori system.
> Oh, no, I haven't lost my interest in sociology.
> Only the other night we went down in the auto and watched the bread line.
> Of course, one can take up *too many* things.

Her misgiving dissolves, and in rapid succession she and her Little Group take up spiritualism, eugenics, genetics, the superman, woman suffrage, welfare work, prison reform, and—with the help of the *vers libre* bard Fothergil Finch, "Poet of Revolt" —the more esoteric phases of the fine arts, including cubist painting, Gertrude Stein, and Sergei Diaghilev. She is an unconscious hypocrite in that she believes herself one of the "Leaders of Modern Thought" but is unaware of the unoriginality of her ideas and the irrelevance and triviality of her motivations. She takes up the "Art of the Future" because "the loveliest man" lectured about it, and she quits the suffrage movement because, "They wanted me to wear one of those horrid yellow sashes." At times her hypocrisy inches toward consciousness. Though she takes up eugenics and longs for a "Cave Man" lover, she never forgets that she is respectable, and she admits that "I don't really *like* discussions of Sex any more than Mamma does. No really nice girl does."

The genteel nature of her hypocrisy checks her "Social Conscience" and leaves the world fairly safe from her "reforms." Her interest in prison reform stops at the notion that her Papa might hire an ex-convict himself—". . . well, really, you know, one must draw the line somewhere!" When she goes down to the breadline, she wears her mink coat and stays in the car. She and her Little Group decide to set the masses an example by not drinking—in public, "if any of the working classes happen to be about where they can see us and become corrupted by our example."

Behind the portrait of Hermione lie standards of sincerity, moderation, and common sense, all misapplied or absent in this girl. Politically, Marquis was at that time a Taft Republican, or rather merely an anti-Wilsonian,[11] but the exaggerated and harmless nature of his version of the New Woman made it possible for both conservatives and liberals to be amused. Morally, Marquis has no grave criticism of Hermione except her pretentiousness. She is respectable but pretends to be daring; Mehitabel is disreputable but pretends to be a "lady." From his citadel of masculine common sense, Marquis satirized both types of erring female.

A CRACKERBOX SAGE

Largely in protest against prohibition, Marquis created a crackerbarrel philosopher in his column and put twenty-two of the sketches about him into *The Old Soak* (1921). The "Old Soak" also yarned and capered through a successful play of that title, produced in 1922, through a second book of sketches (*The Old Soak's History of the World*, 1924), and in magazine stories later included in *When the Turtles Sing* (1928) and *A Variety of People* (1929).

Clem Hawley, the Old Soak, lives out in Baycliff, Long Island, ostensibly a suburb of New York City but actually given a rural flavor that makes it indistinguishable from "Hazelton," Illinois, in *Sons of the Puritans*. In Marquis' fiction all the small towns are essentially the Walnut, Illinois, of his boyhood, as all of Mark Twain's fictional towns were Hannibal, Missouri. Clem's main activity is procuring enough bootleg liquor to keep himself moderately soused, though not sodden. Except for his interest in hootch, he is a bit like Will Rogers, who showed an appreciation of Marquis that was heartily returned, and a good deal like Jiggs and like Ade's breadwinners. He is a family man and has been a hard worker, but may now live without working. "I done all my hard slaving when I was young and I got a little money coming in right along from them two houses I own," he says, revealing himself as a substantial if not large property-holder—William Graham Sumner's Forgotten Man in retirement.

He quarrels constantly with his prim wife, who does not approve of his drinking, and on a trip to Europe he plays the Innocent Abroad. He tells tall tales in frontier style, like the yarn about the "Rev. Mr. Hoskins," a pet bullhead who learned to live out of water and was drowned when he fell into a cistern. He also coins crackerbox aphorisms, like "Neither Prohibition nor booze has much to do with making a mean man mean." He messes up the English language not only in his use of dialect but in malapropisms such as "Bolshevisitors" for Bolsheviks and "Exclusiastics" for Ecclesiastes. In his illiteracy and in his devotion to drink, he is the wise fool. In his tales and aphorisms he appears as the rustic oracle. In his economic stability and family difficulties, he is the solid citizen, and one sees again how traits associated with these three roles may be blended in a single character.

A MAN PLAYS MANY PARTS

Even the use of several different comic masks gave incomplete expression to the contradictions in Marquis' personality. One of these contradictions was between the conventional lyricist and the humorous writer of free verse. "My heart has followed all my days / Something I cannot name," he wrote in *Dreams and Dust* (1915), his first book of serious verse. Thinking of the worship of ideal love and beauty in Marquis' lyrics and of how that worship contrasts with the potboiling which motivated much of his humor, Benjamin De Casseres termed Marquis, "Shelley trying to lasso the Golden Calf." [12] In several books of poems, Marquis wrote lyrics in the sonnet form and in other traditional poetic molds. The more interesting of these poems were satirical, like some of the *Sonnets to a Red-Haired Lady* (1922) and *Love Sonnets of a Cave Man* (1928). The serious ones tended to be sentimental.

A related contradiction existed between Marquis' naturalism and his religious leanings. Most of his significant humor expresses his naturalistic, skeptical bent, and that side of Marquis has consequently received the most emphasis in this discussion. But Christopher Morley, a close friend, called him a "divinity student," and he even tried Christian Science for a short while. In his writing, Don's religious interest manifested itself in a number of short stories (notably those in *Chapters for the Orthodox*) and in *The Dark Hours*, a play about the Crucifixion into which Marquis put years of work—and which failed at the box office, though some reviewers were impressed by the printed version. This contradiction is only partially resolved in his early poem, "The God-Maker, Man," where he avers that ". . . the gods are not / Unless we pray to them," and that

As the forehead of Man grows broader, so do his creeds;
And his gods they are shaped in his image, and mirror his needs.

Therefore all gods are worthy of worship but not of belief, and
"I will bow me down where my brothers bow, / Humble—but
open-eyed!" [13] Even though based on an evolutionary view of
religion, this respect for man's irrational beliefs looks strange
beside the contempt for man voiced by Archy when he tells his
boss that

> . . . when the revolution
> comes i shall
> do my best to save
> you you have so many
> points that are far
> from being human

A third contradiction, related to the discrepancy between
the serious lyricist and the comic free-versifier, is that between
the romantic rebel and the plodding bourgeois. Marquis roman-
ticized, or sentimentalized, the young, eager girl in revolt, in
Ruby Tucker of *When the Turtles Sing* (1928) and Sally Cass
in *Off the Arm* (1930); he even approved of Ruby's "a-takin'
chances" that included leaving a worthless husband and uniting
in joyous adultery with "a travellin' piano tuner." Likewise
Marquis often endorsed the attempts of males to live their lives
in defiance of convention, like the free-loving patriarch Jason
Tucker and the bohemian novelist Hugh Cass, and like those
old loafers Noah and Jonah and Cap'n John Smith, who spend
their time "strummin' golden harps, narreratin' myth." The
adventures of some of these men and women are told by the
Old Soak, and when Marquis is wearing the Old Soak's mask
of wise fool, he is willing to live and let live, but the reckless
Mehitabel gets severe treatment from Mr. Marquis when he
speaks through Archy as solid citizen.

However, by casting Archy also in the role of trickster-
outcast and by making the Old Soak a substantial citizen who
rebels only against a few specific laws, Marquis could exploit
if not resolve his inconsistent attitudes. He could be skeptic
as well as dreamer, philosopher as well as vagabond, rebel as
well as Rotarian—and above all, a somber humorist with a
crooked smile.

PART FOUR

Creators of the Little Man

12

The "Genial Middle Ground"

B. N. Y.*

The year 1915 saw Van Wyck Brooks drawing a distinction in *America's Coming-of-Age* between "Highbrow" and "Lowbrow" culture (the term "middlebrow" had to wait some years for its invention). Brooks maintained that the basic obstacle to the

---

* Before the *New Yorker*.

development of American literature was the gap between these two halves. "Between university ethics and business ethics, between American culture and American humor, between Good Government and Tammany, between academic pedantry and pavement slang, there is no community, no genial middle ground."

By American humor, Brooks apparently meant the humor of the crackerbarrel and the joke page. In the first decade of the century, American humor itself seemed divided much as Brooks felt that the whole American complex was split, Holmes' Autocrat representing one pole and Ade's Artie the other. Bangs' Idiot had his initial poverty and lower-middle-class status in common with Artie, but on the whole, the polished pleasantries of Bangs and of Hayden Caruth, H. C. Bunner, Frank Moore Colby, Gelett Burgess, and Carolyn Wells (among others) diverged far in tone from the more uncouth jesting of Ade, Dunne, Lardner, and Rogers. Mencken enjoyed demonstrating his erudition, but as a humorist he was not yet well known beyond Baltimore, and anyway one would hardly class him with the "university wits." Such relatively pale grinders-out of crackerbox humor as Ed Mott (the "Old Settler," *The Black Homer of Jimtown*), E. N. Westcott (*David Harum*, 1898), Harry Leon Wilson, and Montague Glass could not be said to fill the gap between chalky correctness and the irreverence of Bierce, Howe, "Brann the Iconoclast," and the self-made Chicagoans who in their distrust of the first two items in the American credo—metaphysical absolutes, and progress—broke with textbook morality as well as with textbook language while educators like the superintendent of the Oak Park, Illinois, High School wrung their hands. (This official complained that "Ernie Hemingway was writing like Ring Lardner—and consequently a lost soul.")[1]

Between 1900 and 1950 the crackerbox tradition changed remarkably little, except in adding the automobile, the airplane, the radio, the movies, television, and other outgrowths of the industrial age, to its subject matter. But in other circles, several years before Brooks' essay was written, humorists were moving to create the middle ground of which he spoke. Franklin P. Adams and Christopher Morley were erudite as well as witty, and Adams' column, "The Conning Tower," became a model for other columnists, including Don Marquis. Marquis himself, though he got only part way through high school, allowed Archy to show an acquaintance with literature and history surprising in an unschooled roach, and there is almost as much literary parody in the humor of Marquis as in that of Bangs. Simeon Ford, a hotel manager turned humorist, wrote as a literate and harassed citizen in *A Few Remarks* (1906). Simeon Strunsky, a graduate of Columbia who was not afraid to show it, began to write his column, "The Patient Observer," for the New York *Evening Post* in the same year, and four years later, Clarence Day, Jr., an alumnus of Yale, began to sell the short pieces that eventually made up his first two books, *This Simian World* and *The Crow's Nest*. Also in 1910, Stephen Leacock, a Canadian professor destined to have a wide readership in the United States, made his bow with *Literary Lapses*, which had a direct influence on Robert Benchley. Ring Lardner once referred contemptuously to "correct Crowninshield dinner English," but Frank Crowninshield, after becoming editor of *Vanity Fair* in 1913, encouraged the writing of prose fully as lively if not as boisterous as that of Mencken and Nathan in the *Smart Set*, and just as erudite too, on occasion. *Vanity Fair* was the first commercial magazine to publish verse by Dorothy Parker and prose by Benchley. The supposedly staid *Bookman* published a string of satires by Donald Ogden Stewart that was reprinted as *A Parody Outline of History* (1921). Among the other established periodicals, *Puck* alone died in 1918; *Life, Judge, Harper's, Scribner's,* and the *Atlantic* all continued, publishing contributions from the new generation of cultured humorists along with the work of older writers like Colby. Perhaps the eruption of fresh talent in its pages had something to do with the climbing of *Life's* circulation to 150,000 in 1916 and its reaching a peak of 250,000 in 1921.

This later generation of writers was just as cultivated as the earlier, but less inhibited by genteel taboos about either subject matter or style. Concerning style, they were also less inhibited than the crackerbox writers; they used whatever level of prose served their purpose—say, the language of the half-educated man in the street or of the college-trained man writing a familiar essay for other college-trained men. With regard to ideas and values they were uncertain, and their uncertainty was most effectively embodied in that character type now known as the Little Man.

Before turning a lens on this character as portrayed by humorists of the written word, one might well look briefly at his appearance in certain other media. Doing so may help to explain more clearly just who this Little Man was and what he stood for, as well as to indicate how completely and thoroughly he was becoming part of American popular mythology. The Little Man was not, after all, exclusively the creation of writers of fiction and of essayists; he was part of a general drift in American humor, though the precise extent and nature of the influence of one medium upon another is often impossible to specify.

In the nineteenth century, Artemus Ward, Charles Heber Clark, and Bill Nye had sometimes depicted gentle, bewildered characters trying hopelessly to cope with the immensity and complexity of their environment.[2] In cartoon and comic-strip humor, the average citizen, caricatured neither as solid citizen nor as average dolt, stumbled to prominence during the first three decades of the new century. Here was a figure with whom millions could identify themselves and to whom, at the same time, they could feel superior. Sometimes this Little Man was a lonely tramp or drifter, as exemplified in "Happy Hooligan" (created by Frederick Burr Opper about 1899), "Mutt and Jeff" (created by Bud Fisher in 1907–1908), and "Krazy Kat" (created by George Herriman in 1912). More often he was an inept but more or less appealing husband and father harassed by a strong-willed wife and a houseful of irrepressible offspring and kinfolk. In 1912 Harry Hirshfield invented "Abie the Agent," an "up-to-date Jewish businessman" in a strip of that title, who is "dogged by all the problems of the warmhearted, generous family man with a deep distaste for violence, who lives in a business-is-business world of knavery, egotism, legal complexities and neighborhood disasters."[3] In the same year—a year when Benchley was portraying a Little Man in oral monologues for his fellow students at Harvard—Cliff Sterrett founded "Polly and Her Pals." By 1920 the "family strip" was well established, and during the next fifteen years there appeared, among others, "Gasoline Alley," "The Bungle Family," "The Nebbs," "Winnie Winkle," "Moon Mullins," "Blondie," and "The Gumps."

All of the family strips showed in varying degrees the disillusionment and cynicism that affected many people in the nineteen-twenties. At the same time they tended to negate that cynicism. They showed disillusion, as Stephen Becker points out, by making a "well-meaning imbecile" out of the father,[4] but they negated that disillusion by manifesting the nineteenth-century faith in the solidarity of the family. This solidarity was needed to give point to the zany but harmless deviations of Uncle Willie Mullins, Pa Bungle, and Andy Gump, the ineffectuality of Pa Winkle, and the more frenetic but ultimately harmless blowups within the Bumstead household. The ways in which these comic-strip characters often did *not* act implied certain values that most Americans still clung to. Courage was conspicuous by its absence from Uncle Willie's conduct; industriousness, reason, and right speech by Andy Gump's lack of the same; order and quiet by the din at the Bumsteads'; parental authority by the inadequacy of Pa Winkle and Rudy Nebb as breadwinners and as examples of self-discipline; modesty and competence by the utter lack of these qualities in Pa Bungle. The fact that Jiggs, Paw Perkins (in "Polly and Her Pals"), and Uncle Walt may be classed either as solid citizens or as Little Men—they are at least good providers, and they get their way a fair percentage of the time in family arguments—shows that no hard and fast line existed between the two types, but rather a twilight zone.

The development of the Little Man in still other media can be here suggested only by brief citation. In the movies Charlie Chaplin played his first role of Little-Man-as-tramp in 1914, the same year that Sinclair Lewis, in the field of the novel, depicted a Little Man as white-collar unhero in his first book for adults, *Our Mr. Wrenn*. By 1921, when Benchley's first collection was published, a far more complete exploration of the Little Man than those made by Lewis or Benchley appeared in a novel, part of which was serialized in the *Little Review*. Leopold Bloom, the ad-canvasser in James Joyce's *Ulysses*, had more than a few similarities to the American male of Benchley and Thurber. Bloom's harassment by an aggressive wife, and the hodgepodge of misinformation in his mind may be cited as examples. More basic similarities are his fundamental decency and his warped but still intact awareness of himself and of others as individuals with rights and feelings—an awareness that the Victorians would have unashamedly designated as a "warm heart."[5]

This warmth at the core was compounded of self-consciousness, integrity, and fellow-feeling—vague terms for a complex of intangibles—but the possession of them sharply set off the types here arbitrarily lumped together from the boobs of Mencken and the average men of Lardner. Sometimes a contrast between common man and Little Man appears in the same strip: Mutt is of the former type and Jeff is of the latter; likewise, Ignatius Mouse is an extreme example of the aggressive sort of common man (Common Man as Mouse would be an inappropriate label) and Krazy Kat is a Little Man in feline form, distinguished from victims of the Lardner type by having more concern for others, including his tormentor, than for himself. In their self-centeredness and windy pretentiousness, Pa Bungle, Rudy Nebb, Moon and Willie Mullins, and Andy Gump often suggest the common man, but whenever real evil threatens the family (as in the human predators who are constantly after the wealth of Andy's Uncle Benjamin), these characters will always be found acting on the side of the right, however ineptly. The relative blandness of the comic strip as a medium of satire—except in the hands of an Al Capp or a Walt Kelly—in comparison to the newspaper column or the short story is in part owing to a lack of the devastating portraits of the average man that may sometimes be found in fiction or drama for adults.

As noted, the Ade and Gullible type of household head gradually shades off into the Little Man; however, when one compares Gullible with an extreme example of the Little Man, like Mr. Milquetoast ("The Timid Soul"), one sees the shrinkage of the Little Man in psychological stature. Gullible is still a force, both inside and outside of his family; Mr. Milquetoast is not. The point of these comparisons is that the essentially positive nature of the Little Man as a carrier of values is easier to see in comic strips, cartoons, and early movies than in more complex media. One can usually sympathize with Dagwood even when laughing at him; it is not always so easy to sympathize with the ineptitude, childishness, and perversity of Benchley's narrator, and it is still less easy to sympathize with some of Thurber's drunks and murderers.

Perhaps the greater realism and complexity of written humor over the humor of his earlier slapstick films were what caused Chaplin to misunderstand the positive role of the Little Man, despite his own sensitive portrayals of such a man. "Modern humor frightens me a little," Chaplin said to Max Eastman (James Thurber, Donald Ogden Stewart, and Robert Benchley were among those he mentioned):

> They go in for being crazy. It's a soul-destroying thing. They say, "All right, you're insane, we'll appeal to your insanity." They make insanity the convention. They make humor a premise. Acquiescence in everything disintegrating. Knocking everything down. Annihilating everything. There's no conduct in their humor. They haven't any attitude. It's up-to-date, of course—a part of the chaos.[6]

For once, a theorist has come closer to the truth than a practitioner. Professor Ralph L. Curry has said that both Stephen Leacock and his disciple, Benchley, saw the Little Man as confused and trapped but that "They made fun of the system and not the man who struggled against it."[7] The present writer feels that Benchley and his kind did make considerable fun of the Little Man himself but were definitely on his side and through him made even more fun of the system. The chapters which follow are intended to support this view.

A. N. Y.*

In connection with Day and Benchley, evidence will be offered that, contrary to the popular impression, the humorists associated with the *New Yorker* did not create the Little Man as a type, nor did they originate the kind of humor that centered around his harassment by the modern world. As seen earlier, the character type and the theme of harassment evolved in nineteenth-century humor and in the early years of the twentieth. Between 1920 and 1930 this evolution accelerated. By 1925, when Harold Ross founded the *New Yorker,* Clarence Day and Donald Ogden Stewart had already written a good deal about the Little Man, and Leacock and Benchley were at the height of their reputations. Three others who wrote humor in the role of Little Man—Simeon Strunsky, Alexander Woollcott, and Heywood Broun—had already made their marks as columnists and reviewers. In their treatment and stress of this character, the younger writers who did so much to make Ross's magazine noteworthy were followers, developers, and refiners rather than originators.

Thus the *New Yorker* furnished reinforcement rather than leadership in creating a "genial middle ground" between the consumers of crackerbox humor and readers who preferred the decorum of the university wits. The Little Man who now occupied this ground was far more literate than Lardner's types and often had a college education, yet the problems that confused him were those of every middle-class householder. Mencken and Nathan had helped to create and enrich that ground through the *Smart Set,* and were continuing to do so in the one-year-old

---

* After the *New Yorker.*

American Mercury. Vanity Fair was also helping to fill the gap, and although the *New Yorker* was not especially modeled on either magazine, the cover of the initial number of Ross's periodical bore hints of an influence from both. For this cover, Rea Irvin (who had contributed to *Vanity Fair*) drew a dandy with top hat in the act of peering through his monocle at a butterfly, and Corey Ford named this discriminating dude "Eustace Tilley." Ford, as a writer, often wore the mask of the Little Man, but Eustace looks like one of the nonacademic "civilized minority" for whom Mencken and Nathan were writing, and also like some of the caricatures of "high society" which Irvin and others drew for *Vanity Fair.* Probably all that Ross and Irvin intended was a suggestion of metropolitan "smartness" and a self-caricature of that smartness which would offset any pompous tendency. But in associating the social upper crust with that smartness, Eustace Tilley as a symbol of the *New Yorker* reader was highly misleading. The prospectus of the magazine gave a different account of the aims of Ross:

> The New Yorker will be a reflection in word and picture of metropolitan life. It will be human. Its general tenor will be one of gaiety, wit and satire, but it will be more than a jester. It will not be what is commonly called radical or highbrow. It will be what is commonly called sophisticated, in that it will assume a reasonable degree of enlightenment on the part of its readers. It will hate bunk. . . . Its integrity will be above suspicion. It hopes to be so entertaining and informative as to be a necessity for the person who knows his way about or wants to. . . . The New Yorker will be the magazine which is not edited for the old lady in Dubuque. It will not be concerned in what she is thinking about. . . . It expects a considerable national circulation, but this will come from persons who have a metropolitan interest.[8]

The emphasis was partly on taste and partly on a certain geographical area. The final sentence showed an awareness that urban taste rather than rural might be coming to dominate the national scene.[9] However, in promising lightness of tone and a general sophistication, Ross signified that he planned to be more highbrow than the *Daily News* but less so than perhaps the *Dial* or the *Little Review*. "Nobody's going to make me arty,"[10] he once said.

Along with the image of the Little Man, respect for an urbane but lively style and for competence in achieving that style had, as noted, become the rule among the more high-powered humorists. One breeding-ground for this respect during the early nineteen-twenties was the Vicious Circle of lunchers at the Hotel Algonquin. "F. P. A.," Dorothy Parker, Benchley, Woollcott, Broun, and George S. Kaufman flashed brightest among these wits, and the standards of style in writing which they upheld became the goals of proficiency aimed at by the future stars of the *New Yorker*. One of Thurber's early aims was to get pieces into F. P. A.'s "The Conning Tower," and Thurber wrote of Benchley that, ". . . there was nobody whose praise a cartoonist or humorist would rather have had."[11] What Ross and his magazine did accomplish was to give the highly literate but nimble humorists their most important outlet of publication and to carry respect for competence in general and for stylistic smartness without brashness in particular to an extreme that amounted almost to fetishism concerning the right word and the precise phrase.

Ross did more than any other editor in the twenties and thirties to encourage compression, the *mot juste*, informality, suavity, and irony in the writing of humor, and people now use the term *"New Yorker* style" to designate any writing that shows these attributes, whether it has appeared in the magazine or not. But Ross originated neither these standards nor the Little Man.

13

Life With Clarence Day, Jr.

Clarence Day, Jr., the oldest of the new brigade of suave humorists (if one excepts Leacock, the Canadian), numbered men of
distinction among his ancestors. Benjamin H. Day, the father of
"Father," founded the New York *Sun* and the humorous weekly
Brother Jonathan (1842–1843). An uncle of the author invented

the Ben Day process for color printing. However, to the Astors, Vanderbilts, Renssaelaers, and other pillars of New York "society," the Days and their ilk were strictly middle class. Clarence and his Mother had that fact impressed upon them when they discovered that "their" butcher "was catering to the fashionable Fifth Avenue families and didn't care a rap about ours."

Father Day was a stockbroker who, despite his family connections, had made his own way almost entirely. He resembled H. L. Mencken's father in being the self-made owner of a highly successful small business and in loudly voicing a respect for the ancient qualities of integrity, solvency, thrift, and industriousness. He was like H. L. in seeing himself as a plain, hard-working citizen much abused (though not, in Father Day's case, amused) by the stupidities of 99 per cent of the people around him.

HUMORIST AND LIBERAL

Clarence Day, Jr. went to St. Paul's school and to Yale, and then became a partner in Wall Street with his father. He went off to join the Navy in the Spanish-American War, and from this experience dated his arthritis, "which from middle age made him a complete cripple, unable to leave his bed or move more than a finger."[1] Day endured his affliction courageously; no trace of bitterness or self-pity colored the amused asperity with which he often satirized himself in his writings. He died in 1935, four years before the curtain went up on the dramatized version of *Life With Father*.

He may first have written humor in order to enliven his chores as secretary of the Yale Class of 1896. In compiling biographies of his classmates for the *Decennial Record,* Day was not only uncomfortably candid at times but threw in bits of satiric drollery. Of one classmate he wrote, ". . . he seems to be a Big Gun in the lumber business, and . . . is said to resemble in appearance a Methodist bishop."[2] Day explained that he canceled a visit to another classmate, in Duluth, Minnesota, because of a headline: "Must not Shoot Bear Within City Limits," and he described the effect of this headline by mangling a passage from *Hamlet*: "The Secretary's game leg shivered at this announcement. It harrowed up his soul, froze his young blood, made each particular hair to stand an [*sic*] end like frills upon the fretful concubine."[3] A trifle, but it foreshadows Day's later picture of himself as a normally unheroic fellow, not quite a Milquetoast but no Teddy Roosevelt either.

After his experience in the "splendid little war," Day returned to business for some years, but by 1910 he was a free-lance writer and a professional book reviewer. Before his ailment laid him low, he conducted a book department in the *Metropolitan*, a sophisticated monthly supported by the wealthy socialite Payne Whitney and described by Louis Filler as "quasi-Socialist"[4] (Theodore Roosevelt, however, also contributed to this magazine from about 1914 until his death in 1919). Day also wrote for the *New Republic* after its founding in 1914, and in his humor he both satirizes and defends the reformers who wrote for and read these two magazines. The reformers assumed the existence of a citizenry fundamentally rational and moral in their impulses. Day went so far as to doubt, with other humorists of his time, the rationality and morality of these impulses. In *This Simian World* (1920), the opening theme was that ours is a "simian civilization." Day's *persona* is a man who has not really made up his mind about human worth but is stirred to clarify his attitude by the pessimism of a friend. "I myself feel differently at different times about us human beings: sometimes I get pretty indignant when we are attacked . . . (for there is altogether too much abuse of us [humans] by spectator philosophers) and yet at other times I too feel like a spectator, an alien: but even then I had never felt so alien or despairing as Potter." Gravely the speaker examines the possibility that the ants and bees might have made better rulers of the earth; then he discusses the sort of overlords the cats, dogs, elephants, and other animals might have made. He reflects that man's origin as a simian is responsible for his gregariousness, energy, aimlessness, love of gabble, and above all, for his curiosity. Day (after the first few paragraphs the speaker and the author seem to become one and the same) has misgivings about this animal's ability to solve the problems raised by the excess of his inquisitiveness. "Each simian will wish to know more than his head can hold, let alone ever deal with. . . . It would stretch a god's skull to accomplish such an ambition, yet simians won't like to think it's beyond their powers."

Yet Day finally places himself with the optimists and, by implication, with the reformers rather than with the conservatives who carried on the tradition his Father stood for.[5] We simians, Day says, lack appreciation of beauty, love, and creativeness, and yet, "This is no world for pessimists. An amoeba on the beach, blind and helpless, a mere bit of pulp,—that amoeba has grandsons today who read Kant and play symphonies. . . . This world, and our racial adventure, are magical still." Day's brand of Darwinism stresses the upward evolution of man rather than mere brutish conflict. There were essentially two ways of accepting Darwinism and of applying it to human society. Day is less like Herbert Spencer, Benjamin Kidd, William Graham Sumner, and H. L. Mencken, and more like Emerson, Whitman, and Sandburg. The former emphasized man's selfishness and the struggle for survival, and drew antidemocratic implications therefrom. The latter stressed man's evolutionary progress toward perfection and hence toward democracy.[6] However, Day also resembled his fellow humorist in the reform movement, Finley Peter Dunne, in distrusting the slightest excess in either optimism or zeal among his Progressive colleagues.

In *The Crow's Nest* (1921), which was augmented and revised for posthumous publication as *After All* (1936), Day collected a number of informal magazine essays, reviews, poems, and drawings on a wide variety of subjects, including the life of Thought compared with the life of Action, medieval knights, Bernard Shaw and other authors, the wealthy, the lady anthropologist Elsie Clews Parsons, the lives and scandals of the English statesman Charles Dilke and the Irish statesman Parnell, grammar and grammarians, Edward Lear, Henrik Ibsen, J. Henri Fabre, Egyptian archaeology, and George Washington as a farmer. On controversial matters Day's view was consistently moderate, as in "Sex, Religion and Business," where he compared free love as promoted in Mikhail Artsybashev's novel *Sanine* to asceticism as described in some poetry of India (probably by Tagore). Day stressed his own normal, middle position, saying, "I'm not starved at the moment; but I'm not getting all I want either." (At the time of writing this sentence, he was still single.) In one of his liveliest satires, "The Revolt of Capital," Day knocks together the heads of both capital and labor, and advocates a compromise: labor should be represented on corporation boards of directors—"Both those who do the work and those who put in the money should rightfully be represented in these governing bodies." The proposal seemed radical at the time, and indeed, the principle that labor should help run the company has not yet been accepted in some quarters; however, labor's right at least to sit with management and with the public on arbitration boards was enacted into law with the creation of the Railroad Labor Board in 1920 and would gain yet further respectability under the New Deal. Citizen Day, like Walter Lippmann and others writing for the *New Republic,* was merely trying to find the most reasonable plan between the extremes of destructively competitive capitalism and stultifying control by government—searching, one might say, for a true norm in "normalcy."

Day's drawings deserve attention. They enliven *The Crow's Nest* and *After All* and furnish the main interest in *Thoughts Without Words* (into which, however, a few words crept, "Like flies, buzzing around each of the pictures") and in *Scenes From the Mesozoic* (1935). Though Day's cartoons have an over-all flavor wholly different from Thurber's, they share the same grotesque impishness and give the same impression of being childish scrawls instead of the little masterpieces of art they really are. Like Thurber too, Day sometimes drew the frequent spectator, bumbler, or henpecked husband with a face like his own—in his

case, round and bespectacled; whereas Thurber's is lean and has
a thin mustache. That there were limits to Day's "radicalism" is
further suggested by the following jingle under a drawing in
Thoughts Without Words:

> To Pacifists the proper course
> Of conduct is to sit on Force.
> For, in their dreams, Force can't resist
> The well-intentioned Pacifist.

FATHER AND SON

After the success of the play *Life With Father*, Harold Ross
told Frank Sullivan that "if he had never printed anything except Clarence Day's stuff, it would have been enough." Thurber
remarked that Ross probably didn't know that "the central
theme of the play, the baptism of Father Day, was based on two
stories that had appeared in *Harper's* and later in a book called
God and My Father."[7] The appearance of these two pieces in
that magazine (in December, 1931, and January, 1932) offers an
example of how a livelier sort of prose was penetrating the pages
of the older quality monthlies. Some of Day's *New Yorker* pieces
about his family were collected in 1935 as *Life With Father*, and
a posthumous compilation followed, *Life With Mother* (1937).[8]

In many ways Father is an obtuse tyrant and bully. Why
should the stage version of *Life With Father*, by Howard Lindsay
and Russel Crouse—a version weakened in characterization and
atmosphere and jazzed up with a teen-age romance—have had
the longest continuous run of any play ever on Broadway? Brooks
Atkinson has made some shrewd guesses; he was discussing the
play, but his remarks also fit the subject of the present discussion,
namely, the sketches of the Day family as first written by
Clarence, Jr. Father, says Atkinson, has become "one of the representative American figures. . . . His family problems and his
attitude toward them became the familiar experience of most
fathers in the home." Moreover, life was exciting in the Day
household, even when nothing much was really happening. Yet
Father's rages, in spite of their epic proportions, are often in-

effectual; "Father is defeated in nearly every issue that is raised"[9]
—for instance, in his long but fruitless resistance to baptism.

One may add that the life of this family revealed as much
affection as it did tension. The rages of Father Day clearly spring
from what Clarence, Jr. calls a "thoroughly good-hearted, warm-
blooded man." Father may have been arrogant and obtuse, but
he was not mean or malicious.

Atkinson's phrase, "representative figure," needs fuller definition. The time-span covered by the sketches is roughly the
last two decades of the nineteenth century, and Father is a personage around whom there hangs an air of quaintness because
that figure—the stern masculine ruler of the family, the Victorian
paterfamilias—had largely vanished from the American scene,
along with the period environment of horsecars, coachmen in
livery, massive furniture, ornate clocks, and china pug dogs in
which all this human grandeur flourished. This environment
was re-created by Day with affection and yet with criticism. The
following passage shows how he tempered nostalgia with critical
detachment. His discrimination is based on the difference between the baroque tastes of the upper-middle-class Victorians
and the more restrained tastes of the somewhat less prosperous
but more cultivated readers in his own generation for whom he
was writing:

> Our hall had a solemnly dramatic atmosphere about it to all
> of us boys, because that was where the black hatrack stood,
> at the foot of our stairs, and it was usually there that we got
> spanked.
> As this hatrack was the first thing that visitors saw when
> they entered, it had to be, and was, most impressive. It con-
> sisted of a long, black-walnut chest, low enough to sit down
> on, hidden away in which were all the family's galoshes and
> rubbers and two or three baseballs. Mounted on this chest
> was a mirror, seven feet high and five wide, in a fluted
> black-walnut frame, and this frame had a spreading carved
> canopy overhanging on top. At each side were some gleam-
> ing brass pegs, long and straight, on which hung Father's
> hats; and under these were two umbrella racks with deep
> brass pans underneath.

> In the dining-room there was a black-walnut sideboard, much broader and fatter than the hatrack, and with an even loftier top. At the other end of the room, facing this sideboard, was a combination mantel and mirror. The mirror ran up nearly all the way to the high ceiling, and when I climbed up on a chair I could see the black sideboard in it. On each end of the mantel was a heavily ornamented bronze urn, about two feet high, to match Uncle Hal's immense bronze clock which stood in between them. And in the center of the dining-room, between the mantel and the sideboard, was a great round black-walnut table.
>
> Dark red curtains hung in the windows. There was a thick red rug on the floor. The lower three or four feet of the walls was painted a deep chocolate color. Above that they were a dull bronze, with a Grecian pattern made of flat strips of felt molded on them in relief. Two gory battle scenes and a crayon portrait hung on these walls. The cheeriest thing in the room was the fireplace. It was a rather small one however, with a little brass grate in it, and the overhang of the mantelpiece dwarfed it.

The care with which each detail is recalled and presented betrays the nostalgia. The critical temper appears in the emphasis on the hatrack as an article of conspicuous consumption, the mention of the incongruous objects hidden within this fine black-walnut piece, the adjective applied to the battle scenes, and the ironic stress on the disproportionate smallness of the one cheerful fixture in the setting.

But what does Father himself represent? In his rocklike integrity no less than in his bewilderment at the contrariness of his family, Father is enough like Ade's husbands and Mencken's mask of the responsible citizen to qualify as a member of the elite imagined by these writers. However, the basic contrast is not between this elite and a mass of boobs, nor does the author identify himself with Father's type of man. Instead, Day views his Father with the detachment of a younger generation—but not of just any member of that generation; his *persona* is not one of Lardner's suburban yokels but a man of taste and reflection who has been freed by time from the visual grotesqueness and the social conservatism of the Victorian period but has not succumbed to the garishness and conservatism (or radicalism either) of the nineteen-thirties. There is little satire of his own time by Day in these sketches of his family, but possibly without realizing it, he personified a solid, rational citizen of his own generation, liberal in his social views and restrained in his aesthetic tastes, and not otherwise basically different from Father (with whom the son remained on affectionate terms until the older man's death, even though some of Clarence, Jr.'s sketches about Father Day had already been published and been read by their subject). Father's standards of independence, forthrightness, industry, thrift, and obedience were not so much abandoned as redefined, or remodeled, much as a man like Clarence, Jr. might have had a Victorian parlor remodeled to let in light and air without forfeiting the sense of sturdiness conveyed in that room. Father's ideals of integrity, chastity, and family loyalty were accepted without question. The only new ingredients added by his son were humor, detachment, and a more liberal view of the role of women.

Perhaps Clarence, Jr. went furthest from his Father in his interpretation of Mother's role in the household. In Lavinia Day's frequent triumphs over Father, one glimpses yet another phase of the war between men and women, a phase that is neither Ade's social climber corrupting her husband's simple tastes nor Thurber's female browbeating a pliant slave, but something in between that generates less tension and more laughter. Mother needs to assert herself, but she is no climber or cold-blooded schemer. The friction between Mother and Father over her carefree way with money shows all this. Their liberal son has little use for the Victorian subjection of women to the role of household serfs without money or property, and he suggests that his Mother's haphazard spending is the fault of her background—before her marriage ". . . she had never laid eyes on a ledger"—

and from Father's habit of keeping the purse and paying all the bills himself, a habit quite customary at the time. After all,

> Men knew the world. Women didn't. Women were not fitted to deal with the world. A wife's fortune, if she had one, was usually controlled by her husband. And men's manner in supplying women with money was supposed to be tender but firm.

Day underscored his Mother's vague resistance to this legal and financial thralldom. She "seemed to have no great extravagances. But she loved pretty things," and because of the financial inexperience born of her economic dependence, she "was one of those persons for whom charge accounts were invented." Her own genuine confusion and Father's low boiling point usually frustrated his attempts to make her account for her erratic purchases, and eventually Mother absorbed enough of the New Woman's attitude from her younger friends to pry a regular monthly allowance out of Father—an enormous concession, for him. From this she even managed to save a little, secret nest egg, just to have some real money all her own. Concerning this inconsequential hoarding, her son says, "What she—and still less Father—didn't clearly realize was that she was half unconsciously groping toward a life of her own, in a random, haphazard, inactive way." To this end she could manipulate Father but had no wish to dominate him; indeed it was sometimes all she could do merely to offset his domination of her.

Day's stress on the ridiculous elements of the past, including Father's ineffectuality and Mother's "working" of him, does not lessen one's sense that Father Day was a fitting embodiment for the strong, solid values of his time and social group and that his cluttered but massive home was a fitting framework for these values. W. E. H. Lecky, British historian, wrote in 1896 of the middle class that it was "distinguished beyond all others for its political independence, its caution, its solid practical intelligence, its steady industry, its high moral average."[10] Except for Father's "political independence," which may be estimated by his feeling that ". . . it was hard to see why God had made so many damned fools and democrats," Lecky's description fits Father like a driving glove.

    When Clarence Day, Jr. wrote of the present, he often played the Little Man as philosopher and critic. When the economy went to smash in the early nineteen-thirties, Day turned to the past for his subject matter. In so doing he dropped his self-deprecatory role and, reversing the trend in American humor, assumed a firmer stance as a solid citizen of the present who upholds reason and taste. In this capacity he evoked a bygone atmosphere in which life was exciting but ordered, made challenging by duty but warm by love. In this environment he recreated, with amazingly few departures from literal fact, a father-type nearer to the self-made patriarchs of Ade's fables and to the more recent "Father Barber" of the radio perennial "One Man's Family" than to the other beleaguered husbands in the *New Yorker*. This essentially Victorian type was set off by a wife and mother who "got round" her husband only to the extent of making the father-image less formidable and more appealing. To the whole picture, Day added two elements in harmonious contrast: nostalgic respect for the middle-class Victorian atmosphere and values, and a cultivated, modern liberal *alter ego* suggesting how those values needed modification.

THE ONLY TROUBLE WAS THAT THE CAB HADN'T SEEN ME HAIL IT,
AND DROVE RIGHT BY

The attempts of Benchley's Little Man to assert himself usually end in
frustration. For instance, he ignores an overbearing doorman and tries
to hail a cab himself.

Drawing by Gluyas Williams, from Benchley's *No Poems*, Harper (New York
and London, 1932), p. 125. Reprinted by permission of Harper and Row
(New York and Evanston).

14

Robert Benchley's Normal Bumbler

Like Clarence Day, Jr., Robert Benchley grew up in "a piece of Victorian America" [1]—in Benchley's case, Worcester, Massachusetts—and he retained some of its aggressive Victorian morality. Nathaniel Benchley's biography of his father suggests that Benchley owed some of his moral zeal to his ancestors' having

absorbed the do-good spirit of New England's great reformers—
the spirit of John Pierpont, Harriet Beecher Stowe, and Wendell
Phillips. According to Nathaniel, one grandfather of Robert was
a prominent abolitionist and spent several years in a Texas
prison for his work on the Underground Railroad.[2] Moral zeal
certainly burned in Robert's mother, who, despite her sense
of humor, was a fanatical "dry" of the sort that H. L. Mencken
and the Old Soak of Don Marquis abominated. Robert himself
was an ardent Prohibitionist until prohibition waxed arrogant
and corrupt—then he laboriously learned to drink.

Benchley's father was the mayor's clerk in Worcester, and
economically the family were strictly lower middle class. However, through the financial help of a friend, Robert was able to
spend a year at Phillips Exeter Academy and to matriculate at
Harvard. At the university he was active in dramatics and gave
burlesque lectures that foreshadowed some of his later published
pieces. As president of the *Lampoon* he worked with Gluyas
Williams, the future illustrator of all the Benchley books. He
found time for friendships and for plenty of fun, some of which
is recounted entertainingly by Nathaniel, but he also did settlement work for Phillips Brooks House and later, in New
York, for a boys' club. The spirit of "uplift" was alive in Robert,
if at a nonpolitical level.

Robert had trouble with his grades but eventually was graduated (class of 1912), and then plodded through a succession of
unattractive jobs in advertising, feature writing, and public relations. The moral urge which pushed him into social service
work flared up whenever he encountered injustice in authority,
and he resigned from one job on the New York *Tribune Graphic*
in 1917 because his friend Ernest Gruening (later United States
Senator from Alaska) had been fired for allegedly pro-German
sentiments. After the war, his writing for *Vanity Fair* helped
him to the managing editorship of that periodical, of which
Robert E. Sherwood was then drama editor and Dorothy Parker
drama critic, and to which Frank Moore Colby and Stephen Leacock were contributors.

In 1920, Dorothy Parker was fired from *Vanity Fair* for criticizing Billie Burke and other show people, and again Benchley resigned in protest, along with Sherwood. Robert soon landed two other jobs, as writer of a column on "Books and Other Things" for the New York *World* (1920–1921) and as drama editor for *Life*. After the *New Yorker* got under way in 1925, he began to contribute pieces to Ross's new magazine, and in 1927 he started the column "The Wayward Press" for Ross, using the pseudonym "Guy Fawkes." He left the dying *Life* in 1929 and moved to the *New Yorker* as drama critic, a position he held until 1940.

Publication of his humor in book form began with *Of All Things!* in 1921 (the first of fifteen collections, three of them posthumous),* and he soon acquired a measure of fame but no large measure of money. The latter came eventually, through his acting. In a satirical review produced by the Vicious Circle of wits from the Algonquin Round Table—a production that included Jascha Heifetz, Alexander Woollcott, Marc Connelly, Heywood Broun, George S. Kaufman, Franklin P. Adams, and Donald Ogden Stewart—Benchley read his own composition, "The Treasurer's Report." This performance led to a $500-a-week job giving this piece at the Music Box Theater in 1923. Five years later he starred in the same number for the movies in what may have been the first all-talking picture ever made. This film short was the first of forty-six in which Benchley appeared, many of them, such as "The Sex Life of the Newt," based on his own essays or stories.

After 1938, Benchley gradually gave up writing for movie making, chiefly to earn more money. His last movie, "I'm a Civilian Here Myself," was made for the Navy in 1945. The title

---

* *Of All Things!* (1921); *Love Conquers All* (1922); *Pluck and Luck* (1925); *The Early Worm* (1927); *20,000 Leagues Under the Sea, or David Copperfield* (1928); *The Treasurer's Report* (1930); *No Poems* (1932); *From Bed to Worse* (1934); *My Ten Years in a Quandary* (1936); *After 1903—What?* (1938); *Inside Benchley* (1942); *Benchley Beside Himself* (1943); *Benchley—or Else!* (1947); *Chips Off the Old Benchley* (1949); *The Benchley Roundup* (1954). *Inside Benchley, Benchley—or Else!,* and *The Benchley Roundup* are largely made up of material from the earlier collections.

was doubtless suggested by that of Ogden Nash's *I'm a Stranger Here Myself.* In that same year, Benchley died of a cerebral hemorrhage.

BOWED BUT UNBROKEN

It is impossible to say just when the bemused householder and white-collar man became really prominent in American humor, but by 1910 Stephen Leacock, Simeon Strunsky, and Clarence Day, Jr. were writing pieces in which the disguise of each author was just that. As noted before, one of Benchley's direct models was Leacock, whose *Literary Lapses* appeared in that year. "Leacock [to quote Ralph L. Curry] found much of his fun in the little man beset by advertising, fads, convention, sex, science, cussedness, machinery—social and industrial—and many other impersonal tyrannies."[3] Benchley's favorite piece of humor was "My Financial Career," in *Literary Lapses,* where a bedeviled Little Man of the lower middle class is overawed and confused by a bank and its officials. Robert once stated, "I have enjoyed Leacock's work so much that I have written everything he ever wrote—anywhere from one to five years after him."[4] Leacock wrote of the Little Man in an urbane prose that owed much to the familiar essays of Addison and Lamb, to the English tradition of parody as found in *Punch* (one of whose columnists, A. A. Milne, was another favorite of Benchley), to nonsense humor as exemplified in the verse of Edward Lear and Lewis Carroll, and to the newspaper columnists on Leacock's own side of the Atlantic. In its liveliness, it resembled most perhaps the last-named kind of writing. Despite Benchley's statements of his indebtedness, he might conceivably have written much as he did had he never read Leacock, but his work included all of the elements that went into Leacock's humor. The nonsense element, expressed by such bits as the line from Leacock's *Nonsense Novels,* "Lord Ronald said nothing; he flung himself from the room, flung himself upon his horse and rode madly off in all directions," was to recur with special effectiveness in Benchley's writing. Through the probable influence of Leacock on Benchley, the urbane tradition in American humor, which had always shown a tendency to imitate British humor, received a fresh injection from a new, northerly direction.

In stressing the irrational side of Benchley, Thurber, and Perelman, Walter Blair calls them "Crazy Men" and says that "Benchley constantly assumes the role of 'Perfect Neurotic.' " [5] Blair cites *My Ten Years in a Quandary,* in which the main character "cannot leave a party at a decent time, cure hiccoughs, wear a white suit, smoke a cigarette, or read while eating . . ." A worrier over trifles, this man with his "persecution complex" and his fear of dementia praecox is "just a mess of frustrations and phobias." All of this is true, and one can add to Blair's examples indefinitely. In *Of All Things!,* the Little Man as a suburbanite is stalled by the furnace, stumped by auction bridge, and strapped by household expenses; as a family man he is badgered by children and relatives. His middle-class status augments his frustration: ". . . when I am confronted, in the flesh, by the 'close up' of a workingman with any vestige of authority, however small, I immediately lose my perspective—and also my poise." Out-of-doors, he is thwarted by "Old Step-Mother Nature" as much as was Mr. Dooley or the *persona* of Day in *After All:* when he tries to garden he will allow that nature is wonderful only if something he has planted grows—and that is unlikely.

In recounting the collapse of his efforts to learn to drive a car, this Little Man says, "Frankly I am not much of a hand at machinery of any sort . . . the pencil sharpener in our office is about as far as I, personally, have ever got in the line of operating a complicated piece of mechanism with any degree of success." In *No Poems,* he admits that even such simple articles as bedroom slippers conspire against him, as do also "the hundred and one little bits of wood and metal that go to make up the impedimenta of our daily life—the shoes and pins, the picture books and door keys, the bits of fluff and sheets of newspaper." Nature, technology, people—all give him a hard time.

But he is not really licked, though he says he is. Nor is he "crazy," in the sense of having fostered an image of himself and a picture of the world that are out of touch with reality. He has moments of aberration—as who does not? Benchley's narrator is the normal man, with the ordinary degree of neurosis slightly exaggerated. Except during these brief moments, this character is acutely conscious that his images of self and of the world have lost contact with realities, and the loss worries him. He is usually quite aware that there *are* realities other than his images, and at moments his illusions vanish and he sees truth with painful clarity. Between these moments, his frequent if vague awareness that a difference exists between his actual self and the self-image that he wishes were valid (but knows is not) produces a continual flow of comic irony.

In an ethical sense, he is never seriously aberrant. Benchley's Little Man has an integrity that can be strained but never quite broken; it gleams sullenly through his foggiest notions. In *The Neurotic Personality of Our Time,* Karen Horney says that one refuge of the intellectual sort of neurotic is a detachment in which he refuses to take anything seriously, including himself. The self-mockery of Benchley's fictive double is never carried to the point where he loses his wholesome awareness that man's environment was made for man, not he for it, and if things don't seem that way (here the reformer speaks)—well, things had better be changed. Miss Horney also states that the neurotic feels a compulsion to be liked. Benchley's double is less concerned with being liked than with preserving his integrity and his ethical vision.

Applied to nature this statement is certainly fatuous, and the Little Man looks littlest—he is most consistently rebuffed and humiliated—in his conflicts with the nonhuman environment. Benchley's friend and fellow-humorist Frank Sullivan once said (in referring to Robert himself rather than to the Benchley *persona*), that nature "had him stopped cold." [6] Benchley felt heckled by pigeons, and once he was attacked by terns on the beach at Nantucket. But his Little Man, though afraid of thunder, could at least take the stand that "Nature can go her way and I'll go mine." Thus, loosely speaking, Benchley is

"naturalistic" in the same sense as Stephen Crane, Theodore
Dreiser, and Ernest Hemingway. To these writers, man was all
but helpless in the grip of vast nonhuman forces and was lucky
if these forces seemed merely indifferent, as in Crane's "The
Open Boat," rather than malignant. But far from yielding to
nature more than he had to, man still must live as man. This un-
sentimental view of man's relation to nature is the source of the
irony in Benchley's numerous parodies of the "Hail, vernal equi-
nox!" school of nature writing.

In a sense, Benchley's view of man's relationship to nature was
more pessimistic than the Darwinian attitude that nature is a
ruthless struggle for the survival of the fittest. Such a view implies order and purpose in nature, however irrelevant to man's
desires, a view that Benchley did not hold. He is more like
Will Cuppy in distrusting both the "hearts-and-flowers" and the
"tooth-and-claw" approach. To both humorists, nature is pur-
poseless and chaotic as is much of man's "civilization."

Behind some of Benchley's parodies of nature writing lies an
attack on both the sentimental and the scientific, or at least the
Darwinian, approaches to nature. Examples of this attack may
be seen in the futility of "The Social Life of the Newt" and in
the remarks on eggs in *The Early Worm,* where the utter purpose-
lessness of the shape of the egg is pointed out:

> If you will look at these eggs, you will see that each one
> is *Almost* round, but not *Quite.* They are more of an "egg-
> shape." This may strike you as odd at first, until you learn
> that this is Nature's way of distinguishing eggs from large
> golf balls. You see, Mother Nature takes no chances. She
> used to, but she learned her lesson. And that is a lessson
> that all of you must learn as well.

It was not that Benchley actively disbelieved in evolution but
that he had not (like fellow-Yankee Robert Frost) himself worked
up "that metaphor" and was not much interested in it—except
as material for parody. His narrator cannot defeat nature but
can at least laugh at it even as he laughs at his own losing struggle
with natural phenomena.

THE LITTLE MAN AS LITERARY CRITIC

If Benchley's man can do little about nature he can occasionally make headway against certain man-made phenomena—for instance, letters. One of Benchley's more revealing pieces is "Mind's Eye Trouble," in *No Poems.* Here Benchley (wearing his mask) confesses with ostentatious humility that, "I seem to have been endowed at birth by a Bad, Bad Fairy with a paucity of visual imagination which amounts practically to a squint." This limitation causes him to picture the events in any book he reads as taking place in the home town of his youth. Victor Hugo may not have had Yankee-land in mind when he wrote *Les Miserables;* "However, regardless of what Hugo had in mind, *I* have Front Street, Worcester in mind when I read it." All scenes from classical Roman life are vivified for this reader only in the driveway of the House at May and Woodland Streets where lived the girl he courted, and the mob of Romans listening to Antony's famous speech "extended 'way over across the street to the front lawn of the Congregational Church parsonage." Similarly, the characters of Charles Dickens "all made their exits and their entrances by the door at the left of the stairway and delivered all their speeches in front of the fireplace in the 'sitting-room' of this house at No. 3 Shepard Street." The yard on one side is fixed in this Little Man's mind as the Solid South and as the place where "Werther wrestled with his sorrows." In "this stunted imagination of mine," the yard of his Aunt Mary Elizabeth is the West, "and the West had better accommodate itself to my whim." Scenes from the works of Byron, Samuel Richardson, Mark Twain, Katherine Mansfield, Frank Swinnerton, and Hugh Walpole are inevitably re-created in the playground of the Woodland Street School or its vicinity. The narrator even finds himself "sending Proust walking up and down Woodland Street with Albertine."

The "confession" of this well-read wise fool is the literary equivalent of Mr. Dooley's testing the validity of political ideas by showing how they would operate in Archey Road. Benchley

is implying that if certain overrated works of literature do not
retain their reality and power when their characters and events
are imagined within the frame of the normal, modern man's
everyday experience, it is these works that are at fault, not the
man. Uncritical readers may worship this stuff without putting
it to the test, but not Benchley's narrator.

According to Nathaniel Benchley, his father had burrowed
through Dr. Eliot's "Harvard Classics" and "concluded that it
hadn't been worth the effort." Robert's own comment was, "If
one adopts the Missourian attitude in reading the masters, and,
laying aside their reputation, puts the burden of proof on them,
many times they are not so impressive." The views of Robert are
similar to those reflected by his narrator in "Mind's Eye
Trouble"; Benchley's mask in that piece distorts his true self only
by exaggeration. The confession is no *mea culpa* but an affirmation of Benchley's faith in his own tastes as an educated but
not academic reader.

Benchley's attitude toward Shakespeare too is that of the
cultivated fellow who reads or goes to a play for pleasure and
not to worship the highbrowed god of scholarship. Benchley
scoffs at Shakespeare revivals and insists that on the stage Shakespeare brings out the worst in actors (he excepts certain specific
productions from this criticism, including most of the efforts of
Maurice Evans and Orson Welles). He is particularly severe with
Shakespeare's humor, condemning his low comedy as "horsy and
crass" and claiming that, "It is impossible for a good actor, as
we know good actors today, to handle a Shakespearean low
comedy part, for it demands mugging and tricks which no good
actor would permit himself to do." If alive today, the Bard
would write slapstick movie scripts for Mack Sennett. In "Shakespeare Explained," Benchley parodies the dissection of Shakespeare by pedants in editions overburdened with footnotes. The
way to enjoy Shakespeare, he suggests elsewhere, is to read
snatches from his plays now and then when you want to, and
stop reading when you want to. This attitude will at least be
one's own, not borrowed from some teacher.

Benchley spoke for a more literate type of man than did Ade, Dooley, or Lardner, but his point of view toward letters was scarcely less middlebrow, especially when he dealt with contemporary authors. Like Marquis and Lardner, he parodied many of them, although in Benchley's case parody did not necessarily imply a dislike of the writer thus treated. For instance, he satirized Sinclair Lewis' "flair for minutiae" but elsewhere praised "the remarkable accuracy with which he reports details in his 'Main Street.'" Other moderns whom he parodied included Robert Louis Stevenson, H. G. Wells, Mencken and Nathan, James Branch Cabell, and Marcel Proust. Benchley had no patience with flamboyant, arty, or grotesque styles. He said of William Faulkner, "A writer who doesn't make his book understandable to a moderately intelligent reader is not writing that way because he is consciously adapting a diffuse style, but because he simply doesn't know how to write." Not caring whether he was accused of lack of imagination or not, Benchley insisted on testing all literature, both classic and modern, by trying to fit it into his familiar frame of reference, and by setting it against the standards of his *persona*. In spite of the Little Man's absurdities, Benchley felt that this man was the only possible measure of things. The "great" writers did not "live" in the notes of a few scholars but must overcome a perfectly natural resistance to the new, archaic, or unfamiliar by a substantial body of practiced but nonprofessional readers-for-pleasure.

At various times, Benchley ran the theater department in three publications: the *Bookman, Life,* and the *New Yorker.* As a drama critic, he let others speak for show business or the intellectuals while he consciously tried to represent the man who goes to plays for pleasure (not necessarily amusement). Benchley's comments on Bernard Shaw's *The Apple Cart* and on some Chinese pantomimes amount to a theater-goer's credo. To the argument that we shouldn't be bored by traditions of theater not our own but should make allowances for them, Benchley replied, "Why *need* we be bored? Why should we have to make allowances for *anything* when we go for entertainment? Why is it incumbent on the audience which has paid its money for an evening in the theatre to adjust itself to Shaw or to Mei Lanfang? Other playwrights and other actors have to adjust themselves to their audiences if they want to hold their attention. . . . My suggestion would be that *nobody* be allowed to bore us." [7]

The limitations of this view were surely those of most audiences. One might argue that every tradition was new to its public once and that Benchley's attitude would stultify the attempts of any experimental playwright to reach an audience beyond the narrow circle of professional theater folk and arty bohemians. One might further protest that the sort of playgoer who takes the trouble to read drama reviews usually does not just pay his money for an evening at any play; he at least knows that G. B. Shaw and George M. Cohan purvey different kinds of fare, whatever he may think of either, and he is at liberty to neglect whichever kind he fears will bore him. However, in his practice as reviewer, Benchley was less strict than in his general pronouncements. He praised many specimens of every kind of play, from musicals by Cohan and comedies by Noel Coward to *Murder in the Cathedral* by T. S. Eliot, though his chief criterion was always whether the piece in question stimulated and held the interest of the audience. Through this criterion, Benchley as drama critic kept Benchley the moralist sternly in check, and when he praised the sociological dramas of the nineteen-thirties, including the "message" plays by Paul Green, Maxwell Anderson, Elmer Rice, and Clifford Odets, and the documentary offerings by the Federal Theater Project, he praised them as effective plays, not as trumpet-calls to reformers. To bad plays he was merciless, whether they were musical fluff, or documentaries about the plight of sharecroppers in the South or Jews under Hitler. He sympathized warmly with the liberal purposes of such documentaries, but they were not necessarily *theater*.

Besides demanding entertainment, Benchley often applied the frame-of-reference test as a dramatic standard. He did much to boost the reputation of Eugene O'Neill, but he criticized the exaggerated picture of misery and crabbedness in *Desire Under the Elms,* and parodied—though he frankly enjoyed—the melo-dramatic aspects of *Mourning Becomes Electra.* In reviewing *Marco Millions* for the *Bookman,* he criticized the author on the ground that

> during his poetic passages designed to set off the idealism
> and aesthetic superiority of the East over the fierce commer-
> cialism and blindness of the West there still runs the de-
> batable thesis that money and numbers and luxury are in
> themselves ignoble things and that, if a man prefers the
> sensuous charms of good food, a buxom wife and bags of
> gold to speculating on Truth and the Idea and consorting
> with a lyric and love-sick princess, he is in a way a bounder
> and fit only to be crushed on the wheel.[8]

Here the Little Man as Broadway playgoer was resisting values that did not meet the test of his experience. In view of Bench-ley's refusal to meet the artier arts halfway, it is not surprising that he cared almost as little for grand opera as did Ade and Lardner and followed their example by largely ignoring it except in parody.

HOW TO BE A SUBURBANITE AND A CITIZEN, THOUGH LITERATE

Benchley's graduation from Harvard had been delayed by difficulties with French and economics, but he was no less a Uni-versity Wit than Bangs in preferring his humor in correct English. Although he admired George Ade so much that when Ade died he went out for an evening of funereal merrymaking, Benchley did not sympathize with or encourage crackerbox writing in general. He called the dramatic version of Don Mar-quis' *The Old Soak* "one part Old Soak and nine parts Old Hokum," [9] and in "The Brow-Elevation in Humor" he pooh-poohed the humorous taste of Mark Twain and his times, when ". . . it was considered good form to spoof not only the classics but surplus learning of any kind," and when ". . . any one who wanted to qualify as a humorist had to be able to mispronounce any word of over three syllables." He denounced the "affectation" in "this homespun frame of mind," and concluded, "In F. P. A. we find a combination which makes it possible for us to admit our learning and still be held honorable men." The main character who emerged from dozens of Benchley sketches was neither the self-made entrepreneur or independent loafer of crackerbarrel humor, and he certainly was not "folksy" in his speech. He was a college-trained, white-collar employee who spoke and wrote informally but correctly, and commuted to an office in the city from a home in the suburbs where he fought the furnace, bumbled around the garden, failed to spend within his income, and coped unsuccessfully with children who were not little angels but more like little devils (see Uncle Edith's Christmas stories). Enough readers liked this picture to keep Benchley at one time "writing . . . three syndicated columns a week, doing the theater reviews for the *New Yorker,* appearing in a weekly radio show, and making shorts and full-length pictures in Hollywood . . ." [10] And, on the side, selling a piece now and then as a free-lance.

Benchley's fumbler resembles Mr. Dooley, Abe Martin, Will Rogers, and Gullible insofar as the author measures the world by the standards of this "crazy" man's common sense—which Benchley does often. Through the reactions of this philosopher in a white collar, Benchley can ridicule zoologists, botanists, physicians, psychoanalysts, economists, political commentators—in short, all "experts" who get too abstruse for the moderately intelligent and educated man to follow. Thus Benchley dons this mask of befuddlement in imagining the thoughts of a couple of primeval cells that have just emerged from the ooze. One asks, "How are you fixed for insurance?" The human narrator speaks good English and he evidently knows the latest speculations of evolutionary scientists, but his interpretation of how primeval cells behave is as naive as Mr. Dooley's rendition of the Dreyfus trial. From behind this façade of naïveté Benchley snipes at both biologists and insurance salesmen. The life sciences are hit again, along with their popularizers, when the narrator in another piece also personifies the primeval cell: "Shortly after the cell decides to go ahead with the thing, it gets lonely and divides itself up into three similar cells, just for company's sake and to have someone to talk to." In both sketches, the author is shamming naïveté in order to poke fun at biologists for their confident pronouncements on matters which he considers highly theoretical, and to show the irrelevance of their theories to the problems of everyday living. Both practices offend his common sense. In yet another sketch, the Little Man and the author merge in scoffing about a new astronomical device, the stroboscope:

> How, you may say, can we tell that a body 92,000,000 miles away jumps? And, if it does, what the hell difference does it make, anyway? Ninety-two million miles is ninety-two million miles, and we have got enough things within a radius of five miles to worry about without watching the sun jump.

After relating how the stroboscope purports to measure the motion of the sun, the narrator says ironically, "The next step is to find out some use to which the 'stroboscope' can be put." Readers in the nuclear age who have quailed at the results of certain "useless" theories and devices may find Benchley's dogma of common sense a bit shortsighted. Benchley at times joins Lardner in merging too thoroughly with his literary double.

In economics, Benchley reduces the problem of "How to Understand International Finance" to a matter of personal accounting. Speaking as wise fool and disregarding the fact that he had more than once followed Leacock in making his *alter ego* too hopelessly incompetent to keep the account books of his own household, Benchley says,

> Now there is a certain principle which has to be followed in all financial discussions involving sums over one hundred dollars. There is probably not more than one hundred dollars in actual cash in circulation today. That is, if you were to call in all the bills and silver and gold in the country at noon tomorrow and pile them up on the table, you

would find that you had just about one hundred dollars, with perhaps several Canadian pennies and a few peppermint life-savers. All the rest of the money you hear about doesn't exist. It is conversation money. When you hear of a transaction involving $50,000,000 it means that one firm wrote "50,000,000" on a piece of paper and gave it to another firm, and the other firm took it home and said, "Look, Momma, I got $50,000,000!" But when Momma asked for a dollar and a quarter out of it to pay the man who washed the windows, the answer probably was that the firm hadn't got more than seventy cents in cash.

This is the principle of finance. So long as you can pronounce any number above a thousand, you have got that much money.

In thus reducing current discussions of German reparations to a family scale, Benchley showed his distrust of large-scale credit and of high finance, a distrust shared by more than one crackerbox philosopher. Will Rogers said, "We will never have any prosperity that is free from speculation till we pass a law that every time a person sells something he has got to have it setting there in a bucket, or a bag, or a jug, or a cage, or a rat trap or something."

The Little Man also uses this reduction method in showing his distrust of most goings-on in politics. Early in his career (1915), Benchley compared the election campaign of a little citizen for a post on the local School Committee to the mouthings of bigger politicians about a "business administration." Much later, when the Hoover Dam was on paper, Benchley's double cut the job down to a domestic scale—go ahead and build it, fellow, and "you will find the sugar and coffee on the top shelf in the kitchen closet." Thus the author implied that the proposal to spend $100,000,000 was being made far too casually. During the Smith-Hoover campaign of 1928, some of the disillusionment of the times burst forth from Benchley with surprising acidity. He stood up as the *bonum vir,* the good plain man of Horace, Juvenal, Pope, Swift—and H. L. Mencken—forced by the deplorable state of public affairs to raise his voice against the *canaille* in and out of office:

> In respect of the three leading issues of the campaign, Prohibition, Farm Relief and Water Power, it was found that the average voter likes Prohibition best because he knows what the word means. He doesn't *dis*like Farm Relief and Water Power, mind you, but he gets them mixed up with the Gold Standard and Nullification, which aren't issues at all in this election. All four are more or less grouped in his mind under the general head of "The Tariff," which makes it easier to remember.
>
> But he *knows* Prohibition means that, for every drink he buys, a certain percentage of the price must be paid to the Government for protection. And he likes the idea of this, for your American is a docile soul and craves paternalism; and the thought that a benevolent government is watching over him and protecting him is worth the added seventy-five cents.

Mencken might have written more stridently and Lardner might have used more slang, but neither could have adopted the role of the thinking citizen more completely in order to pour scorn on the booboisie.

In the nineteen-thirties, Benchley's attitude toward government activity became more flexible, but his use of reduction gear when pretentiousness or folly in public affairs was involved remained frequent, and he always retained a distrust of Big Government and Big Business. After the depression hit, Benchley satirized recovery proposals that seemed to encourage spending instead of the thrift of crackerbox times: "Every theory of economic good is based on *my* wearing out shoes, on *my* looking in store windows, on *my* spending money. . . . In the Perfect State, Benchley pays." Sumner had said of the Forgotten Man, "He always pays, yes, above all, he pays," [11] and Benchley here becomes the Forgotten-Man-as-consumer. When Benchley's narrator speaks out on social and political matters, the crackerbox sage and the rational *bonum vir* often merge with the new Little Man.

THE WISE FOOL AS SANE NEUROTIC

The crackerbox philosopher and the solid citizen were usually certain of their identities as persons, and one important difference between them and the Little Man is that the latter is often not certain of his. Instead, he is in quest of self, or of a self-image, all his own, in the validity of which he can believe. He is thus related to such diverse heroes of modern fiction and drama as Joe Williams, Jay Gatsby, Martin Arrowsmith, Eugene Gant, and Oran Mannon. The idea that the modern environment invades and tends to erode or to break up one's personality juts out in Benchley's humor whenever he satirizes psychologists and psychoanalysts. For these he gave his knife an extra whet. He generally depicts a narrator so confused by the theories of the analysts that he must struggle to retain his identity, let alone his common sense. When the "Subconscious" has been brought to this man's attention, he worries about how ". . . my Subconscious is getting to be a better man than I am." For one thing, he doesn't know whether he or his subconscious is on the job. If he is reading something and dozes off, his subconscious may take over, and "The worst of it is that my Subconscious's version makes just enough sense for me to believe that I have actually read it, and makes me liable to assert the next day that I saw in 'Time' where Ambassador Bullitt had blown up the Kremlin." He worries too about what the analysts might think about his inability to "toddle along" home when it is time to leave a party:

> The obvious explanation to an analyst would be that I have an aversion to going *home,* because I have a sister fixation or am subconsciously in love with my parrot and am seeking an escape.
> This, as I am so fond of saying to analysts, is not true. I would much rather be at home than at most parties. In fact, I don't go to many parties, and for that very reason.

Maybe it is true that his inability to leave a party "is a sign of a general break-up" in which the next step is "that I won't be able to find myself at all." But meanwhile he has poked some very

sane fun at psychoanalysts and at people who wear out their
host's welcome; moreover, in his fretting about the subconscious
he has ridiculed the phobias of William C. Bullitt and other ex-
tremists regarding the U.S.S.R. Nor do the Little Man's alleged
persecution complex and fear of dementia praecox prevent him
from making digs elsewhere at the mental diagnosticians. "We
didn't know about 'inhibitions' in my day. They came in with
horn-rimmed glasses and Freud." He points out too that anyone
might be considered insane according to the symptoms of
dementia praecox as given in a certain psychiatric monograph.
The fact is that this Perfect Neurotic is a variety of wise fool; he
speaks wisdom despite symptoms of being not "right" in the head.
He is not so much losing his identity as resisting deprivation of
it by a mad world, and Benchley makes this man's struggle an
instrument for satirizing the madnesses that are tending to de-
prive him of that identity. These madnesses include not only
psychoanalysis but modern gadgetry, fads in sport, art and advertising, and sentimentalization of the home, children, and
nature. Unlike the characters of Lardner and Thurber, those of
Benchley are partially successful in acquiring and recapturing
valid self-images—though their grip on themselves is always precarious—and Benchley's humor is consequently less grim and less
poignant than that of his two contemporaries.

THE LITTLE MAN AS LIBERAL

In *A Preface to Morals* (1929), Walter Lippmann looked at
the demoralized state of American values, and quoting Aristoph-
anes observed that "Whirl is king." Benchley, as noted a few
pages back, could heap scorn upon the mob with the zeal if not
the shrillness of a Mencken. More clearly than that iconoclast,
Benchley thereby implied an ideal if not an elite to carry the
banner of that ideal. In 1924, a year of general disillusion in
America, Benchley wrote,

> He [Paul Revere] saw a hundred and ten million people,
> the men in derbies, the women in felt hats with little bows

on the top. He saw them pushing one another in and out of trolley-cars on their way to and from work, adding up figures incorrectly all morning and subtracting them incorrectly all afternoon, with time out at 12:30 for frosted chocolates and pimento cheese sandwiches. He saw fifty million of them trying to prevent the other sixty million from doing what they wanted to do, and the sixty million trying to prevent the fifty million from doing what *they* wanted to do. He saw them all paying taxes to a few hundred of their number for running the government very badly. He saw ten million thin children working and ten thousand fat children playing in the warm sands. And now and again he saw five million youths, cheered on by a hundred million elders with fallen arches, marching out to give their arms and legs and lives for Something to Be Determined Later. And over all he saw the Stars and Stripes fluttering in the artificial breeze of an electric fan operated behind the scenes.

So tugging at the reins he yelled, "Whoa, Bess. We're going back to the stable."

Similar accusations of the mass appear elsewhere: Benchley anticipates Thurber's "Interview With a Lemming" when he reports the comment of a migrating moth that New York City is "nothing but a settlement of human beings, who, on hot days, sometimes appear in large numbers and beat themselves blindly against whatever happens to be in their way." His narrator also claims that *Alice in Wonderland* fits the present "because the present-day situations are sheer nonsense in themselves." It is not strange that the Little Man often seems out of step. Usually it is the "army" that's out of step but doesn't know it. When the Little Man does go wrong he usually suspects that he's wrong, and the suspicion bothers him. Even when (unlike the solid citizen) he cannot master himself and do what is right and rational, he has not lost sight of the ideals of rightness and reason.

In his quieter way Benchley could equal Mencken in the art of satirical invective, but his denunciations differed from Mencken's in that his zeal was accompanied by a genuine desire to right what was wrong. In the long diatribe just quoted, the com-

ment about the thin children and the fat ones implies an urge
to better the situation—Benchley pinpoints this social inequality
as a moral outrage; Mencken rarely mentioned such inequalities
without stressing that they were but the working out in human
affairs of invariable natural law. Benchley was not skeptical of
the moral absolutes of reason, justice, and democracy so much as
he was disappointed in the failure of the American people, himself included, to live up to these ideals. His son wrote that
Robert "brooded over the fact that he was making no substantial
contribution to Progress. He didn't care what kind of Progress it
was—whether it was social or literary or spiritual—he just wanted
to feel that he had done something to make things a little
better." [12] His urge to right wrongs appeared many times in
personal acts; twice he resigned jobs he badly needed because
of injustices done to friends. With the help of such biographical
evidence, one can see the reformer's motivation behind many of
Benchley's comments on public affairs—comments which are more
frequent than is generally supposed. The chastising flame of
"Guy Fawkes" leaped often in the "Wayward Press" pieces, and
elsewhere Benchley once wrote that ". . . instead of taking
over a protectorate of Armenia we might better take over a protectorate of the State of Georgia, which yearly leads the proud
list of lynchers." He poured alum on the smugness and obsession
with success of *The Americanization of Edward Bok,* and
attacked the banning of Cabell's *Jurgen,* a censorship which had
come about through action by the Society for the Suppression of
Vice. In "The Tariff Unmasked" and in his "short histories" of
American politics he yielded nothing to the conservative
Mencken and the politically indifferent Lardner in his contempt
for the ignorance and apathy of the common man.

Mencken too denounced the venality of the press and (despite
his belief in Negro inferiority) the extreme racial chauvinism of
the South; he too defended *Jurgen* against the prudes, but some
of his elaborate disclaimers of reformist aims have been cited
earlier. Lardner, be it recalled, wrote *The Story of a Wonder
Man* in part to satirize Bok's autobiography. But Benchley's

social satire was not merely that of the aloof observer or disillusioned ironist. He referred to himself as a "confused liberal" and usually registered as a Republican but voted Democratic; he belonged to several guilds and unions, and worked actively with Dorothy Parker, Muriel Draper, and others on behalf of Loyalist refugees from the Spanish Civil War. He definitely wanted to help change things for the better.

Robert E. Sherwood stressed Benchley's inconsistencies, referring to his various roles as a "penurious, homebound commuter, who didn't appear to have a worry or concern in the world beyond the precarious state of his bank balance," as a "laboriously irresponsible flâneur," and "as a violent crusader for civil rights, a marcher in the picket lines for Sacco and Vanzetti, a passionate pacifist." But under the motley, Sherwood says, "he always remained indelibly the same person, Benchley." [13] And in his writing, the same *persona*, despite many variations, consistently portrays the haphazard but stout resistance of the normal man (with a college education) to the chaos of his sick society, and his acceptance of the challenge offered by that sickness.

15

Dorothy Parker's
Idle Men and Women

Of the humorists whose personal conduct seasons any history of the nineteen-twenties, Dorothy Parker stands out. It is said that, just to get some company, she tacked a sign reading "Men" on her office door, and that once when Harold Ross wondered why she hadn't come into the *New Yorker* office to write a certain

piece, she told him that "Somebody was using the pencil." Upon
hearing that Coolidge was dead, she asked, "How can they tell?"
And there was the time she leaped to her feet in an open cab
and shrieked to passers-by, "Help! Help! This man is abducting
me!" "This man" was Robert Benchley, and he whipped off his
scarf and proceeded to gag her with it.[1] Her quips and capers
were recounted at the Algonquin and wherever else two or
more were gathered together in the name of humor, but some of
her best forays and retorts have doubtless been lost to posterity.

She was born Dorothy Rothschild, but after her divorce from
Edwin Pond Parker, she retained his surname. From 1916 to
1920 she wrote verse, humor, and drama reviews for *Vanity Fair*,
which functioned in those years as an incubator of talent for the
New Yorker. In January, 1920, Miss Parker wrote of Billie
Burke's performance in *Caesar's Wife*, by Somerset Maugham:
"She is at her best in her more serious moments; in her desire
to convey the girlishness of the character, she plays her lighter
scenes rather as if she were giving an impersonation of Eva
Tanguay." [2] For this comment and for others less bland, Miss
Burke's husband, Florenz Ziegfeld, producer David Belasco,
and other powers of the theater demanded of Condé Nast and
Frank Crowninshield, the editor and publisher respectively of
Vanity Fair, that Miss Parker be fired. She was, and her colleagues, Benchley and Robert E. Sherwood, resigned in protest. She then free-lanced and worked at a variety of jobs,
contributing some verse and a little prose to the *New Yorker*
after that magazine was founded in 1925. In October, 1927,
she began a book-review column for the *New Yorker* which
she signed "Constant Reader." She did not like book reviewing
—said it interfered with her reading[3]—and soon gave it up as a
regular job.

What doubtless attracted readers of *Enough Rope* (1926), *Sunset Gun* (1928), and *Death and Taxes* (1931)[4] were the light, sar-
donic, often hedonistic stanzas in which she played the role of
romantic adventuress, a role in which she was often star-crossed

but remained steadfastly in love with ideal love after the fashion
of the young Edna St. Vincent Millay.[5] However, Miss Parker
tempered her sentimentality with wit and irony. Frequently
she started a train of sentimentality and then demolished it
with an ironic turn:

> Always I knew it would come like this
>   (Pattering rain, and the grasses springing),
> Sweeter to you is a new love's kiss
>   (Flickering sunshine, and young birds singing).
> Gone are the raptures that once we knew,
>   Now you are finding a new joy greater—
> Well, I'll be doing the same thing, too,
>   Sooner or later.

Such cocktails led Alexander Woollcott to call her a combination of "Little Nell and Lady Macbeth."

HUMORIST AND CRUSADER

In the early twenties, a growing social conscience began to
gnaw at Miss Parker's hedonism. Before Clarence Day, Jr.,
turned mainly to reminiscences of his family, he, Donald Ogden
Stewart, Heywood Broun, and Miss Parker were the most militant political and social liberals among the humorists, both in
person and in writing, and Miss Parker has credited Stewart with
a major influence in the growth of her passion for social justice.[6]
Among other activities, she took part in a demonstration in favor
of Sacco and Vanzetti and was arrested. After the Spanish Civil
War began in 1936, she headed the Joint Anti-Fascist Refugee
Committee to raise funds for the Spanish republicans, and wrote
temporarily for the Marxist *New Masses*. She went to Hollywood to write scenarios and became politically active in the
movie colony. After the victory of fascism in Spain and the on-
set of World War II, she declared that, "There is nothing funny
in the world any more," [7] but her talent for impromptu oral
wit and humor, though glinting less frequently than during the
lunch hours at the Algonquin, reportedly cuts as sharply as
ever, and satire of a bitter variety remains the basic element in
her fiction.

Her short story "Big Blonde" won the O. Henry prize for 1929, and during the next fifteen years she wrote the majority of the stories on which her reputation as a prose writer rests. She has never been prolific, and since the middle nineteen-forties her output in fiction has been small. War work, politics, screenwriting, and personal problems largely account for this, but the legitimate theater too has taken up part of her time. In 1924, she collaborated with Elmer Rice on a play, "Soft Music," which had a short run in 1929 as *Close Harmony*. She substituted for Benchley as drama critic for the *New Yorker* in 1931, and later tried playwriting again, this time in partnership with Ross Evans. The result was "The Coast of Illyria" (1949), which was tried in Dallas, Texas, but never reached Broadway or print. She and Arnaud D'Usseau (co-author with James Gow of the antifascist play *Tomorrow the World*) wrote *Ladies of the Corridor* (1953), and the two scored a fair success on Broadway with this play about lonely middle-aged ladies in a resident hotel.

SMUG, PATHETIC, USELESS WOMEN

In her early years, Miss Parker often appeared as an "orthodox" humorist—that is, a sensible person who chose the middle way and avoided extremes, as in her remarks on the actors' and stagehands' strike of 1919 which had closed all theaters in New York and Chicago:

> The managers, who, but a few brief weeks ago, were vowing that sooner would they run elevators, have enthusiastically recognized the Equity Association, thus generously conceding that actors are people; the stagehands, who, it seems but yesterday, were only waiting to see the whites of the Shuberts' eyes before walking out of every theatre in America, are now humming happily about their work.[8]

Even after the development of her social conscience, Miss Parker could not be called a "proletarian" writer in the doctrinaire sense of Jack Conroy, Albert Maltz, Albert Halper, Mary Heaton Vorse, and Grace Lumpkin. Miss Parker was no sectarian when literature was concerned. She called Upton Sinclair "one of the American great," but she disagreed with his criticisms of American authors for not always writing of "sweatshops and child-labor, of mill-slaves and strikes and wages," [9] and in her own stories her acidity bit most often into the gilt and brass of a certain type of American personality, the self-absorbed female snob. This happened to be a type she knew best in its middle-class manifestations. Ring Lardner—whom she admired as second only to Hemingway among contemporary American writers[10]—dissected the "idle common man," the middle-class male who, having climbed part way up the economic ladder, devotes his increased leisure time to the pursuit and enjoyment of status symbols that will ease the inadequacy he dimly feels because his real self does not match his inflated self-image. Miss Parker invites comparison with Lardner in her focus on the female companion of Lardner's idle middle-class man, also in her frequent use of the diary form, the monologue, and trivial dialogue. Sometimes her idle, middle-class females are smug and aggressive; sometimes they are pathetic like Lardner's "victims"; sometimes both. Occasionally they are more amusing than anything else.

The "woman with the pink velvet poppies" in "Arrangement in Black and White," and Mrs. Ewing in "Clothe the Naked," both of whom showily patronize Negroes, are examples of the aggressive sort. So are the doll-like Mrs. Lanier of "The Custard Heart"; the aristocratic Mrs. Matson of "Little Curtis"; and the "Lady With a Lamp" who drives a nervous patient into hysteria by saying exactly the wrong things about the girl's having been jilted by her lover. The monologue of this woman especially reminds one of Lardner's egocentric males:

> Well—if that's the way you want to be to me, that's the way you want to be. I won't say anything more about it. Only I do think you might have let me know that you had—well, that you were so *tired,* if that's what you want me to say. Why, I'd never have known a word about it if I hadn't run bang into Alice Patterson and she told me she'd called you up and that maid of yours said you had been sick in bed

for ten days. Of course, I'd thought it rather funny I hadn't
heard from you, but you know how you are—you simply let
people go, and weeks can go by like, well, like *weeks*, and
never a sign from you. Why, I could have been dead over
and over again, for all you'd know. Twenty times over. Now,
I'm not going to scold you when you're sick, but frankly
and honestly, Mona, I said to myself this time, "Well, she'll
have a good wait before I call her up. I've given in often
enough, goodness knows. Now she can just call me first."
Frankly and honestly, that's what I said!

This person belongs with the girl who broke up the marriage of
"Cousin Larry," and with the "New York lady" who, in her
diary, records her pursuit of pleasure "During Days of Horror,
Despair, and World Change." (In form, the latter story resembles
Anita Loos's *Gentlemen Prefer Blondes,* but the scorn with which
Miss Parker infused her portrait is largely absent from Miss
Loos's lighthearted sketches of 1926.) Equally smug and self-
absorbed are the couple who make fun of the homely spinster
tending their children in "Horsie," and the wealthy Mrs. Martindale of "Song of the Shirt 1941," whose attempts at sewing hospital bandages are so completely a pose of *noblesse oblige* that
she ignores the needs of a seamstress with a crippled child, to
whom she could just as well have given the work for pay.

Women who are mainly pathetic include Mona in "Lady
With a Lamp," little Mrs. Murdock in "Glory in the Daytime,"
the jilted girl who sits hopefully by the telephone in "A Telephone Call," the girl in a similar plight who finally does call
her boy-friend—unfortunately—in "New York to Detroit," and
Hazel Morse, the "Big Blonde" who has neither the will nor
the self-consciousness even to reflect on her difficulties with men,
much less to solve them.

Pathos and folly, or at least inadequacy, are mixed in varying
ratios in several other women, among them the girl in "Senti-
ment" who wallows in self-pity as she relives certain tender
moments while riding in a cab down "Sixty-Third" street.
The language of her reverie is a parody of Elinor Glyn and
other sentimental novelists, and perhaps also a mocking of the

sentimentality which Miss Parker could often have found in her own work without looking very far:

> And I waiting for him in the dusk, thinking he would never come; and yet the waiting was lovely, too. And then when I opened the door to him—Oh, no, no, no! Oh, no one could bear this. No one, no one.
> Ah, why, why, why must I be driven through here? What torture could there be so terrible as this? It will be better if I uncover my eyes and look. I will see our tree and our house again, and then my heart will burst and I will be dead. I will look, I will look.

Her sentimentality has heretofore kept her from looking, but when she does uncover her eyes, she finds that the street is Sixty-Fifth, not Sixty-Third. Pathetic in their inadequacy are the Weldons of "Too Bad," whose marriage has gone on the rocks from sheer boredom even as the marriage of the Taylors in Lardner's "Anniversary" was going; pathetic in their self-absorption are the wife in "The Banquet of Crow" [11] who is encouraged by a quack lay-analyst to believe that it is merely change of life that causes her husband to walk out on her after eleven years of stale marriage, and the wife of the World War II pilot in "The Lovely Leave" whose possessiveness ruins what few hours she and her husband can have together. In all of these cases, the "victims" are largely self-victimized.

Amusement overbalances pathos in "The Sexes," where a pair of sweethearts quarrel and make up—but show promise of quarreling again at the drop of a hatpin. Amusement is also the dominant effect of "The Standard of Living," in which two office girls pretend they have a million dollars to spend instead of their tiny salaries, and of "Just a Little One," in which a flapper in a speakeasy insists on only one drink at first but gradually gets tanked and begs her date to let them "go out and get a horsie, Freddie—just a little one, darling, just a little one." There is much humor and little pathos in "Here We Are," a scene in which a newly wedded couple unknowingly foreshadow their married life by quarreling suddenly over trifles and making up just as fast (the possibility of tears in the future is hinted at, of course). There is even less pathos in "The Waltz," in which a girl keeps on dancing with a tangle-footed lout while inwardly abusing him and wondering ". . . why I didn't tell him I was tired," or ". . . why I didn't suggest going back to the table." Equally light is "The Little Hours," in which a female night-owl for once goes to bed at ten o'clock. The result—creeping insomnia, but like the girl in "The Waltz," she is not so miserable that she can't mock at herself:

> People pick up those scholarly little essays that start off "Was it not that lovable old cynic, La Rochefoucauld, who said . . ." and then they go around claiming to know the master backwards. Pack of illiterates, that's all they are. . . . I'll stick to La Fontaine. Only I'd be better company if I could quit thinking that La Fontaine married Alfred Lunt.

The darker vein is never entirely absent however, even in "The Waltz" and "The Little Hours," where the two main characters are self-victimized by their own giddiness and lack of perspective. "A humorist, I think, is just balancing on the edge of the dumps," [12] Miss Parker said in 1936. Even her most playful pieces hint at this view.

Occasionally Miss Parker shifts her spotlight to a Little Man somewhat like Benchley's or Thurber's. Once in a long while, she portrays this man as morally sound and mentally equipped with a share of common sense, though ridiculous and/or pathetic in other ways. In the play *Close Harmony*, Ed Graham is described thus: "He is about forty, a little shabby, a little nearsighted—one of ten million. His manner is apologetic—he is scared of the scolding that awaits him." His shrewish wife and sister almost goad him into running off with the mismated wife of a neighbor, but at the moment of decision Ed backs down. However, he shows new force in resisting his wife's demands and in sending the sister packing. Dullness, domesticity, and good-heartedness are incarnate in Ed; indeed, he has too much "heart," and the playwrights do not avoid mawkishness.

More often Miss Parker's males are nondescripts and function chiefly as the victims or exploiters of her females, than whom, as a group, they are no more sympathetic. The fellow who is bewildered at being actually married (in "Here We Are") is comparatively amusing; somewhat less so is the man who cuts embarrassing capers when he gets oiled ("You Were Perfectly Fine"). The colorless fellows who victimize the "Big Blonde," and the passive gigolo in "Dusk Before Fireworks" are fair samples of Miss Parker's more "aggressive" men. An unusually weak and selfish seducer is "Mr. Durant," an "immovably married man of forty-nine" who, despite his insipidity, manages to have his way with a secretary in the office.

THE MIDDLE CLASS

In the concern for status of many of her characters, the author shows an interest in class conflict as an influence on character and action. "Mr. Durant was assistant manager of the rubber company's credit department; his wife was wont to refer to him as one of the officers of the company" (the specification of the company's product is a nice touch, considering the sexual activities of Mr. D.). His middle-class outlook is closely related to his predatory amours: when he decides that Rose should have an abortion, his envy and misunderstanding of the upper class aid him in rationalizing that she ought not to mind—"New York society women, he understood, thought virtually nothing of it." When the operation is over, he says to himself, "Well, that's that," because this expression has "something stylish about it; it was the sort of thing you would expect to hear used by men who wore spats and swung canes without self-consciousness." Thus he tries to play the role of a type socially "above" him; on the other hand, he makes use of his small prestige as a low-ranking executive in the company hierarchy to seduce Rose, who, as a secretary, looked up to him.

Miss Parker's women too are often preoccupied with status.

This is true not only of such specimens of the leisure class as Mrs. Lanier of "The Custard Heart," Mrs. Martindale of "Song of the Shirt 1941," and Mrs. Whittaker of "The Wonderful Old Gentleman," but of the white-collar girls in "Standard of Living." When the loafers whistle at Annabel and Midge, these office girls hold their heads high "and set their feet with exquisite precision, as if they stepped over the necks of peasants." The nub of the story consists in their discovery of how much the maintenance of upper-class prestige really costs—they knew a double rope of pearls could cost as much as a thousand dollars, but the actual price—a quarter of a million—takes their breath away.

Even where class-consciousness is not explicitly a topic, it runs just under the surface. When the boy-friend in "The Sexes" refers to the girl as "snotty," she says, "I'm really not in the habit of hearing language like that," and he has to apologize. The girl in "The Waltz" is dancing with a free-spender who is ready to give the orchestra twenty dollars to keep on playing. Surely this lavishness has something to do with her assurance that "I'd simply adore to go on waltzing."

In "Clothe the Naked," class conflict and the poverty that underlies it are shown as interrelated with white condescension to Negroes. Class-consciousness is also important in "Little Curtis," where Mrs. Matson's pretensions to upper-rung status recall George Ade's idle matrons and the wives of Lardner's Gullible and of the narrator in *The Big Town*.[13] Mrs. Matson is proud that ". . . she had been Miss Laura Whitmore, of the Drop Forge and Tool Works Whitmores," and she refrains from wearing new clothes "for every day," although she can well afford it, because ". . . there was an unpleasant suggestion of extravagance and riotous living in the practice. The working classes, who, as Mrs. Matson often explained to her friends, went and bought themselves electric ice-boxes and radios the minute they got a little money, did such things." The middle-class ethic of Ben Franklin thus drives her into conspicuous thrift—conspicuous consumption in reverse.

Her stinginess is also associated with frigidity; the Matsons have no children and it is suggested that they have little taste for "carnal intimacy." Moreover, they are obsessed with the notion that predatory relatives are after their money, and partly to foil these, they adopt a little boy. Mrs. Matson scolds him for playing with "a furnaceman's child" and in other ways tries to bring him up according to her notions of propriety, but he shows his hopelessly asocial boyishness by laughing when one of his foster-mother's tea guests, who is a little deaf, drops her speaking-tube.

Summarizing a few of Miss Parker's stories does not fully illustrate how she can satirize the language of the idle, middle-class female. The aimlessness and vacuity of polite conversation among such climbers is re-created in this chitchat of Mrs. Matson's friends:

> Mrs. Kerley and Mrs. Swan vied with each other in paying compliments to the day.
> "So clear," said Mrs. Kerley.
> "Not a cloud in the sky," augmented Mrs. Swan. "Not a one."
> "The air was just lovely this morning," reported Mrs. Kerley. "I said to myself, 'Well, this is a beautiful day if there ever *was* one.'"
> "There's something so balmy about it," said Mrs. Swan.
> Mrs. Cook spoke suddenly and overloudly, in the untrustworthy voice of the deaf.
> "Phew, this is a scorcher!" she said. "Something terrible out."
> The conversation went immediately to literature. It developed that Mrs. Kerley had been reading a lovely book. Its name and that of its author escaped her at the moment, but her enjoyment of it was so keen that she had lingered over it till 'way past ten o-clock the night before.

Miss Parker does for these idle women what Don Marquis had done for their daughters in *Hermione* and what Lardner did for their husbands and sons. One may compare the conversation at Mrs. Matson's with that of two baseball fans in one of Ring's early columns:

"Well, that was a great game, wasn't it?"

"It sure was."

"I don't see many games, but I'd like to."

"I'd see more if I had the time."

"That's the trouble with me. I don't have the time."

"Neither do I. I haven't got time to get out to many games."

"Neither have I."

"I do like a good ball game, though."

"So do I. I always have."

"I have, too. I've always been a great lover of the game. It's a clean sport. I used to play it myself, years ago."

"I never played much, but I've always followed it pretty close."

"Yes sir, I used to play, but it was a good many years ago."

"Is that so?"

"Yes, but it was years ago. I wasn't a professional or anything like that. Just played for the fun of it."

"I'd rather see a game than play."

"Oh, I don't know. It's a great exerciser. I remember I used to—."[14]

Lardner's satire was motivated by no strong urge for social reform, whereas Miss Parker's indignation and guilt feelings led her into social crusades and into praise for the fighting peasants of loyalist Spain (in "Soldiers of the Republic"),[15] whom she depicted with an emphasis on simplicity, courtesy, and self-lessness that seldom appears in her profiles of idle Americans. Yet, in subject matter and in technique, the fiction of Lardner and Miss Parker shows enough mutual resemblance to raise the question of the relationship between satire and social reform— a part of the larger question of how humor and satire are related to values in general and what values, if any, are peculiarly conducive to humor. A close study of these knotty questions forms no part of this writer's task, which is merely to set forth those values as he finds them in the work of certain American humorists within a limited time span. In a sense, this book is intended to provide some of the raw material for anyone wishing to undertake such a study. Whoever he is, he will have his work cut out for him.[16]

"Well, Who Made the Magic Go Out of Our Marriage—
You or Me?"

Home

*Sometimes Thurber's male is the aggressor but more often he is the
victim in the marriage relationship.*

Both drawings are from *The Thurber Carnival*, Harper (New York and London, 1945), p. 348. Reprinted by permission of Harper and Row, (New York
and Evanston).

16

James Thurber's
Little Man and Liberal Citizen

"James [Grover] Thurber was born," wrote the humorist, "on a night of wild portent and high wind in the year 1894, at 147 Parsons Avenue, Columbus, Ohio." In *My Life and Hard Times* he portrayed his family as a collection of psychotics, but it must be understood that this book is humor, not autobiography. In

"Lavender With a Difference," Thurber depicted his parents
again, this time showing his father as a businessman with political interests and his mother as an affectionate, witty woman with
a flair for telling yarns and playing practical jokes. Referring
to his mother's sense of humor, Thurber once stated that
without her he never would have been able to write what he
had managed to write.[1] Thus he offered one more proof
of the family affection which was a part of Thurber the man
and tended to mitigate the bitterness that often seemed to dominate Thurber the humorist.

FROM OHIO TO NEW YORK

Thurber attended Ohio State University off and on until
1919. Interruptions included one year out "just to read" and
another to work as a code clerk in Washington and Paris during World War I (his weak eyes eliminated him as a possible
member of the Armed Forces.) Having failed physical education and several other subjects, he took no degree. He worked
on the Columbus *Dispatch* (1920–1924), the Paris edition of the
Chicago *Tribune* (1925–1926) and the New York *Evening Post*
(1926–1927). During this period of knocking about, he got
some pieces into the *Detroit Athletic Club News, Harper's* "The
Lion's Mouth" department, *Sunset* magazine, the Sunday New
York *World,* and the Sunday New York *Tribune,* and sold his
first short story to the Kansas City *Star* Sunday magazine (1923).
Reprinted in *Thurber's Dogs* (1955) "Josephine Has Her Day"
includes two themes that were to figure importantly in Thurber's
later writing—dogs with "character" and mild men who can become aggressive if provoked—but it also shows that in literary
style Thurber was still mainly a good newswriter, and not yet
the artist in prose that he became after he had worked for a while
with Harold Ross and with one of Ross's assistants, E. B. White.
    Thurber felt White had an influence second to none in shap-
ing his style. White went to work for the *New Yorker* in 1926
and was soon writing the "Talk of the Town" department, the
most permanent feature of the magazine, and the most highly

stylized. After his return from France, Thurber wrote and tried unsuccessfully to peddle a book-length manuscript entitled "Why We Behave Like Microbe Hunters." This work was a parody of two popularizations of science, George Dorsey's *Why We Behave Like Human Beings* and Paul de Kruif's *Microbe Hunters*. A piece rejected by the *New Yorker* was accepted by Franklin P. Adams and constituted an entire column of F. P. A.'s "The Conning Tower" in the *World*; shortly thereafter, two poems and a prose piece were accepted by the *New Yorker*, and in February, 1927, Thurber finally met White, who, five minutes later, introduced him to Ross. Ross tried Thurber as managing editor, but after six months Thurber got out of that job and, in his own words, "was safe in the 'Talk of the Town' department,"[2] to which he soon gave a pattern and tone indistinguishable from that of White.

Any discussion of Thurber as a humorist needs comment on his drawings. Thurber informed Alistair Cooke that he had begun both writing and drawing when he was seven. At Ohio State University, Thurber became editor-in-chief of the campus magazine (coincidentally named the *Sun-Dial*), and a wartime scarcity of artists caused him also to take over most of its art chores. He had not yet actively sought publication of his drawings when E. B. White began submitting them—on his own initiative but of course under Thurber's name—to the Tuesday afternoon "art meetings" of the *New Yorker* staff. In 1929, the two friends collaborated on the text of *Is Sex Necessary?*, the first book of prose for both writers. At White's urging, Thurber did thirty or forty drawings in one evening for this volume. The editors at *Harper's* thought at first that these were rough sketches of drawings yet to be submitted, but White, who could be aggressive on behalf of someone else, soon convinced them that these were the actual drawings to go in the book.[3] Thurber's production of scrawly cartoons that looked as simple as they often were complex ceased only in the late nineteen-fifties, when his one eye failed to the point of total blindness.

SEX AND THE THURBER MALE

Thurber has acknowledged the influence on his humor of both Robert Benchley and Clarence Day, Jr., as well as of White. All four writers frequently wear the mask of a bewildered, more or less meek Little Man of the white-collar class. In Thurber's case, the Little Man is bothered most of all by Sex, with its marital concomitant, but also by all disciplines whose names begin with "psych"; by mechanical devices; by the upper-middle-class ceremonials of suburbia; by the bureaucratic organization of modern society, and by the deterioration of communications between man and man and between man and woman.

Certain glib popularizers of Freud and Jung were the main targets of *Is Sex Necessary?* although an important mechanical device, the airplane, was also sniped at. In 1909 Freud and Jung had introduced their theories to Americans through lectures given in person. Translations of their major works followed, and by 1915 William Marion Reedy (the St. Louis editor who published Edgar Lee Masters' *Spoon River Anthology*) could remark, "It's sex o'clock." [4] In 1950, White recollected that the literature of the late twenties "blossomed with deep and lugubrious books on sex and marriage. The Freudian concept had been accepted quite generally. Doctors, psychiatrists, and other students of misbehavior were pursuing sex to the last ditch, and the human animal seemed absorbed in self-analysis." [5]

Thurber and White claimed that two factors in our civilization had been overemphasized: "One is aviation, the other is sex." In hitting at this overemphasis they also struck at the prudishness responsible in part for such overcompensation. In the opening chapter, entitled "The Nature of the American Male: A Study of Pedestalism," Thurber set the tone of the book with a suave parody of the style in which such volumes as Samuel Schmalhausen's *Why We Misbehave* and Dr. Joseph Collins' *The Doctor Looks at Love and Life* and *The Doctor Looks at Marriage and Medicine* were written, an oily, bland style that purported to be "scientific" and was studded with polysyllabic terms, often in foreign languages. With tongue in cheek (as it was not always in later works when he compared the present unfavorably with the past), Thurber cast a look backward at a stabler, happier time: "There was not a single case of nervous breakdown, or neurosis, arising from amatory troubles in the whole cycle from 1800 to 1900, barring a slight flare-up just before the Mexican and Civil wars. This was because love and marriage and children stood for progress, and progress is—or was—a calm, routine business." Nobody bothered about the "Pleasure-Principle." However, this "stability" was not good; it bred its own overcompensating reaction:

> This direct evasion of the Love Urge on the part of Americans of the last century was the nuclear complex of the psycho-neurosis as we know it today. . . . At the turn of the century, the nation was on a sound economic basis and men had the opportunity to direct their attention away from the mechanics of life to the pleasures of living. No race can leap lightly, however, from an economic value to an emotional value. There must be a long period of *Übertragung*, long and tedious.

During this period, said Thurber, man went in for such sex-substitutes as baseball, prize fighting, horse racing, and bicycling. Since women, "naturally introverts," did not take readily to these pastimes, they drew away from men and "began to surround the mere fact of their biological destiny with a nimbus of ineffability. It got so bad that in speaking of birth and other natural phenomena, women seemed often to be discussing something else, such as the Sistine Madonna or the aurora borealis. . . . This could not go on."

After this jab at the prudery of the previous generation of females, the authors described the "diversion subterfuges" practiced by these women to ensnare the amorous male anyhow. These included fudge-making and charades. The result was "Pedestalism," a state of complete separation between the male and the female and also between the "physical and psychic" aspects of love. Thurber says, "This condition nowadays would lead directly to a neurosis, but in those days men were unable

to develop a neurosis because they didn't know how." Instead
they "sublimated" their sex urges by retiring to their dens, and
"The Panic of 1907 was a direct result." The chapter thus turns
out to be a satire of the genteel, repressive approach to sex as
well as of the popularizers of Freud.

When they wanted to, Thurber and White could and did
write and think much alike, and it does not matter much which
author wrote which chapters in this book.[6] For the record,
Thurber wrote "Pedestalism," "A Discussion of Feminine
Types," "The Lilies-and-Bluebird Delusion," "Claustrophobia,
or What Every Young Wife Should Know," and "Glossary"—
Chapters I, III, V, VII, and the second section of Chapter VIII.
White wrote the "Introduction" (1950), "Foreword," Chapters II,
IV, VI ("How to Tell Love From Passion," "The Sexual Revolution," "What Should Children Tell Parents?"), and the first
and third parts of Chapter VIII ("Answers to Hard Questions"
and "A Note on the Drawings in This Book"). The titles of most
of the chapters suggest that the question asked by the title of the
book be answered thus: yes, of course sex is necessary, but overemphasis and oversimplification of it are not. Various chapters
also amplify the prefatory statement that ". . . the authors of
this remarkable book subscribe to the modern ideal of freedom
in sex but do not believe that marriage has yet been proved a
failure in every case, nor that sex can profitably be examined
entirely apart from that old institution." Taken literally, this
statement could pass for a sensible norm, but in an interpretation
of the last two clauses, allowance should be made for understatement. Even so, to Bangs, Ade, Lardner, and possibly even
to Benchley (who told Thurber he didn't believe in second marriages), so lukewarm a statement about marriage would have
seemed a compromise with morality. And the differences between
their domestic ethic and that of Thurber and White in 1929
illustrate the considerable variation possible among humorists
who depicted the American male and who believed essentially in
marital stability and family solidarity.

In his own writing later, Thurber tried to maintain the

same middle position between prudery and prurience, which is to say that he stressed the sexual element as the chief but by no means only force in the lives of his men and women. His moderation should be kept in mind; by comparison with Benchley's humor, Thurber's quivers with sex and with the tensions related thereto. In consequence, one is apt to overlook Thurber's restraint in handling the theme that fascinated him above all others.

About five years after *Is Sex Necessary?* appeared, Thurber told Max Eastman that his humor was about one thing, ". . . beaten-down married people. 'The American woman is my theme . . . and how she dominates the male, how he tries to go away but always comes back for more, being romantic and everlastingly nice and having an almost religious feeling about marriage.' " [7] However, in "Mr. and Mrs. Monroe," which made up about half of *The Owl in the Attic* (1931), the emphasis falls on the male—on Mr. Monroe, who, as Walter Blair says, is humiliated by "the Machine" as well as by "the Woman"—and by the Organization too, whether it is the modern corporation or the modern State. Mr. Monroe's method of conquering a balky shower-bath spray is to yell "Woo! Woo!" at it, and it is "little Mrs. Monroe" who, though not fully equal to many situations herself, solves the problems of finding a dog at a freight terminal and of smuggling a dozen bottles of Benedictine past customs at the dock. Simply by telling "the very blonde lady" about the incident of the shower bath, she even foils an attempt by her confused spouse to philander. Mr. Monroe is trapped by a wife who understands him thoroughly and yet forgives, thereby committing the final indignity against his manhood.

Yet Mr. Monroe is in a sense his own unwilling captor. Like Benchley's man, he is baffled by the little problems of everyday living: he is reduced to jelly by a bat in his bedroom, paralyzed by the middle-class problem of directing the workmen who come to move the furniture, terrorized by having to spend an evening alone in their isolated summer cottage. Most of all, he is like Benchley's narrator in continually forming a high estimate of himself which collapses under pressure. He sees himself as an "imperturbable spirit" but is perturbed by any responsibility, and the mere possibility of making some extramarital time with a lovely lady causes his image of himself as a man of the world to evaporate, bit by bit, during a day of procrastination. One effect of his various humiliations is to drive him back to the protection of his mate.

The chief difference between Benchley's man and Thurber's male is that Thurber much more often gives the female a direct and central part in the male's humiliation by his world. Benchley wrote a number of pieces about children (whom Thurber largely ignored, despite his many portrayals of household life), but the humiliation of Benchley's man rarely comes from his spouse, and marital difficulties, including sexual tension, are almost never a major factor in Benchley's writing. His Little Man is almost sexless, and the wife is a shadowy figure. Benchley's wildest fantasies are underlaid by a certain placidity when compared to the sexuality that charges Thurber's males and their environment.

Not only is Thurber's man a captive of his wife and of his own inadequacies, he is also enslaved by time. Thurber usually depicts his males as middle-aged or verging thereon, and their aging is often related directly to their sexual and marital problems. Concerning the lovely lady, Mr. Monroe thought,

> Of course if it came to impetuosity, he would show 'em who was impetuous. But, at thirty-five, to make the right effect, one had to go slow. Besides, he was a little tired, the party having lasted infernally late. He was glad that someone else was seeing the lady home this particular night. It was devilishly cold.
>
> He had quite a sneezing spell when he got home, which somehow marred his admiration of himself in a glass.

Thus the age of Thurber's males is another of their handicaps in the marital scheme of things as well as in the world at large.

AGGRESSION AND WITHDRAWAL

As do Benchley's characters, Thurber's Little Men sometimes become aggressive, and their aggressions tend likewise to be futile or disastrous to one or both parties. In the series of drawings entitled "The War Between Men and Women" the men win a Pyrrhic victory. In a short story, "The Indian Sign," Mr. Bentley accomplishes nothing except a momentary release of what Freud called psychic energy. To express his disgust with his wife's interest in a sturdy ancestress who had killed nineteen Indians (male), Mr. Bentley cuts loose with a Pequot war whoop, "Ah-wah-wah-wah-wah!" Even in his rebellion he thus reveals his unconscious identification with the victims of the pioneer matron. In another story, when Mrs. Brush and her female friends try to play poker with all sorts of wild cards, Mr. Brush, exercising dealer's choice, invents an absurd variation in which "The red queens, the fours, fives, sixes and eights are wild." Mr. Brush defeats his wife for the moment, but the reader feels that her revenge will come somehow.

Sometimes the husband's "aggression" manifests itself as withdrawal (if that statement is not a descent into psychoanalytic jargon). Mr. Bidwell takes to holding his breath, even at parties; the result is extreme connubial tension—"They knifed each other, from head to stomach, with their eyes"—and finally, divorce. In "The Curb in the Sky," the male's aggression takes the form of telling an outlandish dream he has had. When his wife begins "correcting" his dream, he withdraws into insanity. "The Secret Life of Walter Mitty" depicts the withdrawal by a henpecked husband who, like Mr. Monroe, Mr. Pendly, Tommy Trinway, and other Thurber men, is baffled by the automobile as well as by his wife. Mitty retreats into his own world of wish-fulfillment fantasies in which he is the hero of various adventures. His daydreams are unwitting parodies of several plots and character types overworked in the movies and in trashy fiction: the naval hero, the great surgeon, the icily calm defendant and his "lovely, dark-haired girl" at a murder trial, the daring combat aviator, the hero who dies in defiance—"To hell with the handkerchief." Mitty's fantasies also reflect his worship of science and machinery. In his waking life he cannot park his car properly or put on the tire chains, and his daydreams reveal that his scraps of technical information are mostly misinformation—"Throw on the power lights," says Commander Mitty. "Obstreosis of the ductal tract. . . . Coreopsis has set in," is the verdict of Dr. Mitty. His "inner" life is thus revealed as a meager collection of stereotyped images and trite or inaccurate material assimilated largely (and badly) from the outer world. All he has left is the desire for ego-gratification, and his final dream suggests that even this desire may be weakening. In this dream Mitty dubs himself "Walter Mitty the Undefeated, inscrutable to the last," yet he is defeated in the dream as well as in reality.[8] Thurber has been called a "comic Prufrock," [9] and he shares Prufrock's inner futility, but he is more like James Joyce's Leopold Bloom in his position as a harassed and ineffective husband. Like Bloom too, Mitty serves his author as an agent of unconscious parody and irony.

On the rare occasions when the male's rebellion improves his situation with respect to the female, there are always circumstances that have mitigated his original plight. In "The Catbird Seat," Erwin Martin, an office worker, foils a dominating woman who has wholly captured his boss with her notions of efficiency. Mr. Martin eliminates this threat to his routine and to his job— but Mr. Martin is not married to Mrs. Barrows; they are merely colleagues. In "Am Not I Your Rosalind?" the husband tempts his wife and the wife of a guest into trying to read Shakespeare aloud while high on cocktails. The two wives make fools of themselves, but afterwards the tempter and his wife forget their differences in criticizing their guests:

> They got up and Thorne turned out the lights. "Does he know *anything*? Has he got a brain in his head?" she demanded.
> "Fred? God, no!"

> "If he'd only yawn and get it over with, instead of working his mouth that way."
>
> Halfway up the stairs, Ann turned suddenly. Thorne stopped and looked up at her. "Do you know the most ghastly thing about her?" she asked.
>
> "That moo-cow voice?"
>
> "No. Heaven knows that's bad enough, but can you possibly imagine her in doublet and *hose?* Those *legs,* George, those *legs!*"
>
> Thorne jumped a step, caught up with her, and they went the rest of the way to their bedroom arm in arm.

George and Ann achieve a precarious truce in their own war by having become allies in a cold war on their friends. The irony of their "adjustment" gets a double edge in that Fred and *his* wife, as they drive away, have in their turn been making snide comments about their hosts.

Occasionally the repressed husband breaks out violently. Mr. Preble, "a plump, middle-aged lawyer in Scarsdale," decides to dispose of his wife and run away with his stenographer in a story based perhaps on the celebrated case of Dr. Crippen, who did both. Mr. Preble tries to lure his wife down-cellar (where the doctor had disposed of Mrs. Crippen's body). Mrs. Preble says, "I knew you wanted to bury me the minute you set foot in this house tonight," but she agrees to go down in the cellar and be buried, just to have "a little peace." As she starts down, she complains, "It's *cold* down here! You *would* think of this, at this time of year! Any other husband would have buried his wife in the summer." In order that he not leave a clue, Mrs. Preble advises her spouse to find a weapon out in the street—a piece of iron or something. This weird fantasy ends with her screaming after him to shut the door—"Where were you born—in a barn?"

In "The Whip-poor-will," Kinstrey, already neurotic, is pushed into psychosis by the constant "whipping" of that night bird whose call foreshadows death. Some of Thurber's wives all but smother their husbands with too merciless an understanding coupled with a sympathy that is half contempt ("My great big wonderful husband," Mrs. Monroe says with gentle irony). Madge Kinstrey, however, has contempt without sympathy or understanding; she calls her husband "a spoiled brat" who is "fussing about nothing at all, like an invalid in a wheel chair." Kinstrey finally begins to show signs of schizophrenia: ". . . he had the oddly disturbing feeling that it wasn't he who had spoken but somebody else. . . ."[10] The next morning he suddenly kills his wife, the two servants, and himself. He goes far beyond Lardner's husband in "Ex Parte" who merely smashed up the furniture, but the principle is the same: the male who is misunderstood and feels oppressed may revolt in blind, destructive violence.

Quite often the husband's aggression merely takes the form of bedeviling his mate in little, spiteful ways, a tactic at which she is equally adept and willing. In "A Couple of Hamburgers," a tired couple nag each other with growing viciousness. Their marriage is probably headed for the same fate as that described in "The Breaking Up of the Winships." The Winships parted over a trifle that "seemed to me, at first, as minor a problem as frost on a windowpane." Their "problem" was a difference of opinion about Greta Garbo, and the silly quarrel that grew from this was merely the last straw—as the cry of the whippoorwill was to Kinstrey, except for the minor detail that neither of the Winships committed physical murder.

Mary McCarthy, another frequent contributor to the *New Yorker,* refers in one of her works to "the thrifty bourgeois love-insurance, with its daily payments of patience, forbearance, and resignation."[11] Thurber deplores marriages without these qualities, but he is not attacking marriage as an institution in his tales about the Prebles, the Winships, and the Kinstreys any more than he and White did in *Is Sex Necessary?* If there are any males worse off than his subdued husbands, they are the forlorn bachelors of "Evening's at Seven" and "One Is a Wanderer." The plight of the male in the latter story is especially pathetic; he drinks and thinks, "One's life is made up of twos, and of fours. The Graysons understood the nice little arrangements of living, the twos and fours. Two is company, four is a party, three is a crowd. One is a wanderer." Man can live neither with woman nor without her.

THE HUMOR OF DESPAIR

In his nonfictional essays Thurber sometimes wears the mask of the same figure who cowers in his fiction, with the minor difference that the Little Man of the essays often writes for a living. As a writer, he may easily be portrayed as a wise fool and sad clown:

> Authors of such pieces ["light" pieces running from a thousand to two thousand words] have, nobody knows why, a genius for getting into minor difficulties: they walk into the wrong apartments, they drink furniture polish for stomach bitters, they drive their cars into the prize tulip beds of haughty neighbors, they playfully slap gangsters, mistaking them for old school friends. To call such persons "humorists," a loose-fitting and ugly word, is to miss the nature of their dilemma and the dilemma of their nature. The little wheels of their invention are set in motion by the damp hand of melancholy.

Saddened by his own ineptitude and by his encounters with women, psychiatrists, business, bureaucracy, gadgets, and automobiles,[12] this *persona* was further depressed by the disasters of the nineteen-thirties at home and abroad. "I suspect that nothing is going to get us anywhere," Thurber wrote in 1937, in opposition to those who felt optimistic about the international situation.[13] Elsewhere his comments place him in the broad streams of literary naturalism and pessimism. Man, he says, is merely a part of nature and not necessarily the best part at that:

> Man is simply the highest form of life on his own planet. His superiority rests on a thin and chancy basis: he has the trick of articulate speech and out of this, slowly and laboriously, he has developed the capacity of abstract reasoning. . . . Man has aspired higher than the attainment of natural goals; he has developed ideas and notions; he has monkeyed around with concepts. The life to which he was naturally adapted he has put behind him; in moving into the alien and complicated sphere of Thought and Imagination he has become the least well-adjusted of all the creatures of the earth, and hence the most bewildered . . .

Clarence Day had said something like that in *This Simian World* but had not altogether rejected reason and hope. Thurber's attitude has some of the blackness of Don Marquis, and shows affinity also with writers outside the sphere of humor who disparage reason and stress the maladjustment of man when he moves beyond his animal origins. Sherwood Anderson envied the lot of children and illiterate Negroes; the crew in O'Neill's *The Hairy Ape* advise Yank to "Drink, don't think!" Hemingway's Nick Adams and Frederick Henry are better off when they are fishing, swimming, drinking, or fornicating than when the wheels of their reflection are spinning. Being more cerebral than Yank and more inhibited than Hemingway's males, Thurber's characters find little solace in drink—though not from lack of trying—and their sexual ventures seldom get beyond wishful thinking. But they too are specimens of nature; the introductory quotation for *The Beast in Me* concerns "the beast inside, the beast that haunts the moonlit marges of the mind."

Charles Child Walcutt has emphasized the intimate relationship between naturalism and Freudianism,[14] and an orthodox Freudian would see Thurber's Little Man as tormented by the conflict between the unconscious "beast" of sex and the repression of it by the superego, which is shaped and dominated by this man's "civilized" environment. The repressed animal finds its outlet in anxieties, fixations, and obsessions. Basically, society is at fault for repressing rather than channeling the primary urge.

As hinted earlier, some of Thurber's ideas about sex and personality are not necessarily in conflict with those of Freud. Thurber feels that the male animal is unduly repressed by his environment, an environment which includes another animal, his wife, who both abets and conceals her ruthlessness by means of more resolution, solicitude for her mate, and competence in the small matters of everyday living than he shows. Part of his environment is also a society going mad through a misapplication of technology; so-called neurosis is often merely "a natural caution in a world made up of gadgets that whir and whine and whiz and shriek and sometimes explode." Thurber differs from Freud in ignoring the Oedipus complex, whereas Freud regarded this is the major component of sex. He also differs in feeling that it is futile for man to expect to throw off his repressions or even to sublimate them satisfactorily. The civilized (or repressing and repressed) elements in the Little Man's character and environment often have the same cosmic finality as the natural traits. Thurber's people rarely succeed in changing any aspect of either their surroundings or themselves, and such "adjustment" as the male achieves usually comes only through complete withdrawal, as in the cases of Mitty, and of Grandfather in *My Life and Hard Times.*

One can hardly blame them, so full of terror is their world. The naturalistic portrait of man as the helpless creature of chance, heredity, and environment was conducive to the view that he was the frequent prey of violence and disaster, as Malcolm Cowley and others have pointed out.[15] The violence and terror in Thurber's work is also part of a tradition in American humor that stretches back into the frontier of pre-Civil War days, with its tales of backwoods bullies in crude, dangerous circumstances. Davy Crockett helped to burn forty-six Indians alive in a barricaded hut. Readers thought it funny when Mike Fink shot off a Negro's heel. *Streaks of Squatter Life* by John S. Robb, the *Sut Lovingood Yarns* by George Washington Harris, and the two volumes of backwoods humor collected by William T. Porter[16] were full of rough practical joking, rib cracking, eye gouging, knifing, and shooting. Though written a generation later than most of these works, *Huckleberry Finn* too is full of terror and death. The Bureau of the Census may have pronounced the frontier dead in 1890, but the persistence and revival of violence in humor was encouraged by the strain of naturalism in some twentieth-century humorists—including several writing outside the frontier or crackerbarrel traditions. Ring Lardner, Don Marquis, Will Cuppy, and S. J. Perelman depict episodes of violence that take place against the backdrop or with the collaboration of an indifferent or hostile universe. This approach is not wholly absent from the satire of Robert Benchley and Dorothy Parker.

To be impressed by the proportion of violence in Thurber's narratives, one need only look at *The Thurber Carnival,* a cross section of his writing and drawing up to 1945. The first four sections of this book contain thirty-three pieces. Fifteen—or nearly half of these—deal with terror, violence, and disaster, including a nightmare in which gangsters are about to bump off the dreamer and his wife; a woman who goes violently insane; a man who does likewise; several other people who are on the verge; a man who dies by accident; and two who are murdered (three if one counts "The Macbeth Murder Mystery"). The fifth section is *My Life and Hard Times,* complete, a fictionalized autobiography of certain episodes in the life of Thurber and his family. This section includes three chapters about panic in the home, one about mass panic in the streets ("The Day the Dam Broke"), one about various family servants—most of whom go berserk— and one about a vicious dog.

The sixth section consists of pieces from *Fables for Our Time.* The brief allegories in the book of that title (first published in 1940) and in *Further Fables for Our Time* (1956) are, as a group, the most violent and bitter of Thurber's satires. Like Bierce and Ade, Thurber often gives an old adage a new and ironic twist, but Ade's fables are spiritual milk for babes by comparison with those of Thurber. In one, for example, a chipmunk is safe from the shrikes so long as he loiters in his cave, but when his energetic wife—a typical Thurber female—persuades him to go out, they are both killed. The moral is, "Early to rise and early to bed makes a male healthy and wealthy and dead." Other old saws retooled to show the vanity of human wishes and the irrelevance of mortals' morality are: "He who hesitates is sometimes saved"; "Fools rush in where angels fear to tread, and the angels are all in Heaven, but few of the fools are dead"; and "It is not always more blessed to give than to receive, but it is frequently more rewarding."

Several of the fables carry a message also found in *Is Sex Necessary?* and *Let Your Mind Alone:* namely, the naturalistic theme that man, in trying to act as if he were above his place in nature's order, has muddled himself into disaster. A "seal" leaves his natural habitat to join a circus; when he returns home to impress the stay-at-homes he tries to swim, but

> . . . he was so hampered by his smart city clothes, including a pair of seventeen-dollar shoes, that he began to founder at once. Since he hadn't been in swimming for three years, he had forgot what to do with his flippers and tail, and he went down for the third time before the other seals could reach him. They gave him a simple but dignified funeral.
>
> *Moral:* Whom God has equipped with flippers should not monkey around with zippers.

Likewise, a crow falls in love with an oriole and "pleaded his cause—or should we say cawed his pleas?" All he gets by this is the loss of his proper crow-wife. "Moral: Even the llama should stick to mamma." A tiger and a leopard stage a prize fight and end up killing each other. "Moral: If you live as humans do, it will be the end of you." But since the animal kingdom can match the human race in showing an irrational urge to destroy itself— witness the lemmings—there is little consolation or wisdom to be found in the nonhuman world, except for the courage and tranquillity of certain dogs.

Although Thurber meant *The Last Flower* (1939) to be a message of hope, it is easier to find the central idea of this sequence of cartoons and captions, done hastily on the eve of World War II, in the depiction of civilization as doomed to emerge from one meaningless cycle of self-destruction only to plunge into another. This fable might be termed one of those "Ironic points of light" which W. H. Auden in "September 1, 1939" said were flashing out "wherever the Just/Exchange their messages."[17] Any optimistic implication is overshadowed by the somber content of Thurber's sequence and by its implicit determinism.

ONE OF THE JUST

A pessimistic naturalism has thus permeated Thurber's depiction of the Little Man, but in the late nineteen-thirties, as the economic depression persisted and war began to threaten, he began to say things about public affairs that call for classifying his literary double also with the heirs of the Progressive "New Citizen," that is, with the liberals of the thirties and forties and with the active opponents of McCarthyism in the frightened fifties. In the anger of *The Last Flower* itself one senses—again, in Auden's words—"an affirming flame" of zeal and hope which is scarcely consistent with despair, and for over a quarter of a century Thurber was outspoken in his attacks on authoritarianism of both left and right.

In the "Preface" to *My Life and Hard Times,* Thurber had insisted that as a writer he was just another Little Man with little interests:

> Such a writer moves about restlessly wherever he goes, ready to get the hell out at the drop of a pie-pan or the lift of a skirt. His gestures are the ludicrous reflexes of the maladjusted; his repose is the momentary inertia of the nonplussed. . . . He talks largely about small matters and smally about great affairs. His ears are shut to the ominous rumblings of the dynasties of the world moving toward a cloudier chaos than even before, but he hears with an acute perception the startling sounds that rabbits make twisting in the bushes along a country road at night and a cold chill comes upon him when the comic supplement of a Sunday newspaper blows unexpectedly out of an areaway and envelops his knees. He can sleep while the commonwealth crumbles . . . but he keeps looking behind him as he walks along darkening streets out of the fear that he is being softly followed by little men padding along in single file, about a foot and a half high, large-eyed, and whiskered.

> It is difficult for such a person to conform to what Ford Madox Ford in his book of recollections has called the sole reason for writing one's memoirs: namely, to paint a picture of one's time. Your short-piece writer's time is not Walter Lippmann's time, or Stuart Chase's time, or Professor Einstein's time. It is his own personal time, circumscribed by the short boundaries of his pain and his embarrassment, in which what happens to his digestion, the rear axle of his car, and the confused flow of his relationships with six or eight persons and two or three buildings is of greater importance than

what goes on in the nation or the universe. . . . He is aware
that billions of dollars are stolen every year by bankers and
politicians, and that thousands of people are out of work,
but these conditions do not worry him a tenth as much as
the conviction that he has wasted three months on a stupid
psychoanalyst or the suspicion that a piece he has been
working on for two long days was done much better and
probably more quickly by Robert Benchley in 1924.

This preface written in 1933 was outdated by 1940 as a reliable source of information about Thurber's interests. In the
latter year, he wrote a column for *PM*, a militantly antifascist
daily in New York City, "twice a week until I went into a nervous tail spin following my fifth eye operation."[18] The play *The
Male Animal*, by Thurber and Elliot Nugent, was produced in
the same year, and the playwrights proved that they most certainly did hear "the rumblings of the dynasties," especially those
reverberations that sounded near home. This play has two rather
awkwardly interwoven plots: in one of them Professor Tommy
Turner is the usual confused Thurber husband, but in the other
his integrity as a teacher makes him stick to his plan of reading
in class the letter of Vanzetti about the significance of his own
and his partner Sacco's execution, despite the threats of a Babbitt
type of trustee that Tommy will be fired for this action. In standing up for academic freedom, Tommy is not merely a male animal but the liberal citizen behaving as a citizen ought to behave
when freedom is threatened.

Some of the *Fables for Our Time* also suggest a citizen-writer
for whom all is not lost, practicing the eternal vigilance cited by
the forefathers as the price of liberty. In "The Birds and the
Foxes," the latter animals "civilize" the geese and ducks, and
"liberate" the orioles by killing and eating them. "Moral: Government of the orioles, by the foxes, and for the foxes, must
perish from the earth." Even closer to the lesson of *The Male
Animal* is the fable in which a gander is unjustly set upon because somebody has complimented him for being a "proper
gander." Somebody else, however, thinks that this bird is being
accused of propaganda. The ironic moral is: "Anybody who you

or your wife thinks is going to overthrow the government by violence must be driven out of the country."

In certain nonhumorous pieces, Thurber also has shown his
social and political involvement. He criticized *The Moon Is
Down* (1942), John Steinbeck's novel about the Nazi conquest of
Norway, for its allegedly sympathetic portrayal of the conquerors.
Thurber declared in the *New Republic* (Clarence Day's old employers) that ". . . this book needs more guts and less moon," and
that it softened the true story of "hell, horror and hopelessness."
Neither here nor in his defense when criticized in his turn was
there any of the naturalistic defeatism and passivity associated
with the Little Man.[19] Naturalism was likewise in eclipse during
a lecture on humor given in his native Columbus in 1953, where
he said, "There used to be men among us who could brandish
the shield of humor with telling effect in the now sensitive area
of politics and government . . . the H. L. Mencken of an earlier
and bolder day, and the late Will Rogers, and William Allen
White, and old Ed Howe . . ." Besides praising the militancy of
two conservatives (Mencken and Howe), a New Dealer (Rogers),
and a writer best classified as both and neither (White), Thurber
threw a punch at McCarthyism with ". . . [comedy] sickens in
the weather of intimidation and suppression, and such a sickness could infect a whole nation. The only rules comedy can
tolerate are those of taste, and the only limitations those of
libel."[20] In an interview given during the previous year, Thurber
called himself "an Eisenhower man,"[21] and his attitudes on
McCarthyism and on the presidential election added up to those
of a man who felt close to the middle of the political road but
very much in that road—not off to one side, detached, paring his
fingernails.

Thurber's humor in his last decade shows the same inconsistent mixture of despair and of militancy with its concomitant
of hope. In *Further Fables for Our Time* (1956), one finds some
of the older, skeptical pessimism about the human race—see
"The Human Being and the Dinosaur"—but one also finds that
at least ten out of the forty-seven fables in this book are disguised

tracts in defense of free expression. In "The Peacelike Mongoose," an animal of that species is persecuted for his use of "reason and intelligence" by those who cry "Reason is six-sevenths of treason." Two more fables are likewise thrusts at McCarthyism: "The Trial of the Old Watchdog" and "Ivory, Apes, and People," but at least two of these *Further Fables* are satires of Soviet communism, which Thurber hated as much as he disliked professional Americanism ("The nature of humor is anti-communistic," he declared in his Ohio lecture). In *Lanterns and Lances* (1960), the pessimistic theme that man embodies the worst aspects of nature is prominent, but Thurber praises the late Elmer Davis, of whose New Deal and Fair Deal sympathies there was no doubt, and Edward P. Morgan, sponsored by the CIO-AF of L, for "intelligence, devotion to American ideals, courage, and wit." In this, his last book before his death, Thurber evidently felt these phenomena were still worth a few broken lances.

The liberal citizen would lead no forlorn hope either. In his "Foreword," the author says the perceptive will detect in these pieces "a basic and indestructible thread of hope. . . . It is lighter than you think."

Thurber's liberalism resembles that of Day and Benchley in being sharply limited by his middle-class angle of vision. Most of his neurotic males and females are suburbanites with hired "help" and summer cottages; people who earn their living with their hands are among the threats to this white-collar cocktail crowd. Mr. Monroe shrinks before the furniture movers; Walter Mitty is buffaloed by the parking-lot attendant; Mr. Pendly by garage mechanics, and several of Thurber's protagonists by waiters, maids, or butlers. In 1934 Thurber served on a committee for the welfare of waiters during a strike by these workers, but he admitted that he didn't have the slightest idea of what waiters do when they go home. In his essays, Thurber or rather his *persona,* has difficulty with waiters, office help, street-gang laborers, house-servants, and hired yardmen. Oftener than any humorist of note since Bangs, Thurber makes comedy out of "difficult" servants. The maid in *The Male Animal* is a nineteenth-century stereotype. If their employers are neurotic, Emma Inch, Barney Haller, and several Negro maids are "odd," cross-grained, stupid, or downright psychotic. The servants of the Thurber family in *My Life and Hard Times* usually seem even more unbalanced than their employers, and in a revealing piece called "A Friend of the Earth," Thurber's *alter ego* psychologically grapples with Zeph Leggins, a village roustabout, philosopher, and joker who can also be taken as a symbol of the author's rejection of crackerbarrel humor.

Only occasionally are the manual workers shown as mentally healthy, in contrast to the neurotic persons with more money and book-learning. One such worker is the cabdriver who tells Kirk in "One Is a Wanderer" that "I got a home over in Brooklyn and a wife and a couple kids, and, boy, I'm tellin' you that's the best place . . ." The point is not that Thurber makes a principle of relating neurosis to social class, but that nearly all manual workers in his writings are seen only from the viewpoint of their employers, and the author does not seem interested in any other viewpoint. When not butts of satire, they are mere foils for his educated, middle-class neurotics.

TWO TYPES OF THURBER MALE

Thus, one of Thurber's masks has been that of a Little Man helpless in the grip of nature, his wife, and his own nature; the other, used somewhat less often, has been that of a militant of the Progressive–New Deal stamp. (One recalls that many Progressive–New Dealers were conservative in their values and liberal in their advocation of reforms to conserve those values.) The two attitudes existed simultaneously throughout Thurber's career, although most of his pessimistic pieces appeared in the earlier part of his career and most of his more optimistic pieces were written since about 1939. In 1953 he implied that even his satirical portraits of women had been made with a reformer's intent:

> Almost any century now Woman may lose her patience with black politics and red war and let fly. I wish I could be on earth then to witness the saving of our self-destructive species by its greatest creative force. If I have sometimes seemed to make fun of Woman, I assure you it has only been for the purpose of egging her on.[22]

These statements may be mellow afterthoughts during a happy second marriage, but a contradiction remains between the view of man as a helpless bit of animated earth and the view that he can and ought to achieve his freedom and improve his lot. This contradiction is reduced but not resolved by the fact that Thurber's pessimistic determinism appears chiefly in his writings about personal and domestic matters, whereas his belief in free will and freedom crops out mainly in his pieces dealing with social and political topics. Rarely, as in *The Male Animal*, does he try to fuse the two realms of subject matter and the two philosophies, and when he does try, the result is not convincing either as ideology or as art.

In the work of Benchley one sees a family man and citizen who is seldom victorious and often defeated but who rarely gives up his theoretical hold on certain hard and fast values. In Thurber's writing, this figure is more often driven over the brink to psychosis and separated from any sense of values. The *persona* who fights the liberal fight for a freedom he refuses to consider dead in theory or in practice is separate and distinct from the beaten-down Little Man. Faced with the dilemma of naturalism—the belief that man is an animal whose character and fate are predetermined by his heredity and his environment— and the contradictory need for some form of belief in free will and morality if one is to live harmoniously among one's fellows or to write humor, Thurber solved the problem no better than did Mencken. Mencken blithely ignored the dilemma; Thurber divided his conception of man and embodied each conception in a separate image inconsistent with the other. Ring Lardner too had suffered from the same ideological schizophrenia, but Lardner never warmed to the humanitarian tradition, and a nearly complete pessimism took hold of him. Don Marquis was affected by the same split, though his nagging wish that things might be better in spite of the naturalistic cosmos was born of religious idealism rather than secular humanitarianism. Marquis too attempted to disguise the problem by the use of more than one comic mask.

All these writers may be called pre-atomic pessimists, but since 1945, the dilemma with which they struggled has not changed in kind—only in urgency.[23]

17

E. B. White, "Farmer/Other"

A brief biography of Elwyn Brooks White before he joined the *New Yorker* staff reads like that of many upper-middle-class Americans in his generation. He was the youngest of eight children at a time when large families were still common among the solid citizens. His birthplace was Mt. Vernon, New York, a "carefully zoned suburb," and his father was "a God-fearing man" who "never missed a copy of the New York *Times* either." White entered Cornell University, but as soon as he was old enough he dropped out to join the Army during World War I. Eventually he returned to the campus, where in his senior year he edited the Cornell *Daily Sun*.

REPORTER AND WANDERER

In 1921 White got his A.B. and took off for the West Coast, guiding westward the Model T Ford which he and Richard Lee Strout later depicted as a symbol of adventure in the pioneer years of the auto age. The young pioneer, like Milt Daggett, the mechanic in Sinclair Lewis' *Free Air,* wound up in Seattle, where he worked on the *Times* of that city, discovered he was of little use as a mere reporter, and was soon put to writing features in which some quaint or colorful detail gave the budding stylist a chance to display his highly personal approach, a chance not offered by the reporting of straight news. Before long, he left the *Times* and sailed to Alaska, working part of his passage as a mess boy. After this adventure he came back to New York and lapsed into advertising—with an occasional stab, he confesses, at ghostwriting. In this suburban background, university education, uneventful military service, and mild wanderlust, there was little thus far to set White apart from large numbers of his fellow men, and in later years an important feature of his life and thought has been his sustained attempt to recapture and retain a sense of connection with as large a number of Americans as possible. Despite his cultural equipment and polished prose style, he has not intended to appeal only to an elite.

Like Don Marquis, Ring Lardner, Dorothy Parker, and James Thurber, White placed a few early contributions in F. P. A.'s column, "The Conning Tower." In 1925 he began to sell poems and short prose pieces to the *New Yorker*. Two books of verse, *The Lady Is Cold* (1929) and *The Fox of Peapack* (1938) were in the so-called "light" vein, but some of this verse is explicitly as well as implicitly serious. Thirteen volumes of prose and verse now bear his name. None of them is large but he has written over a million words for the "Talk of the Town" department in the *New Yorker,* most of it anonymously.

In 1926 Katharine Sergeant Angell, one of Harold Ross's most valued assistants on the *New Yorker,* hired White for Ross at a salary of thirty dollars a week. She eventually became White's wife, and his collaborator in editing an anthology, *A Subtreasury of American Humor.* Twenty-one years later, Thurber said that White had been the "number one wheel horse" of the magazine.[1] Among the jobs White did for the *New Yorker* in the early years were these:

(1) He edited the "Talk of the Town" and for many years wrote the first page of that section, subtitled "Notes & Comment."[2] Thurber says that " 'Notes and Comment' . . . did more than anything else to set the tone and cadence of the *New Yorker* and to shape its turns of thought . . ." If this is true, White has been one of the most influential prose stylists in the twentieth century. Thurber also pays tribute to "White's skill in bringing this page to the kind of perfection Ross had dreamed of . . ." [3]

(2) He played a part in getting Ross to hire Thurber.

(3) He encouraged Thurber to publish his drawings and to keep on drawing in his unique, deceptively simple style.[4]

(4) He wrote most of the one-line captions for the column "Slips That Pass in the Type," having shown a knack for making quips about slips that no one else has consistently duplicated.

(5) From the first months of the magazine's life he contributed poems and "casuals" (pieces not written on assignment). The first number of the *New Yorker* appeared February 22, 1925, and White's initial contribution appeared on May 9, 1925, nearly a year and a half before he joined Ross's staff.

CITIZEN OF THE CITY

White's first casual in the *New Yorker* was an exercise in quaintness entitled "Defense of the Bronx River." His second was "Child's Play," a brief essay in which he describes how a waitress spilled buttermilk over him in a Child's restaurant and how rattled she got. White here selected an episode from his real life in which he could appear with only slight distortion as the Little Man to whom miniature disasters happen, a role in which he consciously resembled Benchley. White's early sketches were the kind of thing Benchley and his other imitators (including Thurber at that time) were doing for *Vanity Fair, Life, Judge,* and the *Bookman;* Dale Kramer says that most of the early pieces by White and others in the *New Yorker* owed something to the style of *Life* and *Judge.* Kramer thus documents the view taken in this book that the *New Yorker* style was not a mutant or "sport," but a direct outgrowth of its journalistic and humorous milieu. In Kramer's view, White differed from Benchley "in that, beneath the whimsy, he had tried to insert beauty." With his buttermilk piece "White had made a dent in the contemporary *Life* and *Judge* pattern of the 'funny' writer." [5] White added a touch of the poet to prose humor, a lyric note to the style of Benchley and his followers. Because of White's lyricism and his interest in nature, Warren Beck is probably right in suggesting that White did much to keep the *New Yorker* from merely baiting the booboisie as Mencken and Sinclair Lewis were doing.[6]

Certainly White often took pains to resemble in print the ordinary literate citizen rather than Mencken's illiterates. The Lardner type of character, with an idiom that suggested incomplete servitude in a small-town grade school, was still numerous in the early nineteen-twenties, but the number of citizens with some college or university background was on the increase. These were the readers White was aiming for.

However, the *New Yorker* assumption of "a reasonable degree of enlightenment on the part of its readers" did not prevent White from making frequent use of the technique so often employed by Dunne (a crackerbox humorist) and Benchley (another university man) of reducing broad problems to their effect on any humble citizen. In *Alice Through the Cellophane* (1933), a collection of "Notes & Comment" material, White said of the New Deal plan to cut production and raise farm prices:

> The farmers are to be asked to withdraw some of their land from cultivation, to save their own skins. This is a toothsome paradox. . . . I have been thinking about the allotment idea particularly in relation to my own agricultural life, which has found expression in the burgeoning of a rubber plant's acreage, and I doubt if farmers will be happy in their restrictions either.

That there was no excess acreage of rubber plants in most homes and that the analogy with commercial crops was faulty anyway, merely lent a wise-foolish tinge to White's comment. What he stressed was the *feeling* that anyone who keeps even a single house plant may experience if he identifies himself with those commercial farmers whose rights may be violated by economic planners. Moreover, such a feeling would tend to bridge the gap between the metropolitan reader of the *New Yorker* and his country cousin.

In other ways too, White kept insinuating that he was just an ordinary fellow trying to puzzle things out. In *Every Day Is Saturday* (1934), another collection from "Notes & Comment," he remarked that "in a small way" he was against the isolationism of Father Coughlin, a radio commentator with a sizable following in the thirties. White said, ". . . there stands Father Coughlin in front of the microphone, his voice reaching well up into Canada, his voice reaching well down into Mexico, his voice leaping national boundaries as lightly as a rabbit—there he stands, saying that internationalism will be our ruin, and getting millions of letters saying he is right. Will somebody please write us one letter saying that he is wrong—if only so that we can employ a secretary?" White here sets himself in opposition to millions of plain people who he feels have been misled, but he also suggests that he himself is somewhat absurd despite his sensible ideology. Mencken and Benchley used the same technique, often with even more abrupt switches from good sense to absurdity.

The views of the solid citizen and the Little Man are valid, but their authors are primarily writing humor, not sermons or moral essays.

In "Notes & Comment," White tried to be less often a political or economic oracle than a commentator on quaint, colorful trivia about life in New York City. In some of his paragraphs he reminds one of what George Ade had done for Chicago in "Stories of the Streets and of the Town," although White showed a delicate intensity in drawing large implications from these trivia, whereas Ade used cruder strokes. In making the small momentous, White used exactly the reverse of his political technique of reducing the momentous to the small, but in either method his spotlight usually focused on himself as Little Man:

> Coming out into Eighth Avenue from the Rodeo, fresh from the jousts and the great scenes of prowess, with the noise of the hooves of death still in our ears and in our head the respect for the strong-kneed of the world and the lean-hipped and stilt-legged; coming out we got caught alone in the middle of the charging hordes of cars from the north and the stampede of cars from the south, and as we stood there, firm, never yielding, never flinching, letting them brush the nap right off our coat, we realized how special an Eastern feat that was; and for a second we were blood brother to a bronc-rider, and his nerves of steel were our nerves of chromium, one and the same.

Into this one graceful sentence about an experience duplicated by millions of people every day, White packs implications about technology, the East, the "wild" West, and the integrity as well as the role-playing tendencies of the Little Man.

White's narrator tried to cope with a world in which the harmony and order of nature contrasted with the confusion and discord of the man-made environment. While living in New York City, White searched constantly for evidence that even here nature was the abiding reality, and he delighted in his discoveries of that reality. On spotting a thrush near Turtle Bay, he declared, "There is a special satisfaction to a city person in such a visitation; we took twice the pleasure in this thrush that we would have felt had we discovered him in the country." There were instances when the blend of natural and man-made beauty stimulated White to prose-poetry:

> Sometimes, just before nightfall, the buildings and roofs and chimneys come to rest in a calm bath of light which makes them seem suddenly clear and good. The sun being gone, there is no glare, no distortion of shadow; the city is touched with a clarity which gives it a feeling of direction, almost of serenity. There is no moment in the day quite like it—the terraces stand firm in flat colors against a west in which quiet clouds are moored. Dogs and children cry out, distinctly, crisply, then cease—the sounds sharp as country sounds. Windows stand open and curtains stir in the imperceptible air; and when the "L" goes by, the murmur it makes down the street is as significant, as mysterious in its own right, as the bucolic dialogues of katydids.

That White put many such lyrical bulletins from nature into "Notes & Comment" indicates his judgment that city readers were as eager to re-establish their contacts with trees and grass and birds as he was. Paragraphs like this also reveal that long before White moved to Maine, he was striving to banish his sense of alienation from the natural cosmos, in contrast to the wistful resignation of Don Marquis and the distrust of or indifference to nature shown by Benchley and Thurber.

It is not surprising, then, that the first collection of White's longer essays, *Quo Vadimus? or the Case for the Bicycle* (1939), is partially unified by the incongruous contrast between natural harmony and man-made discord. Caught between these two worlds, the average man, says White—and this includes himself—struggles half blindly, but he does struggle. Though often absurd, he becomes strong whenever he recaptures for a moment the mystic oneness with the universe that is his if he wills to feel it. In the title piece of this volume, the narrator asks a

man in a crowd where the hell he is going—"Quo vadis?" He
gets this answer:

> "I'm on my way to the Crowbar Building, Forty-first and
> Park, in Pershing Square, named after General Pershing in
> the Grand Central zone, zone as in Zonite, because I forgot
> to tell Miss Cortright to leave a note for Mr. Josefson when
> he comes in, telling him he should tell the engraver to
> vignette the halftone on page forty-three of the salesmen's
> instruction book that Irwain, Weasey, Weasey, & Button are
> getting out for the Fretherby-Quigley Company, which is to
> go to all their salesmen on the road."

The narrator says, "All you really want is a decent meal when
it comes mealtime, isn't it?" The man adds, "And a warm place
to sleep when it comes night." These needs are "natural" in
their simplicity, but this white-collar unhero has been caught
in the same welter of commercial and mechanical trivia that
entrapped Benchley's man. White as narrator sounds a note
of cosmic doom with a characteristically light touch—"Paths
of glory, leading to the engravers, my man."

The narrator gets his answer to the main question only after
he has amended "Quo vadis?" to "Quo Vadimus?" (Where are
we going?). It turns out that the narrator (and the reader,
hypocrite lecteur!) is in the same fix; he too is bound on a trivial
errand that has nothing to do with his need of a decent meal
and a warm place to sleep. However, the mutual recognition of
each other's plight is not enough to release either of them from
that plight; the moment of communion dissolves, and they continue on their "lonely and imponderable ways."

Elsewhere in *Quo Vadimus?* White is again the bemused but
thoughtful citizen among citizens as he ponders on "How to
Tell a Major Poet From a Minor Poet"; is moderately confused
by the meaningless overuse of "Thank you," "Please," and
other polite mouth-noises; lingers over the problem of how to
pronounce word-coinages in *Time* magazine such as "cinemad-
dict" and RFChairman"; listens skeptically to his thirteen-year-
old nephew's account of the Chicago World's Fair and its evi-

dence of a "Century of Progress"; ponders the problem of choosing an Arthur Murray dance instructor on the basis of the glowing ads; writes an angry letter to the "Association of National Advertisers"; admits he can't get along with women; doubts that a certain pretentious writer in *Harper's* gets along any better; makes pithy pronouncements on public affairs ("The Economics of Abundance means that there is an abundance of economists."); exults, Benchley-fashion, over having survived a visit to the dentist, and squirms when nurses and dental nurses try to sooth him with false phrases.

In his struggles with environment this man sometimes loses, sometimes wins. With the help of "Baby," his pet bird, he vanquishes a life-insurance salesman, but he is victimized by the craze for "organization" of one's work, "being happily disorganized by nature." Doilies are among the trivia of an unnecessarily complex age that bother him. He makes the Benchleyish mistake of carrying his ice skates into a model home on exhibit, under the impression that he is entering a public rink; he sympathizes wordlessly with a man whose wife has led him into the trials of building a house. He shares the exuberance of nature as manifested in his child, who has "a certain intensity," and in his dog with its "idiot love of life," but he reacts coldly to the comments of the boy's teacher at a "progressive" school. In brief, the author-citizen of these pieces is often befuddled by practical problems but never confused for long in his sense of values, and whenever he feels that some event or observed detail is right and good, it is likely to be in some way associated with natural phenomena rather than with phenomena perpetrated by men.

Thus, in "Irtnog," the narrator describes how the mass production and consumption of printed matter resulted first in readers' digests, then in digests of these digests, and so on until all printed matter was condensed into one (nonsense) "Word of the Day." People, he observes, then quit reading, with the result that nature's harmony was restored and man's life regained the goodness it had lost through his correlated abuse of nature

and of himself: "Forests, which had been plundered for news-
print, grew tall again; droughts were unheard of; and people
dwelt in slow comfort, in a green world."

CITIZEN OF THE TOWNSHIP

White's friend, the humorist and scholar Morris Bishop,
says that "In 1938, E. B. White went through some sort of inward
upheaval." [7] As his favorite writer Thoreau had done, White
left the city and went to the woods and pastures in search of
reality. Having found it, partly on a salt-water farm near
Brooklin, Maine, and partly in the perpetual search itself, he
quietly examined the march of the world into war. *One Man's
Meat*, a series of essays most of which appeared in *Harper's*
magazine from July, 1938, to January, 1943, contains the fruits
of that examination.

Perhaps intensification is a better word than upheaval, insofar as White's intellectual life is concerned. The essays in *One
Man's Meat* show a concentration of elements that had been
important in his work long before his removal to the Maine
coast. One was his presentation of himself as citizen-writer, a
role changed only in that this Little Man was now attempting to
gain inward stature by working a small farm. Another was
White's method of discussing public affairs by showing how they
affected this man. A third was his continued urging that all men
need communion with nature.

White was aware that the "back to the land" movement was
not free from affectation. In earlier pieces he had satirized well-
to-do urbanites who "take up" farming, remodel old farmhouses,
and clutter them with all the modern gimcrackery these remod-
elers are supposedly escaping from. In *One Man's Meat* therefore, White continued to present himself as a Little Man tainted
by absurdity. By means of this role he conducted a semidetached,
public examination of himself and his experiment, despite his
basic involvement with that experiment. In the first essay
he told of his efforts to get rid of a large, ugly, gold mirror, "a
sort of symbol of what I was trying to escape from." He couldn't

even give it away, and finally he had to slip it into a doorway and just leave it. On the farm, he was plunged into comic chagrin because his hens produced so many eggs that ". . . we now had a first-rate farm surplus problem on our hands." He mused ruefully over how the profit motive lured him into unloading the extra eggs "on a storekeeper who used to be my friend." He pooh-poohs those who claim that farm life is simple and relaxed—"Pressure! I've been on the trot now for a long time, and don't know whether I'll ever get slowed down." He makes no pretense at living the simple life—the Whites have an electric pump, heater, lights, and refrigerator—or even to being a good farmer: "I have been fooling around this place for a couple of years, but nobody calls my activity agriculture. I simply like to play with animals." In a "letter" to Thoreau he lists the expenses of his own visit to Walden Pond and apologizes to the Concord apostle of simplicity for spending so much on shoes, shelter, and food; however, he defends the purchase of a baseball bat and glove for his son—"You never had to cope with a short-stop." White writes as a family man, not as a loner. The good life must be achieved without the sacrifice of normal, healthy domesticity.

White's relations with his immediate neighbors were evidently good, and his sense of having become part of the community was one of the rewards of his changed life. "The Flocks We Watch by Night," written in November, 1939, three months after the Nazis had rumbled into Poland, is a low-pitched account of how he and a neighboring farmer handled a sick sheep and afterwards talked a bit. "Town Meeting" is an account of that ancient and honorable New England phenomenon from the point of view of E. B. White, participant. Possibly White overstresses the degree of his acceptance by the local citizenry. Yet his satisfaction at being accepted by Charles the farmer, Dameron the lobster fisherman, and other blunt Maine folk does not prevent him from reporting evidence that he was not thus accepted by everybody in the township. When a rumor got around that White was running for the school board, the author gleefully quoted Dameron's comment, "You would have been murdered." White implies that suspicion is the normal reaction for many years of the community as a whole to the outlander in a Maine township.

On the other hand, the average man is above as well as below some of the people. After all, White was a university man writing for *Harper's* and the *New Yorker*. He pokes fun at the illiteracy of the folks who compose letters to the *Rural New Yorker,* his favorite farm journal—fun that is tempered by his admiration of that periodical's ability to interpret modern scientific farming and yet "to preserve and transmit a feeling for the land . . ." Under the wise-foolish mask of "a middle-aged hack," he shows the solid citizen's suspicion of Dr. Francis E. Townsend's old-age pension plan as presented at a Methodist camp-meeting—". . . he wanted to keep the Plan simple and beautiful, like young love before sex has reared its head." Mencken did not damn the fundamentalists in Dayton, Tennessee, more effectively with abuse than White does the Townsendites through faint praise and ironic metaphors. And although White in certain moods admires farmers' "healthy suspicion of book learning," his choice of the following quotation as an example of "practical" folk wisdom is surely satiric: " 'The time to cut hay,' he [a neighbor] said firmly, 'is in hayin' time.' "

Politically, White insisted that his own tendency in times of strain was "toward the spineless middle ground." He has never been a party man, but neither has he been a drifter. In *One Man's Meat* his standard for judging any public event or proposal continued to be: how will it affect me, the ordinary citizen, in my day-to-day experience? The battle of France moved him to imitate Don Marquis' *The Almost Perfect State* and present in dialogue form some propositions on democracy and freedom. One comment was:

> VOICE: How do you know what's good for the people?
> STINGING REPLY: I know what's good for me.

In essay after essay White brought great public affairs down to the level of his average narrator. The question of how far the Government can go in aiding farmers or anyone else without undermining self-reliance vexed White when he received his allotment of free limestone fertilizer under a provision of the Agricultural Adjustment Act. "Thus the New Deal came home to me in powdered form." He heard someone admire the "fine alert faces" of the young German soldiers, and fascism came to him as the disturbance in the stomach which he felt on hearing this remark. America's participation in the war became real to him when he got his occupational questionnaire from Selective Service headquarters—he proudly put himself down as "Farmer / other," the only farm classification on the blank besides "Farmer dairy." The war also became real when he took the post of air-raid warden and raced through the blacked-out countryside, blowing his horn to warn his neighbors of the "attack." Some essays in this book are wholly devoted to the foreground of daily matters, with no reference to the shattering events in the outside world, but more often White's pictures of daily life include carefully interspersed comment on these events: "At 8:55 exactly the Russians resume their withdrawal, the Germans resume their advance, the Japs resume their position along the Siberian border, and it's time to shut the pullets up . . ." White felt that the war was being fought so that individuals could go on doing such tasks and experiencing the elemental as manifested in the simple cycle of the day's activities and the grand cycle of nature's year:

> I sit and feel again the matchless circle of the hours, the endless circle Porgy meant when he sang to Bess: "Mornin' time and evenin' time." . . . It's almost midnight now. Nothing has meaning except the immediate moment, which is precious and indisputable. . . . This gate is dewy on a man's behind. . . . The tenderness of March, the brutality of August. . . . In the west, from the other side of town, the church bell rings, so far away that I can barely make it out, yet there it is. Give me to hold the beloved sound, the enormous sky, the church bell in the night beyond the fields and woods, the same white church near which I stood my watch this afternoon. That was before the sky had cleared. The sky is now intemperately clear. Ring bell. . . .[8] forever ring!

Global war, White felt, tended to make men forget that "the land, and the creatures that go with it, are what is left that is good." Throughout *One Man's Meat* White was trying to stimulate the ordinary man's awareness of world-wide social problems (as the Progressives had tried to do) and to reawaken his sense of relationship with the earth as part of the cosmos. White was also trying to make him feel the interrelatedness of the social and natural realms and the significance of that related- ness for the average man's fate: ". . . a man's free condition is of two parts: the instinctive freedoms he experiences as an animal dweller on a planet, and the practical liberties he enjoys as a privileged member of human society . . ." Without either, true freedom is impossible. The need for stressing freedom through harmony with nature at a time when the admittedly important struggle for political freedom was getting all the headlines was the justification White offered for writing mostly about farm and household chores while "Countries are ransacked, valleys drenched with blood."

Even so, in 1943 White returned to the city in order to par- ticipate more directly in the war effort. In *Here Is New York* (1949), written after the war for *Holiday* magazine, he showed that his ability to find dignity, color, and humor in the city as well as in the country had not waned. He did not, however, abandon his farm or his agrarian philosophy, nor did he aban- don another view, to which he had gradually come in the closing months of his stay on the farm. This view may be extracted by implication from his early writings, but it is one of the few major ideas "produced" by White on the farm in the sense of first finding overt expression during his years there.

"The earth is common ground," he wrote in *One Man's Meat*, "and we are all overlords, whether we hold title or not; gradually the idea is taking form that the land must be held in safekeeping, that one generation is to some extent responsible to the next . . ." Paradoxically, White's individualism had led him to an agrarian collectivism of a traditional American sort. A hundred years earlier, the United States had been dotted with experimental colonies that included in their ideologies the common right of all men to all the land, from the Fourieristic "consociations" to the "United Orders" among the Mormons. Among writers, Thoreau had held the surprisingly anti-individualistic view that the State must protect forests and wildlife by regulating trappers and loggers, and that townships should preserve some wild land as public property.[9] Henry George had maintained that ". . . the common right to land has everywhere been primarily recognized . . ." [10] William Faulkner was not interested in George's single-tax theory, but through Uncle Ike's cogitations in *Go Down Moses*, Faulkner too has suggested that individuals can only hold the land in trust, not really own it, because it belongs to all men in common. The roots of White's agrarian communalism reach far back, and into some odd corners.

CITIZEN OF THE WORLD

Despite his distrust of Father Coughlin's isolationism, White during the early thirties could himself be described as moderately isolationist. An early poem, "Statement of the Foreign Policy of One Citizen of the United States," expressed a view held by Will Rogers and much of the public of both humorists in the late nineteen-twenties and early thirties. White's little citizen says,

> I have no plan
> Involving Japan.
>
> I do not wish to crush
> Soviet Rush . . .
>
> Germany, as far as I am concerned,
> Can consider the other cheek turned . . .

But White did not consider the problem of world peace solved by such passivity. In the same volume (*The Fox of Peapack*, 1928–1938), he prophesied that war would yet take many lives. Any confusion in his mind vanished before World War II was very old. During the battle of France, in June, 1940, White suggested in *One Man's Meat* that planning a "perfect state" would involve designing an all-inclusive world society. Later he hinted that isolationism died when the Japanese attacked on December 7, 1941, and internationalism would have to be its replacement. He warned that, "Before you can be an internationalist you have first to be a naturalist and feel the ground under you making a whole circle," but from a feeling of unity with nature one might progress to a sound interest in the unity of man. Thus White's urging that world government was the possible redeeming force in global politics was closely related to his belief in nature as the source of personal redemption.

Beginning on April 19, 1943, White intermittently used his "Notes & Comment" section in the *New Yorker* as a blackboard for essays of usually no more than three or four paragraphs encouraging "a federation of democratic countries, which differs from a league in that it has a legislature that can legislate, a judiciary that can judge, and an executive that can execute." These essays were collected in book form in *The Wild Flag* (1946). In these pieces he supported the budding United Nations, though he believed it fell short in not requiring any nation to get rid of the great stumbling block to global unity: national sovereignty.

How far White was ahead of the average reader of the *New Yorker* it would be hard to say, especially as White had no blueprint for achieving a workable world government and mainly confined himself to general principles. He rejected the old-style nationalism of one newspaper of mass circulation, Hearst's New York *Daily Mirror,* but he liked to feel that he spoke for "Pfc. Herbert Weintraub" and other millions of people who "are groping toward something which still has no name but which keeps turning up . . . the yet unclaimed triumph: justice among men of all races, a world in which children (of whatever country) are warm and unafraid." White tried to make this groping articulate.

In his role of spokesman for the ordinary man, White did not flatter the man's capacity for "supranationalism," rather, he cited

Thurber's "The Day the Dam Broke" as an example of how liable the people are to panic, and he warned that "World government is an appalling prospect. . . . Certainly the world is not ready for government on a planetary scale. In our opinion, it will never be ready. The test is whether the people will chance it anyway, like children who hear the familiar cry, 'Coming, whether ready or not!'" Man might make a botch of world federation and so perish, but without trying it he would certainly perish. One course was risky, but the other was fatal.

In voicing what he hoped the people felt, White usually spoke as an insignificant fellow who, however sure of his values, was bewildered by the facts. He portrayed himself as "just a nervous little homebody in a sack suit, trying to unravel supply lines, spearheads, flank movements . . . and the whole impossible mystery of modern tactical warfare." Once in a while he dropped the mask of meekness and hurled political epigrams with cracker-barrel deftness:

> One nation's common sense is another nation's high blood pressure.

> Bear in mind always that foreign policy is domestic policy with its hat on.

> Remember, an intelligence service is, in fact, a stupidity service.

Had they been White's contemporaries, Ade, Dunne, and their fellow wits of the Whitechapel Club would have applauded their colleague on the *New Yorker*.

THE MAZE, AND THE WAY OUT

White showed his feeling for rural ways in two narratives for children that are probably read more often by adults, *Stuart Little* (1945), and *Charlotte's Web* (1952). After *The Wild Flag*, the fullest and most forthright statements of White's main ideas appeared in *The Second Tree From the Corner* (1954).[11] This collection included short stories, essays, prefaces, parodies, poems, and extracts from "Notes & Comment." White's concern with the acceleration of change in our time shows in his choice of titles for the first two groups of pieces in this book. Group I is headed "Time Past, Time Future," and the second group is labeled "Time Present." The choice of these phrases from T. S. Eliot's "Burnt Norton" does not, however, imply any special interest on White's part in the intellectual as a superior being. White's basic theme is still the common citizen trying to preserve his integrity, and he still believes that the chief anchor for that citizen must be nature in all its regularity and mystery.

In "A Weekend With the Angels," the troubles of the narrator are largely those of Irvin S. Cobb in *Speaking of Operations—*" i.e., hospital troubles. In "The Door," a man is making arrangements for his own commitment to a mental institution and possibly for a lobotomy. Unlike Walter Mitty, White's man in "The Door," though disturbed, is still sane ethically; it is environment that has taken leave of reason and integrity:

> Everything (he kept saying) is something it isn't. And everybody is always somewhere else. Maybe it was the city, being in the city, that made him feel how queer everything was and that it was something else. Maybe (he kept thinking) it was the names of the things. The names were tex and frequently koid. Or they were flex and oid or they were duroid (sani) or flexsan (duro), but everything was glass (but not quite glass) and the thing that you touched (the surface washable, crease-resistant) was rubber, only it wasn't quite rubber and you didn't quite touch it but almost. The wall, which was glass but thrutex, turned out on being approached not to be a wall, it was something else, it was an opening or doorway—and the doorway (through which he saw himself approaching) turned out to be something else, it was a wall.

To thus abandon reality as this man's environment has done is to become, in the words of the cartoonist Jules Feiffer, "Sick, sick, sick." Religion, science, and sex have all offered "doors" out of this sick society—doors that turned out to be blank walls.

The man feels like a rat trapped in a maze and deliberately tricked by a high priest of this society—a scientist—for some end known only to that scientist, if to him.

Even the reader is thrown into a daze by "The Hour of Letdown," in which a man carries a mechanical "brain" into a bar and buys drinks for it.[12] In contrast, the alleged psychoneurotic in "The Second Tree From the Corner" suddenly discovers what Walt Whitman, an author whom White has parodied but respects, once called the "primal sanities" of nature. Paradoxically but not surprisingly, what touches off Trexler's revelation is his sudden awareness that his analyst too is on the ragged edge. When Trexler throws the analyst's own question, "What do you want?" right back at him, the doctor says, "I want a wing on the small house I own in Westport. I want more money, and more leisure to do the things I want to do." At this expression of commonplace and mutually contradictory aims, Trexler's self-absorption and fear is suddenly replaced by pity. "Poor, scared, overworked bastard," he thinks. With this rush of feeling comes a restoration of his solidarity with nature. He catches sight of a small tree in the twilight, and ". . . his sickness seemed health, his dizziness stability." He announces, "I want the second tree from the corner, just as it stands," and the renewed communion restores his courage.

Trexler's rediscovery of nature is part of a personal revolt, but man in the mass can revolt too. "The Decline of Sport" is a satiric parable in which radio, television, and sky-writing have made each passive mass of spectators emotionally the prey of several sporting events at once. The result is catastrophic and then a rediscovery of simpler, more contemplative pleasures like "old, twisty roads that led through main streets and past barnyards, with their mild congestions and pleasant smells." Here, as in "Irtnog," the New-Citizen-as-consumer of whom Walter Weyl spoke in 1912 has finally expressed his resentment in a boycott. The difference between the optimism of the first Progressives and the more cautious, less political outlook of White some forty years later is seen in that mass catastrophe is needed to provoke the consumers' revolt, and nature, not politics, turns out to be the chief restorative.

In "The Morning of the Day They Did It," White warns of what may happen should man go too far in manipulating nature through technology. At a time perhaps not so far in the future, toxic disinfectants like "Tri-D" (a name suggested, no doubt, by DDT)[13] have rendered the earth dangerous for human habitation. Two average Americans, from Brooklyn and from Iowa, who happen to be U.S. Army officers flying with a secret weapon, suddenly experience the intoxicating detachment induced by stratospheric flight. They feel like "doing a little shooting," and civilization is thereby destroyed. The few survivors move to another planet where the people do only what genuinely holds their interest and where the unsprayed apples are often wormy but have "a most wonderful flavor." The narrator, just another white-collar man who in this case happens to be a video newscaster, had been fed up with the scientific nightmare of life on earth, but White reminds us of the confusion that often blurs the average man's insight: the fellow says nostalgically, "I would be lying if I said I didn't miss that other life, I loved it so." White believes that the ordinary man can, if pushed, discover nature and its harmonies, but the insight that leads to this discovery isn't permanent; it must be perpetually renewed.

The third group of sketches in *The Second Tree From the Corner* is entitled "The Wonderful World of Letters" and includes some provocative remarks on humor and a discussion of Don Marquis, whom White admired as a satirist and as a poet, and of whose idealism White had more than a touch (the protagonist in "The Door" quotes from Marquis' *Dreams and Dust*, "My heart has followed all my days something I cannot name," and suggests that disappointment in this quest killed Marquis).[14] White, as seen, does not share the complete disillusion of this protagonist or of Marquis. Nine poems comprise the fourth group in this book. The magic of nature in both city and country is the main subject of "The City and the Land," the fifth and last group of sketches in this volume. In this group appears the mock-epic "Death of a Pig," in which E. B. White, farmer, copes with the cosmic mysteries of life and death as they disrupt his works and days through the sickness and demise of an animal. As usual, White draws a sweeping moral from a small incident: ". . . I knew that what could be true of my pig could be true also of the rest of my tidy world." The writer-farmer is moved, though not upset, by the basic insecurity of all things.

Moved but not upset—this is true of White whether he is dissecting the follies of an age of gadgetry or pondering on the butchery of a lamb or the death of a pig. For all his interest in nature, White was not a pessimistic Darwinian like Dreiser, Dos Passos, or Hemingway, or like Marquis or Thurber, despite his agreement with Thurber on so many other matters. Despite his realism about nature's brutality to farm animals, White's over-all view is more like that of the great romantic writers than like the Darwinians'. Blake with his ability to see eternity in a grain of sand, Wordsworth recalling the glimpses of immortality he had had as a child, Thoreau hearing "an Iliad and Odyssey in the air" when a mosquito hummed, Whitman inviting his soul by observing a spear of summer grass, Frost finding in the use of an ax "My avocation and my vocation"—these are among White's spiritual predecessors. He belongs also with the eloquent naturalists who, in spite of Darwinism, felt that man must achieve a oneness with nature beyond merely scientific understanding, and with present-day ecologists like Aldo Leopold and Paul Errington who feel, as Joseph Wood Krutch has put it, that "conservation is not enough." [15] In an early poem White had asked "The God I half believe in" to

> Keep most carefully alive in me
> Something of the expectancy
> That is somehow likeliest to be
> In a child waking,
> A day breaking,
> A robin singing,
> Or a telephone ringing . . .

The last item suggests that White will find intensity in the man-made environment if given half a chance (Wordsworth had found it on Westminster bridge as well as among the Cumberland lakes), but he looks more hopefully to a cosmic order of which man could be a harmonious part if only he would. White denies the premise of the literary Darwinians that nature is indifferent to man. It could be so only if man remains indifferent to it. The view of Wordsworth and Emerson that as a child man felt his unity with nature but lost it as he grew older was strongly felt by White. In *One Man's Meat* he declared of his "love affair" with freedom: "It began with the haunting intimation (which I presume every child receives) of his mystical inner life; of God in man; of nature publishing herself through the 'I.' " White's two books for children amplify this view. One of the chief ends of man, he felt, was to recapture this unity and in a sense, to put it to work straightening out the inevitably "unnatural" confusions of civilization.

At home in both the country and the city, E. B. White helped the *New Yorker* to combine small-town informality with cosmopolitan breadth and refinement. The prose and some of the poetry of this Cornell graduate suggest a neighbor leaning on the fire escape to talk to another neighbor. His main *persona* is the urban white-collar man attempting to recapture the "sanity and repose of nature," [16] and this character is yet another version of one met with among White's humorous predecessors and colleagues, particularly Finley Peter Dunne, Clarence Day, Jr., Donald Ogden Stewart, Robert Benchley, Frank Sullivan, Wolcott Gibbs, John McNulty, and James Thurber—the Little Man who, even in his deteriorated condition, represents the closest we can get to the ideal, rational citizen.

18

Will Cuppy:
The Wise Fool as Pedant

In Will Cuppy one finds another humorist reared in the Midwest who went to New York and eventually became known in
print as a little citizen of urban America in general. Cuppy was
born in 1884 at Auburn, Indiana, and as a child he passed most
of his summers on a farm near South Whitley in that state,

". . . where I acquired my first knowledge of the birds and the flowers and all the other aspects of animate nature which I have treated none too kindly in some of my writings."[1] Another literary descendant of the University Wits, Cuppy took a B.A. at the University of Chicago (1907) and stayed around the campus for seven more years, "taking courses in practically everything, with or without bothering to go to examinations." He claimed "I wanted rather desperately to learn something about life and I thought that was the way to go about it." He added that he was saved from getting a Ph.D. by difficulties with "Old High Middle Gothic and other linguistic riddles," but Burton Rascoe, who knew him both as a student in Chicago and as a writer in New York, says that Cuppy's real reason for staying so long at the university "was that he was obviously afraid of the great world outside."[2] According to Rascoe, a huge inferiority complex was the source of Cuppy's fear and this complex also made him so diffident about writing that none of his books would ever have been published were it not for the constant encouragement of Isabel Paterson, a novelist and a colleague of Cuppy on the New York *Herald Tribune*. Certainly the shrinking Little Man whose role Cuppy played in his humor does, at times, resemble the person with a chronic sense of inferiority described by Rascoe.

A LIFETIME STUDENT

Cuppy finally settled for an M.A., and cut the collegiate cord. Later he made good use of his long wandering in the groves of Academe, and probably worked off some personal hostilities, in his satiric comments on pundits of all kinds. Yet he himself was a thorough scholar, meticulous beyond all ordinary necessity. His friend Fred Feldkamp says of Will:

> Before writing a line on any topic—or even thinking about what he might write—he would read every volume and article on the subject that he could find—including, in many cases, obscure books no longer available in this country. This was standard operating procedure, whether the topic in question was the Giant Ground Sloth or Catherine the Great.

After having absorbed this exhaustive amount of material, he would make notes on little 3-by-5 index cards, which he would then file under the appropriate subheading in a card-file box. Usually he would amass hundreds and hundreds of these cards in several boxes, before beginning to block out his piece. In some cases, he would read more than twenty-five thick volumes before writing a one-thousand-word piece. Cuppy felt that he must know his subject as thoroughly as was humanly possible before going to work on it.[3]

Cuppy carefully concealed his literary erudition behind the mask of a fellow who has nothing against prose but has a healthy suspicion of poetry, the most literary of literary disciplines:

I would say more about Milton's work, but I'm a poetry-skipper myself. I don't like to boast, but I have probably skipped more poetry than any other person of my age and weight in this country—make it any other *two* persons. This doesn't mean that I hate poetry. I don't feel that strongly about it. It only means that those who wish to communicate with me by means of the written word must do so in prose.[4]

Cuppy may not have enjoyed poetry, but one does not ordinarily get an M.A. in English by skipping that much of it. As had Dunne, Rogers, Marquis, and sometimes E. B. White, Cuppy wooed readers with less erudition in the humanities than himself by concealing his learning. In history and the sciences, he lured readers by the opposite method of displaying his learning in order to make fun of it and of himself as a Little Man turned pompous pedant.

Cuppy's first book was *Maroon Tales* (1909), a set of short stories about fraternity life at the University of Chicago. Rascoe says that Cuppy wrote these tales at the request of university authorities who wished him thus to make up some "traditions" for the recently inaugurated fraternity system there. In New York, Cuppy's routine job for many years was conducting a book-review column, "Mystery and Adventure," in the *Herald Tribune,* a column devoted mainly to detective novels and other books about crime. He came late to the field of humor; Thurber, White, and Cuppy published their first prose collections of humor in the same year (1929), but Cuppy was five years older than Thurber and ten years older than White.

In 1921, Cuppy moved out to an abandoned cabin near Zack's Inlet on Jones Island, off Long Island, and lived for over seven years in what he felt was his real home—". . . 'I have been here before,' and I care not if the alienists have a long, insulting name for that particular feeling." He anticipated E. B. White in renewing his contact with nature, "my ancient home," simplifying his life and enjoying wildness without cutting himself off from his friends in town, though unlike White, he had no manual aptitude for farming or interest in it. Cuppy ended his full-time retreat in 1929 when most of Jones Island was turned into Jones Beach and made a New York state park. However, his shack seems to have been outside the park limits, and until his final illness Cuppy often returned for visits lasting up to several weeks.

A number of sketches written during his seven-year "exile" were collected in his first book of humor, *How to Be a Hermit* (1929).[5] In this work, which went into six printings in six months, Cuppy used the problem of keeping bachelor's hall in a beach shanty as a peg on which to hang satires of naturalists, psychologists, architecture, cookery, the too-well-organized home, unwelcome visitors, and writers who deal pretentiously with these subjects, such as the columnists in *Good Housekeeping* and *Better Homes & Gardens*. Before this book was published he had begun amassing material for several volumes of parody and satire on field manuals for amateur nature-chasers. *How to Tell Your Friends From the Apes* (1932), *How to Become Extinct* (1941), and *How to Attract the Wombat* (1949) appeared during Cuppy's lifetime.[6] Possibly owing something to Oliver Herford's irreverent *A Child's Primer of Natural History* (1899) and to Robert Benchley's parodies of nature writers, these books are largely made up of epigrams and one- and two-paragraph essays on birds, fish, reptiles, and mammals, including primitive man and modern man. The paragraphs are often bewhiskered with satirical footnotes.

Cuppy's satires were not, as some readers claimed, just "little pieces about animals," any more than were Thurber's zoological wonders in *Fables for Our Time* and *The Beast in Me*. Cuppy wrote about animals as if they were people, and said of this tactic, "Why do you suppose I did that unless it was to get in all those dirty cracks about the human race, a form of life I suppose I am a little too much inclined to look down upon?" [7] Typical of these cracks was, "Ants operate by instinct instead of intelligence. Intelligence is the capacity to know what we are doing and instinct is just instinct. The results are about the same." [8]

Cuppy died in November, 1949. A student to the last, he left some two hundred thousand cards of notes in several hundred card-file boxes. From this huge mass of material Fred Feldkamp quarried two more books. *The Decline and Fall of Practically Everybody* (1950) was a burlesque history of the human race, suggested perhaps by *1066 and All That* (1931), a comic history of Great Britain by W. C. Sellar and R. J. Yeatman.[9] *How to Get From January to December* (1951) was a comic almanac; in language it did not much resemble the almanacs of Josh Billings and Abe Martin, but the cynicism of some of its comments did recall the horse sense of these crackerbox sages, especially in the occasional references to political and historical topics. Cuppy used the murder of Marat by Charlotte Corday to jibe at political agitators of both extremes: he shed no tears for Marat, but "I can see Charlotte's side of it, too; she thought she was doing good, and she didn't mind attracting a little attention at the same time." [10] However, this book, along with Cuppy's bestiaries, is less like crackerbox humor and more like Day's *This Simian World* and the pieces in which Benchley's narrator is baffled by gadgets. All three writers stress man's preoccupation with complicated trivia.

A SOCRATIC NEUROTIC

Cuppy's unusual life as a scholarly recluse did not deter him from presenting most of his humor in the familiar guise of the badgered Little Man who is also a wise fool. In *How to Be a*

Hermit Cuppy depicts his *alter ego* as harassed by the big city and its gadgetry but aware that it, and not he, has wandered from sensible norms: ". . . a hermit is simply a person to whom civilization has failed to adjust itself." Cuppy's narrator hates to think of being called a misfit, and he is aware that psychoanalysts would consider him deviant and try to "cure" him. The problems of getting along in the Gadget Age confuse him as much as they baffle Benchley and Thurber—"Hermits loose in Manhattan use more of these [nickels] than the native since they are likely to drop another one in the dujingus when they exit, from sheer inability in the excitement to know whether they are going or coming." Nevertheless, even on his island he is, "scientifically speaking, one of the by-products of the Machine Age. My one culinary talent lies in thinking up new, novel and palatable ways of opening tin cans."

In this book Cuppy attacks pretentiousness, especially of the intellectual kind, from the disarming viewpoint of the harmlessly conceited wiseacre—Jones Beachcombing variety. He boasts that a movement exists among architects to use his shack as "a textbook example of what's wrong with their business. The sooner the better—that will give the dome of St. Paul's a rest." Shortly thereafter, he says of his beloved bungalow, "A snippy author is fond of remarking that its architecture shows a quality of brute force rather than an association of many intellects. Yes, and I have more than a suspicion that if the intelligentsia had designed my residence it wouldn't be here to tell the tale." From behind his wall of inordinate pride, the speaker snipes with his common sense at those writers who prescribe elaborately for the average family on home maintenance, budgeting and cookery— all those busy minds who would make the daily life of the Little Man and his household more cluttered with trivia than it already is. In place of elaborate prescriptions by slick writers, Cuppy solemnly proposed the "Cuppy Plan of Motionless Housekeeping."

In subsequent collections, Cuppy often wore the same wisefoolish mask. Ignoring, with airy inconsistency, his own statements of affection for the beach, the ocean, and the simple life, Cuppy often acts the part of a narrator who resembles Benchley's in being disturbed to the point of psychosis by what sentimental writers call Nature or the Great Outdoors: "The Robin is called the harbinger of spring because he makes so much noise. He starts singing under your window before daylight in March and continues with brief intermissions for lunch until you are taken to Bellevue." [11] Cuppy and Benchley both used their *personae* as ways of ridiculing the gushy approach to this subject.

When scientific or literary erudition is the target, Cuppy shoots at it by having his Little Fellow, now operating as pedant, get all balled up in his efforts to sound as though he knew his subjects. Cuppy's darts are thus blunted; savants may be amused by this fellow's bungling, and laymen may be amused at the satire on the savants. This satire comes in part through the shrewdness with which this Little Man, for all his inadequacy in matters of mere fact, evaluates the specialists' reasoning: "Plesiosaurs had very little fun. They had to go ashore to lay their eggs and that sort of thing. They also tried to get along with gizzards instead of stomachs, swallowing pebbles after each meal to grind their food. At least, pebbles have been found near fossil Plesiosaurs, and to a scientist that means the Plesiosaur had a gizzard." [12]

Other mixtures of foolishness and common sense appear when Cuppy's man earnestly belabors the dead theories of Aristotle, Buffon, Cuvier, and other superseded naturalists. He is acute in pointing out their dogmatism; he is obtuse in showing as much zeal as if their statements were contemporary. He is the fool also in the simplicity and wrongheadedness of his refutations:

> Too often, when discussing the feelings of fish, their desirability as pets, or their value as citizens, he [Cuvier] would run on like this: "The inhabitant of the water does not attach itself. It has no language, no affection; it does not know what it is to be husband or father, or to make an abode for itself." Rubbish, Baron Cuvier!
> Every single thing in that little lecture is wrong, Baron,

excepting possibly the part about language, and that is extremely shaky. How do you know that fish have no language?
In my opinion they have, but you wouldn't understand it because it isn't full of accents like your own. As for fish not
knowing what it is to be a husband and father, where do you
think Minnows come from, anyway?[13]

On the other hand, Cuppy jeers at people who cling to myths
that have been disproved by proper investigation, notions such
as that the earth is flat and there are no germs. His over-all view
is a mean between extremes and is intended to represent the majority of fairly literate people.

NATURE, AND NATURE'S DOOM

Cuppy often depicts the Little Man as a slightly superior
beast doomed by natural forces which are manifested within
him by the lusts for wealth, violence, and power, and which
operate outside him as the impersonal grinding of the cosmos.
In these moods Cuppy resembles Marquis, Thurber, and other
exponents of pessimistic naturalism. Cuppy's depiction of man
the animal is untempered by Day's hope that the animal will
progress in the future as he has progressed in the past; communion with ocean and sky on Jones Beach did not lead him to
see the benevolence E. B. White found in the cycle of the seasons
and in the bluntness of his Yankee neighbors. Cuppy made
friends with the Coast Guardsmen and a few of the summer residents near his hermitage, but he saw the human race in general
as distinguished mainly for their garrulity and ferocity:

> The Modern Man or Nervous Wreck is the highest of all
> mammals because anyone can see that he is. There are about
> 2,000,000,000 Modern Men or too many. The Modern Man's
> highly developed brain has made him what he is and you
> know what he is.[1] The development of his brain is caused by
> his upright or bipedal position, as in the Penguin, the
> Dinosaur and other extinct reptiles. Modern Man has been
> called the Talking Animal because he talks more than any

three other animals chosen at random. He has also been called the Reasoning Animal but there may be a catch in this. The fissure of Sylvius and the fissure of Rolando enable him to argue in circles. His main pursuits in the order named are murder, robbery, kidnapping, body-snatching, barratry, nepotism, arson, and mayhem. This is known as the Good, the True and the Beautiful. Modern Men are viviparous. They mature slowly but make up for it later, generally from July first to June thirtieth inclusive. The females carry nickels and pins in their mouths. They are fond of glittering objects, bits of ribbon and olives.[2] All Modern Men are descended from a Wormlike creature but it shows more on some people. Modern Man will never become extinct if the Democrats can help it.[3]

[*Cuppy's footnotes*] [1]It is because of his brain that he has risen above the animals. Guess which animals he has risen above.

[2]Each male has from 2 to 700 females with whom he discusses current events. Of these he marries from 3 to 17.

[3]To be perfectly fair, Modern Man was invented on October 25, 4004 B.C., at 9 o'clock in the morning, according to the statement of Dr. John Lightfoot (1602–1675) of Stoke-upon-Trent, Vice-chancellor of the University of Cambridge. Dr. Lightfoot's *Whole Works* comes in thirteen volumes.

Perhaps Cuppy's philosophy may be summed up thus: man is a concentration of the worst aspects of a meaningless universe, and he has worsened his lot still more by creating for himself an environment divorced from the nonhuman world through its new and strange modes of becoming more irrational, complex, and brutal than that world. Toward the unworthy end of creating this environment, man has exercised the superior cranial capacity that might instead have furthered the uses of reason. Yet the individual, if he is not too damned intellectual, may struggle to achieve a kind of balance consisting of one part acceptance of the nonhuman aspects of nature, one part honesty, one part humility, and several parts of skepticism concerning his species—including himself—and its works. This balance is a valid ideal, and though he may never achieve it, the struggle itself may help him to stave off the complete disorder of self forced upon him by a technical but still primitive age.[14]

The division of society into a mindless mob and a small elite of good men trying to think rationally is explicit in Mencken and implicit in several other humorists looked at thus far, including Will Cuppy. This division is not, of course, a peculiarly American one; Cuppy resembled Horace and Swift in finding for himself the friendship of a few choice individuals. Fred Feldkamp was one, and so was Isabel Paterson, "to whom I always dedicate my books." Cuppy also found a vocation in playing the role of wise fool as pedant, a role that enabled him to combine scholarship and humor and to make the most of his limitations as a writer through use of the paragraph, the epigram, and the footnote as his chief humorous weapons (like Will Rogers, Cuppy could not tell a story). But the depth of Cuppy's pessimism rivaled Lardner's; he stressed that nothing worked well in alleviating *la condition humaine*. He could see only one final solution: "I would go so far as to say that becoming extinct is the perfect answer to everything and I defy anybody to think of a better. Other solutions are mere palliatives . . ."[15]

19

The Sane Psychoses of S. J. Perelman

As if American fiction thrived on impending disaster, 1929, the year of the Great Crash, saw the appearance of Hemingway's *A Farewell to Arms,* Wolfe's *Look Homeward, Angel,* Faulkner's *The Sound and the Fury,* and Sinclair Lewis' *Dodsworth.* The production of "light" literature was no less interesting than that of "heavy." Three "first" books of humor were published by writers destined for prominence in that field: *Is Sex Necessary?* by Thurber and White, *How to Be a Hermit* by Will Cuppy, and *Dawn Ginsbergh's Revenge* by S. J. Perelman.

Sidney Joseph Perelman was born in Brooklyn (1904), but grew up mainly in Rhode Island. At the Classical High School in Providence he was chairman of the debating society, to which he once contributed what he calls "a philippic entitled 'Science vs. Religion,' an indigestible hash of Robert Ingersoll and Haldeman-Julius." He went on to Brown University, where he had "a brief, precarious toehold as assistant art editor" of *Casements,* a literary magazine. At Brown he became part of a group of literary hopefuls that included Israel Kapstein, Quentin Reynolds, and Nathanael West, whose sister Laura he married and whose fiction he undoubtedly influenced.[1]

SCENARIO WRITER

Perelman was graduated from Brown in 1925 and by December of that year was "settled" in Greenwich Village, drawing cartoons and writing parodies and burlesques. For awhile he was on the staff of *Judge,* and some of his early prose appeared in that magazine as well as in *College Humor,* the "old" *Life,* and other periodicals. Most of these early pieces deserve not to have been reprinted in *Dawn Ginsbergh's Revenge.* Despite the weakness of its contents, however, this book evidently did not hinder—and may have helped—Perelman's breaking into scriptwriting for the movies, "an occupation which, like herding swine, makes the vocabulary pungent but contributes little to one's prose style." Perhaps for humorous effect Perelman was deliberately underestimating his improvement as a writer for magazines during those first years in Hollywood; certainly the magazine pieces published after he had begun his movie work show a marked rise in quality over the strained and tasteless burlesques in his first book and in *Parlor, Bedlam and Bath* (1930), a satire done in collaboration with Quentin Reynolds. Working on wildly comic scripts for the Marx brothers, such as *Monkey Business* (1931) and *Horsefeathers* (1932), may have made him defter in handling nightmarish farce in the essay form. Probably his interest in film writing and in the legitimate drama are responsible for the frequency with which his essays include brief scenarios; undoubtedly the influence of the *New Yorker,* for which he began writing in 1932, helped also to give his prose a high compression and crackle which it had shown only at moments before that date.

The "I" in Perelman's essays is often on the verge of a nervous breakdown, and the author himself has had his share of personal problems, but the fact that he has been a hard and prolific worker should discourage the reader from casually identifying the author with his *alter ego.* Besides doing films for the Marx brothers, Perelman worked on *Sweethearts* (starring Nelson Eddy and Jeanette MacDonald), *Ambush* (1939), and a number of scenarios never filmed. In 1956 he helped producer Mike Todd to adapt Jules Verne's *Around the World in Eighty Days* for a film that won an Academy Award as the best picture of the year. Perelman has also written for the legitimate stage, doing an unsuccessful piece called *The Ladders;* a revue entitled *Sherry Flip* (1932) which, he says, "set the American theater back a hundred years"; and *Sweet Bye and Bye* (with Al Hirschfeld, Ogden Nash, and Vernon Duke). With his wife, Perelman did *The Night Before Christmas* (1941), and with Ogden Nash and Kurt Weill he wrote the successful *One Touch of Venus* (1943). In addition to his dramatic work, he has turned out a stream of magazine pieces, most of which have appeared in the *New Yorker,* and which to date fill fourteen volumes.[2]

In 1932 the Perelmans followed the trail of Bangs, Cobb, Lardner, Benchley, and Thurber from Manhattan to the outskirts. Preceding Dorothy Parker, they bought land in Bucks County, Pennsylvania, an area which A. C. Spectorsky insists is too far from New York City to be a suburb and must be classed as an "exurb."[3] The Perelmans' move resulted in *Acres and Pains* (1947) and a number of shorter pieces. Ocean voyages by Perel-

man after World War II were described in *Westward Ha!* (1948)
and *The Swiss Family Perelman* (1950).

CRAZY—LIKE A FOX

Perelman has been readier than some humorists to acknowledge influences on his writing. He has told an interviewer
that his major debts are to Ring Lardner's nonsense plays, to
Robert Benchley—"about Benchley I am practically idola-
trous" [4]—Stephen Leacock, George Ade, and James Joyce, whom
he considers "*the* great comic writer of our time." To the mention of these writers and of Perelman's movie jobs, one should
add that at his wackiest, Perelman shows some resemblance to
Thurber. In turn, Perelman's humor has drawn praise from
Dorothy Parker and from Benchley. In her "Introduction" to
The Most of Perelman, Miss Parker says that Benchley and Lardner are Perelman's only worthy predecessors, and in a foreword to
Strictly From Hunger, Benchley asserted that "Perelman took
over the *dementia praecox* field. . ." [5]

To disentangle the specific influences of the writers named
would be as fruitless as impossible. In general, Perelman resembles the Lardner of the plays in his frequent use of a dramatic
framework; Leacock, Benchley, and Joyce in his talent for parody
and monologue; and the Marx brothers in his controlled wildness
of incident and metaphor. In his emphasis on a bedeviled Little
Man of the white-collar class as his *alter ego,* he resembles all of
the writers mentioned—including Joyce—except for Ade, who
had more often stressed the self-made entrepreneur. Moreover,
Perelman also stands in the mainstream of American humor by
virtue of his frequent contrasting of the Little Man with the
crass and venal executives, salesmen, ad-writers, and movie-makers
who harass him—those who might be called the *lumpen* middle
class. In Perelman's version of the elite versus the mob, the
archetype who represents the elite is defeated and disturbed, but
he is still a battler against odds for his sanity, as have been the

protagonists of such diverse humorists as Mencken. Benchley, White, Cuppy, and at times, Ogden Nash.

Once in a while Perelman uses Jewish dialect, and at such times he belongs to a branch of a once important but now dying tradition: dialect humor based on the uncouth English of immigrant minorities. In the twentieth century this tradition was represented earlier by George V. Hobart and his "gonversationings" of Mr. and Mrs. Dinkelspiel; the stories by Montague Glass about Potash and Perlmutter,[6] and later by the work of Milt Gross with his "Nize Baby" series; Arthur Kober with his tales about Bella Gross and her family; and Dr. Leo Rosten (Leonard Q. Ross) in his stories about H*Y*M*A*N K*A*P*L*A*N.

Perelman's use of Jewish dialect is most frequent in *Dawn Ginsbergh's Revenge,* where he employs many Yiddish words or Yiddish-English turns of phrase in puns or in bits of parody—"If you must vex somebody, why don't you go home and vex the floors?" Other examples are, "What It Minns to Be a Minnow," and "It was a veritable fairyland as we drove homeward in the cutter with the bells tinkling and Irma's cheeks red like two apples her cheeks were red." In his later books Perelman limits this dialect to an occasional Yiddish word, like "momzer," "zoftick," or "nebich," and to a few Yiddish turns of English phrases, as in the title, "You Should Live So, Walden Pond." He uses a good many Jewish proper names, and the total effect of these devices is to suggest the forced and incongruous merging of the most resistant elements in the Anglo-Saxon and Jewish cultures. This incongruity has been a fertile source of humor to writers for the Yiddish theater, and a historian of that theater could doubtless find that it contributed as well to Perelman's development.

Those who see only despair and insanity in Perelman's humor have not looked hard at his major type-figure. The Little Man may be pushed toward the gulf, but he rarely loses his sense of values—values which the author behind the mask emphatically shares. Sometimes the author as such explicitly endorses the stand of this character; thus, in *Dawn Ginsbergh's Revenge*, Perelman presents a "Fairy Tale for Bored Bar-Flies" which features

> a certain Moorish bimbo in the great wastelands along the upper Bronx River by the name of Etta Falcovsky who had become twenty-three years of age *without* changing her name to Yvette Falconer and who did *not* comb her hair straight back and sag from her hips in order to look like Edna Best. . . . The boy friend did *not* wear striped shirts with stiff bosoms and there were *no* pleats in his waistband. He had *not* read "The Mansions of Philosophy" and he was *not* taking journalism courses at Columbia.

The tale is merely about how they met and married and lived simply and happily thereafter. They brought up two kids in a Bronx flat and did not change their way of life even when the boy's grandfather left them half a million dollars. In short, they lived in sober, frugal contrast to the stereotypes in fiction and films of the twenties, and when they died, in old age, "The newspapers gave them a line apiece and their neighbors gave them the bird and called them tight. And if you go out to visit them, you will find that their children have honored them with a twenty-foot tower of streaked red marble ornamented with cupids and wreaths and engraved with hand-made sentiments from the Elks' Magazine."

The ending of this tale about two solid citizens is ironic, but the story does not encourage despair. The author maintains that their values are part of a satisfying life. That this sort of life lacks proper appreciation by the masses in no way implies it is not full and good.[7]

More commonly, Perelman speaks in the first person from behind a narrator's mask the nature of which can be indicated by the proposed title of this narrator's memoirs—"Forty Years a Boob"—and by the apter title of one of the author's books—*Crazy*

Like a Fox. Perelman's wise fool might be called the Sane Psychotic, in view of the fantastic images that swirl in this figure's consciousness and suggest insanity to the unwary reader. These aberrations plus the egotism of the Sane Psychotic make him a clown, but behind the clown's mask and among the dancing images lurk the same values found in Benchley's bumbler—integrity, sincerity, skepticism, taste, a respect for competence, a striving after the golden mean, and a longing for better communication and understanding among men. These values are found too in Mr. Dooley, Abe Martin, and Will Rogers, despite the enormous difference between the unpolished dialect of the crackerbarrel and the dazzling vocabulary of Perelman's narrator. The neighborhood oracle and the college graduate may define some of these values differently, but they agree that the values do exist and can be defined.

To further disarm the reader, Perelman uses the familiar technique of tempting him to laugh at the narrator. In an introduction to *The Best of Perelman,* "Sidney Namlerep" pokes fun at his own conceit, which is all too typical of that found in authors:

> In any consideration of S. J. Perelman—and S. J. Perelman certainly deserves the same consideration one accords old ladies on street cars, babies traveling unescorted on planes, and the feeble-minded generally—it is important to remember the crushing, the well-nigh intolerable odds under which the man has struggled to produce what may well be, in the verdict of history, the most picayune prose ever produced in America. Denied every advantage, beset and plagued by ill fortune and a disposition so crabbed as to make Alexander Pope and Dr. Johnson seem sunny by contrast, he has nevertheless managed to belt out a series of books each less distinguished than its predecessor, each a milestone of bombast, conceit, pedantry, and strutting pomposity.

"Sidney Namlerep" is only somewhat more of a self-burlesque than are Perelman's other narrators, but if they represent the author's faults in exaggerated form, they also present the values he strongly feels—in underplayed form. These narrators—or rather the narrator, for they are all one—the narrator carries a torch for sanity and good taste, but the author half hides that torch by making the carrier "foolish" in the sense of making him neurotic to the point of insanity.

This half-concealment of values is easily traced in the pieces with the running title "Cloudland Revisited," in which novels or movies that were best sellers or box-office hits in Perelman's youth are ridiculed through selective summary, ironic paraphrase, and direct analysis. The satiric digest itself is usually set in a narrative framework consisting of three parts: (1) the circumstances associated in the narrator's mind with this movie or novel many years ago (2) the circumstances under which he has been exposed to it again recently, and (3) the effects on him of the re-exposure. For example, in "Sodom in the Suburbs," the narrator opens with, "The closest I ever came to an orgy, aside from the occasion in Montparnasse twenty years ago when I smoked a cigarette purported to contain hashish and fainted dead away after two puffs, was at a student dance at Brown around 1922" (held under the auspices of the Brown Christian Association). "Attired in a greenish Norfolk jacket and scuffing the massive bluchers with perforated toe caps and brass eyelets considered *de rigueur* in that period, I spent the evening buffeting about in the stag line, prayerfully beseeching the underclassmen I knew for permission to cut in on their women and tread a few measures of the Camel Walk." Every so often he withdrew to a cloakroom and tossed off a small shot of gin from a pocket flask. "Altogether, it was a strikingly commonplace experience . . ."

Next Sunday he learned he had been involved in "a momentous debauch. . . . In blazing scareheads, the Hearst Boston *American* tore the veil from the excesses tolerated at Brown University dances." Alcohol, ragtime, and sex, according to the newspaper, reigned supreme at Brown. "Worst of all, and indicative of the depths to which the Jazz Age had reduced American womanhood, was the unwritten law that each girl must check her corset before the saturnalia."

Perelman's narrator is reminded of this exposé as he sits turning the pages of *Flaming Youth,* by "Warner Fabian," ostensibly a physician but said to be a "top-drawer novelist" (if Perelman knew that "Warner Fabian" was really Samuel Hopkins Adams, he gave no sign). The style of this book, "at once flamboyant, euphuistic, and turgid, suggested nothing quite so much as melted marzipan." Of the plot, the narrator says,

> Stripped of its gingerbread, the story concerns itself with the amours of the three Fentriss daughters, Constance, Dee, and Pat, whose adolescence has been colored by their mother's reckless hedonism. She, while delectable, sounds from Fabian's thumbnail description very much like an early Cubist portrait by Picasso: "She was a golden-brown, strong, delicately rounded woman, glowing with an effect of triumphant and imperishable youth. Not one of her features but was faulty by strict artistic tenets; even the lustrous eyes were set at slightly different levels." Mona Fentriss's life of self-indulgence has done more than throw her features out of whack; in the opening stanza, we see her being told by her physician and devoted admirer, Dr. Robert Osterhout, that there are fairies at the bottom of her aorta and that her days are numbered. Osterhout is a gruff, lovable character in the best medico-literary tradition: "Like a bear's, his exterior was rough, shaggy, and seemed not to fit him well. His face was irregularly square, homely, thoughtful, and humorous." Ever the heedless pagan, Mona turns a deaf ear to the voice of doom and, over the single shakerful of cocktails the doctor has restricted her to daily, confesses no remorse for her numerous extramarital affairs. Her husband, she confides, is equally unconcerned at her peccadilloes ("They say he's got a floozie now, tucked away in a cozy corner somewhere"), and it is a lead-pipe cinch that, given this profligate environment and dubious heredity, the Fentriss girls are going to cut some pretty spectacular didos once the saxophones start sobbing.

Most of these didos are cut by Pat, the youngest of the Fentriss girls. She falls in love with a romantic stereotype named Cary Scott who is an old flame of her mother's and is already married. After some nude mixed bathing, a long lapse of time, "a thirty-one page renunciation jam-packed with rough tenderness, eyes shadowed with pain, and germane claptrap," and a succession of debauches and fiancés on the part of the girl, the two lovers are reconciled. Cary's impossible wife has conveniently died, "and, oblivious of the dead and dying syntax about them, the lovers go forth in search of Ben Lindsey and a companionate marriage." The narrator's final reaction to this mishmash is as follows:

> It may be only a coincidence, but for a whole day after re-reading *Flaming Youth*, my pupils were so dilated that you would have sworn I had been using belladonna. My complexion, though somewhat ruddier, recalled Bartholomew Sholto's in *The Sign of the Four* as he lay transfixed by an aboriginal dart that fateful night at Pondicherry Lodge. Luckily, I managed to work out a simple, effective treatment I can pass on to anyone afflicted with star-dust poisoning. All you need is an eyedropper, enough kerosene to saturate an average three-hundred-and-thirty-six-page romance, and a match. A darkened room, for lying down in afterward, is nice but not absolutely essential. Just keep your eyes peeled, your nose clean, and avoid doctors and novels written by doctors. When you're over forty, one extra bumper of over-ripe beauty can do you in.

This piece has been quoted in some detail because it contains several features typical not only of the "Cloudland" satires but of Perelman's work as a whole. First, he caricatures himself through a *persona*. Second, this fictitious individual is one type of average man, despite his highbrow vocabulary, his sometime attendance at an Ivy League university, and his having been abroad. Elements in his conduct that suggest Mr. Milquetoast as he might have behaved at dear old Siwash during the Jazz Age are not lacking. However, the Little Man of Perelman is chronically more upset than Mr. Milquetoast, as well as more aggressive. The Sane Psychotic, or at the very least, the "Balanced Neurotic," are better labels for him than is "The Timid Soul." An occasional timidity is the least complicated of his reactions.

Third, this wise fool or Sane Psychotic has a stubborn

integrity, and a sense of what is appropriate in prose, that cause
him to be repelled by the shrill exaggerations he encounters in
the Hearst paper and the sensational gimcrackery of Warner
Fabian's novel. Presumably, years and experience have brought
him a measure of wisdom and taste. Many other pieces by Perelman likewise show a Little Man who is emotionally disturbed
but who nevertheless resists and criticizes the phony aspects of his
environment.

Fourth, most of this Little Man's foes are among the mass
media, which are, on the whole, the offspring of technology's un-
consecrated marriage with Big Business. These foes include any
prose style which murders reason and clarity. It is not surprising
that advertising, radio, and television, as well as movies and bad
fiction, are among Perelman's chief targets.

PERELMONTAGE

Perelman's interest in psychological imbalance is partly expressed through an atmosphere of nightmarish zaniness which
he achieves by loading his prose with wildly incongruous contexts, often superimposed one upon another in highly condensed
form. Sometimes he does this superimposing by means of puns,
especially in his titles—"To Sleep, Perchance to Steam," "A Farewell to Omsk," "It Isn't the Heat, It's the Cupidity." Sometimes
he does it through telescoping two or more well-known quotations, titles, clichés, or catch-phrases, some of which are altered
almost but not quite beyond recognition. Again his titles furnish
examples—"Short Easterly Squall, With Low Visibility and Rising Gorge," "I Am Not Now, Nor Have I Ever Been, a Matrix of
Lean Meat," "The Yanks Are Coming, in Five Breathless Colors,"
"No Starch in the Dhoti, S'il Vous Plaît." "Free association" is
a misleading term for this technique, because Perelman's superimposition of contexts is not really free but is rigidly controlled;
anyhow, this incongruous juxtaposition on a larger scale is ex-

emplified in the following passage from "Amo, Amas, Amat, Amamus, Amatis, Enough:"

> The other day I surfaced in a pool of glorious golden sunshine laced with cracker crumbs to discover that spring had returned to Washington Square. A pair of pigeons were cooing gently directly beneath my window; two squirrels plighted their troth in a branch overhead; at the corner a handsome member of New York's finest twirled his night stick and cast roguish glances at the saucy-eyed flower vendor. The scene could have been staged only by a Lubitsch; in fact, Lubitsch himself was seated on a bench across the street, smoking a cucumber and looking as cool as a cigar.

The simple act of waking up and looking at the plaza outside is fused with the notion of rising to the surface of a pool, also with the idea of cocktails ("laced") and with the actual remnants of what nice people have been feeding the pigeons. Other realistic details about the scene are given in language that parodies the popular sentimentalizing of the season. Suddenly introduced into the scene is an object with only a farfetched and hypothetical relationship to that scene—a well-known producer of movie comedies, whose actions are indicated in two trite but ludicrously mixed metaphors. The composite picture is an incongruous blend of the relevant with the irrelevant and of precise detail with worn-out phrases, all for the purpose of satirizing at least three different phenomena: overemphasis on spring, writing in clichés, and the triteness and artificiality of certain situations in films.

Sometimes the blend of incongruities is achieved by the use of a phrase or statement simultaneously in both a literal and a figurative meaning:

> SWICKARD: Which it's the hallmark of every industrial wizard worth a hoot.
> THIMIG: You can say *that* again. *(Swickard starts to say it again, trails off as Hyssop rises and stands plunged in thought.)*

Such double usage was characteristic of Benchley's more whimsical pieces and could also be found in the nonsense plays of Lardner:

> First Glue Lifter: Well, my man, how goes it?
> Second Glue Lifter: *(Sings "My Man," to show how it goes.)*

A variation of this literal-and-figurative usage is the occurrence of a word or phrase in a figurative but commonplace and accepted sense followed without warning by a switch to one or more usages of that same word or phrase which are extraordinary. Thus, "The color drained slowly from my face, entered the auricle, shot up the escalator, and issued from the ladies' and misses' section into the housewares department." Here Perelman uses "color" first in a hackneyed, commonplace fashion and then in a sense highly unusual.

Perelman's respect for James Joyce becomes more understandable as one recalls that Joyce too made basic use of the superimposition of multiple contexts and for this purpose developed the pun into a major artistic device, especially in *Finnegan's Wake*. Perelman's use of stream-of-consciousness also suggests Joyce, and at least once, in "Pale Hands I Loathe," Perelman specifies that in imagining the stream-of-consciousness of a business executive, he is using "the kind of tackle Mr. Joyce employed on Leopold Bloom." Another piece, "Scenario," is a monologue composed of the trite language of movie-makers as it might be heard on a dozen different sets and read in any number of publicity releases during the making of a dozen different but monotonously similar historical "epics." In its blend of violence and triteness, "Scenario" suggests the Walpurgis Night episode in *Ulysses,* an episode Perelman has called "the greatest single comic achievement in the language:" [8]

> Fade in, exterior grassy knoll, long shot. Above the scene the thundering measures of Von Suppe's "Light Cavalry Overture." Austerlitz? The Plains of Abraham? Vicksburg? The Little Big Horn? Cambrai? Steady on, old son; it is

Yorktown. Under a blood-red setting sun yon proud crest is
Cornwallis. Blood and 'ouns, proud sirrah, dost brush so
lightly past an exciseman of the Crown? Lady Rotogravure's
powdered shoulders shrank from the highwayman's caress;
what, Jermyn, footpads on Hounslow Heath? A certain party
in the D.A.'s office will hear of this, you bastard. There was a
silken insolence in his smile as he drew the greatcoat about
his face and leveled his shooting-iron at her dainty puss.
Leave go that lady or I'll smear yuh. No quarter, eh? Me,
whose ancestors scuttled stately India merchantmen of their
comfits and silken stuffs and careened their piratical craft
in the Dry Tortugas to carouse with bumboat women till
the cock crew? Yuh'll buy my booze or I'll give yuh a hand-
ful of clouds. Me, whose ancestors rode with Yancey, Jeb
Stuart, and Joe Johnston through the dusty bottoms of the
Chickamauga? Oceans of love, but not one cent for tribute.
Make a heel out of a guy whose grandsire, Olaf Hasholem,
swapped powder and ball with the murderous Sioux through
the wheels of a Conestoga wagon, who mined the yellow dirt
with Sutter and slapped nuggets across the rude bars of
Leadville and Goldfield? One side, damn your black hide,
suh, or Ah'll send one mo' dirty Litvak to the boneyard. It's
right up the exhibitor's alley, Mr. Biberman, and you got to
hand it to them on a platter steaming hot. I know, Stanley,
but let's look at this thing reasonable; we been showing the
public Folly Larrabee's drawers two years and they been cool-
ing off.

The influence of Joyce is clear enough, but one recalls that Perelman's violent yoking of associations also owes much to the techniques of the very movie-makers that he satirized, especially the
technique of montage, in which fragments of two or more
pictures are combined in space by the superimposition of one
upon another, partially or entirely, so that highlights of each and
all may stand out and other details of each shot may be glimpsed
through the intervening details of the other pictures. A variation
in time of this technique is the rapid succession of shots of extreme brevity. In humorous writing, the equivalent effect of
either technique might be called Perelmontage.

Perelman's prose reflects a civilization which is dizzying in
its speed, complexity, and disorder, and staggering in the sheer,

oppressive *quantity* of things and forces with which it bombards the average consciousness. The use of multiple contexts is one way of indicating this quantity; the use of contexts that are also incongruous is a way of suggesting both complexity and discord.

"Things close in," Walter Mitty says, and the apparent derangement of Perelman's Little Man likewise arises from the closing in on him of forces that invade and corrupt his personality and impel him toward neurosis. But he hasn't yet given in completely. The fact that his resistance is sometimes wrongheaded often obscures his essential good sense in really important matters. His reaction to dentistry, for instance, resembles that of Benchley's narrator, but the fear and trembling of both characters is neurotic only insofar as it is carried beyond the "normal" dislike of having dental work done. When it is so carried, this reaction makes Perelman's man look pretty foolish, but his equally extreme reaction to bad taste in advertising and in window display includes rational and humanistic reflections that should give pause to all who pretend to mental and political health. He observes, in a shoe-store window, the skeleton of a human foot wired to a hidden motor that makes it move. The sight makes him want to rush home and lie down, and as he thinks about it later, "with a vinegar poultice on my forehead," he realizes that, "That little bevy of bones had been oscillating back and forth all through Danzig, Pearl Harbor, and the North African campaign; this very minute it was undulating turgidly, heedless of the fact the store had been closed two hours." Are his reactions neurotic? Possibly, but the display itself is more neurotic, and the meditation on how (during days of "horror, despair, and world change" as Dorothy Parker had put it) this bit of grotesque commercialism has as much or more of permanence and "stability" as most higher and worthier phenomena—this meditation lifts the narrator's reactions above the level of mere neurosis.

Perelman's dental patient reacts to persecution with a desire to escape and an aggressive desire to retaliate, though the aggression actually manifested is the merely negative act of refusing to go back to the dentist again. Patterns of withdrawal and aggression are common in the disturbance of Perelman's main character. Withdrawal may be manifested by an overpowering desire to flee, physically, from the scene of one's torment. Discomfort and poor service on the Santa Fe railroad's "Super Chief" cause Perelman's man to slide down an arroyo, crawl up a mesa, and hide behind a mesquite bush until the train has left. A magazine column of hints on how to consume more conspicuously sends this moderate consumer into a mad flight from Brentano's basement into "the cool, sweet air of Forty-Seventh Street." Advertisements in *Vogue* for clothes made of synthetics and having *"an individual life of their own"* [9] scare him into a more passive withdrawal: "For two days now I have been crouching in a corner of this coal bin, enjoying a peace I never thought possible." Since looking into a book entitled *Cosmetic Surgery,* he has been "confined to my rooms in the Albany with a fairly constant attack of the rams." Both aggression and flight, the latter manifested as a suicidal urge, appear in his reaction to Maxwell Bodenheim's erotic novel *Replenishing Jessica*: after referring to himself as "hysteroid," he reports that, "Unlike the average hypnotic subject, the central character was fully conscious at all times, even while asleep. He ate a banana, flung the skin out of the window, flung the book after the skin, and was with difficulty restrained from following."

The aggressions of Perelman's narrator run the gamut from futility to violence. He will wear a cord to hold up his pants rather than use a Talon fastener. The style of a certain female fashion-analyst causes him to fling the New York *Times* from him with a force that demolishes a lamp. An ad that represents food as articulate ("I am a matrix of lean meat with my trimmings ground and worked back into me.") stimulates him into planting a microphone and a tape recorder in the refrigerator. Then, beset by hallucinations about what has been "recorded," he rushes to the refrigerator, intent on throwing out the contents.

Small wonder that his wife locks herself in the henhouse. The skeletal foot in the shoestore window leads him to propose bombing the store, anarchist fashion, and to anyone who follows the advice given in a book on *How to Crash Tin-Pan Alley* he will gladly give a "just reward"—two hundred lashes with a blacksnake whip.

Obviously Perelman's Sane Psychotic is less sane and more psychotic than the Little Man of some other writers. But does the fault lie in the man or in his environment? His need for "a good five-cent psychiatrist" arises from his reading about the possibilities for getting a fatal shock from an electric blanket. Is this man sicker than the men who make and advertise such gadgetry? A certain store clerk gradually comes to feel that he is being watched by a mannequin. So he is—by a movie director hidden in this dummy. However, because the clerk thinks he must be going mad, he does go mad. This narrative grew out of an actual suggestion by a film critic that scenes could be shot in stores and other places of business with concealed cameras, and it has political implications concerning censorship and snooping. Perelman is suggesting that such tactics on the part of movie-makers—or anybody—would invade the right of privacy of the unfortunate citizens thus photographed, as well as drive them batty. (He has yet to give full expression to what he probably thinks about "Candid Camera.")[10] The clerk's "hallucinations" are all too real; the aberration is that of a society which would countenance such spying. Through his narrator, Perelman mocks the weaknesses of himself, and by implication, of his readers, but he is also insisting that his own irrationalities should not be abetted and compounded by those of society and its mass media. If they are so compounded, what (he implicitly asks) is left for the harassed man of sensitivity but aggression and/or withdrawal?

THE EXURBANITE, AND THE INNOCENT ABROAD

Escape to the country has not helped Perelman's man much. In *Acres and Pains* and in shorter pieces dealing with life in

Bucks County, Perelman (or rather, his double) shows that he has, on the whole, merely added to his troubles by becoming a part-time farmer. He says, "In a scant fifteen years [of country living] I have acquired a superb library of mortgages, mostly first editions, and the finest case of sacroiliac known to science." This little "exurbanite" has been affronted or victimized by the climate, by the soil, by workmen, by the natives, by fellow ex-urbanites, by architects, by machinery, by house servants, by ghosts (or so he thinks), by pets, by his own elaborate plans, by cruel chance and malign fate. However, like E. B. White, Perelman admits wryly that rural life has brought him into contact with certain realities unknown to the city dweller:

> For my money, the most parochial, unwholesome aspect of contemporary civilization is the life led by the average urban dweller. Cooped up in a stuffy, over-heated hotel suite with nothing but a bowl of cracked ice, a blonde, and a fleet bell-boy poised on his toe like Pavlova waiting to run errands, he misses the rich, multiple savor of country living. He never knows the fierce ecstasy of rising in a sub-zero dawn to find the furnace cold and the pipes frozen, or the exhilaration of changing a tire by flashlight in an icy garage. No wonder his muscles atrophy as he lies abed until noon, nibbling bits of toast over the latest edition. No wonder his horizons shrink and his waistband swells. And no wonder he'll live twice as long as I will.

Yet Perelman did not rush to sell his place as soon as this was written. No less than Cobb or Benchley, he valued those realities.

In his two travel books, Perelman's narrator shows his affinity with the wise American fool of Mark Twain's *Innocents Abroad* and with dozens of other equally shrewd but parochial tourists, including the narrator in Cobb's *Europe Revised,* the Old Soak of Don Marquis, and at times, Sinclair Lewis' Sam Dodsworth. Perelman as tourist refuses to see anything new or exciting in foreign parts; when he isn't recalling the dirt and the heat, or the discomforts of travel and the obnoxiousness of his fellow travelers, he is insisting that the fabled sights of far countries are no more exciting than various commonplace scenes at home. Perelman's traveler describes his first sight of China as "a sullen range of hills disturbingly similar to those we had left behind in Southern California." Just as Mark Twain had compared Lake Como unfavorably with Lake Tahoe, Perelman's man finds the scenery about Chinwangtao "reminiscent of the less attractive suburbs of Carteret, New Jersey." The Oriental night club where the deposed Emperor of Annam, Bao Dai, took his pleasure "turned out to be a somewhat sedater version of Broadway's Roseland . . ." Of all the Oriental cities he saw, only Bangkok impressed him, and of all the great sights, only the Taj Mahal.

In the *Swiss Family Perelman* this wiseacre has his family along, and his problem becomes one of getting the little woman and two children past such perils as the ship's menu, their fellow passengers, friendly foreigners, and assorted sights on shore. In the fashion of Lardner, Day, Benchley, and Thurber, much emphasis is given to father's attempts to preserve his ego from demolition by his family when things go wrong, as they usually do. The wife's comments at one dismal moment are typical:

> "Did I ever tell you," she went on, "that in order to marry you, I jilted an explorer?"
> "Honestly?" I asked. "What did you tell him?"
> "I wish I could remember," she murmured. "It sure would come in handy."

The rich cultural allusiveness of Perelman's discourse should not blur the basic traits which establish as his central figure a superior type of American, a man of sensitivity and intelligence who remains ordinary in the sense of sharing the faults and foibles of most of his countrymen, and of humankind. His normal quota of foolishness is exaggerated into psychosis for the

purpose of satirizing the madnesses of this man's environment.
Whether he appears as writer, exurbanite, traveler, or mere consumer of mass media, this type exercises his reason and taste in
pointing out the disorders of his civilization. In so doing, he re-
enacts the revolt of the consumer hoped for by Walter Weyl in
1912, and in spite of irrational responses to some of these disorders, he fights to retain his loosening grip on ideals of clarity,
honesty, common sense, and the right to his own personality—
which includes the right to be foolish and undignified in his own
way, not in the more effectively lethal ways forced on one by an
environment madder than he. He still knows the good, though
he cannot always will that good which he knows or do that good
which he wills.

He is a shade better off than "Miss Lonelyhearts" in the novel
of that title by Perelman's brother-in-law, Nathanael West.
"Miss" Lonelyhearts goes completely to pieces in his disordered
environment, but Perelman's narrator retains a measure of sanity
in a world which suffers from what Erich Fromm has called "the
pathology of normalcy" [11]—a world where even visions of the
Hereafter include "time clocks, Kardex systems, and for all we
know, conferences in which ghostly Corona-Coronas are chewed."
In such a world, the faith of Perelman's narrator in the decency
of at least a small number of human beings may seem fatuous
but it will not down. That faith saves him from the fate of West's
anti-hero—that faith, and a sense of humor.

20

Some Questions

The end of this book is a strategic place in which to make a few generalizations about American humor and humorists during the first half of the twentieth century. One is that most of these humorists came into their field through journalism. Of the sixteen surveyed in this book, all but one were journalists by profession, and that one, Will Rogers, became a part-time journalist. Six—Dunne, Hubbard, Rogers, Mencken, Lardner, and Cuppy—were still on the payrolls of newspapers, magazines, or features syndicates when illness, retirement, or death ended their careers. The proportion of journalists among men of humor far outweighs that among "serious" novelists or poets.

The journalistic background of modern humor is surely related to the fact that both the crackerbox philosophers and the humorists of the less rural tradition have observed certain taboos more strictly than many of the serious novelists. Barnyard humor is out; and sex too gets along without benefit of four-letter words. Another taboo is religion; implicit criticisms of religious faith and orthodoxy may be found in the more naturalistic writers, but only Dunne, Marquis, and Mencken habitually made theology, churches, and churchgoing a subject of direct, humorous treatment. Dunne, a Catholic, presents Father Kelly as a sympathetic character but makes little of Mr. Dooley's faith except to suggest that he is within the fold. Marquis is sympathetic to religious faith almost as often as he is critical. Thurber's view is perhaps typical: "I share [Harold] Ross's deep conviction that major blasphemies have no place in comedy."[1] Most humorists have been, like Thurber, unorthodox in private, though some are not without religious feeling. But most have avoided any discussion of religious doctrine and institutions, and only Mencken made the kind of direct and specific attack found in Sinclair Lewis' *Elmer Gantry*.

The relation between journalism and gentility arises partly because the journalist knows that if he wishes to prosper he must attract and hold a large readership. Consequently he tends to have a fairly humble conception of himself as a tradesman in words rather than as an artist for whom his art is all. He will lose readers if he jolts their prejudices too severely or too often, or if his style becomes esoteric. He cannot afford the lonely dedication to "pure" literature of a Flaubert, a Joyce, or even a Dreiser; he cannot, in the name of art or of private truth, reject conventional morality. There have been no Henry Millers among humorists of the printed word except, at times, Miller himself.

Gentility has not, of course, been strictly or even mainly a bread-and-butter proposition. Frequently these humorists took risks and made sacrifices in order to write more competently or more honestly. Ring Lardner continued to write his radio column, "Over the Waves," for the *New Yorker* despite the niggling pay because "I would rather write for the *New Yorker* at five cents a word than for *Cosmopolitan* at a dollar a word."[2] Granted that Mencken and Nathan rejected some pieces for the *Smart Set* because "nice" readers wouldn't approve of them; they wrote and accepted enough unsettling material to injure the circulation of the magazine. The point is that these writers sincerely shared the views of many of the readers for whom they felt themselves to be writing—as what writer does not?

Stylistically there is no question but that most of these humorists were dedicated to achieving perfection in their chosen modes. However, their ideas of perfection in style, like their ideas of good morals, did not ordinarily shock many subscribers into canceling their renewals.

Whether small, independent businesses are making a comeback in numbers, as a onetime advisor of the Eisenhower Administration has claimed,[3] or whether they are not, the cracker-box philosopher of the "old" middle class of entrepreneurs is largely a holdover from the nineteenth century[4] and he is not likely to be revived in the twentieth. To a somewhat less degree, the same is true of the substantial citizen denoted by Sumner as the Forgotten Man. The Little Man of the "new," white-collar class stands as the representative American in the humor of the twentieth century. Yet he has close ties with his predecessors; he indicates continuity, not a break, in the development of American humor. In his embodiment of an imperfect being's struggle to attain and to retain integrity, sincerity, reason, common sense, and taste, this character resembles the two earlier types.

He also resembles these types in his loneliness, but he differs from them in showing that quality more overtly than did the crackerbox characters.⁵ Despite his political, social, and personal resemblance to millions of fellow beings, the Little Man is a lonely figure. It is not merely that he is contrasted sharply with the depersonalized environment created by the machine and with the mindless mob of depersonalized beings in that environment who harass him. In an age of improved mass communications, one of the themes of his creators is the lack of communication between man and man. All of the Little-Man humorists have featured monologues and dialogues in which nothing passes between people but misunderstanding. Benchley's treasurer merely exposes his own incompetence and incoherence; many of the folks in Thurber's panic-stricken crowd think the soldiers are saying, "The dam has now broken!" when actually they are saying, "The dam has *not* broken"; Perelman's narrator dates a girl who spends the evening "yacketing in the wilderness," so to speak, about nothing and doesn't even get his name right. Husbands and wives murder understanding with mutual hostility. David Riesman's image of the "lonely crowd" matches too well that of the better sort of Average American in American humor.

Along with loneliness, melancholy, and terror, another ingredient of earlier American humor, violence, is found also in the world of the Little Man. True, melancholy has probably always been important in humor; *Don Quixote, Gulliver's Travels,* and *Tristram Shandy* have plenty of it. In *Intellectual America,* Oscar Cargill has commented on the "sour note in western humor" with reference to the cynicism of Josh Billings and his crackerbarrel brethren. E. B. White says, ". . . there is a deep vein of melancholy running through everyone's life and . . . the humorist, perhaps more sensible of it than some others, compensates for it actively and positively. Humorists fatten on trouble. They have always made trouble pay." Likewise, violence and terror are a permanent part of the world's humor. The fables of Aesop, the bloody adventures of Reynard the Fox and other trickster-heroes, and the many scenes of physical violence in *Tom Jones* come at once to mind. The roughness of life on the American frontier offered plenty of encouragement to the "dark" impulse in the humorists of that area; and through Mark Twain, who drew heavily on the frontier tradition, a continuity of violence was established between the backwoods tale-tellers and those later humorists whose use of melancholy and terror was encouraged by their pessimistic world view. Ade and Mencken were keen students of Mark Twain, and Mencken especially appreciated the pessimism of his later writings. Lardner too, though he denied any conscious influence, was a close reader of Mark Twain, with whose work his own bears many resemblances.[6] Don Marquis shared Twain's pessimism, and in both his first and last novels he used many of Twain's techniques as well. Without looking further for specific debts to Mark Twain, one easily recalls the naturalism and pessimism of his later years when one encounters the scenes and images of terror, violence, disaster, and death in the work of Parker, Thurber, Cuppy, Perelman, and, to a somewhat less degree, in Benchley and White. Such scenes and images are not surprising in a world where even the comic books cause the Little Man, as Perelman says, to "do his sleeping with the lights on." Ironically, this habitual use of terror in humor and satire may have better equipped a future crop of humorous writers to find humor in the nuclear age, if there is a future crop.

If, then, the Little Man is so much like the earlier types, in what ways is he different in kind rather than degree? The difference in his economic status has already been noted. Other differences may be summed up in the statement that he is *dominated*—by gadgets, by his boss, by his associates on the job, by the problems of maintaining a home, by his wife and children. Ade's men often lost but they often won too, even in the home. Mencken's rational conservative faced heavy odds, but at least he controlled his own mind and was a happy man. Father Day is often balked, but he is continually on the offensive, his personality fills the house, and it is Mother, not he, who gives the impression of struggling against odds. But from Cobb's hospital patient through Perelman's Sane Psychotic, the Little Man is always in retreat, psychologically as well as externally, except for those moments when he demonstrates his futility by acts of aggression as ill-timed as they are ineffectual. The crackerbox oracle was self-assured and "strong," the solid citizen was powerful if sometimes beaten, but the Little Man has been dwarfed by the monsters of industry, science, business, and government.

One aim of this commentator has been to drop certain questions in the reader's lap and leave them there. Why, for instance, has so little humor worth survival been written concerning war and wartime conditions in the two world conflicts? Loss of topical interest cannot be the answer; the frontier too has passed but certain frontier humorists continue to be read by a small audience that of late has been growing. Perhaps mass slaughter and misery are too overpowering to allow much humorous treatment within the bounds of respectable taste. Another question: Why did not the depression of the nineteen-thirties give rise to more humor about the social and economic problems of those years?[7] Less convincingly, some will advance the same general answer as that about the dearth of war humor: certain conditions are just too big and serious for humor. More specifically, unemployment, poverty, and bread lines aren't very humorous in themselves. Neither are deteriorating marriages and broken homes, yet much humor continued to be made out of those situations.

A vast amount of humor about depression and war has died with the topic—who now reads *Dere Mable; See Here, Private Hargrove!* or *How to Lose Your Money Prudently?* Only Will Rogers and E. B. White have written durable humor about war, and White deliberately underplayed the international conflict itself. In the poverty and unrest of the thirties only Rogers found a major source of enduring humor and satire.

Why too was much of the best humor of the last sixty years produced during the central portion of this period, roughly, between the two wars? Answers to any or all of these questions would have to include a detailed comparison of American humor with its environment. Such a comparison would involve literature, psychology, history, politics, economics, sociology, anthropology, and linguistics on a far larger scale than the present introductory effort. Even then, such correlations as it established between humor and fact would be only speculative.

THE PAST AND FUTURE OF AMERICAN HUMOR

A man writing in the nineteen-sixties about American humor from 1900 to 1950 does not have a long perspective on the chosen period. To the questions, What is the state of American humor at present? and, What are its prospects for the future? one mumbles that much of the best humor of the last ten years or so is still embedded in the periodicals of its first appearance, and other duties have prevented him from ferreting it out. Of the humorists discussed in this book who are still living, E. B. White and S. J. Perelman have published recent collections, *The Points of My Compass* (1962) and *The Rising Gorge* (1961) respectively. A book by the late James Thurber has appeared posthumously— *Credos and Curios* (1962). No startlingly new departures of theme or idea appear in any of the three books. Certain other humorists active before 1950 who were squeezed out of this volume for lack of room are still writing and have published books within the last five years. Among them are Corey Ford, Arthur Kober, Frank Sullivan, Ogden Nash, Phyllis McGinley, Margaret Halsey, H. Allen Smith, Max Shulman, Emily Kimbrough, Cornelia Otis Skinner, Edward Streeter, and Leo Rosten. Humorists who published little in book form before 1950 and who are among the more interesting now active include Peter DeVries (recruited for the *New Yorker* by Thurber), Art Buchwald, Mac Hyman, Richard Armour, Ken Purdy, Shel Silverstein, and Ira Wallach. Many names might be added, but an up-to-the-minute survey of American humor would have to take into account the large amount of still uncollected magazine material by the authors listed and by writers whose works have not yet appeared between hard covers.

The outlets for humorous writing seem to be growing in number, and although this growth complicates the job of bringing one's survey up to date, it suggests that in bulk at least,

American humor is not diminishing. Critics of the *New Yorker* have claimed that the success of the magazine in attracting humorous talent has tended to kill off other outlets. *Collier's* and *The Country Gentleman*, mass-circulation magazines which published considerable humor, have gone under (not, one hastens to add, because of competition for manuscripts from the *New Yorker*, a somewhat different type of magazine), and their demise has reduced the number of periodicals who paid well for unashamedly "light" stuff. On the other hand, the magazine *Playboy* has been founded, making at least one new worthwhile outlet for writing by the right humorists, and *Esquire* and the *Saturday Review* have increased the amount of humor by free-lance writers in their pages.

Further, many daily and weekly newspapers still publish humorous columns—in widely varying degrees of quantity and quality. (How much the decrease in the absolute number of dailies and weeklies has affected the output of column humor cannot be determined.) Some of these columns are syndicated: Harry Golden of the *Carolina Israelite*, William E. Vaughan ("Senator Soaper"), Fletcher Knebel ("Potomac Fever"), Sydney Harris ("Strictly Personal") and James Stevens ("Out of the Woods") are among the humorists who started writing for a single newspaper and have achieved fame through syndication. In addition, hundreds—possibly thousands—of newspapers and house organs feature regular columns of "light" prose or poetry by writers known only locally.

One may safely suggest that American humor of the printed word will undergo no immediate decline in quantity. One may also predict that the *New Yorker* tradition of urbane, allusive wit and satire will continue to flourish alongside a modified form of crackerbox humor, and there will continue to be some mutual interpenetration. A number of writers who publish in the *New Yorker* also appear in *Playboy*, and the style of the department "Playboy After Hours" is modeled closely upon that of the "Talk of the Town." One is reminded that the "Talk" itself shows a tinge of crackerbarrel influence; and the combined effect of the

"Talk" and the crackerbox column of brief, disconnected quips, of paragraphs, and of essays up to four or five hundred words in length may also be seen in the *Saturday Review,* which indeed has encouraged chattiness, brevity, and astringence in no less than five departments. "Offhand" by Niccolo Tucci was dropped after a short run, but "Trade Winds," "Manner of Speaking" (by John Ciardi), "The Phoenix Nest" (edited by Martin Levin), and "The First of the Month" (by Cleveland Amory) continue. In the *Saturday Evening Post,* the one-page section, "Post Scripts," has for many years furnished an outlet for verse, pithy sayings, and brief, informal essays.

If the less citified sort of crackerbox humor is dying, its death is of the slowest. Even the casual reader of small-town papers during a trip across the continent will spot a column in dialect from time to time, and most of the rural papers he picks up will contain at least one column in prose so colloquial as to earn the crackerbox label. By chance, this author once looked at the *Budget,* of Douglas, Wyoming (the home town of a nineteenth-century oracle, M. C. Barrow, who rates mention in Blair's *Native American Humor),* and found a crackerbox column entitled "Chatter." A few unsyndicated columns in dialect, like John Tatsey's "Heart Butte News" in the *Glacier Reporter* of Browning, Montana, are quoted far beyond the local orbit of subscribers.[8]

At present there seems to be no radically new genre of humor growing within the shell of the crackerbox or suave traditions (this statement does not refer to humor in the movies, television, or night clubs). Has this lack of new forms inhibited the rise of talent to the levels reached during the nineteen-twenties and thirties? Few will grant that any humorist in the *New Yorker* tradition who has published most of his material since World War II has attained the stature of Lardner, Marquis, Benchley, Thurber, White, or Perelman, or that any crackerbarrel sage writing since Will Rogers has had Rogers' wide appeal. Perhaps another burst of talent will have to await a new approach, as fresh in its way as were the crackerbox and *New Yorker* approaches at one time. Undoubtedly any new approach will reflect, for better or for worse, the influence of the vast amount of humor purveyed on television screens; another influence may be the rise of satirical picture magazines like *Mad* and *Cavalier*.

Perhaps the new approach will include re-evaluations of the American as man and as citizen of an international community with new frontiers in outer space—or, as the case may be, of a decimated humanity reduced to primitive conditions in a radio-active wasteland. The pessimistic note predominates in the wildly comic novels of such relatively new writers as J. P. Donleavy, Joseph Heller, John Barth, and Thomas Pynchon. However, sharp breaks with the past are as rare in humorous writing as in other kinds, and whatever the nature of the re-evaluation, humorists may want to embody their values in new character types that will yet have recognizable continuity with those created earlier.

Notes

PART ONE

Genteel Humor and Some History

Chapter 1.
Humor in the Nineties

1. In particular see Whitlock's *J. Hardin and Son* (1923). Abe C.
   Ravitz, "Brand Whitlock's Macochee: Puritan Theo-Politics in the
   Midwest," *Ohio Historical Quarterly,* LXVIII (July, 1959), 257–
   275 includes discussion of Whitlock's criticism, in his novels, of an
   archetypal small town.

2. First published as *The Cynic's Word Book* (1906).

3. The fullest discussions of the crackerbarrel tradition are in Jennette Tandy, *Crackerbox Philosophers in American Humor and Satire*, Columbia University Press (New York, 1925), and Walter Blair, *Horse Sense in American Humor*, University of Chicago Press (Chicago, 1943). See also Blair, *Native American Humor*, Chandler (San Francisco, 1960), pp. 3–147, and Constance Rourke, *American Humor*, Harcourt, Brace (New York, 1931), Chs. I and II.

4. M. C. Barrow, editor of the magazine *Sagebrush Philosophy* (1904–1910) in Douglas, Wyoming, was an example of how the crackerbox type of editor-humorist continued to operate in the twentieth century.

5. Quoted in Blair, *Native American Humor*, p. 427.

6. *Loc. cit.*

7. Blair, *Horse Sense in American Humor*, pp. 157, 161–168.

8. Walter Lippmann, *A Preface to Politics*, Mitchell Kennerly (New York and London, 1913), p. 196.

9. Frank Luther Mott, *A History of American Magazines, 1885–1905*, Harvard University Press (Cambridge, Massachusetts), pp. 556–558.

10. Samuel S. Cox, *Why We Laugh*, Harper (New York, 1876), p. 100.

11. Mott, *loc. cit.*

12. *Puck*, XXXVI (August 22, 1894), 4; XXXVI (November 14, 1894), 198.

13. Frederick Lewis Allen, "American Magazines, 1741–1941," *Bulletin of the New York Public Library*, XLV (June, 1941), 439–445; Frank Luther Mott, *American Journalism*, Macmillan (New York, 1941), p. 507.

14. Henry Luce bought the title of the "old" *Life* in 1936 in order to give it to the news-picture magazine he was founding.

15. William R. Linneman, "Satires of American Realism 1880–1900," *American Literature*, XXXIV (March, 1962), 80–93.

16. Carolyn Wells included contributions by Herford, Loomis, and George T. Lanigan, another of these minor contributors to the weeklies of the nineties, in her *Nonsense Anthology*, the latest reprinting of which is by Dover (New York, 1961). This collection is worth looking into particularly for the pieces taken from R. H. Russell (ed.), *Ruthless Rhymes for Heartless Homes* (1901)—an early type of "sick" humor. An out-of-print collection in which many minor writers of genteel humor appeared is *Men and Things*, Harper (New York and London, 1905).

17. *The Colby Essays*, Clarence Day, Jr. (ed.), Harper (New York, 1926), I, 49.

18. Thomas D. Clark, *The Southern Country Editor*, Bobbs-Merrill (Indianapolis and New York, 1948), p. 83.

19. James Gray, "The Journalist As Literary Man," in May Brodbeck, James Gray, and Walter Metzger, *American Non-Fiction 1900–1950,* Henry Regnery (Chicago, 1952), p. 141.

20. Between 1900 and 1929 the number of pupils enrolled in secondary schools beyond the sixth grade more than tripled. See I. L. Kandel, *History of Secondary Education,* Houghton Mifflin (Boston, 1930), p. 449.

Chapter 2.
The Decline of the Common Man

1. Don Marquis, *The Lives and Times of Archy and Mehitabel,* Doubleday, Doran (Garden City, New York, 1935), p. 297.

2. Richard Hofstadter, *The Age of Reform,* Vintage (New York, 1960), pp. 217–218; C. Wright Mills, *White Collar,* Oxford University Press (New York, 1951), p. 63. Cf. Erich Fromm, *Escape From Freedom,* Rinehart (New York, Toronto, 1941), pp. 124–213.

3. Woodrow Wilson, *The New Freedom,* Doubleday, Page (New York and Garden City, 1913), pp. 80, 288.

4. Nicholas Murray Butler, *The American As He Is,* Scribner (New York, 1915), pp. 37, 49.

5. *McClure's* XL (1912–1913), 120, qu. in Henry F. May, *The End of American Innocence 1912–1917,* Knopf (New York, 1959), p. 26.

6. William Allen White, *The Old Order Changeth,* Macmillan (New York, 1910), p. 191.

7. Butler, *The American As He Is,* pp. 54–55.

8. Qu. by Irvin G. Wyllie, *The Self-Made Man in America,* Rutgers University Press (New Brunswick, N.J., 1954), p. 26.

9. White, *The Old Order Changeth,* p. 249.

10. Paul H. Douglas, *Real Wages in the United States 1890–1926,* Houghton Mifflin (Boston, 1930), p. 230. In 1903 the United States Bureau of Labor found that about two-thirds of a large sample of working-class families received less than $700 annually, and nearly one-half less than $600. The minimum "subsistence-plus" income needed for a family of five was estimated to be $700. See Harvey Wish, *Society and Thought in Modern America,* Longmans (New York, London, and Toronto, 1952), p. 196.

11. *Life,* XXVII (January 16, 1896), 35.

12. Douglas, *Real Wages in the United States,* p. 359.

13. Meredith Nicholson, *The Valley of Democracy,* Scribner (New York, 1918), p. 60.

14. Randolph Bourne, *History of a Literary Radical,* B. W. Huebsch (New York, 1920), pp. 133–135.

15. George Ade, *Stories of the Streets and of the Town* . . . *1893–1900*, Franklin J. Meine (ed.), The Caxton Club (Chicago, 1941), p. 75.
16. *Sumner Today*, Maurice R. Davie (ed.), Yale University Press (New Haven, 1940), pp. 3–26.
17. Walter E. Weyl, *The New Democracy*, Macmillan (New York, 1912), pp. 249–251.
18. Qu. by Morton White, *Social Thought in America*, Beacon Press (Boston, 1957), pp. 48–49. C. Wright Mills remarks that in *Public Opinion* (1922), Walter Lippmann was stressing the extreme difficulty of educating the common man to the point of understanding the complex world he now lived in (see Mills, *White Collar*, pp. 324–325).
19. Calvin Coolidge, *Autobiography*, Cosmopolitan Book Corporation (New York, 1929), p. 60.
20. Louis D. Brandeis, *Business: A Profession*, Small, Maynard (Boston, 1925), p. 27.
21. Qu. in Frederick William Conner, *Cosmic Optimism*, University of Florida Press (Gainesville, 1949), p. 153.
22. White, *The Old Order Changeth*, p. 193. Lippmann became more pessimistic later.
23. Qu. in Granville Hicks, "Marquand of Newburyport," *Harper's*, CC (April, 1950), 106.
24. Rod W. Horton and Herbert W. Edwards, *Backgrounds of American Literary Thought*, Appleton-Century-Crofts (New York, 1952), p. 246.
25. May, *The End of American Innocence*, pp. 232–236.
26. Max Eastman, *The Sense of Humor*, Scribner (New York, 1921), p. 38. In that chapter, "Humor and Sexuality" (pp. 38–41), Eastman implies that on the whole Freud's theories have been beneficial, but in "Freud's Contribution" (pp. 190–205), he is quite critical of Freud's views.
27. Mills, *White Collar*, p. 328.

Chapter 3.
John Kendrick Bangs, University Wit

1. John Kendrick Bangs, "John Phoenix and His Work," a preface to *Phoenixiana*, Appleton (New York, 1903), pp. vii–viii. "John Phoenix" was Captain George Horatio Derby, U.S.A.
2. "The Confession of John Kendrick Bangs," in *Our American Humorists*, Thomas L. Masson (ed.), Dodd, Mead (New York, 1922), pp. 40–41.

3. *Ibid.*, p. 41. The statement does not, in context, seem ironical in intention.

4. John Kendrick Bangs, "A Word Concerning American Humor," *The Book Buyer*, XX (April, 1900), 205; Francis Hyde Bangs, *John Kendrick Bangs*, Knopf (New York, 1941), p. 272.

5. *The Enchanted Typewriter* (1899) contains an interesting antici- pation of Don Marquis' way of introducing Archy. Bangs' narrator, like that of Marquis, is mystified by a typewriter that seems to tap out messages by itself. He finds that the spirit of Boswell has been operating the machine. Bangs' use of the occult as a subject of humor was even more frequent than Marquis'. Bangs also planned to write some pieces on a cockroach but gave up the idea because his illustrator could not draw roaches.

6. *Coffee and Repartee* (1893), *Three Weeks in Politics* (1894), *The Idiot* (1895), *The Idiot at Home* (1900), *Inventions of the Idiot* (1903), *The Genial Idiot* (1908), *Half-Hours With the Idiot* (1917).

7. Francis Hyde Bangs, *John Kendrick Bangs*, p. 131.

8. In *Over the Plumpudding*, Harper (New York and London, 1901).

9. It is only fair to note that Bangs heaped praise on "the ineffable Mr. Dooley, not to have read whose sage reflections and comments on life is not to have lived." Dooley, he said, was "humor boiled down," the "pure, undiluted essence of humor"; moreover, "Mr. Dooley is no more of Erin than Thackeray is of Hindustan, and in his own way is as wholly American as was old Hosea Biglow him- self." See Bangs, "A Word Concerning American Humor," pp. 207–208.

PART TWO

Crackerbarrel Survivals

Chapter 4.
George Ade, Student of "Success"

1. John T. McCutcheon, *Notes and Reminiscences*, Holiday Press (Chicago, 1940), qu. by Franklin J. Meine, "Introduction" to George Ade, *Stories of the Streets and of the Town*, p. xv.

2. Fred C. Kelly, *George Ade, Warmhearted Satirist*, Bobbs-Merrill (Indianapolis and New York, 1947), p. 16.

3. Reprinted in Kelly, *George Ade,* pp. 43–45.

4. Besides Kelly's book, the chief source of material for the preceding paragraphs has been Philip Nordhus, "George Ade," unpublished doctoral dissertation, State University of Iowa, Iowa City, 1956, p. 21. Nordhus' work is especially useful in its examination of Ade's plays and of Ade's part in developing musical comedy in America. The scanty amount of contemporary biographical and critical material on Ade also includes Bergen Evans, "George Ade: Rustic Humorist," *American Mercury,* LXX (March, 1950), 321–329, and J. A. Clark, "Ade's Fables in Slang: An Appreciation," *South Atlantic Quarterly,* XLVI (October, 1947), 537–544; Van Wyck Brooks, *The Confident Years,* E. P. Dutton (New York, 1955), pp. 183–186, and R. Balfour Daniels, "George Ade As Social Critic," *Mississippi Quarterly,* XII (Fall, 1959), 194–204. See also Dorothy Russo, *A Bibliography of George Ade,* Bobbs-Merrill (Indianapolis, 1947), and Fred C. Kelly (ed.), *The Permanent Ade,* Bobbs-Merrill (Indianapolis and New York, 1947). Another collection is Jean Shepherd (ed.), *The America of George Ade,* Putnam (New York, 1960).

5. *Stories of the Streets and of the Town,* pp. xxiv–xxv.

6. Many of the stories were republished by the *Record* in a series of eight pamphlets under the running title *Stories of the Streets and of the Town* (1894–1900).

7. George Ade, "Keep on Being a Country Boy," *Hearst's International,* LXXIX (December, 1925), 56, qu. by Nordhus, "George Ade," p. 23.

8. Meine (ed.), *Stories of the Streets and of the Town,* pp. xvi–xx.

9. The Albany *Journal,* qu. in an advertisement on an unnumbered back page of George Ade, *Pink Marsh,* Herbert S. Stone (Chicago and New York, 1897).

10. Cf. Norris W. Yates, *William T. Porter . . . a Study of the "Big Bear" School of Humor,* Louisiana State University Press (Baton Rouge, 1957), pp. 152–153. The frontier version quoted here is more imaginative than Ade's.

11. Mark Twain praised *Pink Marsh* extravagantly, saying in a letter to William Dean Howells, "Pink—oh, the shiftless, worthless, lovable black darling! Howells, he deserves to live forever." Qu. in George Ade, *One Afternoon With Mark Twain* (Mark Twain Society of Chicago, 1939), pp. 8–9, and reprinted in *Mark Twain—Howells' Letters,* Henry Nash Smith and William M. Gibson (eds.), Harvard University Press (Cambridge, 1960), II, 832.

12. In *The Social Secretary* (1905), David Graham Phillips portrayed a white-collar girl whose job is a springboard to marriage with a multi-millionaire.

13. Kelly, *George Ade,* pp. 136–137.

14. Of these books, all or part were fables in the vernacular: *Fables in Slang* (1899), *More Fables* (1900), *Forty Modern Fables* (1901), *The Girl Proposition* (1902), *People You Know* (1903), *Breaking Into Society* (1904), *True Bills* (1904), *Knocking the Neighbors* (1912), *Ade's Fables* (1914), *Hand-Made Fables* (1920). One more, *I Knew Him When* (1910), is a nonfictional essay written in slang.

15. Nordhus, "George Ade," pp. 136–137. Ade's fables, of course, are not true fables, since the characters are not animals, but he evidently thought of a fable as any short tale with very simple character types and with a moral at the end. See also George Kummer, *Harry Leon Wilson,* The Press of Western Reserve University (Cleveland, 1963), pp. 30–31.

16. George Ade, "The Champion of Walpole Township," [a poem] *Puck,* XXXVII (March 6, 1895), 35.

17. *Life,* XXVII (April 16, 1896), 308. Other titles in the series were "The Tiger and the Deer" (aimed at Tammany Hall), "The Baa-Sheep and the Lion," "The Ambitious Hippopotamus," and "The Fox and the Grapes." All of Phillips' fables in *Life* were illustrated with line drawings by T. S. Sullivant.

18. This remark of Ade's was recalled by J. M. Chapple, "Ade as a Playwright and Chauffeur," *National Magazine,* XIX (February, 1904), 560. Qu. by Nordhus, "George Ade," p. 109.

19. The formula got pretty well-worn; in fact a British critic referred to *Hand-Made Fables* as "Machine-Made Fables." See Nordhus, "George Ade," p. 4.

20. Qu. in Mark Sullivan, *Our Times,* II, Scribner (New York and London, 1927), 25.

21. Henry James, *The American Scene,* Harper (New York and London), p. 164.

22. Qu. in Kelly, *George Ade,* p. 71.

Chapter 5.
Mr. Dooley of Archey Road

1. "Mr. Dooley was as clearly of the tradition of the crackerbox philosopher as was Hosea Biglow, Abe Martin, or Will Rogers." So says Elmer Ellis, *Mr. Dooley's America, a Life of Finley Peter Dunne,* Knopf (New York, 1941), p. 302. Cf. Blair, *Horse Sense in American Humor,* pp. 240–255.

2. Blair, *Horse Sense in American Humor,* p. 241.

3. Most of the sketches about Mr. Dooley were eventually collected in *Mr. Dooley In Peace and In War* (1898), *Mr. Dooley in the Hearts of His Countrymen* (1898), *What Dooley Says* (1899), *Mr. Dooley's Philosophy* (1900), *Mr. Dooley's Opinions* (1901), *Observations by Mr.*

Dooley (1902), *Dissertations by Mr. Dooley* (1906), *Mr. Dooley Says* (1910), *New Dooley Book* (1911), *Mr. Dooley on Making a Will and Other Necessary Evils* (1919), *The "Mr. Dooley" Papers* (1938). Later compilations of Dunne's work are Elmer Ellis, *Mr. Dooley at His Best,* Scribner (New York, 1938), with a foreword by Franklin P. Adams; Louis Filler, *Mr. Dooley: Now and Forever,* Academic Reprints (Stanford, California, 1954); *Mr. Dooley on Ivrything and Ivrybody,* Dover (New York, 1962), and *The World of Mr. Dooley,* Collier (New York, 1963).

4. Hofstadter, *The Age of Reform,* p. 260.

5. *Ibid.,* p. 261.

6. As qu. by Fred C. Kelly, *The Life and Times of Kin Hubbard, Creator of Abe Martin,* Farrar, Straus and Young (New York, 1952), p. 179, Abe said, "If capital an' labor ever do git t'gether it's good night fer th 'rest of us.'"

7. Qu. by Blair, *Horse Sense in American Humor,* p. 248.

8. Ellis, *Mr. Dooley's America,* p. 262.

9. *Ibid.,* pp. 240–241; Filler, *Mr. Dooley: Now and Forever,* pp. xii-xiii.

10. However, in some of the longer narratives rendered by Dooley, Dunne could be sentimental to the point of bathos.

Chapter 6.

Kin Hubbard of Brown County, Indiana

1. George Ade, "Abe Martin of Brown County," *American Magazine,* LXX (May, 1910), 46–48.

2. Qu. by Blair, *Horse Sense in American Humor,* p. 262. In addition to the quotations from Hubbard's prose used by Blair, fifty maxims from three of Hubbard's almanacs are reprinted in John T. Flanagan and Arthur Palmer Hudson (eds.), *Folklore in American Literature,* Row, Peterson (Evanston, Illinois, and White Plains, New York, 1958), pp. 477–478.

3. Fred C. Kelly, *The Life and Times of Kin Hubbard,* Farrar, Straus and Young (New York, 1952), p. 86. Most of the biographical information in this chapter comes from this volume. Riley's poem is reprinted on pp. 95–96.

    Hubbard was so little interested in reproducing the dialect of any specific region that his use of local English amounts to little more than elisions and cacography. Moreover, he is often inconsistent in using these devices. I have made no attempt to "correct" his inconsistencies.

4. Qu. by Blair, *Horse Sense in American Humor,* p. 252.

5. Robert S. Lynd and Helen Merrell Lynd, *Middletown in Transition,* Harcourt, Brace (New York, 1937), p. 26.

6. Preston William Slosson, *The Great Crusade and After, 1914–1928,* pp. 96–98, has interesting data that in the main corroborate Hubbard's views on the relationship between crime and the automobile.

7. Kin Hubbard, "Abe Martin on the War," *American Magazine,* LXXXI (January, 1916), 23.

Chapter 7.
The Crackerbarrel Sage in the West and South: Will Rogers and Irvin S. Cobb

1. Homer Croy, *Our Will Rogers,* Duell, Sloan and Pearce (New York, 1953), pp. 173–179. Collections of Rogers' writings and sayings in book form include *The Cowboy Philosopher on Prohibition* (1919); *Rogers-isms, the Cowboy Philosopher on the Peace Conference* (1919); *What We Laugh At* (1920); *The Illiterate Digest* (1924); *Letters of a Self-Made Diplomat to His President* (1926); *There's Not a Bathing Suit in Russia* (1927); *Will Rogers' Political Follies* (1929); *Ether and Me* (1929); *Wit and Philosophy From the Radio Talks of America's Humorist, Will Rogers* (1930); Jack Lait (comp.), *Will Rogers, Wit and Wisdom* (1936); *The Autobiography of Will Rogers* (1949); *How We Elect Our Presidents* (1952); *Sanity Is Where You Find It* (1955). The last three compilations were made by Donald Day. Day has recently completed *Will Rogers: A Biography,* David McKay (New York, 1962) in which, among other new material, is recorded the fact that Will tried without much success to publish some of his jokes in *Life.*

2. P. J. O'Brien, *Will Rogers,* John C. Winston (Chicago and Philadelphia, 1935), p. 274.

3. Irvin S. Cobb, *Exit Laughing,* Bobbs-Merrill (Indianapolis and New York, 1941), pp. 406–407; Croy, *Our Will Rogers,* p. vii. Other major biographical sources include William Howard Payne and Jake G. Lyons (comps.), *Folks Say of Will Rogers,* Putnam (New York, 1936), and Betty Rogers, *Will Rogers, His Wife's Story,* Bobbs-Merrill (Indianapolis and New York, 1941).

4. Eastman, *Enjoyment of Laughter,* p. 338.

5. Progressives in this sense, the Progressives who gave the era its name, agreed with their opponents that progress was natural—even almost inevitable—but they wanted to speed it up. "Most of the political differences among Americans in this age of political conflict reflected no difference in ideology more basic than this" (May, *The End of American Innocence 1912–1917,* p. 21). Rogers, as will be seen, belonged to the generation of skeptics in a somewhat later period who were having doubts about progress.

6. Despite his isolationism, Rogers was a firm advocate of preparedness and clairvoyant in his stress of air power. In 1923 he warned that "the Nation in the Next War that ain't up in the Air, is just going to get something dropped on its Bean." His first airplane ride was given him by General Billy Mitchell after the latter's court-martial.

7. One of the accounts by Rogers of his interview with Mussolini may be found in *Letters of a Self-Made Diplomat to His President*, Albert and Charles Boni (New York, 1926), pp. 128–143. Detailed, mainly favorable comments on Mussolini and his policies follow (pp. 143–152).

8. Robert S. Lynd and Helen Merrell Lynd, *Middletown in Transition*, p. 481.

9. *The Life of Davy Crockett Written by Himself*, Signet (New York, 1955), p. 69.

10. Cf. Donald Day (ed.), *The Autobiography of Will Rogers*, Houghton Mifflin (Boston, 1949), pp. 248–249, and Will Durant, *On the Meaning of Life*, Ray Long, Richard L. Smith (New York, 1932), pp. 60–62. Durant has considerably abridged Will's comments. Day says that Will was "basically a crusader" (*Will Rogers: A Biography*, p. 338); if so, Rogers' frequent denials that he had any "mission" suggest yet another inconsistency shared by many of his fellow citizens.

11. Fred G. Neuman, *Irvin S. Cobb, His Life and Letters*, Rodale Press (Emaus [sic], Pennsylvania, 1938), pp. 37–38.

12. Elisabeth Cobb, *My Wayward Parent*, Bobbs-Merrill (Indianapolis and New York, 1945), p. 162.

13. *Folks Say of Will Rogers*, p. 78; Cobb, *Exit Laughing*, pp. 333–347.

14. Irvin S. Cobb, *Back Home*, Review of Reviews Corporation (New York, 1912), p. ix.

15. Cobb's ideas about the South and Americanism were shared by certain intellectuals whom he may well have mistrusted *because* they were intellectuals. In the symposium *I'll Take My Stand*, Harper (New York and London, 1930), twelve southerners defended the "humanistic" culture of America, saying ". . . we believe that this, the genuine humanism, was rooted in the agrarian life of the older South and of other parts of the country that shared in such a tradition" (p. xvi). Cf. Donald Davidson, *The Attack on Leviathan*, University of North Carolina Press (Chapel Hill, 1938), p. 284. Davidson's ideal southerner, the planter "Cousin Roderick," is much like Judge Priest in his character, tastes, and relation to the community, if not in his specific occupation. Cf. also "The Life and Death of Cousin Lucius," by J. D. Wade, in *I'll Take My Stand*, pp. 265–301.

16. Cobb was condemning the methods of the revived Klan, not necessarily their aims, which coincided in part with his own hopes. In

1926, the Imperial Wizard of the Klan demanded "a return of power into the hands of the . . . unspoiled and not de-Americanized average citizen of the old stock." Qu. by Hofstadter, *The Age of Reform,* pp. 295–296.

17. William Allen White, "The Humor of the Self-Kidder," *Saturday Review of Literature,* XXIII (March 22, 1941), 5.

18. After an operation for gallstones, Will Rogers imitated *"Speaking of Operations—"* in *Ether and Me* (1929).

19. Gilbert Seldes, *The Seven Lively Arts,* Harper (New York and London, 1924), p. 51.

PART THREE

"Sophisticated" Skeptics

Chapter 9.
The Two Masks of H. L. Mencken

1. Frederick Lewis Allen, *Only Yesterday,* Bantam Giant Edition (New York, 1952), p. 209. The reaction to Mencken's "baseballs" tended toward violent resentment, as shown in Sara Haardt Mencken (ed.), *Menckeniana: A Schimpflexikon* [dictionary of abuse] Knopf (New York, 1928), but Carl Van Doren was only the first of a number of critics to appreciate Mencken as a humorist; see *Many Minds,* Knopf (New York, 1924), p. 135. Cf. Brooks, *The Confident Years,* p. 462; Alastair Cooke, "Introduction" to *The Vintage Mencken,* Vintage (New York, 1950), p. xi; Ernest Boyd, *H. L. Mencken,* Robert M. McBride (New York, 1925), pp. 82–83; Isaac Goldberg, *The Man Mencken,* Simon and Schuster (New York, 1925), p. 276, and Charles Angoff, *H. L. Mencken: A Portrait From Memory,* Thomas Yoseloff (New York, 1956), p. 13. Two biographies of recent years are Edgar Kemler, *The Irreverent Mr. Mencken,* Little, Brown (Boston, 1950), and William Manchester, *Disturber of the Peace,* Harper (New York, 1951). Valuable for study of the *Smart Set* during the editorship of Mencken and Nathan is Carl Richard Dolmetsch, "A History of *The Smart Set* Magazine, 1914–1923," unpublished doctoral dissertation, University of Chicago, 1957, and the supplement by the same author, "An Index to *The Smart Set* Magazine," unpublished ms. on microfilm, University of Chicago, 1957. Other additions to the growing body of Mencken scholarship are M. K. Singleton, *H. L. Mencken and*

the American Mercury *Adventure,* Duke University Press (Durham, N.C., 1962), and *H. L. M.: The Mencken Bibliography,* comp. by Betty Adler asst. by Jane Wilhelm, Enoch Pratt Free Library, Johns Hopkins Press (Baltimore, 1961). Selections of Mencken's writings are available in three compilations in paperback format: Cooke (ed.), *The Vintage Mencken;* Malcolm Moos (ed.), *H. L. Mencken on Politics,* Johns Hopkins (Baltimore, 1956) [in hard cover], Vintage (New York, 1960) [in paper cover]; James T. Farrell (ed.), *H. L. Mencken Prejudices: A Selection,* Vintage (New York, 1958).

2. Brooks, *The Confident Years,* pp. 452–453. Brooks' last statement is perhaps misleading. For the record, Mencken traveled extensively, and from the time of his marriage to Sara Haardt in 1930 until several months after her death in 1935, he lived in an apartment at 704 Cathedral Street, not far from the house at 1524 Hollins Street to which Brooks undoubtedly refers and in which he did reside for most of his life, including the years of his final illness.

3. Brooks, *The Confident Years,* p. 452; cf. p. 454, also Robert E. Spiller *et al., Literary History of the United States,* Macmillan (New York, 1948), II, 1142–43; Arthur Hobson Quinn *et al., The Literature of the American People,* Appleton-Century-Crofts (New York, 1951), p. 853, and Kemler, *The Irreverent Mr. Mencken,* pp. 27–28.

4. Cooke, *The Vintage Mencken,* p. ix. Mencken himself sheds little light on his debt to the German philosopher. Edward Stone wrote an M.A. thesis for the University of Texas on "H. L. Mencken's Debt to F. W. Nietzsche," and after seeing the manuscript, Mencken wrote to Stone, "As you know, I was under the impression that my debt to Nietzsche was very slight. I must say now that your argument rather shakes me. Such influences are exerted, it appears, very insidiously. I was picking up Nietzscheisms without being aware of them, and they undoubtedly got into my own stuff. Certainly you maintain your thesis with immense plausibility, and, as I say, I am half inclined to confess conversion to it." See Guy J. Forgue (ed.), *Letters of H. L. Mencken,* Knopf (New York, 1961), p. 417. I have not seen Mr. Stone's thesis.

5. Cf. Mencken's comment two years later that, "His 'good' meant, not 'holy' or 'meek,' but 'able.' His god was 'efficiency.'" From "The Literary Heavyweight Champion," *Smart Set,* XXX (March, 1910), 153–160.

6. A useful, brief study of Sumner's thought is Richard Hofstadter, "William Graham Sumner, Social Darwinist," *Social Darwinism in American Thought,* University of Pennsylvania Press (Philadelphia, 1945), pp. 37–51.

7. May, *The End of American Innocence,* p. 208. The quotations within the quotation are from H. L. Mencken, *The Philosophy of Friedrich Nietzsche,* 2nd ed. (Boston, 1913), p. 159.

8. Qu. by Dolmetsch, "A History of *The Smart Set* Magazine," p. 49.

Cf. Mencken's letter to Ellery Sedgwick, *Letters of H. L. Mencken,* p. 49. In this letter to the editor of the *Atlantic* Mencken was defending the *Smart Set* policy of satire and the light touch. In another letter, to Dreiser, Mencken said, "My whole life, once I get free from my present engagements, will be devoted to combatting Puritanism" *(Letters of H. L. Mencken,* p. 87). However, in this letter Mencken was advising Dreiser to compromise in deleting or altering certain passages in *The Genius,* and the quoted statement is by way of excusing his own pessimism regarding Dreiser's ability to beat the censorship of his novel without such a compromise. Despite his blatancy, Mencken was a man of consideration and tact in most of his personal relationships and a man of tactics in his public writings, and any statement he made about himself, either in public or in private, should be evaluated only within its full context.

9. H. L. Mencken, "Postscript by H. L. Mencken," in anon., *Three Years 1924 to 1927, The Story of a New Idea and Its Successful Adaptation,* the *American Mercury* [publisher] (New York, 1927), p. 36.

10. *Letters of H. L. Mencken,* p. 188.

11. In *Prejudices: Fifth Series,* p. 304, Mencken again claimed that he lived in America rather than Europe because he found more amusement in his own country:

   Q. If you find so much that is unworthy of reverence in the United States, then why do you live here?
   A. Why do men go to zoos?

12. This essay is reprinted in *Sumner Today,* Maurice R. Davie (ed.), Yale University Press (New Haven, 1940), pp. 3–26. To another essay by Sumner in this volume, Mencken contributed an appreciative note, pp. 113–114.
   "The Forgotten Man" presents only a part of Sumner's total philosophy and only a small fraction of the interests which eventually made him eminent in sociology and anthropology as well as in economics. Although Mencken wrote to Albert G. Keller in 1932, "The books of your old chief, Dr. Sumner, made a powerful impression on me when I was young, and their influence has survived" *(Letters of H. L. Mencken,* p. 337), he cited only "The Forgotten Man," and there is little evidence that he was familiar with Sumner's most ambitious works, *Folkways* (1907), and *The Science of Society* (1927).

13. Mencken wrote an introduction for Howe's *Ventures in Common Sense,* Knopf (New York, 1919), in which his description of Howe suggests the same type of rational conservative Mencken was depicting as his own *persona.* In *Letters of H. L. Mencken,* he refers to Howe as "the very best type of American" in contrast to "the Judaized New Yorker" (p. 186).

14. He probably did not mean the *Atlantic*. Within the year, Mencken wrote Ellery Sedgwick asking for a copy of the *Atlantic* style sheet. Presumably he intended to use it as a style guide for the *Mercury*. Earlier he had written articles for the *Atlantic* and had expressd to Sedgwick his hope that he and Nathan could make the *Smart Set* "a sort of frivolous sister to the *Atlantic*." See *Letters of H. L. Mencken*, pp. 49, 272. As a writer, Mencken honored decorum and taste almost as much in the observance as in the breach—his tactics in any given essay or editorial depended largely on his purpose in that item. As an editor, he was even more calculating.

15. Singleton, *H. L. Mencken and the* American Mercury *Adventure,"* pp. 156, 183*n*, 228*n*.

16. The periods at the end of the quote are Mencken's.

17. In heartily approving of Sinclair Lewis' plan for *Babbitt*, Mencken declared that "The big city right-thinker seems to me to be even more typical of the Republic than the Main Street right-thinker." See *Letters of H. L. Mencken*, p. 233.

18. At the time he wrote *In Defense of Women*, Mencken was a bachelor and would remain one for quite awhile. Whether Mencken's life with Sara Haardt, to whom he was married in 1930 at the age of fifty and who died of tubercular meningitis in 1935, bore any resemblance to the "ideal" relationship depicted in that book is not within the scope of inquiry of this work.

Chapter 10.
The Isolated Man of Ring Lardner

1. In 1905 it was estimated that the percentage of first-graders who would eventually be graduated from the twelfth grade was about ten. See *Report of the Commissioner of Education for the Year Ended June, 1914*, Government Printing Office (Washington, D.C., 1915), p. xiv. In 1910, about one million pupils were in secondary schools beyond the sixth year. This figure had almost doubled by 1920, and more than quadrupled by 1928. The rapid increase in school attendance during these eighteen years indicates how low the general level of school training was in the populace at the time Lardner started his writing career. See I. L. Kandel, *History of Secondary Education*, p. 449.

2. Donald Elder, *Ring Lardner*, Doubleday (Garden City, New York), p. 14.

3. Howard W. Webb, Jr., "The Development of a Style: The Lardner Idiom," *American Quarterly*, XII (Winter, 1960), 482–492.

4. Elder, p. 112. See also Charles A. Fenton, *The Apprenticeship of Ernest Hemingway*, Viking (New York), pp. 22–26, 59–60.

5. Elder, p. 183.

6. Howard Webb, "Ring Lardner's Idle Common Man," *Bulletin of the Central Mississippi Valley American Studies Association,* I (Spring, 1958), 6–13. Mr. Webb's interpretations of Lardner supplied one of the kernels of my thesis in this book as a whole. He is not responsible for the ways in which I have modified his views while extending them to cover other humorists. Cf. Maxwell Geismar, *Writers in Crisis,* Houghton Mifflin (Boston, 1942), pp. 3–36.

7. Concerning the wise boob, Elder adds *(Ring Lardner,* p. 169), "But the character is deceptive. It is really a burlesque of all wise boobs, of all humorists and commentators; it is a burlesque of Ring himself."

8. Webb, "Ring Lardner's Idle Common Man," p. 13.

9. Howard W. Webb, Jr., "The Meaning of Ring Lardner's Fiction: A Re-evaluation," *American Literature,* XXXI (January, 1960), 434–445. Professor Webb is also compiling the unreprinted works of Lardner.

10. *Ibid.,* p. 437.

11. *Ibid.,* p. 436.

12. The Grosses are revived in several as yet uncollected stories in the same magazine.

13. The characterization of Gullible is not entirely consistent; for instance, in "Three Without, Doubled," he is more of a boor than in "Gullible's Travels." In all, five stories were written about Gullible and appeared in the *Saturday Evening Post:* "Carmen" (February 19, 1916), "Three Kings and a Pair" (March 11, 1916), "Gullible's Travels" (August 19, 1916), "The Water Cure" (October 14, 1916), and "Three Without, Doubled" (January 13, 1917). Lardner was writing much else during this period, and he may not have planned originally to integrate these stories in a book. Anyway, he collected them in *Gullible's Travels,* Bobbs-Merrill (Indianapolis, 1917). The title story and "Carmen" were included in *The Portable Ring Lardner,* Viking (New York, 1946); the title story and "Three Without, Doubled" may also be found in *The Ring Lardner Reader,* Maxwell Geismar (ed.), Scribner (New York, 1963). The latter volume also includes a good, brief introduction by the editor.

14. Such comparisons do not mean that Thurber is a better artist and more effective humorist than Lardner. This discussion, like the book in general, has to do mainly with who and what certain humorous characters are, and what values they embody, not with how skillfully these characters and their values are rendered.

15. *Say It With Oil* was reprinted upside down within the same covers as Nina Wilcox Putnam, *Say It With Bricks,* George H. Doran (New York, 1923). (Or Mrs. Putnam's essay was reprinted upside down, depending on how one picks up the volume.) *Say It With Bricks* was a defense of wives.

16. Compare Mr. and Mrs. Babbitt at the breakfast table and the Taylors of "Anniversary" in the evening:

> "And it says here a fellow was inaugurated mayor in overalls—a preacher, too! What do you think of that?"
> "Humph! Well!" (*Babbitt*, Ch. II)

> "Think of it!" he said. "Nearly twenty-eight million automobiles!"
> "Heavens!" said Mrs. Taylor.

17. Elder, *Ring Lardner*, p. 309. A possible exception to Elder's generalization that Ring never portrayed wives favorably is Mrs. Drake in "Liberty Hall."
18. *Ibid.*, p. 358. See Ernest Hemingway, "In Defense of Dirty Words," *Esquire*, II (September, 1934), 19, 158B, 158D.
19. In stating that isolation has been a common theme in American letters, I do not mean that all writers have dealt with the same aspects, causes, or effects of that isolation. Lardner, for example, was rarely concerned—at least on paper—with the loneliness of the truly creative artist, a theme that stimulated Hawthorne and Henry James, or with the isolation of the seeker for absolutes in an inscrutable universe, as was Melville.
20. Geismar, *Writers in Crisis*, p. 18.
21. John Dos Passos, *The Big Money*, Vol. III of *U.S.A.*, Random House (New York, 1937), p. 191.
22. Robert Frost, "To a Thinker," *Complete Poems*, Henry Holt (New York, 1949), p. 431.
23. Elder, *Ring Lardner*, p. 291.
24. Ring Lardner, "Sport," in Harold Stearns (ed.), *Civilization in the United States*, Harcourt, Brace (New York, 1922), p. 461.

Chapter 11.
The Many Masks of Don Marquis

1. Edward Anthony, *O Rare Don Marquis*, Doubleday (Garden City, New York, 1962), p. 645.
2. E. B. White, "Don Marquis," *The Second Tree From the Corner*, Harper (New York, 1954), p. 187. Incidentally, White capitalizes the first letter of Archy's name because Marquis did likewise whenever he referred to this character in his prose columns (p. 183). I follow White's lead.
3. *Danny's Own Story*, Doubleday, Page (Garden City, New York, 1912)—in many episodes an almost slavish imitation of *Huckleberry Finn*—and *Sons of the Puritans*, Doubleday, Doran (New York, 1939), with a preface by Christopher Morley.

4. Other plays by Marquis include "Words and Thoughts" in *Carter and Other People* (1921), *The Dark Hours* (1924), *Out of the Sea* (1927), *Master of the Revels* (1934), "A Moment in Hell" in *Chapters for the Orthodox* (1934), and "Everything's Jake" (unpublished). *Shinbone Alley*, a musical comedy based on the poems about Archy and Mehitabel, was produced on Broadway in 1957.

5. Hamlin Hill, "Archy and Uncle Remus: Don Marquis's Debt to Joel Chandler Harris," *The Georgia Review*, XV (Spring, 1961), 78–87. Cf. Anthony, *O Rare Don Marquis*, p. 142. The idea of endowing a roach with human attributes did not necessarily originate with Marquis; John Kendrick Bangs had tried it once and dropped the notion because Peter Newell, at that time his most frequent illustrator, could not draw roaches. See Christopher Morley, "Don Marquis: An Appreciation," *Tomorrow*, IX (May, 1950), 52–53. George Herriman, the creator of Krazy Kat, illustrated reprint editions of all three of the Archy books. Herriman's pensive roaches and raffish cats do more than supplement the text; they are an attraction in their own right.

6. Margaret Case Harriman, *The Vicious Circle: The Story of the Algonquin Round Table*, Rinehart (New York, Toronto, 1951), p. 53.

7. Judge Ben B. Lindsey and Wainwright Evans, *The Companionate Marriage*, Garden City Publishing Co. (Garden City, New York, 1927, 1929), p. xiii.

8. Hill, "Archy and Uncle Remus," 82–86, has suggested that Archy resembles the trickster-heroes of Uncle Remus in several ways, and possibly also the rogue-heroes of nineteenth-century American humor—Jack Downing, Simon Suggs, Artemus Ward, and Josh Billings. In general, Marquis felt that he owed more to Eugene Field and George Ade. See Anthony, *O Rare Don Marquis*, p. 66.

9. Don Marquis, "The Farmer of Snap-Bean Farm," *"Uncle Remus's the Home Magazine*, XXIV (September, 1908), 7.

10. Charles Child Walcutt, *American Literary Naturalism, a Divided Stream*, University of Minnesota Press (Minneapolis, 1956), pp. 10–20. As a boy, Marquis read Darwin's *The Origin of Species* and *The Descent of Man*, and some of the work of Herbert Spencer. See Anthony, *O Rare Don Marquis*, pp. 39, 54.

11. Marquis once told Morley that "In 1916 I again returned to the Republican party. This time it was for the express purpose of voting against Mr. Wilson." See Morley's *Shandygaff*, Doubleday, Page (Garden City, New York, 1918), p. 39.

12. Qu. in Stanley J. Kunitz and Howard Haycraft, *Twentieth Century Authors*, H. M. Wilson (New York, 1942), p. 913.

13. Cf. *Prefaces*, Appleton (New York, London, 1923), pp. 147–148, where Marquis wrote, "The creeds that have endured have endured because of the truth in them; and this truth has always been a courage about life on earth and a high thought concerning the ultimate destiny of the spirit." His language is not entirely clear; he could mean that the spirit does have a destiny other than dust, or merely that men are most noble when they believe this about the spirit. Marquis himself had a hard struggle to retain the courage of which he speaks, and one of his attempts to do so was his precarious conversion, under the influence of his second wife, to Christian Science, around 1927 or 1928. Anthony *(O Rare Don Marquis,* p. 418) thinks that this conversion lasted about a year.

PART FOUR

Creators of the Little Man

Chapter 12.
The "Genial Middle Ground"

1. Fenton, *The Apprenticeship of Ernest Hemingway,* p. 24.

2. Blair, *Horse Sense in American Humor,* pp. 274–277.

3. Stephen Becker, *Comic Art in America,* Simon and Schuster (New York, 1959), p. 39.

4. *Ibid.,* pp. 54–86.

5. To satisfy the more careful students of Joyce, let it be stated that I am aware of enormous differences between Bloom and the Little Man of American humor. Discussion of these differences is beyond the scope of this book.

6. Eastman, *Enjoyment of Laughter,* p. 108. The comment by Chaplin is reprinted by permission of Simon and Schuster, Inc.

7. Ralph L. Curry, "Leacock and Benchley: An Acknowledged Literary Debt," *American Book Collector,* VII (March, 1957), 14.

8. Taken from Margaret Case Harriman, *The Vicious Circle,* Rinehart (New York, 1951), pp. 176–179, and reprinted by permission of the *New Yorker.* Cf. Theodore Peterson, *Magazines in the Twentieth Century,* University of Illinois Press (Urbana, 1956), p. 237. A brief discussion of the *New Yorker* is that by James Playsted Wood, *Magazines in the United States,* Ronald Press (New York,

1949), pp. 209–233. "Advisory Editors" whose names appeared in connection with the prospectus were Ralph Barton, Heywood Broun, Marc Connelly, Edna Ferber, Rea Irvin, George S. Kaufman, Alice Duer Miller, Dorothy Parker, Laurence Stallings, and Alexander Woollcott. Some of these people, however, had little connection with the magazine *(The Vicious Circle,* p. 180).

9. According to the U.S. Census of 1920, urban residents outnumbered rural for the first time during that year.

10. James Thurber, *The Years With Ross,* Little, Brown (Boston and Toronto, 1959), p. 77.

11. *Ibid.,* p. 54.

Chapter 13.
Life With Clarence Day, Jr.

1. Kunitz and Haycraft, *Twentieth Century Authors,* p. 357.

2. *Decennial Record of the Class of 1896, Yale College.* Compiled by Clarence S. Day, Jr., Class Secretary. De Vinne Press (New York, 1907), p. 639.

3. *Ibid.,* p. 201. Cf. *Hamlet* I.v.15.

4. Louis Filler, *Crusaders for American Liberalism,* Harcourt, Brace (New York, 1939), pp. 370–371.

5. However, Day was so little the partisan in politics that he wrote a moving account of the death and burial of Calvin Coolidge, reprinted as *In the Green Mountain Country,* Yale University Press (New Haven, 1934).

6. Hofstadter, *Social Darwinism in American Thought,* p. 31 and *passim;* Walcutt, *American Literary Naturalism,* pp. 10–20. Concerning the connection between optimistic beliefs about human nature and the belief in democracy, Herbert Croly, the founder of the *New Republic,* wrote, "Democracy must stand or fall on a platform of possible human perfectibility," and proclaimed his own assumption of this possibility. See *The Promise of American Life,* Macmillan (New York, 1909), p. 400.

7. Thurber, *The Years With Ross,* p. 174.

8. A third collection, *Father and I,* was listed by Kunitz and Haycraft as published in 1940, but I have found no further evidence of its publication.

9. Brooks Atkinson, "Introduction" to Howard Lindsay and Russel Crouse, *Life With Father* (play), Knopf (New York, 1940), p. vii–xi.

10. Qu. by C. Wright Mills, *White Collar,* p. 32.

Chapter 14.
Robert Benchley's Normal Bumbler

1. Nathaniel Benchley, *Robert Benchley,* McGraw-Hill (New York, Toronto, London, 1955), p. 20. This book includes a "Foreword" by Robert E. Sherwood, pp. xiii–xvi.
2. A Texas student of Benchley contends that Robert's grandfather was not an abolitionist and may even have been pro-Confederate, though Robert may not have known this. See Andrew Forest Muir, "The Skeleton in Bob Benchley's Closet," *Southwest Review,* XLIII (Winter, 1958), 70–72. According to Muir, in 1863 Henry Benchley even "got up" a musical entertainment to help raise the morale of Texas Confederates.
3. Ralph L. Curry, *Stephen Leacock,* Doubleday (Garden City, New York, 1959), p. 83.
4. *Ibid.,* p. 135. For further details of Benchley's debt to Leacock, see pp. 84, 133–134, also the article by Curry cited in Ch. XII, note 7.
5. Blair, *Horse Sense in American Humor,* pp. 274–283; *Native American Humor,* p. 171.
6. Frank Sullivan, "Introduction" to *Chips Off the Old Benchley,* Harper (New York, 1949), p. xi.
7. Robert Benchley, "The Theatre," *New Yorker,* VI (March 8, 1930, 27–28. Besides resurrecting some of Benchley's sprightliest prose, a selective compilation of his uncollected drama reviews would make available further data on the American theater during the nineteen-twenties and nineteen-thirties.
8. Robert Benchley, "Glorifying the American Flea," *Bookman,* LXVII (March, 1928), 64–66.
9. Robert Benchley, "Drama," *Life,* LXXX (September 14, 1922), 20.
10. Nathaniel Benchley, *Robert Benchley,* p. 3. According to Blair in *Horse Sense in American Humor,* p. 280, Benchley's books had sold "well above 120,000 copies" by 1942. He was reaching several times that number of readers through magazines.
11. *Sumner Today,* p. 23.
12. Nathaniel Benchley, *Robert Benchley,* pp. 168–169.
13. *Ibid.,* pp. xv-xvi.

Chapter 15.
Dorothy Parker's Idle Men and Women

1. Harriman, *The Vicious Circle,* pp. 14–16. Miss Parker denied the "Men" story in an AP interview. See the Des Moines *Sunday Register,* October 13, 1963, pp. 1-W, 4-W.
2. *Ibid.,* pp. 14–15; Nathaniel Benchley, *Robert Benchley,* p. 143.
3. Kramer, *Ross and the* New Yorker, p. 116.
4. These three volumes were combined in *Not So Deep As a Well*

(1936). The fullest available collection of her work is *The Portable Dorothy Parker,* Viking (New York, 1944). Many of her early poems and sketches in *Vanity Fair* and in *Life* remain uncollected.

5. Edmund Wilson compares her with Housman and Millay in "A Toast and a Tear for Dorothy Parker," *New Yorker,* XX (May 20, 1944), 75–76.

6. Dorothy Parker, "Not Enough," *New Masses,* XXX (March 14, 1939), 3–4.

7. Qu. in "Where'd the Money Go?" *Newsweek,* XLV (March 7, 1955), 25–26. In this story *Newsweek* also charged that Miss Parker was part of the "Red tinted ferment" in Hollywood.

8. Dorothy Parker, "The Union Forever!" *Vanity Fair,* XIII (November, 1919), 37. The title of this piece is ironic.

9. "Constant Reader" [Dorothy Parker], "Reading and Writing," *New Yorker,* III (December 10, 1927), 122–124.

10. See "Constant Reader" [Dorothy Parker], "Reading and Writing," *New Yorker,* III (December 17, 1927), 109–110; (February 4, 1928), 74–77; (February 18, 1928), 76–79; see also Dorothy Parker, "Profiles / The Artist's Reward" [a profile of Hemingway], *New Yorker,* VI (November 30, 1929), 28, where she calls Hemingway "far and away the first American artist."

11. Dorothy Parker, "The Banquet of Crow," *New Yorker,* XXXIII (December 14, 1957), 39–43.

12. Eastman, *Enjoyment of Laughter,* p. 331. Referring to the way the world seemed to be drifting toward fascism, she also said, "A humorist in this world . . . is whistling by the loneliest graveyard and whistling the saddest song." See *Newsweek* XLV (March 7, 1955), 25–26; Cf. Stanley J. Kunitz, *Twentieth Century Authors* (First Supplement), H. W. Wilson (New York, 1955), p. 753.

13. Cf. Dorothy Parker, "Lolita," *New Yorker,* XXXI (August 27, 1955), 32–35, another study of a domineering mother of the upper class.

14. Qu. from Lardner's "In the Wake of the News" by Howard Webb, "Ring Lardner's Idle Common Man," *Bulletin of the Central Mississippi Valley American Studies Association,* I (Spring, 1958), 8.

15. Yet she could also write a story on that old chestnut of American humor, the "servant problem." In "Mrs. Hofstadter on Josephine Street," the middle-class employers are portrayed sympathetically. Dorothy Parker remained, as she herself doubtless has realized, a member of the middle class.

16. My colleague, Dr. Leonard Feinberg, has completed an exhaustive study of the satirist and his relation to value-systems. Feinberg's tentative conclusion is that there is no *necessary* relationship between satire and any special ethic or ideology. See Leonard Feinberg, *The Satirist: His Temperament, Motivation, and Influence,* Iowa State University Press (Ames, 1963).

Chapter 16.
James Thurber's Little Man and Liberal Citizen

1. James Thurber, *Thurber on Humor,* The Martha Kinney Cooper Ohioana Library Association (Columbus, Ohio, [1953] p. 14. This fourteen-page pamphlet was Thurber's response to his award of the Ohioana Sesquicentennial medal. A "Foreword" states that in commemoration of Ohio's 150th anniversary, the association directed preparation of this medal and designated that it be awarded to Thurber, "native Ohioan, in recognition of his distinctive contributions in the field of art and literature and in appreciation of the prestige he has brought to Ohio." Thurber was unable to attend the presentation ceremony, and the lecture was read by George A. Smallsreed, editor of the Columbus *Dispatch.* Part of this lecture (not including the comment on his debt to his mother) was reprinted in *Lanterns and Lances,* Harper (New York, 1960), pp. 210–215. The lecture was direct and serious, not humorous or ironic.

2. Kunitz and Haycraft, *Twentieth Century Authors,* pp. 1404–05. Thurber's first publications in the *New Yorker* appeared on February 26, 1927, and March 5, 1927.

3. Thurber, *The Years With Ross,* p. 56. Thurber recalls that once White caught him trying to elaborate his simple scrawls with some solid black and crosshatching, and warned him, "Don't do that. If you ever got good you'd be mediocre" (p. 56). Cf. "James Thurber in Conversation With Alistair Cooke," *Atlantic,* CIXVIII (August, 1956), 36–40.

   More systematic study of Thurber's life and work than has yet been published is needed. At present, the most thorough examination of Thurber is Robert E. Morsberger, "The Predicaments and Perplexities of James Thurber," unpublished doctoral dissertation, State University of Iowa, Iowa City, 1956.

4. Mark Sullivan, *Our Times,* III, Scribner (New York and London, 1930), 520; IV, Scribner (New York and London, 1932), 174.

5. E. B. White, "Introduction" to *Is Sex Necessary?* Dell (New York, 1950), p. 12.

6. White says in the 1950 "Introduction" (p. 16) that Thurber wrote the chapter on "Pedestalism." Ch. VI, "What Should Children Tell Parents?" appeared under White's name in *Harper's,* CLX (December, 1929), 120–122. Ch. VII, "Claustrophobia, or What Every Young Wife Should Know," appeared in the *New Yorker,* V (October 12, 1929), under the name of James Thurber. The first part of Ch. VIII appeared in the *New Yorker,* V (September 28, 1929), under the name of E. B. White and with the title "Frigidity in Men," a title given in the book to the entire chapter. A section of Ch. VIII entitled "Answers to Hard Questions" appeared under the name of E. B. White in the *New Yorker,* V (July 6, 1929). Mrs. James Thurber states that Thurber wrote the "Preface" to the 1929 edition and Chs. I, III, V, VII, and the glossary (letter from Helen

Thurber to Norris W. Yates, March 22, 1963). White wrote the "Introduction" to the 1950 Dell edition.
An essay that looks as if it may have been left over from material prepared for *Is Sex Necessary?* is Thurber's "Freud: or the Future of Psychoanalysis," in *Whither, Whither or After Sex, What? a Symposium to End Symposiums,* Walter S. Hankel, (ed.), The Macaulay Company (New York, 1930), pp. 111–130.

7. Eastman, *Enjoyment of Laughter,* p. 105. Thurber then, according to Eastman, quoted this stanza from Clarence Day, Jr., *Thoughts Without Words:*

> Who drags the fiery artist down?
> Who will not let the sailor roam?
> Who keeps the pioneer in town?
> It is the wife, it is the home.

Pedants may check Thurber's slight misquotation in *The Best of Clarence Day,* p. 437.

8. In addition to a radio version of "Walter Mitty" in which Benchley played the title role, a movie, "The Secret Life of Walter Mitty," was produced despite several strong objections by Thurber to changes made in his story by the film producers. See Kramer, *Ross and the* New Yorker, p. 260. In the movie Danny Kaye played the title role.

9. Peter DeVries, "James Thurber: The Comic Prufrock," *Poetry,* LXIII (December, 1943), 151–152. Cf. Otto Friedrich, "James Thurber: A Critical Study," *Discovery No. 5,* Pocket Books (New York, 1955), pp. 158–192.

10. The last period and ellipses are Thurber's.

11. Mary McCarthy, "Cruel and Barbarous Treatment," *The Company She Keeps,* Weidenfeld and Nicolson (London, 1943, 1957), p. 16.

12. In case anyone should confuse Thurber with his *persona* of Little Man, a comment by Wolcott Gibbs is worth quoting: "The essence of Thurber is such that in any real contest of personalities everyone else would be well advised to take to the hills." Qu. in "Thurber and His Humor," *Newsweek,* XLIX (February 4, 1957), 56.

13. James Thurber, "Pepper for the Belgians," *New Yorker,* XIII (December 18, 1937), 20.

14. Walcutt, *American Literary Naturalism,* pp. 20–21.

15. Malcolm Cowley, "Dos Passos and His Predecessors," *New York Times Book Review,* January 19, 1947, p. 1. Cf. Walcutt, *loc. cit.*

16. *The Big Bear of Arkansas,* Carey and Hart (Philadelphia, 1845), and *A Quarter Race in Kentucky,* Carey and Hart (Philadelphia, 1846).

17. From "September 1, 1939," by W. H. Auden. Copyright 1940 by W. H. Auden. Reprinted from *The Collected Poetry of W. H. Auden,* by permission of Random House, Inc.

18. Thurber, *The Years With Ross,* p. 121.

19. See "What Price Conquest?" *New Republic,* CVI (March 16, 1942), 370; "Correspondence," (March 30, 1942), 43. The controversy stirred up by Thurber's review is discussed by Peter Lisca, *The Wide World of John Steinbeck,* Rutgers University Press (New Brunswick, New Jersey, 1958), pp. 186–188, 305–306. Replying to one reader who called his review a "slap in the face," Thurber wrote, "I am sorry about that slap in the face. I didn't realize my hand was open."

20. *Thurber on Humor,* pp. 10–11; Lanterns and Lances, pp. 211–212. Cf. James Thurber, "The Case for Comedy," *Atlantic,* CCVI (November, 1960), 97–99.

21. Harvey Breit, "Talk With James Thurber," *New York Times Book Review,* June 29, 1952, p. 19, repr. in Breit, *The Writer Observed,* Collier Books (New York, 1961), p. 167.

22. *Thurber on Humor,* p. 10; *Lanterns and Lances,* p. 211.

23. A posthumous collection of Thurber's sketches, stories, and tributes to contemporaries is *Credos and Curios,* Harper and Row (New York, 1962). A comprehensive selection of his writings and drawings is Helen Thurber (comp.), *Vintage Thurber,* 2 vols., Hamish Hamilton (London, 1963). Thurber's writings have also furnished the material for two musical revues, *The Thurber Carnival* and *The Beast in Me.*

Chapter 17.
E. B. White, "Farmer/Other"

1. Thurber, *The Years With Ross,* p. 92.

2. In 1912, before he started "The Sun Dial" column, Don Marquis wrote a section of the editorial page for the New York *Evening Sun,* entitled "Notes and Comment," which seems to have been similar in character to the "Notes & Comment" section of "Talk of the Town" in the *New Yorker.* See Anthony, *O Rare Don Marquis,* pp. 137, 355–356.

3. Thurber, *The Years With Ross,* pp. 95–96.

4. *Ibid.,* p. 56.

5. Kramer, *Ross and the* New Yorker, p. 153.

6. Warren Beck, "E. B. White," *College English,* VII (April, 1946), 367–373.

7. Morris Bishop, "Introduction" to E. B. White, *One Man's Meat,* Harper (New York, 1950), p. viii. The first edition of this book was published in 1942 and contained fewer essays than the 1944 edition. Bishop's introduction was written for the 1950 edition.

8. The period and ellipses in this instance and the second instance are White's.

9. John C. Broderick, "Thoreau's Proposals for Legislation," *American Quarterly,* VII (Fall, 1955), 285–290.

10. Henry George, *Progress and Poverty,* [first published 1879] Robert Schalkenbach Foundation (New York, 1946), p. 369.

11. A later collection of White's work is *The Points of My Compass,* Harper and Row (New York and Evanston, 1962).

12. This story has faint overtones of an article by Poe, "Maelzel's Chess-Player," concerning a mechanical "man" that was attracting much attention in the eighteen-thirties.

13. Ironically, an article sympathetic to the continued widespread use of DDT appeared in the *New Yorker* in the same year that *The Second Tree From the Corner* was published. See Robert Rice, "DDT," *New Yorker,* XXX (July 17, 1954), 31–56.

14. I am indebted to my colleague, Professor John F. Speer, for tracing the source of this quotation after I had overlooked White's use of it.

15. Joseph Wood Krutch, *The Voice of the Desert,* Sloane (New York, 1954), pp. 186ff. Cf. Aldo Leopold, *A Sand County Almanac,* Oxford University Press (New York, 1949), pp. 201–226, and Paul L. Errington, *Of Men and Marshes,* Macmillan (New York, 1957), pp. 116, 124, 125–139.

16. John Burroughs, *Whitman: A Study,* Houghton Mifflin (Boston and New York, 1904), p. 5. If White is a "naturalist," he is in the mode of Burroughs rather than of Dreiser. In addition to his scientific observations, Burroughs became a farmer, and in work with his hands on the land he found a stimulation that he had not previously got from nature. See *Literary Values and Other Papers,* Houghton Mifflin (Boston and New York, 1902), pp. 244–256.

Chapter 18.
Will Cuppy: The Wise Fool as Pedant

1. Kunitz and Haycraft, *Twentieth Century Authors,* p. 341.

2. Burton Rascoe, *Before I Forget,* Doubleday, Doran (Garden City, New York, 1937), p. 177.

3. Fred Feldkamp, "Introduction" to Will Cuppy, *The Decline and Fall of Practically Everybody,* Dell (New York, 1950), pp. 1–2, reprinted by permission of Holt, Rinehart and Winston, Inc. See also Feldkamp's "Introduction" to *How to Get From January to December,* Henry Holt (New York, 1951), pp. vii–ix.

4. *Ibid.,* p. 236. Reprinted by permission of Holt, Rinehart and Winston, Inc.

5. *How to Be a Hermit or a Bachelor Keeps House,* Horace Liveright (New York, 1929).

6. *The Great Bustard,* Farrar and Rinehart (New York, 1941), is a republication under the same cover of *How to Tell Your Friends From the Apes* and *How to Become Extinct.* Many of the pieces in the books that Cuppy published during his lifetime appeared first in the *New Yorker, Bookman, Saturday Evening Post,* and other magazines. In his "Preface" to *How to Tell Your Friends From the Apes,* Cuppy parried the question of whether he had borrowed the title from a humorous volume of verse and drawings by Robert Williams Wood, *How to Tell the Birds From the Flowers* (1917). Certainly Wood's gay little tome, republished by Dover (New York, 1959), contributes nothing but the title—if that—to Cuppy's mordant collection.

7. *How to Attract the Wombat,* Rinehart (New York and Toronto, 1949), pp. 15–16. Reprinted by permission of Holt, Rinehart and Winston, Inc.

8. *Ibid.,* p. 138. "But we do it on purpose" [Cuppy's footnote]. Reprinted by permission of Holt, Rinehart and Winston, Inc.

9. Cuppy supplied humorous footnotes for the American edition of W. C. Sellar and R. J. Yeatman's tilt at amateur gardening and at nature-lovers, *Garden Rubbish and Other Country Bumps,* Farrar and Rinehart (New York, 1937).

10. *How to Get From January to December,* p. 153. Reprinted by permission of Holt, Rinehart and Winston, Inc.

11. *The Great Bustard,* p. 55. Reprinted by permission of Holt, Rinehart and Winston, Inc.

12. *Ibid.,* p. 154. (Cuppy's footnote is, "This is Gimmick's Law.") Reprinted by permission of Holt, Rinehart and Winston, Inc.

13. *Ibid.,* pp. 68–69. Reprinted by permission of Holt, Rinehart and Winston, Inc.

14. Cf. José Ortega y Gasset, "The Primitive and the Technical," in *The Revolt of the Masses,* Third Printing, Mentor (New York, 1952), 55–63. Though he seems to have Europeans primarily in mind, Ortega postulates a mass-man remarkably like the American

boobs of Mencken, Lardner, Cuppy, Perelman, and other humorists who emphasize a discrepancy between the average man's limited mentality and the enormous powers placed in his hands by modern technology. Ortega also has his version of the elite.

The reader will note in Cuppy the same contradiction between determinism and the idea of a will free to struggle that appears in other naturalistic writers.

15. *The Great Bustard*, p. 146. Reprinted by permission of Holt, Rinehart and Winston, Inc. The periods are mine.

Chapter 19.
The Sane Psychoses of S. J. Perelman

1. Richard B. Gehman, "Introduction" to Nathanael West, *The Day of the Locust*, Bantam (New York, 1958), p. xiii. Gehman says that ". . . his [Perelman's] shadow can be detected in *A Cool Million* in particular."

2. *Dawn Ginsbergh's Revenge* (1929); *Parlor, Bedlam and Bath* (1930) with Quentin Reynolds; *Strictly From Hunger* (1937); *Look Who's Talking!* (1940); *The Dream Department* (1943); *Crazy Like a Fox* (1944); *Keep It Crisp* (1946); *Acres and Pains* (1947); *Westward Ha!* (1948), *Listen to the Mocking Bird* (1949); *The Swiss Family Perelman* (1950); *The Ill-Tempered Clavichord* (1952); *The Road to Miltown* (1957); *The Rising Gorge* (1961). Much of the material in these volumes, along with several pieces not previously collected, has been reprinted in *The Most of S. J. Perelman*, Simon and Schuster (New York, 1958). A play, *The Beauty Part*, based largely on material from some of Perelman's essays and sketches, had a run on Broadway during 1962–1963.

3. For a discussion of Bucks County as an "exurb," see A. C. Spectorsky, *The Exurbanites*, Berkeley Publishing Corp. (New York, 1955), pp. 47–59. A recent analysis of humor that makes use of contemporary trends in sociology is Russell W. Nash, "Max Shulman and the Changing Image of Suburbia," *Midcontinent American Studies Journal*, IX (Spring, 1963), 27–38.

4. John K. Hutchens, "On an Author," *New York Herald Tribune Book Review*, XXIX (January 11, 1953), 2. *The Best of Perelman*, Modern Library (New York, 1947), is dedicated to Benchley. This volume, by the way, is a reissue of *Crazy Like a Fox*, Random House (New York, 1944), with four pieces added from *Keep It Crisp*, Random House (New York, 1946).

5. Qu. in Kunitz and Haycraft, *Twentieth Century Authors*, p. 1092.

6. See George Vere Hobart, *D. Dinkelspiel, His Gonversationings,* New Amsterdam Book Company (New York, 1900), and *Heart To Heart Talks Mit Dinkelspiel,* G. W. Dillingham Company (New York [1900]). Other "Dinkelspiel" volumes appeared in 1904 and 1908. See also Montague Glass, *Potash and Perlmutter,* Doubleday, Page (New York, 1911)—the first of a string of volumes about these two Jewish businessmen. Some of these stories were made into a successful play, *Potash and Perlmutter* (1913).

7. In *One Touch of Venus* the "hero" is a barber who is compared favorably with supposedly more impressive types. Venus, though a goddess, is in love with him and says, "All my other men have been such heroic figures. I want somebody nobody's ever heard of." Barber and goddess do not marry, but this Little Man gets *a* girl if not *the* girl.

8. Hutchens, *loc. cit.* It has been suggested too that Perelman's work is akin to that of the French Surrealists. They evidently regarded him as "a kindred spirit, especially when they discovered the screen plays he wrote for the Marx brothers" (Gehman, *loc. cit.*).

9. The italics are Perelman's.

10. A recent satirical novel, *Golk,* by Richard Stern, concerns "Candid Camera."

11. Erich Fromm, *The Sane Society,* Rinehart (New York and Toronto, 1955), pp. 12–21.

Chapter 20.
Some Questions

1. Thurber, *The Years With Ross,* p. 228.

2. *Ibid.,* p. 50.

3. Arthur F. Burns, "An Economist's View of Our Unfinished Business," *Reporter,* XXIII (November 24, 1960), 30–31. Mr. Burns was chairman of the President's Council of Economic Advisors during Eisenhower's first term.

4. Irvin G. Wyllie, in *The Self-Made Man in America,* pp. 168–169, says that in the nineteen-twenties the ideal of success in the vast literature on how to succeed had changed from owning one's own business and being one's own boss to merely rising into the "managerial elite" of top-salaried executives. "The success cult's glorification of hired managers during the 1920's represented at the very least a retreat from the traditional ideal of independence" (p. 169).

5. In a lively introduction to *The America of George Ade* (pp. 9–12, 21), Jean Shepherd stresses the element of loneliness in Ade's life and humor. However, Ade himself did not specifically emphasize the loneliness of his characters; their isolation was a part of their total condition but rarely an overt topic in the sense that it is the topic of Thurber's "One Is a Wanderer" or White's "The Door."

6. Believers in the scapegoat theory of humor could probably have it that in neither the two wars nor the depression could any definite and simple "goats" be found. But the Germans (as "Huns" in World War I and as Nazis in World War II) were available; yet little satire good enough to survive was hurled in their direction. One would have expected the Nazis to be especially tempting targets.

7. Howard Webb, Jr., "Mark Twain and Ring Lardner," *Mark Twain Journal*. XI (Summer, 1960), 13–15.

8. Mr. Tatsey is a Blackfoot Indian and writes in an idiom utterly his own. My colleague, Dr. Phillips G. Davies, first called his column to my attention.

Index

Index

Truth, 30

Tucci, Niccolo, 359

Turner, Frederick Jackson, 63, 64

Twentieth Century Authors, 128, 379*n*,
381*n*, 384*n*, 387*n*, 389*n;* First Supplement, 383*n*

Ulysses, 224; Perelman and, 343–44

Uncle Remus, 23; *Uncle Remus's the Home Magazine*, 34, 197, 198

University Wits, 30–31, 49–50, 220, 226, 252, 322

U.S.S.R., the, 258

Vanderbilts, the, 54

Van Doren, Carl, 373*n*

Van Doren, Mark, 144

Vanity Fair, 29, 31, 139, 221, 227, 242, 243, 263, 302, 383*n*

Vaughan, William E., 101, 358

Verdict, 30

Virchow, Rudolf, 147

Vogue, 346

Voltaire, 146

Von Bismarck, Otto. *See* Bismarck, Otto Von

Vorse, Mary Heaton, 265

Wade, J. D., 372*n*

Walcutt, Charles Child, 210, 288

Wall Street, 166

Wallach, Ira, 357

Walnut, Illinois, 196, 208, 214

Walpole, Hugh, 248

War, 91, 356; *see also* World War I, World War II

Warner, Charles Dudley, 29

"Warner Fabian," 339, 341

Washington, D.C., 276

Washington, George, 105, 232–33

Washington Square, 342

Wave, the, 30

Webb, Howard, W., Jr., 168, 173, 391*n*

Weill, Kurt, 333

Welles, Orson, 249

Wells, Carolyn, 15, 32, 364*n*

Wells, H. G., 55, 250

Wesleyan University, 50

West, Laura, 332, 333

West, Nathanael, 332, 350

Westcott, E. N., 220

Weyl, Walter, 43, 68, 168, 317, 350

Wharton, Edith, 75

White, Elwyn Brooks (1899–   ), 6, 11, 32, 46, 47, 54, 82, 196, 199, 210, 276, 277; chapter on: 299ff.; 354, 355, 356, 359, 386*n*–387*n;* and Rogers, 117; and Lardner, 189–90; and Cuppy, 323, 324, 328; and Perelman, 335, 348

—*The Fox of Peapack*, 300, 313; *The Lady Is Cold*, 300; *A Subtreasury of American Humor* (ed., with K. S. White), 301; *Alice Through the Cellophane*, 302; *Every Day Is "Saturday*, 303; *Quo Vadimus?* 305–8; "How to Tell a Major Poet From a Minor Poet," 306; "Irtnog," 307, 317; *One Man's Meat*, 308ff., 320; "The Flocks We Watch by Night," 309; "Town Meeting," 309; *Here Is New York*, 312; *The Wild Flag*, 314; *Charlotte's Web*, 315; *The Second Tree From the Corner*, 315ff.; *Stuart Little*, 315; "Time Past, Time Future," 316; "Time Present," 316; "The Door," 316–17, 318; "A Weekend With the Angels," 316; "The Decline of Sport," 317; "The City and the Land," 318; "The Hour of Letdown," 318; "The Morning of the Day They Did It," 318; "The Wonderful World of Letters," 318; "Death of a Pig," 319; *The Points of My Compass*, 357, 387*n*

White Katharine Sergeant (Angell), 6

White, Morton, 366*n*

White, William Allen, 41, 42, 44, 130; praised by Thurber, 294

White Sox, Chicago, 192

Whitechapel Club, 65, 315

Whitlock, Brand, 20

Whitman, Walt, 232, 317, 319

Why We Behave Like Human Beings, 277

Why We Laugh, 364*n*

Why We Misbehave, 278

Wilcox, Ella Wheeler, 44

Wilhelm, Jane, 374*n*